BLACK HORSE RIDE

THE INSIDE STORY OF LLOYDS
AND THE BANKING CRISIS

IVAN FALLON

Biteback Publishing

This edition published in Great Britain in 2015 by
Biteback Publishing Ltd
Westminster Tower
3 Albert Embankment
London SE1 7SP
Copyright © Ivan Fallon 2015, 2016

First published in Great Britain in 2015 by
The Robson Press (an imprint of Biteback Publishing Ltd)

Ivan Fallon has asserted his right under the Copyright, Designs and Patents
Act 1988 to be identified as the author of this work.

ISBN 978-1-78590-023-5

10 9 8 7 6 5 4 3 2 1

A CIP catalogue record for this book is available from the British Library.

Set in Adobe Garamond Pro

Printed and bound in Great Britain by
CPI Group (UK) Ltd, Croydon CR0 4YY

MIX
Paper from
responsible sources
FSC® C020471

CONTENTS

FOREWORD

The story of the failure of HBOS is important both to provide a record of an event which required a major contribution by the public purse, and because it is a story of the failure of a bank that did not undertake complicated activity or so-called racy investment banking.

Bank of England Report, 'The Failure of HBOS', December 2015

The financial crisis of 2008/09 turned just about every banker in the world into a social pariah. Driven by greed, egotism and vaulting ambition, they were blamed for wrecking the global economy, destroying jobs, wiping out huge swathes of wealth and savings and ushering in the biggest recession in a century.

Although many of them deserved what they got, not all bankers were bad people. A profession, once highly respected, did not change overnight and there were some banks – not many – that refused to get involved in sub-prime mortgages, never got carried away by soaring property and asset values and ignored the siren call of the huge fortunes being accumulated in the more glamorous world of investment banking.

This is a story about one such bank, run by a group of cautious, experienced and professional bankers who steered well clear of the activities which caused the financial system so much financial grief. While more highly rated banks were coining it, they plodded their weary way along a self-chosen path of probity and conservatism, earning themselves no accolades in the City or with their own investors who regarded them as staid and boring. Yet, in September 2008, in the immediate aftermath of the crash of Lehman Brothers, this same group of bankers took a decision which is still widely regarded as one of the worst in British banking history. It came close to destroying Britain's most venerable financial institution, a 240-year-old bank which had survived depressions, world wars and banking crises almost as bad as this one.

It is the story of Lloyds TSB's takeover – or rescue if you want to call it that – of Halifax Bank of Scotland (HBOS), the circumstances which led up to it and its bloody aftermath. It is told from the point of view of the Lloyds executives and board rather than from the universally hostile perspective from which almost all commentators have approached this frenetic period of financial history. In the ugly, anti-banker climate which followed the crisis, no distinctions were made, and they found themselves lumped in with the failures, bearing the stigma which attached to all the bankers, good and bad, who accepted government 'bail-out' money at the height of the crisis. They have borne the marks ever since.

None of the former Lloyds directors have spoken about it in public and have only spoken to me on the grounds that I protect their anonymity. Initially they were reluctant to talk at all and it took some time to persuade them to do so. They were not seeking expiation or redemption – in fact they were not seeking anything, preferring to bear in private their own share of the stigma that has attached to them since the HBOS deal went very publicly sour within months of being consummated. These were not innocent, young amateurs but hardened, professional business people who had all climbed up the ladders of their individual professions – lawyers, accountants, senior company directors and bankers who had been around the City and business for decades and knew well the cost of failure. All of them signed off on the deal, all supported their chairman and chief executive to the last and all of them felt that, in the circumstances in which the HBOS decision was taken, it was the right thing to do. They might think differently with the benefit of hindsight but they did not have that luxury in the autumn of 2008.

Because Lloyds took government money – or the 'Queen's Shilling' as a Bank of England official jovially called it – it was put into the same basket as Royal Bank of Scotland (RBS), HBOS and Northern Rock, all of them deeply flawed institutions. Yet going into the crisis, it was the strongest of all the British banks other than HSBC and Standard Chartered. It was making profits of £4 billion a year, was relatively well capitalised, had virtually zero exposure to sub-prime and had shunned the toxic instruments which nearly dragged down the whole system and for which the big banks are still paying (Bank of America has now paid out over $80 billion in fines and the top twenty global banks more than $250 billion). Lloyds had also avoided the more reckless corporate lending which brought HBOS down, the crazed rush for growth of Fred Goodwin at RBS or the irresponsible mortgage lending of Northern Rock. It had also eschewed the easier pickings of investment banking which made Barclays's Bob Diamond one of the highest-paid executives in the world and a hero in the City.

As a result, the Lloyds management had to put up with jibes about being the 'plodding Black Horse bank', or 'the Black Horse bank slows to a trot'. Its urbane chairman, Sir Victor Blank, and its phlegmatic chief executive, Eric Daniels, the two central characters in this book, learned to be thick-skinned. Daniels in particular was convinced that, when other banks were throwing caution to the wind, his day would come. As a result, when the crash arrived in the autumn of 2008, Lloyds was ideally placed to take advantage of it.

That was when the Prime Minister, Gordon Brown, at a now legendary cocktail party, gave Blank the go-ahead to take over HBOS, the 'big prize' that Lloyds had wanted to land for years but which would never have come its way without the financial crisis. Brown thought he was saving the banking system, and maybe he was. Urged on by No. 10, the Treasury, the Bank of England and the Financial Services Authority, and with the support of its own seasoned board and shareholders, Lloyds rescued the stricken HBOS which otherwise would have had to be nationalised with potentially disastrous consequences for the whole economy.

Lloyds was primarily aiming to become the UK's leading retail bank and that only became possible when the banking crisis threw HBOS into its arms. For its part, the government wanted the deal so badly that, over a dramatic weekend at the Treasury in October 2008, it was prepared to make all sorts of promises on Sunday which it seemed to have forgotten about by Tuesday. Six months later the same Treasury officials who had piloted the deal through were engineering the departure of the Lloyds chairman who, up to that moment, had been personally supported by the Prime Minister. Faced with another political crisis if he had taken sides against the Treasury, Brown washed his hands of it.

In November 2015, seven years after the event and six months after the first publication of this book, the Bank of England and the Prudential Regulation Authority published their report 'The Failure of HBOS'. It did not deal with the Lloyds takeover or the events that make up the central theme of *Black Horse Ride*, and was wholly concerned with the regulatory and management failure that led up to the collapse of a mighty institution. As such, it is a fascinating exercise for banking students but did not cause me to change any of my opinions or descriptions.

In writing an account of those events I have interviewed, all on a non-attributable basis, some fifty of the people most concerned, including former Lloyds and HBOS executives, non-executive directors, officials in the Bank of England, FSA and Treasury, some of the ministers involved and City advisers. I have also interviewed, on the same basis, several other bank chairmen and former chief executives. I want to acknowledge their contribution to this narrative, even if I can't mention them by name.

Finally, I want to thank my publisher, Jeremy Robson, and my editor, Victoria Godden, whose patience and endurance were tested to the full.

DRAMATIS PERSONAE

Lloyds TSB

Sir Victor Blank – Chairman, 2006–09

Eric Daniels – CEO, 2003–11

Tim Tookey – Finance Director, 2008–12

Helen Weir – Finance Director, 2003–07; Head of Retail Banking, 2007–12

Sir Philip Hampton – Finance Director, 2002–03 (later chairman of RBS)

Archie Kane – Scottish Widows

Truett Tate – Head of Wholesale Banking

Terri Dial – Head of Retail Banking, 2003–07 (died 2012)

Patrick Foley – Strategy and Chief Economist

Carole Sergeant – Head of Risk

Stephen Roughton-Smith – Deputy Head of Risk

Non-Executive Directors

Wolfgang Berndt
Sir Ewan Brown
Jan du Plessis
Philip Green
Sir Julian Horn-Smith
Lord (Sandy) Leitch
Sir David Manning
Carolyn McCall
Tim Ryan
Martin Sicluna
Tony Watson

Lloyds Chairmen

Sir Jeremy Morse, 1977–93
Sir Robin Ibbs, 1993–97
Sir Brian Pitman, 1997–2001
Maarten van den Bergh, 2001–06
Sir Win Bischoff, 2009–14

CEOs

Sir Brian Pitman, 1983–97
Sir Peter Ellwood, 1997–2003
António Horta-Osório, 2009–present

Halifax Bank of Scotland (HBOS)

Lord (Dennis) Stevenson – Chairman

James Crosby – CEO, 2001–06
Andy Hornby – CEO, 2006–08
Harry Baines – Legal Council
Peter Cummings – Head of Corporate Division
Graeme Shankland – Integrated Finance

Ministers

Gordon Brown – Prime Minister
Alistair Darling – Chancellor of the Exchequer
Lord (Peter) Mandelson – Business Secretary
Baroness (Shriti) Vadera – Business Minister
Lord (Paul) Myners – Financial Secretary

Treasury

Sir Nicholas Macpherson – Permanent Secretary
John Kingman – Second Permanent Secretary; First CEO of UKFI
Tom Scholar – Second Permanent Secretary

Bank of England

Lord (Mervyn) King – Governor
Sir John Gieve – Deputy Governor (Financial Stability)
Sir Paul Tucker – Executive Director
Andrew Bailey – Chief Cashier
Andrew Haldane – Chief Economist

Financial Services Authority

Sir Howard Davies – Chairman, 1997–2003
Sir Callum McCarthy – Chairman, 2003–08
Lord (Adair) Turner – Chairman, 2008–13
Sir Hector Sants – CEO, 2007–12

European Bankers

Rijkman Groenink – CEO, ABN Amro
Count Maurice Lippens – Chairman, Fortis
Jean-Paul Votron – CEO, Fortis
Georges Pauget and Gilles de Margerie – Crédit Agricole
José Ignacio Goirigolzarri – Deputy CEO, BBVA
Michael Diekman – CEO, Allianz
Paul Achleitner – Finance Director, Allianz

Advisers

Matthew Greenburgh – Merrill Lynch (Northern Rock and Lloyds)
Henrietta Baldock – Merrill Lynch (Lloyds)
Simon Robey – Morgan Stanley (HBOS)
William Chalmers – Morgan Stanley (HBOS)
David Hutchison – Dresdner Kleinwort (HBOS)
Stewart Bennett – Dresdner Kleinwort (HBOS)
David Mayhew – JP Morgan Cazenove (Treasury)
James Leigh-Pemberton – CEO (UK) Credit Suisse (Treasury)
George Maddison – Credit Suisse (Treasury)
Roland Rudd – PR advisory to Lloyds TSB

Others

Sir George Mathewson – CEO, RBS, 1992–2002, later Chairman

Sir Peter Burt – CEO, Bank of Scotland, 1996–2001

Ian Harley – CEO, Abbey National

Baroness (Denise) Kingsmill – Deputy Chairman, Competition Commission

Lord (Stephen) Green – Chairman, HSBC

Fred Goodwin – CEO, RBS

Sir Tom McKillop – Chairman, RBS

Glen Moreno – Chairman, UKFI

Lord (Mervyn) Davies – CEO (later Chairman), Standard Chartered

Douglas Flint – Finance Director, HSBC

Peter Sands – CEO, Standard Chartered

John Varley – Chairman, Barclays Bank

Bob Diamond – Chairman, Barcap

Robin Saunders – WestLB and Clearbrook

Anna Mann – Headhunter

Carol Leonard – Headhunter

Ashley Summerfield – Headhunter

Sean Mack – Chairman, Morgan Stanley

Lord (Digby) Jones – CBI

PREFACE

I**T WAS JUST** before eight on the evening of Monday 15 September 2008 when Sir Victor Blank arrived at Spencer House, ancestral home of Princess Diana, in London's St James's Place. He was late for a pre-dinner drinks reception and as the tall, patrician chairman of the Lloyds TSB banking group climbed the stairs to the gilded Great Room on the first floor, he could already hear the excited hum of a dozen conversations all discussing the same subject. Lehman Brothers, one of Wall Street's biggest and oldest banks, had spectacularly gone bankrupt overnight, threatening the entire global banking system with collapse and with it the fortunes of almost everyone in the room that night.

The reception was hosted by Sir Win Bischoff, chairman of the New York-based Citigroup, who had just presided over a two-day board meeting which turned out to be one of the gloomiest in the long history of the American bank, then ranked as the seventh biggest in the world. Bank shares that day had collapsed, with Citigroup's own shares down 40 per cent in a single session and no financial institution, including Lloyds, had escaped the market mayhem. What had been intended as a social evening for his Citigroup board to meet some of the leading figures in Britain's banking and financial communities had been overwhelmed by the events of the past twenty-four hours.

Bischoff was anxiously glancing at his watch when Blank finally appeared. A few minutes earlier he had checked with the organiser to see if everyone was present so they could cut off the interminable drinks session and go next door to dinner. 'All, except for one person,' she answered. 'We're still waiting for Sir Victor Blank.'

'We'll give him five more minutes,' Bischoff decided. 'The Prime Minister wants to disappear but he wants to talk to him first.'

At that moment the Prime Minister, Gordon Brown, was standing a few feet away, deep in conversation with Bob Rubin, a former co-chairman of Goldman Sachs and Treasury Secretary under Bill Clinton who now served on the Citigroup board. Brown knew him well from his days as Chancellor of the Exchequer, and the two of them were animatedly debating the urgent actions their respective governments should be taking to head off financial Armageddon.

The Citibank event had been in Brown's diary for months but he had cancelled the dinner and had come along to the cocktail party to hear what the bankers had to say – and to lend an air of reassurance that the government was staying calm. The atmosphere in the room was anything but calm. Words such as 'scary', 'terrifying' and 'meltdown' could be heard above the hubbub and the word 'Lehman' was on everyone's lips. The events over the weekend were unprecedented in financial history and no one had any illusions about the fall-out, which was going to affect all of them profoundly.

Blank, not a man to panic easily, was as concerned as any of them. He had woken up that morning to the news that Lehman was filing for bankruptcy, the biggest banking failure ever and America's largest bankruptcy. And that was not all: the mighty Merrill Lynch, the legendary

'Thundering Herd' and the largest brokerage house on earth, had suffered such massive losses on its mortgage portfolio that it had to be bailed out by Bank of America before the markets opened. At close of business on Friday there had been four major investment banks on Wall Street: Merrill's, Lehman, Morgan Stanley and Goldman Sachs. By Monday there were two: Morgan Stanley and Goldmans – and even they looked perilously close to the brink too.

Just as seriously, the global insurance giant AIG (American International Group, Inc.) was in deep trouble, desperately trying to scrape together an emergency injection of $50 billion to keep it afloat after its shares fell by 72 per cent in one day. Its collapse, which seemed imminent, threatened the entire world insurance system as well as the banks, whose loans it insured.

Blank had spent the day talking to his executives and board, trying to get a handle on the impact on Lloyds of these momentous, unimaginable events. Lloyds, like every bank, did business with Lehman and he knew there would be a write-off, possibly running into the hundreds of millions. Until twenty-four hours before, Lehman had also been Lloyds's lead stockbroker (Citi was another one) and would have to be replaced at a time when it was needed the most.

As he arrived at the Citigroup reception, Blank was still trying to absorb the fact that the brash, irrepressible Lehman, which was founded in 1850 and had weathered the American Civil War, the Great Depression, two world wars and countless financial crises, was no more, its doors closed forever. Earlier in the day he had watched the TV coverage of disconsolate Lehman employees, among the highest earners in the City just a week before, carrying all that remained of their glittering careers in cardboard boxes out onto the street in Canary Wharf. That stark, unforgettable scene, more than any other, symbolised better than anything the end of the longest and biggest banking boom in history – and presaged the biggest crash which was now under way.

The Lloyds chairman made straight for Bischoff, who tactfully steered Rubin away to leave Brown alone with Blank, out of earshot of the rest of the room. The Prime Minister didn't waste time on pleasantries and went straight to the matter on hand. 'I haven't forgotten that conversation we had on the plane about Halifax Bank of Scotland,' he began, oblivious to the quizzical looks cast in their direction. 'We have been thinking quite hard about it – and we'll do everything we can to help.'

This was momentous news, which Blank had been waiting to hear since he and the Prime Minister talked on a plane coming back from Israel six weeks before. But he hadn't expected to get it at a cocktail party. For two years Lloyds and HBOS, Britain's fifth and fourth biggest banks respectively, had been trying to find ways to merge but had never been able to get past the competition issues involved. In July, with HBOS in serious trouble, Blank had suggested to Brown that the government help clear the way for the merger on the grounds that, unless HBOS was rescued by Lloyds, it would either go bust or have to be nationalised, both equally unpalatable for the Prime Minister. Now he listened, half stunned, as Brown finally gave him his decision.

'We recognise your argument that you could not go through the competitions process, particularly if there was a full review,' the Prime Minister said. 'Halifax Bank of Scotland could not survive it, so if you still want to do it, you should get on with it quickly.' He had, he said, scheduled a meeting the next morning with the new Chancellor, Alistair Darling, and Mervyn King, Governor of the Bank of England, and he would start the process immediately. After once more urging Blank to move fast and keep Downing Street informed, the Prime Minister turned away and, saying his goodbyes, left the room. He was expecting a long evening back at the office.

It took the normally quick-witted Blank a moment to take in the significance of what he had just heard. In effect, he had been given the green light for Lloyds TSB to proceed with the acquisition of HBOS, which at that moment seemed to be heading the same way as Northern Rock, the high-flying mortgage bank which had collapsed the previous year after the first bank run in Britain for more than a century. That day alone the HBOS share price had fallen by 18 per cent, deposits were flowing out at a terrifying rate and the view in the Lloyds boardroom, shared by some of those in Spencer House, was that without government help, or a takeover from a stronger bank, it might not survive the week. With 15 million investors, 5 million mortgage-holders, 2 million shareholders and assets in excess of the annual UK GDP, its collapse could bring down the whole British banking system, turning the developing recession into the deepest depression since the 1930s.

The Prime Minister was aware that, behind the scenes, Lloyds and HBOS had been in merger discussions for months, but he didn't know the details. In fact, they were a long way down the road, and two months earlier the two banks had informally agreed on a basic structure whereby Lloyds, marginally the smaller of the two but with a stronger balance sheet, would take over HBOS. It would be an all-paper deal, a swap of Lloyds's shares for HBOS's, designed to protect every pound in precious capital the two banks could muster between them. Blank would be chairman of the new group and his American-born chief executive, Eric Daniels, would retain executive control. In a single bound, Lloyds, long seen as the staidest and most old-fashioned of all the high street banks, would vault to first place among domestic British banks, a position it had not enjoyed for a decade, the leader in all the major banking retail markets.

To the 65-year-old Blank, in his third year as non-executive chairman, HBOS was 'the big prize', the acquisition which, from the moment he arrived at Lloyds in 2006, he and the board had believed was the best solution to Lloyds's strategic problems. Both HBOS and Lloyds, he had long concluded, were 'marooned', stuck as two mid-sized financial institutions focusing on a mature UK banking market which had barely grown in five years. A decade of trying to expand through cross-border merg-ers in Europe had taken Lloyds nowhere and for some time Blank and Daniels had been focused on a merger with HBOS as their best way to break out of their strategic straitjacket. The financial crisis, and HBOS's looming problems, gave them their window, the one brief moment when the competition rules could be relaxed long enough to let them through, but they had to move fast before it closed again. HBOS, after a period of wild and overaggressive expansion, needed rescue and Lloyds was the only bank around that could bail it out.

Watching the Prime Minister's back recede through the door, Blank caught the eye of his chief executive, who had been observing his inter-action with Brown from across the room, and he gestured for him to follow him outside. Daniels was an obsessive smoker and was delighted to be in the open air where they stood on the steps directly underneath Rupert Murdoch's London apartment and facing (Lord) Jacob Roths-child's headquarters (also at the party).

'Eric, you're not going to believe this,' Blank began as Daniels lit up. He then related the conversation he had just had and its implications. 'It's as firm an assurance as he can give,' concluded Blank.

While Blank went back into the dinner, Daniels wheeled into action, calling his opposite number at HBOS, Andy Hornby, to pass on the news and ask him to assemble his executive team for a meeting first thing in the morning. Later in the evening Blank got hold of the HBOS chairman, (Lord) Dennis Stevenson, to tell him: 'Dennis, we've got the go-ahead from Gordon Brown on the competition issue. But we need to move fast.' Stevenson, contemplating the collapse of his bank and an inglorious end to his career, needed no urging.

The biggest banking merger in British history was under way.

CHAPTER 1

THE PITMAN MANTLE

EARLY IN 2002 Sir Victor Blank had one of his regular lunches with Sir Brian Pitman at the Savoy Grill. Pitman, widely regarded as the shrewdest and most pioneering banker of his generation, had recently retired after a 49-year career at Lloyds TSB, the last eighteen as chief executive and then chairman. His years at the top were generally judged to have been spectacularly successful ones, transforming Lloyds from an old-fashioned, medium-sized institution into, for a few months at least, the biggest bank in the world.

In his last few years, however, his almost-mythical status in the City had slipped as the bank's performance faltered and analysts began questioning Pitman's single-minded focus on the domestic market, his obsessive drive for shareholder returns and his rejection of the more glamorous areas of investment banking and international operations. Lloyds had dropped from first to fifth place among the high street banks, passed first by HSBC after it took over Midland, and then by a more dynamic Barclays. Two newly created groups, HBOS, a merger of the seventeenth-century Bank of Scotland with the Halifax Building Society, and the Royal Bank of Scotland (RBS), which had taken over the National Westminster Bank in 2000, had turned the Big Four clearing banks into the Big Five and Lloyds was steadily being outpaced by all four of its more aggressive rivals.

Nonetheless, Pitman, then aged seventy, still commanded huge respect in the banking community, a giant of the industry whom everyone listened to with reverence – as Blank, ten years his junior, did that day. A bluff, bear of a man with a heavily lined face and imposing polished dome, Pitman had revolutionised the way British banks were run, changing forever the patrician world of a management culture which believed that what mattered was size rather than profitability. His single-minded drive for return on equity, an alien concept in the banking industry until he introduced it the mid-1980s, had created a new generation of highly paid bank executives who put shareholders before customers and turned traditional bank managers into salesmen marketing a broad range of financial products which went well beyond cashing cheques and offering overdrafts. The result was one of the biggest financial success stories in banking history.

Against what he later admitted was 'massive resistance' from his own senior executives, Pitman had imposed a value-creation philosophy on the bank, which basically meant that increasing the share price and dividend should be the bank's first and only target – everything else would fall in behind. The key to what he achieved at Lloyds, he later reflected, was centred around what he called 'a single, well-defined performance measure', against which all decisions, however small, were taken. Initially, he set his team a target of achieving a return on equity of 10 per cent above the prevailing inflation rate of 5 per cent. The problem was no one at the bank had ever worked out what the return on equity (RoE) really was. When they did, they were astonished to find it was 17–18 per cent, already well above their target. Pitman immediately raised the bar, reinforcing the pressure by using it as a measure for determining executive pay. 'After that, the cry "Improve RoE" could be heard all around the organisation,' he joked later.

'The adoption of a value-creation philosophy imposes a tough discipline,' he said in a lecture he gave at Harvard in 2002. 'People, with an eye to their bonuses, will wriggle like mad to avoid goals based on shareholder value, often arguing for alternatives that only appear to be related to it. And beliefs are hard to change.'

In Lloyds's case, that meant abandoning the conviction that it should be a global bank offering all things to all people. 'We had to accept that it was all right to get smaller, to stay close to home, to focus on unglamorous products like mortgages and insurance while getting out of the more prestigious services such as investment banking and currency trading.'

Every action he took flowed from that philosophy. There would, he decreed, be no investment in anything that did not measurably increase shareholder value. The bank, he repeated endlessly, 'has no other goals'. In his hunt for it, he began the wholesale dismantling of the extensive overseas operations which Lloyds had built up over a century, and focused the bank's resources solely on the area where the best returns were to be made: the UK retail market, where he would sell not just banking services but every other kind of financial service too. Lloyds was the first British bank to acquire an insurance company, followed by the acquisition of a building society, another first, and then the big one: the old Trustee Savings Bank, which almost doubled the size of Lloyds's branch network. It could now offer its own pensions, mortgages, insurance policies, tax and investment advice, unit trusts and financial planning through its high street branches which, under Pitman's rule, became mini financial supermarkets, the beginning of the 'bancassurance' model that drives all commercial banks today. Lloyds even led the way in offering payment protection insurance, or PPI, designed to help borrowers who got into financial difficulties with their mortgage or loan payments, a product which, sold in moderation – as it was for a time – was a perfectly legitimate addition to the portfolio. When mis-sold, as it eventually was, it became another matter.

Pitman was also the first to concentrate seriously on costs, pioneering widespread outsourcing of customer services to call centres which were often based in low-cost countries such as India where English was a second language. Baffled customers, used to a Captain Mainwaring-style manager and personal service, complained they were often kept on the line for hours but Pitman was unrepentant – they would, he reasoned, soon get used to it.

The result was a slimmer, more efficient and UK-focused bank (despite the foreign outsourcing) which delivered for shareholders rather better than it did for customers or staff.

Ruminating after his retirement, even Pitman began to wonder if maybe the process hadn't gone too far. Surveys, he grumbled to Blank over lunch, were identifying growing dissatisfaction among Lloyd's customers who missed their old-fashioned bank managers and disliked the much less personalised service they were now offered. 'The retail banker has moved away from being the customer's trusted adviser to increasingly being an individual who sells products,' he complained. The first person he encountered on entering a bank now, he said, was a member of the sales staff. 'Can you imagine giving incentives to staff for selling loans? It's crazy, but it's happening.' Pitman shook his massive head sadly. 'All these call centres and stuff – it doesn't feel right. Somehow we've got to pull it back.'

Gazing across at him, Blank refrained from pointing out that Pitman was the man most responsible for introducing the very practices he was complaining about. He might have sparked a revolution in profitability

for the big banks, but it had also made them the most unpopular institutions in the country – including the tabloid press, which Blank, as
chairman of the Mirror Group of newspapers, was very familiar with.

. . .

Lloyds Bank can trace its origins back to 1765 as Taylors & Lloyds in
Birmingham, a private bank that converted into a joint-stock company in 1865. In its first 220 years of existence it created a shareholder
value of £1 billion. Over the next eighteen, it created another £44 billion,
making Pitman's reign the defining one in the bank's history, setting the
structure and culture which still drove the bank well into Blank's time. As
the most influential commercial banker of his day, it is worth spending
a moment on Pitman, the man who in effect set the scene for the events
of September 2008 which were to have such profound consequences for
the bank he adored.

Born in Cheltenham in 1931, Pitman's background was no different
from that of many of the men (they were all men) who climbed the executive rungs of the clearing bank ladder in the post-war era. He won a
scholarship to his local grammar school, then one of the best schools in
Gloucestershire, where he developed his life-long passion for sport, particularly cricket. He was also a decent musician, playing the trombone
as a youth in a local jazz band and at one stage thought seriously about
turning professional. Instead he got a job in the local Cheltenham &
Gloucester building society, and a few years later, aged eighteen, he moved
to Lloyds Bank where he stayed for the rest of his long working career.

Fast-tracked through the rigid management structure, he was a senior
executive at Lloyds's head office in the City by the mid-1970s when the so-
called 'fringe bank' crisis arrived, a seminal event in his life where he later
remarked he learned the true meaning of risk. He played a leading role

in the Bank of England's 'lifeboat' operation which was set up to bail out the smaller, secondary banks during a crisis which was almost as serious as that of 2008. It was there he met his future chairman, Jeremy Morse, a senior Bank official in overall charge of the operation whose intellect and clear thinking he developed a life-long respect for. A few years later he found himself at the heart of another banking disaster, the great Latin American debt debacle caused by Mexico defaulting on its international debt in 1982, eventually followed by fifteen other Latin American countries. Of all the British – and international – banks, Lloyds was the most heavily involved in South America where it earned half its profits, and Pitman later admitted to the journalist Robert Peston that the bank, in common with several major American banks, would have gone bust if it had been required to tell shareholders and creditors just how much it owed and how little it would get back – 'which would have been the case under the disclosure rules which now apply'. In one year Lloyds had to write off £2.6 billion, plunging it into a loss of £715 million, at that stage the largest ever reported by a British company.

But it survived and Morse and the rest of the Lloyds board were impressed with Pitman's cool handling of the crisis which brought several of the big international banks to their knees (private lenders eventually had to forgive $61 billion in loans to Latin American and other developing countries, about one third of their total outstanding debt). When other banks panicked, Pitman held his nerve, urging the Lloyds board to see it through. 'Lloyds's involvement with South America was quite different from that of any other bank, except Citibank,' Morse would recall later,

> because it was deeply embedded on the ground where it was well-run. The customers ended up all right. That's why we held onto most of the debt and didn't sell it at a discount. Banks which had nothing on the ground and essentially lent to the government suffered much more in the crisis.

A year later, at the age of fifty-two, Pitman was made chief executive and within a few years it looked like the best decision Lloyds had ever made.

For much of his time as chief executive, Pitman worked well with Morse. The more cerebral and socially polished Morse (Winchester and Oxford), whose hobby was setting crossword puzzles and solving chess problems, counterbalanced Pitman's more earthy management style which his staff sardonically characterised as 'genial thuggery'. Unlike Morse, Pitman was no intellectual, rarely venturing opinions about the state of the economy or the wider financial world, but he was an instinctive banker who had lived through crises and understood risk. Throughout their fifteen-year relationship, he and Morse often disagreed – notably over the sale of overseas assets – but they were united in rejecting the temptations of the more glamorous businesses of stock-broking and investment banking, which all the other banks invested in after Big Bang deregulated the markets in the mid-1980s (with generally disastrous results). They also managed to stay clear of the bad property loans which were to bring down the chairmen of some of the other banks, including John Quinton of Barclays.

The real starting point for Lloyds's startling change of pace was Pitman's decision in 1986 to sell the retail banking operation in California which up to that time the bank had regarded as an important strategic foothold in one of the world's most affluent economies. It was probably the most internally controversial decision he would ever make, but it persuaded his team that managing for shareholder value, however 'gut-wrenching', was the right way to go. 'It gave us the mettle we needed to put the interests of the shareholders first, and it set the stage for a resurgence in the bank's fortunes,' he said afterwards. Two years later Lloyds was making record profits and its share price had risen four-fold.

The sale of the California bank marked the beginning of Lloyds's wholesale withdrawal from international markets. Lloyds-Bolsa (Bank of

London and South America) in Latin America, once the flagship of the whole bank, soon followed, as did its interests in Portugal which were highly profitable. When Pitman took over, Lloyds had branches in forty-seven countries. When he retired, it was down to a bank in New Zealand, a few bits and pieces in South America and not much else.

By the late 1980s Lloyds was doing so well that executives were finding it all too easy to achieve their profit targets, comfortably producing higher returns than any of their rivals. So Pitman raised the bar again and went on raising it.

'If we wanted to be world class, we had to benchmark ourselves against world-class corporations – and not just banks,' he said in his Harvard lecture. The most challenging comparison he could find was with Coca Cola, which set itself the target of doubling shareholder value every three years which, even to Pitman, sounded about as stretching as you could get. When he proposed this to his staff as the new metric for determining executive bonuses, he later recounted, he was told he was 'stark raving mad, comparing us to a soft drinks company'.

But it worked. For the rest of the 1980s and through the 1990s, the value of Lloyds doubled every three years, taking its market value flying past every other bank in the world. Most executives had stock options and the City was soon commenting enviously on the large number of new millionaires in the Lloyds ranks. It brought bank salaries and bonuses into the spotlight for the first time, although criticism from the financial press and shareholders was tempered by the fact that bonuses were matched by performance. And it wasn't just executives who benefited – one of the newspapers discovered a Lloyds messenger who held shares worth £250,000.

Even as his wealth and legend grew, Pitman added to his mystique by travelling to work on the London Underground, revelling in the image it gave him as the common man, but at the same time making sure it was widely publicised. Inside the bank, however, he was legendarily obsessed with his own pay package, comparing it constantly with others in the industry. 'He didn't like it when other people in the City, who he didn't think were doing such a good job, were earning more than him, and he insisted on getting more,' says a former Lloyds director who had to engage him in salary negotiations. 'He had that competitive urge, but it was always restrained by a proper retail banker's caution.' Pitman hit the headlines in 1995 when his remuneration, including performance-related bonus, rose by 28 per cent to £581,383, making him for a time the highest-paid commercial banker in the UK. A decade later, so much had bank executive pay soared over this period, it would have made him one of the poorest.

By the early 1990s there was a growing unease among his board at the direction Lloyds was heading in. Jeremy Morse, who stepped down as chairman in 1993, increasingly felt that chasing shareholder value was being taken too far. 'I accepted his advice, and that of Lindsay Alexander, the deputy chairman at the time, that Lloyds had badly under-served its shareholders for twenty years and had been much more careful with our staff and customers than we were with our shareholders,' said Morse, who died in 2016.

> I agreed that we had to do more for them but he didn't think they had a God-given right to get everything they did – and he was completely right about that. It was a great achievement at that time but we all felt it went too far in the end. I think if Brian had stayed on as CEO for longer, his natural caution would have kept it all right.

There was also growing concern inside the bank at the strategic box that Lloyds was getting itself into. Morse initially opposed the sale of the Latin American operations but gave way when Pitman proved to him that the return on equity was half what it was in the UK. Morse was also uneasy about the concentration on one single market, however lucrative it was proving – and strangely Pitman agreed. 'Brian was quite aware of the dangers of getting into what he called "too narrow a water, or channel",' Morse remarked many years later. 'But he was also driven by the idea that the core business was the retail operation in the UK and that is where we should concentrate the resources of the bank.'

Nobody, not even Morse, could argue with the success of the strategy. This was the era of Margaret Thatcher's 'capital-owning democracy' when British citizens were encouraged to own their own homes, build up private pension funds and invest in privatised utilities; when council houses were sold off, taxes were cut and a sustained house-price boom created heavy demands for loans, mortgages and insurance products. After Britain exited the Exchange Rate Mechanism (ERM) in 1992, long-term interest rates dropped sharply, raising the value of the banks' bond and loan portfolios; and rapid employment growth through most of the 1990s reduced bad debts. It was a golden period for British banking and Pitman led the way in taking full advantage of it.

.   .   .

'There's always a better strategy than the one you have; you just haven't thought of it yet,' Pitman liked to say when he was quizzed on apparent contradictions in his philosophy. In this case his new strategy was to acquire other banks at the same time as he was disposing of them, swapping Latin American assets for ones closer to home – or attempting to.

For all his skills as a banker, Pitman proved remarkably inept in the bid arena where cannier rivals ran rings around him. In 1984, soon after he took over, he had a go at the Royal Bank of Scotland, only to be blocked by the Bank of England which was very protective of the big Scottish banks in those days. Two years later he made a hostile £1.2 billion bid for Standard Chartered Bank which ranked as Britain's fifth biggest bank although its main office was in Hong Kong and did business mostly in the developing countries. Pitman was attracted by the similarity in cultures, reckoning that Standard, unlike the Latin American businesses, would produce sizeable synergies and widen the reach of the bank. It was a deal which in a single stroke would have transformed Lloyds into the kind of international British bank, quite different from the Lloyds he had inherited, which he and his successors sought so hard to create in later years. But he fluffed it.

Formed by the 1969 merger of Standard Bank, which operated largely in Africa, and Chartered Bank, whose fiefdom was the Far East, the group had over-expanded in Europe and North America and was highly vulnerable when Pitman mounted his bid, the biggest ever made for a bank up to that time, in 1986. He should have been able to pull it off, but Standard easily out-manouevred him by inviting three famously acquisitive entrepreneurs – the shipping magnate Yue-Kong Pao of Hong Kong, the Australian Robert Holmes à Court of Australia and Singapore's richest man, Khoo Teck Puat – to come to its rescue. Acting separately, these three unlikely 'white knights' bought a 30 per cent stake in Standard Chartered between them and voted it against Lloyds, which received only 44.1 per cent acceptances.

Pitman got another chance three years later when in the spring of 1989 John Richardson, a well-connected Hong Kong-based Australian businessman, came to see him in his office in Lombard Street with a proposition he expected Pitman to leap at. Richardson, previously the chief executive of Li Ka-shing's Hutchison International, had recently been appointed chairman of the ragbag of European companies controlled by the Australian magnate Alan Bond. Richardson explained to Pitman that HSBC had given him an unofficial mandate to reduce Bond's gearing, which he described as 'stratospheric', by selling off some of the assets Bond had acquired over his debt-fuelled business career (he went spectacularly bust a few years later). They included a 23 per cent shareholding in Standard Chartered which Bond had acquired when he bought Bell Securities, the Holmes à Court holding company which ran into trouble after the 1987 stock market crash.

One of Bond's ambitions at the time – he was never short of ambitions – was to create a major financial conglomerate and the acquisition of Standard Chartered would have put him in the big time. But the lesson of the unsuccessful Lloyds takeover attempt was that a hostile bid would not work, and he asked Richardson to approach Standard Chartered's chairman, Rodney Galpin, to test the water. Richardson knew Galpin, a steely Bank of England official put in to rescue Standard after it ran into its problems, but was turned down flat when he mentioned Bond. 'Rodney politely but firmly told me that such a bid would not get Bank of England approval,' says Richardson. Bond had to accept there was no point in pursuing a deal and decided to sell his stake. He gave the job to the resourceful Richardson.

Before approaching Lloyds, the most likely buyer, Richardson went to see his old Singaporean friend Khoo Teck Puat who still had the shareholding he had bought as part of the 'white knight' operation. His proposal, which Khoo approved in principle, was that they pool their stakes, amounting to around 35 per cent of Standard Chartered, and offer them to Pitman.

Richardson then flew back to London, called Pitman and suggested they meet. The Lloyds chairman listened carefully to his proposal, asked a few questions about price (Richardson hadn't decided on one yet but made it clear he would be looking for a premium on the market) and finally said, 'Look, it's very interesting. Let me think about it.' He called back a few days later to say there was too much risk involved and he didn't want to pursue it.

'He blanched when I put the proposal to him, even though I was offering him control of Standard Chartered on a plate,' says Richardson now.

> It was a deal involving two people who had attracted a fair degree of controversy and I don't think he liked that aspect of it. Or maybe it was a case of once bitten, twice shy. But really he didn't have the stomach for it. He just wasn't a risk-taker because he certainly would have got it if he had bought the two stakes.

Early in 1991 Pitman ventured back into the takeover arena again, this time with a clumsy, hostile bid for the struggling Midland Bank which for four years had been involved in on/off discussions about a 'marriage of equals' with Hongkong & Shanghai Banking Corporation (only later did it shorten its name to HSBC). The prize, as with the HBOS bid all those years later, was a vast one. The Lloyds plan was to sell or close 1,000 out of 3,750 branches, the Midland name would disappear and some 20,000 employees out of a workforce of 100,000 in Britain would lose their jobs. The savings were estimated at over £800 million a year by 1996.

Once again Pitman mishandled it from the start, alienating the Midland management which he needed to have on his side, and even turning the Bank of England, which started out supporting him, against him. Midland, once (like Lloyds) the biggest bank in the world, desperately needed a partner. Its disastrous acquisition of the Crocker National Bank in California and a string of poor trading figures since had resulted in the ultimate humiliation of receiving an approach from Saatchi & Saatchi in 1987, surely the cheekiest proposal of all time. It then agreed that HSBC should take a stake of 14.9 per cent on the understanding that the two banks would eventually merge, which the Bank of England initially opposed on the grounds that HSBC was a foreign bank even if it was based in a British colony and not a suitable partner for one of the Big Four. So, for the next two years the two banks had to be content with endless discussions about closer co-operation which they hoped might still lead to a merger. They even discussed new names for the joint bank, the favourite being 'Mercator' which would have replaced both the HSBC and Midland logos.

In the autumn of 1991, with HSBC still in balk, Pitman approached Midland to propose a merger between the two banks. He was, he indicated, being encouraged to make his move by the Bank of England which didn't like HSBC and was increasingly concerned about the state of Midland's finances. He was not welcomed by Midland whose CEO, Brian Pearse, stormed off to the Bank to confront the deputy governor Eddie George, one of the most popular and respected officials the Bank of England has ever had. 'I asked him specifically if the Bank was behind the proposal,' Pearse noted later, 'and he said … they would much prefer the [Midland-Lloyds] solution which is within the family.' According to Pearse, as recorded by HSBC's official biographers David Kynaston and Richard Roberts, in their recently published history of the bank (*The Lion Awakes: A Modern History of HSBC*), George had already informed the HSBC chairman Willie Purves 'that the Bank would fight his proposal on the grounds that they were not financially suitable to own a major bank in the UK'.

After months of dithering, in March 1992 Pitman decided the time had come to bring things to a head and called Pearse to tell him that Lloyds was calling a press conference to announce the two banks were in merger discussions – even though they were not. It provoked a fierce reaction from the Midland CEO. 'I told them that their actions seemed extremely hostile and I hoped he would not suggest at the press conference that I would be part of the combined management team because I would not.'

From that moment on, the Midland management and board, already leaning towards Hongkong Bank, were solidly opposed to the Lloyds bid. When Morse and Pitman pitched their bid to them on 13 March 1992, the meeting, according to the minutes, decided that 'the HSBC proposal offered the best prospect of a combination which would be in the best interests of Midland and its shareholders'.

Pitman had lost the initiative and he never regained it. The Bank of England switched sides, agreeing to allow HSBC to go ahead on the condition that it moved its headquarters – or, as Eddie George put it, 'its mind and management' – to London where it would be regulated by the Bank of England. HSBC, for the first time in its 130-year existence, was about to become a fully fledged British bank. On 14 April it announced a £3.1 billion bid for Midland followed up by an intense PR campaign which turned the press and City strongly in its favour. When Pitman hit back by announcing that Lloyds 'was considering' making a 457p a share counter-offer (against HSBC's 416p), the City and the press were unimpressed. 'Lloyds Play Monopoly', said *The Times* scathingly, and the tabloids, stirred up by the growing opposition from the unions and from small businesses, were downright rude: 'What a Bunch of Bankers' said *The Sun*, while the *Mirror*'s headline was 'Bank on a Mega-Lloyds Being Bad for Britain'. With the economy in a hole and unemployment rising, this was no time for Pitman to boast about the cost savings he was proposing.

The end was in sight when 160 MPs signed an Early Day Motion (EDM) in support of the HSBC bid and on 22 May Michael Heseltine, the Trade and Industry Secretary, applied the *coup de grace* by referring the Lloyds bid to the Mergers and Monopolies Commission while, at the same time, clearing the HSBC offer. When HSBC raised its bid to £3.9 billion Pitman threw in the towel, arguing that if he had topped it again, 'Midland shareholders would have ended up with about half the combined group. That could never have been right.'

. . .

The Midland failure, although it was a huge opportunity missed, scarcely dented Pitman's reputation and may even have enhanced it. Shareholders were prepared to forgive him anything as long as profits and the share price kept growing. And, driven by his bancassurance model and his tight control of costs, they were. In 1988, in between the two Standard Chartered episodes, he had acquired control of the insurance company Abbey Life and began aggressively selling its financial products through its branch network, incentivising bank staff who were paid a commission on each sale. It worked remarkably well and by 1993 Lloyds, with margins the highest in the business, became the first British bank to break the £1 billion profit mark. It was spinning off so much cash that shareholders were already putting pressure on Pitman to return some of it to them – which he did by raising the dividend by 20 per cent, setting another precedent which would haunt his successors.

But he chose to spend some of his cash where he thought he could use it most profitably – on another takeover, this time for one of the new banks which were emerging from the demutualisation of the old building societies. The 1986 Building Societies Act, a seminal event in the history of the 200-year-old building society movement, had created half a dozen new 'banks' with large deposit bases, thousands of branches, millions of customers – the Halifax alone had 7.7 million – and under-performing assets, some of them potentially ripe for the picking if you were a well-heeled bank. Before the act, building societies were old-fashioned mutuals, owned by their members (savers and mortgage-holders), traditionally holding money on deposit and lending it, for a small margin, to prospective homeowners.

The act allowed them to 'demutualise', transforming themselves into fully fledged banks with shareholders, able to offer all the services a commercial bank such as Lloyds did. Nine of the biggest societies, accounting for two-thirds of all building society assets, did so. Abbey National, under its enterprising chief executive, Peter Birch – who had been partly responsible for re-writing the legislation – kicked off the process in 1989, followed by the Halifax, Alliance & Leicester, Bradford & Bingley and other household names, including Northern Rock. This was the area where Pitman now sought his long-awaited major acquisition. In 1995, after more than a decade of trying, two came along at once, doubling the size of Lloyds in a single twelve-month period – three times in terms of market value – and forming the bank which would basically remain unchanged right up to the HBOS takeover.

The first deal was in many ways the most daring, a genuine trailblazer which would become the template for other banks to copy in the years ahead. The Cheltenham & Gloucester Building Society, which had given Pitman his first job when he was only sixteen, had been founded in 1850 by radical nonconformists to enable local working men to pool their savings, buy land and build houses. Its story, like that of so many other building societies and savings banks, was a remarkable one of civic-minded, unpaid people who ran a non-profit-making society solely for the public good. They were local tradesmen, bakers, blacksmiths and carpenters who the working class trusted with their savings without a qualm. Under professional managers, it thrived in the 1930s, survived World War Two – not a great time to be a mortgage lender – and then expanded rapidly in the housing boom of the 1960s, even starting its own building company when the supply of new houses dried up.

By the end of 1994, when Pitman approached its chief executive, Andrew Longhurst, to discuss taking it over, C&G was generally regarded as the most efficient building society in the country. It was still a mutual, owned by its million savers and 265,000 borrowers, but was considering following the others into the public arena. Pitman was treading into new territory, as there had never been an association between a bank and a building society and the legalities of acquiring one were not at all clear. But Longhurst, who would receive 1.4 million Lloyds options in the deal, was keen to go ahead and so was his board. When Lloyds made a £1.8 billion offer, 95 per cent of savers and 75 per cent of borrowers happily accepted. Pitman could not repress a chuckle when, at a crowded meeting in London's Docklands to approve the deal, someone complained that being taken over by Lloyds was 'like a virgin being embraced by an old and proven rake'.

The ink had barely dried on that deal before Pitman was off again, this time with an even bigger acquisition. It was his master-stroke, the bid he would always be remembered for: a £13.6 billion merger with the TSB, or the Trustee Savings Bank, which turned Lloyds into Britain's biggest bank and doubled its profits. It also gave it a new name: Lloyds TSB. Run by Peter Ellwood, a cost-conscious manager who was destined to play a major role in Lloyds's future, TSB was a highly profitable and uncomplicated institution which in the mid-1980s transformed itself from a collection of small individual savings banks into a single corporate entity – which no one owned. In the absence of any other shareholder, the Conservative government claimed dubious rights to the share capital and flogged it to the public in 1986, giving TSB back the proceeds to expand. It did so in profligate style, buying the City merchant bank Hill Samuel for £777 million on the highest multiple the City had ever seen. By the time Lloyds came along, it was beginning to run out of both money and steam and Ellwood was looking for someone to sell it to. 'He saw Pitman coming and took full advantage of it,' says a Lloyds insider sourly. Geographically it was a perfect fit with Lloyds, which had 1,800 branches, most of them in southern England, while TSB had 1,100 branches which were predominantly in the north and in Scotland.

Although Ellwood had stripped large amounts of costs out of TSB, the merger with Lloyds provided even more scope. Pitman reckoned he could make annual savings of £350 million a year by the end of the decade, largely by eliminating overlaps, closing branches (eventually, over fierce opposition from the unions, he closed 150), reducing staff and centralising the back offices and other services. His critics later claimed he never actually got there, and the savings announced were exaggerated by some smart accounting practices. 'He really kitchen-sinked it,' says a former executive, 'and recorded savings which were not savings at all. We were all asked to scrape the barrel, down to the cancellation of newspapers.'

The next two years, Pitman's last as chief executive, were probably his best. The old Lloyds with its overseas operations and traditional branch managers had gone and the new bank was almost entirely UK-based, with a fifth of its profits coming from insurance – primarily life insurance which moved in a different cycle to consumer banking – and another fifth from mortgages. A single set of employees processed transactions conducted under the Lloyds, TSB and Cheltenham & Gloucester brands which were sold under one roof, increasing sales of all three. It had a retail-banking breadth that no other British bank could match, servicing 15 million customers through a network of 2,750 branches, hundreds more than its nearest rival, NatWest. It was the market leader in cheque-writing accounts and personal loans, and the second largest credit card issuer. Profits were £2.5 billion in 1996 and topped £3 billion the following year.

Pitman's declared aim to double the share price every three years had been met and even surpassed, depending on the mood of the market, and return on equity, in single figures when he took over in 1983, was 33 per cent in 1996 and over 40 per cent in 1997, levels never achieved before in Britain and very rarely by overseas banks. Few banks in the world get anywhere near it today.

In 1997, when Pitman, aged sixty-six, finally stepped down as chief executive, Lloyds was the world's most valuable bank, with a market value of £42 billion, more than forty times what it was when he took over, four times what it had been just five years before and three times its size immediately after the TSB deal. Its shares were changing hands at seven times book value, twice that of its British counterparts. Sir Brian Pitman had become a brand name in his own right.

. . .

Beneath the almost mythical status which attached to Pitman when he eventually vacated the CEO's chair, there were serious under-lying problems and potentially fatal cracks in the Lloyds structure. The core business was effectively ex-growth and profits from now on would be driven almost exclusively from savings created by acquisitions. C&G and TSB would keep growth going only for a few more years, but after that they would run out. The combined bank now had more than 20 per cent of personal accounts and 16 per cent of mortgages in Britain, danger territory for competition authorities and difficult to increase. The money-machine needed feeding with new acquisitions every few years and Lloyds would soon find that they were not going to be allowed them.

Under Pitman, the Black Horse bank had run a brilliant race. But his critics would later point to the opportunities he had missed and the problems he had left for his successors. 'Pitman never used the strength of his shares to make an overseas deal, which haunted the group after-wards – and still does,' says a former Lloyds executive. 'He wouldn't do it because it would have damaged his returns. He had been lucky and rode the consumer boom, but by the time he retired it was already over. He really had nowhere to go – and nor did his successors.'

CHAPTER 2

LIFE AFTER BRIAN

STEPPING INTO PITMAN'S shoes was always going to be a daunting task, and Peter Ellwood, although he tried valiantly, never really had much of a chance. In 1997, after two years as deputy chief executive, he moved up to the top job when Pitman, six years past the traditional Lloyds retirement age, finally retired. Except he didn't retire – citing shareholder and City support, he flouted the corporate governance codes and stayed on as chairman, supposedly part-time and non-executive. It was a popular move in the City and with shareholders, who adored him. But, in the long run, it was to prove bad for the bank.

No new chief executive welcomes his predecessor remaining on the board, let alone as chairman, but Ellwood, out of loyalty and respect for the iconic Pitman, chose not to protest. It is pointless now speculating on how he would have performed if he had been able to come out from under the Pitman mantle and pursue his own course. He never really did and his attempts at establishing his authority on the bank fizzled out almost before they had begun. Rival bankers began referring to him witheringly as 'the John Major of banking', and a *Sunday Telegraph* interview started: 'The hardest thing about being Peter Ellwood is not being Brian Pitman.'

Through most of Ellwood's six-year stint as CEO, during which time the market value of Lloyds fell by nearly a half, Pitman's presence and culture hung heavily over the bank and, no natural leader himself, Ellwood didn't possess the skills to tackle the fundamental fault-lines which Pitman had bequeathed him. Inside the bank he was seen, says a former executive, 'as a decent man trying to do the right thing, but with Brian still around, that was just about impossible. People had this snobbish view of him that he was not quite good enough.'

Although Ellwood always insisted that his relationship with his chairman was perfectly amicable, it was far from it. In public he betrayed no resentment towards Pitman but the continual comparisons, which ran all the way through his time as CEO, must have got under his skin. 'The deal with Brian was very clear when I was asked to be CEO,' he insisted, with no hint of anger, when he was asked about the relationship. 'There should be one person running the bank – and that was me.' Time and again he insisted he was not concerned by Pitman's higher profile, however wounding it must have been privately.

> It doesn't worry me as long as I am allowed to run the bank and get on with it. He manages the board, he manages the shareholders and he is there as a sounding board. There is absolutely no ambiguity, irrespective of what you read in the press, about who runs the company. You can't have two bosses.

Yet many people in the City and inside the bank still thought that Pitman *was* the boss and he continued to behave as if he were, giving speeches, attending City dinners, sometimes attending two or three functions in a single evening, all contributing to the general impression, which he didn't discourage, that he was still in charge. 'We've all assumed that, no matter what they tell us, it's Pitman who still wears the trousers,' wrote one commentator, and *The Economist* shared that view: 'Few doubt that Sir Brian is still pulling at least some of the strings. Mr Ellwood has much to prove, and much to lose.'

A short, compact and chunky man, Ellwood always appeared amiable, good-humoured and, as one observer generously noted, 'very likeable, very straight'. But, he added, 'He's not slick – and journalists like slick.' On his desk he kept a well-thumbed copy of Clausewitz's *On War*, which he said helped him plan future conquests – although in reality he was an unlikely military strategist, no Talleyrand to Pitman's Napoleon. 'Peter was never a good strategist,' says one of his former directors. 'Pitman was in a different league.' Ellwood worked hard, was exceptionally well organised, efficient and good with people, at least on a one-to-one basis, but where Pitman could be positively bombastic, he was reticent almost to the point of shyness. Amanda Hall of the *Telegraph* found him almost drying up on her: 'Poor Mr Ellwood,' she concluded at the end of a fairly gentle grilling, 'he really is not having a lot of fun.'

Yet there was a burning ambition in there too and his close colleagues knew him as a driven man intent on leaving his mark on Lloyds's history. 'It's only when he laughs and you see a flash of teeth beneath the grey sweep of hair that you think, mmm, maybe there's more vulpine determination here than you realised,' wrote another interviewer perceptively. He had not climbed to the top of the banking world simply by accident.

Ellwood believed, with some justification, that he had earned the CEO job through hard work and a record which was more than respectable. A life-long banker like Pitman, he had joined Barclays when he left school, did his stint in the regions and arrived in the City head office at the age of thirty. He established his reputation running Barclaycard, then emerging as the leading credit card in the market, before he was headhunted in 1989 to join TSB as chief of its retail operation soon after its privatisation. Within a few years he had done so well that he was rewarded with the CEO role, where over the next six years he built a reputation as an even more formidable cost-cutter than Pitman, closing branches and making thousands of staff redundant in an archaic organisation which was designed for a different age. However, as with Lloyds, he needed acquisitions to keep up his impressive earnings growth but found the door slammed in his face time and again. 'Everyone we approached said "No thanks, you'll just chop costs and we don't want that",' he admitted to Andrew Davidson in a long interview for *Management Today* in October 2001. It was a forerunner to what he would encounter in his time at Lloyds.

He claimed it was he, rather than Pitman – who always saw TSB as a poor second best to the Midland – who conceived the idea of a merger with Lloyds and it was he who made it happen. 'I thought, if we can't buy something it is probably in the best interest of shareholders to sell ourselves to someone else, and I selected Lloyds.' The deal was brokered over dinner with Pitman at JP Morgan, TSB's bankers, and there was some speculation later that Ellwood himself was one of the TSB assets that Pitman was most interested in. Ellwood agreed to run the retail side of the merged bank for a year and take his chances when Pitman, twelve years his senior, retired. There was no talk of Pitman staying on as chairman at that stage, but he made no promises and Ellwood asked for none. 'There were to be two deputy chief executives and I made no requirement that I be made the CEO when Brian moved on.' But as head of the retail operation he was the bookies' favourite from the start. He was also clear that if he didn't get the top job, 'I would have walked' – although he later denied he had ever verbalised that threat to Pitman or the board.

. . .

When Ellwood finally moved into Pitman's office in 1997, he took over a bank which, on the face of it, seemed in amazingly good shape. Profits in the past year had risen by 30 per cent, there was plenty of cash and the ratios used to judge a bank's performance could not have been better: post-tax return on shareholders' funds was 41.2 per cent, a phenomenal figure which it would never see again, and the cost to income ratio stood at 50.8 per cent, again an impressive figure. The share price was still climbing vertically: in January 1996 it was 331p and by the end of 1997 it had risen to 786p, a two-year gain of 137 per cent.

But over the next few years, although the share price topped £10 in 1998 and peaked at £11 a year later, Ellwood found it more and more difficult to maintain the earnings momentum. All the other banks were now copying Lloyds, rationalising bank structures – 3,000 bank or building society branches disappeared between 1995 and 2000, a rate of more than one a week – and selling insurance and mortgages, and there were no easy gains. Pitman had inherited the carcass of the merchant bank Hill Samuel, which had proved a disaster for TSB, confirming his determination to avoid expansion in investment banking as a means of growth. But even that decision, which had looked very clever for a time, no longer appeared quite so wise as the big American banks happily pocketed large profits from it and the UK banks, notably Barclays under Bob Diamond, began to get their acts together. Pitman's decision to pull out of its overseas operations didn't look so brilliant either, particularly as Brazil and some of the other South American economies recovered and repaid their debts (or some of them).

Ellwood's initial strategy was to concentrate on making the bank still more efficient and to sell more products to more customers through a distribution capability which was the largest in Europe. But there was a limit to how many life insurance policies and mortgages his customers could take, or how many branches he could close without damaging the business or Lloyds's market share, which was already beginning to fall. In public he argued that even without acquisitions the bank could continue to grow by cutting still more flab, but in reality he knew he would inevitably have to make a major acquisition, preferably one big enough to transform the bank – which, with Midland, NatWest and Barclays ruled out by monopoly considerations, probably meant a European group.

However much he tried to dampen the City's expectations of a company-transforming acquisition, Pitman cheerfully undermined him, tantalisingly talking about 'lots of opportunities'. There was, he told an audience in the City in May 1999, evidence that rival banks 'are beginning to realise that the current run of record profits can't be sustained'. That, he reckoned, would make them 'more willing to consider an approach'. Back in Lombard Street, Ellwood gritted his teeth and carried on.

In the summer of 1999 one of Lloyds's brokers, ABN Amro, published a lengthy analysis that highlighted the bank's dilemma. 'The outside world can reasonably surmise only one thing about Lloyds's acquisition strategy: the current state of inaction isn't a deliberate policy.' The broker was scathing about its own client's reliance on acquisitions, arguing that the case for Lloyds to increase its investment in its existing business was 'greater than at any time in the last decade'.

For his part, Pitman resolutely ignored the rising tide of scepticism from analysts and shareholders who, only a few years before, believed he could do no wrong. When he was asked about Lloyds's dependence on domestic retail banking and bancassurance, he hit back fiercely at what he called the 'universal' banks, such as Citibank, which had gone into everything from investment banking to expensive overseas acquisitions. 'The returns are pathetic,' he told a City audience. What about cross-border mergers? 'Difficult to do!' With that he grumped off.

In fact by that stage a cross-border merger with a European bank was becoming Lloyds's favoured option and Ellwood's obsession. He was offered banks in Greece, Spain, Belgium and France but didn't like any of them. He had discussions with Fortis, then Belgium's leading bancassurer, looked at France's Crédit Lyonnais and ABN Amro in the Netherlands and also flew several times to the US to see if Lloyds could get back into that market. He talked to several of the big Spanish banks and held brief discussions with a bank in Turkey, one in Iceland and another in Ireland. Every bank he looked at had a problem: either it was too expensive, too risky, offered no synergies (and therefore cost savings) or would dilute shareholder value. Each time he came back empty-handed. An analysis by *The Economist* in April 1999 summed up Ellwood's situation:

> The trouble is that Lloyds TSB's successful strategy in Britain cannot easily be replicated in many other European countries where labour laws make it hard to sack people, so the logic of mergers becomes less compelling. Moreover, in many European countries mutually owned co-operative banks have a big share of the market; unless they decide to go public, as did many of Britain's building societies, they cannot be taken over.

Whereas Pitman's reign had been blessed by benevolent markets and booming house prices, Ellwood soon got a reputation for being an unlucky manager. 'Everything Pitman touched turned to gold,' says a former manager. 'Everything Ellwood touched turned to salt.' He cites two initiatives which the strategic team came up with soon after he took over: an investment vehicle aimed at high net-worth individuals called Create and an internet bank to be known as Evolve. 'The cost-cutting strategy was deeply embedded by then,' says a former manager, 'and people were not good at driving revenues. So when the strategy people came up with these two new initiatives, no one knew how to make them work. We lost around £100 million on them – the culture in the bank was just wrong.'

On another occasion, Ellwood proposed to introduce a mortgage processing service from the US which Pitman didn't think much of. In the middle of a presentation to a sceptical board in the Lombard Street headquarters, the fire alarm went off and everyone had to leave the building. 'And there was Peter standing out on the pavement with his Americans,' says one of the Lloyds team who was there, 'and all the momentum had gone. Pitman just shot it down after that. Peter was just so unlucky with everything.'

In June 1999 Ellwood, more in desperation than anything else, made his one and only significant acquisition: the £6 billion takeover of Scottish Widows, an Edinburgh-based mutual insurer set up two centuries before to support the widows and orphans of the soldiers killed in the Napoleonic Wars. It was paid for out of Lloyds's cash reserves, which at that stage totalled £5.7 billion (more than the Treasury would inject into it in the crisis of 2008). It went down like a lead balloon. The City had been expecting something more imaginative and the shares fell sharply on disappointment that it was not the big deal they had been looking for. 'The market has been waiting for an acquisition for years,' one analyst was quoted as saying, 'and this was all they could do. People are now realising the numbers don't really stack up.'

It was Ellwood's deal but it was Pitman who did most of the talking, trying to counter the air of scepticism which had now set in over Lloyds's growth and acquisition policies. 'We won't be stopping here. We remain an ambitious group, hungry for further expansion.' But the truth is that Lloyds had shot off all its powder and had nothing left for an assault on Europe, even if it could find a target. There were very little savings to be made from the Widows takeover – Ellwood talked about £60 million over three years, a tiny sum in the context of the size of the deal – and as Lloyds already had an insurance arm in Abbey Life, why did it need another one? The City sensed it was an acquisition done more for the sake of doing a deal rather than with any strategic intent – and it was probably right.

The decision looked even worse a few months later when Barclays kicked off a new round of bank takeovers with an agreed £5.3 billion acquisition of the Woolwich, another building society-turned bank, and announced it was on the lookout for more. Ellwood had earlier cast an eye over Woolwich and had rejected it in favour of Scottish Widows and must now have regretted it. John Stewart, the Woolwich chief executive, rubbed his nose in it by saying: 'Woolwich was the prettiest girl in town. We could have a choice and we chose Barclays.'

The Scottish Widows bid was a watershed for Lloyds TSB. In the longer term it made strategic sense, but in the short-term it did little for Lloyds: there were no real cost savings, no synergies, and the cultures were so different that Ellwood basically left it as a standalone operation. Never again would it command the market respect and standing it had enjoyed even two years earlier.

.   .   .

By the autumn of 1999, the whole industry was on the move, driven by the same factors that had motivated Pitman – not always success-fully – a decade before: leaps in technology, the growth of bancassurance and rationalisation of bank networks were producing literally billions of pounds of savings. Size mattered and the pool of potential targets was getting smaller.

In September, NatWest, goaded into action after a decade of lacklustre performance, made a £10.7 billion bid for Britain's second biggest insur-ance company, Legal & General, its forlorn attempt at playing catch-up with Lloyds and the other banks. It was a lame and belated response to pressure from shareholders and, far from cementing its position as

Britain's third biggest bank, it put NatWest in play and brought the two big Scottish Banks, the Royal Bank of Scotland and Bank of Scotland, haring south. Both of them had been watching the banking scene south of the border for years with growing interest but had usually been seen more as potential victims than predators in the consolidation stakes. Now, under younger and more ambitious managers, they both hit on NatWest, which was bigger than both of them put together but vulnerable for all that. Initially they discussed pooling their efforts and making a joint bid, but in September 1999 Peter Burt, chief executive of the Bank of Scotland, decided to fly solo and made a pre-emptive strike before the Royal could get its act together.

Peter Ellwood, along with just about every senior bank chairman and chief executive in the world, was at the IMF annual meeting in Washington when he got the news that the Bank of Scotland had ambushed the unsuspecting NatWest with a hostile £24 billion offer. He awoke to a banking scene humming with rumours of counter-bidders already lining up for NatWest, Abbey National and the Halifax being the favourites.

The Lloyds chief executive cut short his Washington trip and flew back to London, convening an urgent meeting of his advisers to discuss this unexpected foray into English territory. The Bank of Scotland had been performing brilliantly under Burt, eclipsing even Lloyds over the past five years, and if Burt got his hands on the lacklustre NatWest, he reasoned, the whole competitive landscape could change. More immediately, he wanted to know was there any way Lloyds could get involved? As with Midland, the potential benefits of a merger with NatWest were mouth-watering – at least £1 billion of savings – but the obstacles were equally forbidding. Sadly, Ellwood had to accept that there was no chance of getting a merger past the competition authorities. He would just have to watch from the side-lines and sit this one out, even when, two months later, the Royal Bank of Scotland joined in the scrap with a counter-offer for NatWest.

And that's what he did for the next three months while the two big Scottish banks slugged it out and NatWest, forced to drop its bid for Legal & General, desperately fought to keep its independence. All three banks tore each other's performances and balance sheets apart and indulged in such a nasty round of name-calling and personal insults that one analyst was provoked to remark: 'This is about as hostile as you can get without punching the other side in the face. The law of the jungle now presides.'

Royal Bank won by a whisker, throwing up a new star in the shape of the 41-year-old Fred Goodwin who was promoted to take charge of the bid process, with the prize that he would be given the combined retail operation to run if he pulled it off. Already known as 'Fred the Shred' or 'Fred the Impaler' because of his cost-cutting at his previous job at Clydesdale Bank, he had a fan club in the City which liked an ambitious Scot from a humble background (his father was an electrician). They tended to be keener and hungrier than their English, public school counterparts.

A deeply disappointed Peter Burt went back to Edinburgh where he succumbed to flu and took a week off work. He had been back at his desk for only a matter of days when he got a call from Ian Harley, chief executive of Abbey National, asking him if he would be interested in a merger.

Burt didn't much like Harley, for whom the description 'dour Scot' seemed to have been invented, and knew he was already in the market for a bank merger but only on condition that he was the chief executive. However, he agreed to talk – little knowing at the time that Peter Ellwood and Brian Pitman had finally settled on Abbey as the long-awaited acquisition they had been promising for so long.

CHAPTER 3

ABBEY ROAD

ABBEY NATIONAL WAS not quite in the Midland or NatWest league, but it was developing into a significant bank, with ambitions to become the much-talked-about 'fifth force' on the high street (the Halifax was jockeying for the same position, as were several others), when it made its approach to the Bank of Scotland. It was the first building society to convert from mutual status in 1989 and made a big success of it. The shares that it issued to members and listed on the Stock Exchange performed spectacularly well, rising eight-fold over the next ten years. During that time it made fourteen acquisitions for a total of £2 billion, including another large building society, National & Provincial, and by 2000 it was looking for something even bigger. Bank of Scotland, with its reputation as a great corporate bank and enviable customer base, would do nicely.

Ellwood had actually been stalking Abbey from his TSB days but had been unceremoniously shown the door by the truculent Harley who made no secret of his dislike for him. At the end of 1999, with Pitman in tow, he had another go, this time proposing a 'merger of equals' which Harley saw for what it was: a crude euphemism for a takeover without a premium. Abbey was half the size of Lloyds – profits of £1.8 billion against £3.6 billion – and Ellwood made it clear that he and Pitman would be keeping the top jobs. Harley was also concerned about Ellwood's reputation for cutting costs. 'It meant rape and pillage, Harley knew that,' one Abbey insider was quoted as saying. 'It was his worst nightmare. It meant the undoing of everything he had tried to achieve.' It also meant he would be without a job. Once again he turned it down and Ellwood, unwilling to go hostile, gloomily went back to the drawing board to think again.

But he didn't give up and his opportunity came a year later when news of the Bank of Scotland discussions, which had been sputtering along for six months, leaked to the financial press. Word soon reached Ellwood that the negotiations were not going well, largely because, as Burt had feared, of a disagreement over who would be top dog. Bank of Scotland was a proud 300-year-old institution, well run by Burt, with a performance record, reputation and a business which were infinitely better than Abbey's. He was willing to discuss a merger of equals but not a takeover by Abbey, which was bigger and was already throwing its weight about. 'We will be acquiring and we will decide how it goes forward,' insisted an Abbey spokesman, raising the hackles of the Scottish establishment which had already seen two of its great companies, Distillers and Coats Patons, succumb to takeovers from England-based companies and didn't want to lose another one. The talks were on the verge of collapse when Lloyds made its move.

Ellwood called an emergency meeting of the Lloyds TSB board on Sunday 3 December 2000 and presented a detailed plan for making a £19 billion bid for Abbey, bigger than all the bank's previous bids put together. 'The combination of the two businesses would be virtually unassailable,' he pointed out, with 25 million customers and market-leading positions in all personal financial services products. But the biggest attraction, as with TSB, was on the cost side. Ellwood reckoned he could make savings of £950 million a year by closing 600 branches and laying off 10,000 staff at a one-off cost of £1.1 billion. He also believed he could generate an extra £1 billion of turnover by pushing Lloyds TSB's mix of products through a branch network that would be the biggest in Europe.

The board, urged on by Pitman, gave him its backing and Ellwood called Harley to tell him that he and Pitman wanted to see him urgently. They met the next morning at Ellwood's London house and the Lloyds men laid out the terms of their bid, an all-share offer conditional on agreement from the Abbey board and no reference to the Competition Commission. There was no talk this time about a 'merger of equals' and no attempt to disguise it as anything other than a takeover. A furious Harley told them there was no possibility of getting approval from the Abbey board and in any case, contrary to what they might have been told, the talks with the Bank of Scotland were going well and he was not going to be sidetracked by an unwanted offer which didn't have a chance of succeeding. With that he bid them good day.

It was a low moment for both Ellwood and Pitman, who, when the news leaked, were seen to have been publicly humiliated. 'Lloyds has come out with all guns blazing,' wrote one City analyst, 'but it's been slapped down. Being so gung-ho was a mistake and it's now in a corner.' There was even talk that Peter Burt at Bank of Scotland should get out his NatWest plan, ditch Abbey and bid for Lloyds TSB instead.

A measure of Ellwood's desperation was his decision, which he took over the Christmas break, to go hostile, which he must have known would significantly weaken his hand with the competition authorities. On 31 January 2001 Lloyds announced a full, formal offer worth £19 billion, conditional on approval from the Abbey board and the bid not being referred, although by then he knew he was not going to get the first. In fact he got neither. Harley, for the fourth time, flatly rejected him, causing the *Telegraph*'s City editor Neil Bennett to remark, 'The fact is that Abbey's management hates and fears the top team at Lloyds and will do anything to avoid being taken over.' A month later the Trade Secretary, Stephen Byers, referred the bid to the Competition Commission, adding ominously that it 'would lead to the elimination from the market of one of the most significant branch-based competitors to the largest four banks which had over 80 per cent of the current account market between them.' That did not bode well.

Perversely, Ellwood chose to fight on against odds that were now heavily stacked against him. Lloyds shares had fallen by £1 since the start of the battle while Abbey shares had risen, making the acquisition prohibitively expensive even with all the cost savings. If he were allowed to make the bid, he would have to offer the equivalent of half of Lloyds's equity, which would mean a substantial dilution in earnings and a probable cut in the dividend. He was gambling on being able to strip huge costs out of Abbey but even that was looking more difficult because of rising trade union anger, an antagonistic government and a public that was fed up with rising charges and falling services.

The financial press, which had usually supported Pitman, had also turned against the luckless Ellwood. In March the Questor column in the *Daily Telegraph* remarked that he had 'nothing else to show shareholders if the Commission says no. Talk of boosting revenue growth is seen for what it is. Scottish Widows does not look like value for money. Alarm bells have been sounded by the abandonment of Lloyds's rigid cost controls, once the envy of the banking sector.' On the other hand, it added even-handedly, a positive ruling could return Lloyds and Ellwood to what they understood best: stripping costs out of acquisitions. 'A negative ruling will prove a catalyst: a new strategy and perhaps a new management structure.'

Ellwood's fate now rested in the hands of Denise Kingsmill, deputy chairman of the Competition Commission, who would chair the enquiry – and also add a touch of colour to an otherwise dreary process. Slender and tall at almost six foot, Kingsmill was described by one interviewer as 'impossibly glamorous with her blonde hair and enormous bead necklace'. She was also formidably bright, a barrister who, several years before, set up her own law firm which advised some of the biggest companies in the country. She had been a member of the Labour Party since she was eighteen (Gordon Brown later appointed her to the House of Lords), a consumers' champion and, importantly for Ellwood, mightily unimpressed with the banking industry's attitude to its customers over the past decade. Although she would be scrupulously fair in her inquiry, that didn't bode well either.

Even Ellwood was starting to resign himself to defeat when, just as Kingsmill's hearings were getting under way, he was thrown a potential lifeline. The Bank of Scotland, which had temporarily abandoned its talks with Abbey, found a new partner, confirming press leaks that it was in merger discussions with Halifax, once by far the biggest building society in Britain. The aim, it said, was to create the 'real fifth force' in banking. They planned to call the merged company Halifax Bank of Scotland, or HBOS, basically because someone quipped that if Halifax, very much the bigger partner, came last, the new company would be called BOSH – not a good name for a bank.

At the end of 2000, shortly before the creation of HBOS, Lloyds's market value of £32 billion put it in third place among the big four, just behind RBS after its acquisition of NatWest (£35 billion). HSBC, having successfully absorbed Midland and benefited from the booming markets of the Far East, was well out ahead at over £90 billion. Barclays, with a market value of £30 billion, was in fourth place but gaining rapidly after selling off BZW, its loss-making investment banking and market-making business.

HBOS started life with a market value of over £30 billion, level with Barclays, and the eleventh biggest bank in Europe, employing 60,000 people and making a profit of £2.8 billion. By the end of 2001, Lloyds, number one just three years before, was back in fifth place. That is a true measure of how it had lost out in the great bank merger boom which by rights it should have led.

CHAPTER 4

'SCOTTISH SELL-OUT'

THE CREATION OF HBOS brought to the fore three powerful personalities who were to leave an indelible mark – some would say 'stain' – on British banking history over the next decade, eventually bringing down upon themselves, along with Fred Goodwin, a level of public censure and obloquy not seen in the industry up to that point. All three were non-bankers with brilliant academic records who, for a time, were the toast of the City where they were hailed as the acceptable faces of the post-Pitman era of banking. But their ascent to power marked the danger Pitman had warned against many times: non-bankers, with no experience of risk, moving into the top jobs in institutions which had survived for centuries on the principles of prudence and caution. The City, however, was bored with prudence and caution which were not getting Lloyds anywhere, and growth through cost-cutting was out of fashion. The new story was top-line growth, achieved through the use of clever and aggressive marketing techniques designed to sell more financial products through a smaller branch network. A new generation of marketing-oriented managers was offering more risky mortgages aimed at younger wage-earners desperate to get on the housing ladder. Investment banking, with its easier – and larger – returns, was also becoming more highly rated than the slog of squeezing more profit out of an already squeezed retail business. Prudence was out, aggressive lending, investment banking and marketing were in. And Lloyds was only really good at prudence.

Between them the HBOS trio had a total of ten years of banking experience, all at a high level, and none of them had been through a financial crisis of the kind Pitman, Jeremy Morse and bankers of their generation had been tried and tested in. At the top of this talented triangle was the engaging (Lord) Dennis Stevenson, an unorthodox, even eccentric, 56-year-old who, with his left-of-centre leanings and excitable nature, attracted respect and dislike in about equal measure in the City. A thin, stick-like, articulate and voluble man, he was possessed of prodigious energy which reflected in an eclectic range of interests: he was chairman of the Tate Gallery, a decent violinist (he had played in the National Youth Orchestra) and was Chancellor of the London University of the Arts among many other positions. His political connections were immaculate: Peter Mandelson was a close friend, and the Prime Minister, Tony Blair, was something more than a nodding acquaintance.

The son of a farmer and sheriff of Edinburgh, Stevenson won a scholarship to King's College, Cambridge, where he read economics and sociology, played the violin and dabbled in politics. But he only graduated with a humble 2:2 rather than the brilliant first he'd predicted for himself. 'It was the biggest disaster that ever happened to me,' he later recalled. 'I cried for almost a week.' No one, including his tutors, saw it as a reflection on the power of his intellect – just his application. He had too many other interests to occupy his butterfly mind.

None of it stopped him making his mark in the financial world: at the time of the bid he was chairman of Pearson Group, owner of the *Financial Times* and a director of BSkyB, Lazards and *The Economist* among others. Never short of a (usually contrary) view or quip on any subject, he was, as the *Daily Mail* waspishly remarked, 'a man known City-wide for his high opinion of his own worth'. Stevenson preferred to describe himself as 'an unreconstructed 1960s *Guardian*-reading liberal', quite happy to admit he was an 'intellectual snob' who would be 'very cross if anyone came away from meeting me and thought I was dim'. Blair gave him his knighthood in 1997 and he became a life peer two years later.

Soon after it demutualised, Halifax, thinking he might liven up a dull board, invited Stevenson to become chairman, intending the role to be a non-executive one. Stevenson, as he made clear later, never saw it quite like that. 'I can understand a mindset which regards a "non-executive chairman" as sailing above the battle, not concerned with the detailed day-to-day realities,' he wrote to the head of the Financial Services Authority in 2008. 'Can I make it plain that I do not regard myself as that kind of chairman. Yes, I am part-time (but not non-executive). I am legally responsible for the business and with the modesty for which I am not famous regard myself as being knowledgeable and well briefed.' They were words which would come back to haunt him.

The other two members of the top Halifax team were equally bright but, importantly for the future of the new combine, also from non-banking stables. The chief executive, James Crosby, was a 45-year-old Oxford-educated mathematician who had trained as an actuary and then moved into fund management at Rothschild Assurance. Almost totally bald, the joke about his egg-shaped head was that his brain was so big it had pushed out all his hair. He had joined the Halifax in 1994 to run the developing insurance side of the Yorkshire-based building society and took over as chief executive five years later, around the time Stevenson arrived.

Crosby's brief was to transform the Halifax from being a one-product mortgage company into a fully fledged high street bank and he started by following the Pitman bancassurance formula, spending £1 billion to beef up the Clerical Medical insurance subsidiary and aggressively selling its insurance products through the Halifax network. Internet banking was taking off and he created a new telephone and internet bank called Intelligent Finance; he also bought into the wealth management business St James's Place Capital (where Stevenson was a director). All of them were sensible and well-planned moves, properly implemented. The assiduous Crosby was nothing if not competent. But even in the early stages there was some concern among City analysts at the speed at which he was expanding the bank, rapidly eating into his huge deposit base and lending long-term at a far faster rate than the money was coming in.

To run the Halifax's retail operation, where the easiest short-term gains lay, Crosby hired one of the emerging stars of the supermarket industry, the first time a serious retailer had been brought into a bank. Andy Hornby was at least as bright as Crosby, with a first (in English) from Oxford and an MBA from Harvard where he graduated top out of 700 in his year. He joined Boston Consulting, the management consultancy business which took on only the cream of American business graduates – *Fortune* magazine rated it the fourth best company in the world to work for in the late 1990s – before moving on to Blue Circle Cement and finally Asda, the supermarket group where the visionary chief executive Allan Leighton had created what was in effect his own business school. The personable Hornby was one of his brightest graduates and by the time he left to join the Halifax in 1999 he was responsible for 14,000 people and had been appointed to the management board. If Crosby, at forty-five, was young to be the chief executive of a major bank, Hornby, at thirty-two, was a mere baby, soon earning himself the sobriquet 'boy wonder' in the financial press which liked him from the start. No one seemed to wonder how his skills at selling groceries could be translated successfully into banking, but he argued they were both retailing operations requiring pretty much the same disciplines. By the time of the crash in 2008, he had been a banker for just eight years.

This was the trio that set about building the Halifax into what they termed 'a new force in banking' which would have such an impact on the history of British banking in the new millennium.

. . .

The fourth member of this little cast, indeed the man who by rights should have had top billing, was Peter Burt, chief executive designate of the new HBOS. Burt was already fifty-seven, three years short of the Bank of Scotland's normal retirement age, and he had no desire to stay on as chief executive beyond that point. He agreed to serve for three years and then make way for the ambitious Crosby who was said to have wanted the job from the beginning and swallowed his disappointment only reluctantly when he didn't get it immediately.

A professional banker to the core, Burt was also proudly Scottish, a product of one of the smaller public schools (Merchiston) and St Andrews University. He got his MBA at the Wharton business school in Philadelphia, joined the computer company Hewlett Packard and then returned to Scotland where he worked for one of the small secondary banks, Edward Bates, which went bust in the financial crash of 1975. Out of work for three months, he was taken on by the Bank of Scotland where his career flourished in the booming North Sea oil financings market in which the bank did spectacularly well in the 1980s. A favourite of the chief executive, and later Governor, Bruce Pattullo, in 1990 Burt was appointed to run the group's domestic bank.

The Bank of Scotland in the 1990s epitomised all that was staid, cautious but professional in British banking, and Burt, with his down-to-earth,

common-sense approach, was very much at home there. When it cel-
ebrated its tercentenary in 1995, the *Financial Times* described it as 'the
most boring bank in Britain', which it intended as a compliment: 'The
business's steadiness helps explain 300 years of consistent profitability and
more recently how the Bank has outperformed the sector by nearly 100
per cent since 1980.' Over the next five years it increased its profits by an
average 20 per cent a year and it could boast – and did – that its return
on equity of 36 per cent was the highest in the industry, getting close to
the 40 per cent Pitman had managed at his peak. In 1997, the year Burt
took over as chief executive, its share price rose by 85 per cent, making
it the best performing FTSE 100 share.

But the failure of his adventurous NatWest bid, which started so aus-
piciously in 1999, put the Bank of Scotland 'in play', unlikely to retain its
independence in the fierce round of bids that were reshaping the industry. By that stage the bank's rapid expansion had outgrown its deposit
base and it had begun borrowing from the wholesale market where banks
with surplus cash lent to other banks. Most of these loans were relatively
short-term, five years or less (or just overnight in some cases), whereas
mortgage lending was much longer-term. No prudent banker wanted to
become too dependent on the wholesale market, a fact Burt was keenly
conscious of.

After their NatWest rebuff, Burt and his team considered splitting
the bank in two, selling off the retail side altogether and using the proceeds to create what would be the country's leading niche commercial
bank, building on the skills and reputation it acquired from its successful North Sea oil business in the 1980s. But the sums didn't add up and
they rejected the idea and looked for something else.

That was when Burt received the unwanted attentions of Abbey
National and was reluctantly forced to enter into discussions with Harley before, to his considerable relief, the Lloyds bid for Abbey rescued

him. Burt was basically in limbo, waiting for the Competition Commission process to run its course, when in February 2001 he got a call from David Mayhew, the senior partner of the City stockbrokers Cazenove and the most powerful stockbroker in the City, at the centre of many of the big privatisations and takeover bids of the past twenty years (including Guinness).

Mayhew had a proposition which was far more interesting than Abbey: Halifax was interested in talking to him about a merger. It was a perfect fit, he urged. The Halifax had, in the words of one commentator, 'deposits coming out of its ears', the answer to Burt's mounting concern about his dependence on the wholesale market. Mayhew's proposal was that there would be a 'nil-premium merger', with neither side paying a premium above the market price for the other's shares and the top management jobs would be split more or less evenly. Would he be willing to meet James Crosby?

As it happened, Burt had some history with the Halifax, which he had been pursuing for several years with a view to a deal of his own. In the mid-1990s, Burt and his then chief executive Bruce Pattullo made two separate merger approaches to the Halifax to propose a takeover. The first time they got a flat 'no', but on the second occasion the Halifax chief executive, Mike Blackburn, saw the logic in putting the Halifax's savings base together with the Scottish bank's acknowledged banking skills, but his highly conservative board turned it down. Now the boot was on the other foot and the Halifax was the aggressor, this time approaching him.

From the start, although both parties agreed that the senior jobs in the new bank would be split equally, the negotiations were dominated by the Halifax, much the bigger of the two (the shareholding split would be 70/30). As a gesture to the Scottish lobby and the so-called 'Edinburgh Mafia', it was agreed the headquarters would remain in Scotland, one of the few wins for the Scottish side (although the real head office, where all the work was done, would remain in the Yorkshire town of Halifax). Stevenson would be chairman and Crosby deputy executive chairman, and early in the negotiations it was accepted that the Halifax's Mike Ellis would get the chief financial officer role. Hornby would run the retail bank and personal banking. So, in effect, four of the top five jobs would go to Halifax people. The balance, such as it was, was to be made up by Burt becoming chief executive, the single most important role by a long way.

Then, without warning even his colleagues, Burt announced he had had enough and would not take up the job of chief executive, even for three years. He would see the merger through, stay on for a year as executive deputy chairman and then retire. That meant that all the top jobs would go to the Halifax.

A severely shaken Mayhew and the other advisers, fearing a backlash from investors, tried hard to persuade Burt to change his mind, but he was adamant. 'He was tired, not physically, but years of mental strain wrestling with the problems of the bank's future and dragging down the country to proposition potential suitors had been draining,' wrote Ray Perman in his book *Hubris: How HBOS wrecked the best bank in Britain*. 'He had had fruitless talks with a dozen companies and come close to securing NatWest, only to have the prize stolen away from him. Now at last he had found a solution [in Halifax].'

Parliamentary commissions, bank historians and commentators would later look back at this point in the history of both venerable institutions and pinpoint it as the moment the seeds of their catastrophic failure were fatally implanted. The decisions which resulted in a board structure so skewed towards the Halifax were, in the mind of one Scottish banker (later a board member), 'mind-boggling'. The Scottish bank's board, he asserted angrily, 'just rolled over – gave way to Stevenson, who in my book did more damage to Scotland than anyone since King George II. It would just have been inconceivable under Alistair Grant, the former governor.'

Sir Alistair Grant, governor of the Bank of Scotland for just two years, was, perhaps, the spectre at the feast, the missing force whose presence and personality would almost certainly have tipped the balance back to some semblance of parity. Highly regarded in both the Scottish financial community and in the City, Grant was a veteran of many contested takeover battles and was a tough and shrewd negotiator who took no prisoners. Oddly enough, he too, like Hornby, had made his reputation – and fortune – in the supermarket industry where he and his fellow Scot, the more pugnacious James Gulliver, built up the Argyll Group, operating under the Safeway supermarket brand (it later became part of William Morrison). It was Grant, more than Gulliver or the third member of the team, David Webster, who masterminded the £2.4 billion bid for Scotland's greatest company, Distillers, the biggest bid ever made in Britain up to that point, which also became the most controversial in City history when Argyll lost to Guinness. By an odd coincidence, Victor Blank acted as merchant bank adviser to Argyll during the bid and was a good friend of Grant's, whom he played cricket with.

In 1997, by now a pillar of the Scottish establishment and fully fledged member of the Edinburgh Mafia, Grant became chairman – or governor – of the Bank of Scotland. An imposing figure, he worked well with Burt, five years his junior, until tragedy struck. In 1999 he informed the board he had terminal cancer and within eighteen months he was dead. His successor was the nondescript Jack Shaw, an accountant who lacked Grant's authority and flair, so when it came to choosing the chairman of the new joint company, it was no contest. Stevenson got the job.

'For me the whole HBOS tragedy starts with Alistair's illness,' says the Scottish banker. 'I don't believe for a second he would have accepted that management split. Never!'

When Burt's decision to step aside was announced, the reaction in

Edinburgh was one of horror. 'People in Scotland could not believe it,' says the former director,

> and with hindsight it's absolutely incredible that this happened. The combination of Peter Burt ducking out, for whatever reason, and a very weak chair agreeing that Stevenson and Crosby should get the top jobs was simply unbelievable. As far as we were concerned, control had just passed. This bank, which was founded in 1695, had basically gone.

If Burt had stayed on, even for three years, would the subsequent history of HBOS (and Lloyds TSB) have been different? He would still have been outnumbered on the executive committee but he was an experienced hand at managing boards and delicate situations and could have finessed that. Both Crosby and Hornby might have learned something from him, and he would have been a steadying influence on Peter Cummings, the head of the corporate business who had worked under him for years and who respected him greatly. Even before the takeover, Burt was already concerned by his dependence on the wholesale market, which was a mere bagatelle compared to HBOS's borrowings in its final few years. When crisis struck, it was HBOS's Achilles heel.

We will never know whether he would have led HBOS away from disaster. But what is indubitably true is that his absence, and the lack of banking experience on the HBOS executive, was a major contributing factor to the situation which HBOS found itself in when Lehman Brothers went down in September 2008.

In November 2015, the damning Bank of England report heaped blame on the bank's board and top management, and concluded that they 'failed to set an appropriate strategy and also failed to challenge a flawed business model'. It added: 'The paradox of the story is that at the time, and indeed up until near its failure, HBOS was widely regarded as a success story.'

CHAPTER 5

MAROONED

ON **18 APRIL** 2001, Brian Pitman gave his valedictory chairman's address at Lloyds TSB's annual meeting which, as usual, was held in Glasgow. Loyal shareholders turned out in force to say goodbye to him – pensioners, widows and fund managers alike, most of whom had made handsome profits on their investment despite the fall in the share price in recent years. Regardless of the lacklustre performance of the bank in his last few years, he was still their hero and the resounding applause as he rose to speak clearly moved him.

That day he struggled to find any good news for his faithful fans. The Abbey National bid was in limbo, the merger of the Halifax and the Bank of Scotland was galloping ahead with seemingly no obstacles and profits growth had dried up. Nothing seemed to be going right for the Black Horse bank.

Sir Brian tried to make the best of it, describing 2000 as a 'successful year' when the bank had taken over Scottish Widows and profits were (marginally) up. The New Year, he said, had started well enough, the bank was ahead in the first quarter and there was plenty of opportunity left in the domestic market. Analysts, struggling to see where growth was going to come from, were not convinced and there were more bears than bulls among the bigger investors.

The shares that day were 700p, a third off their peak, and someone calculated that they had been the equivalent of 32.2p on the day Pitman became chief executive. Even if he couldn't summon any great message of cheer, that at least was a reasonable note to go out on.

His successor as Lloyds chairman, who he had personally headhunted and recruited, was the 59-year-old Maarten van den Bergh, a man who had spent more than thirty years in the oil industry, ending up as president of Royal Dutch Petroleum, one of the top jobs in Holland. He was the scion of the Van den Bergh margarine family, one of the Dutch founders of Unilever which was almost a family business. His father was the last of a long line of Van den Berghs to sit on the Unilever board. Maarten was a sophisticated, well-connected and widely travelled man who lived outside his native Holland most of his life and now served on half a dozen international boards. But, as he openly confessed, he knew nothing about banking. 'I don't think in the chairman's role you necessarily have to be a banker. You have to be an experienced business person and understand how the world of business works.'

Pitman had recruited him for a specific purpose: to use his European contacts and knowledge to help Lloyds make the major acquisition on the continent he and Ellwood were so keen on. Pitman seemed to have reluctantly accepted, even if Ellwood hadn't, that the acquisition of Abbey was doomed, that expansion in the UK had run out of steam and the bank had to look overseas for its next move. 'You've got to remember,' he said in an interview that weekend with the *Daily Telegraph*, 'that banking – the pure milk of banking – isn't growing very fast. The real growth has been in financial services.'

The British banking market, Pitman added, 'was a reasonably cosy market, protected by regulation – the more regulation, the more difficult it is to get in. Deregulation has brought a flood of competition into this market, all entirely healthy in my view.' But it was becoming harder for Lloyds to maintain its competitive edge. 'You can have the right product, but products can be copied faster than ever before. In financial services if you introduce a new product today, give it a day or two and somebody will copy it. We've got to provide more value for less money – it's true of everything.'

. . .

All this time Ellwood was winding his weary way through the obstacle-laden competition process, becoming more despondent by the day. His mood was made even worse by the speed at which the HBOS merger was merrily sailing along, given a fair wind by just about everybody. The two companies only began talking in February 2001, the news leaked – to a generally favourable reaction – in April and on 4 May the deal was formally announced. By July the circulars had gone out to both sets of shareholders who formally approved the merger in August – and it was done and dusted by September. It was all relatively painless, blessed by the Office of Fair Trading (OFT), the Bank of England, the Financial Services Authority, shareholders and the financial press – everyone, it seemed, except for a few grumpy bankers in Edinburgh who didn't like Stevenson and mourned for their lost bank. But in the euphoria that reigned around the new joint entity, no one paid the Jeremiahs much attention.

The Halifax-Bank of Scotland merger brought to an end the greatest wave of consolidation in British banking history, wholly reshaping the industry in just a few years. It had begun with NatWest bidding for Legal & General; that caused the Bank of Scotland to make a surprise hostile bid for NatWest which it lost to Royal Bank of Scotland. In the meantime Lloyds bid for Abbey National which then approached Bank of Scotland – which merged with Halifax. It seemed like a great game of musical chairs, with Lloyds, which had earlier lost Midland to HSBC, the one left out.

Having committed himself to the fight, Ellwood did everything he could, short of dropping his bid, to win over Denise Kingsmill and her commission, even offering to sell off Abbey National's two million current accounts while retaining the mortgage, savings and credit card businesses. 'You have to wonder what is in it for Lloyds TSB if they are actually willing to give up so much,' one banking analyst pondered. Inside Lloyds, some of the senior executives were asking the same question.

Kingsmill finished her report at the end of June 2001 and sent it to the new Trade Secretary, Patricia Hewitt, who on 10 July delivered her verdict: the merger should be blocked on the grounds that it 'would reduce competition in the markets for personal current accounts and banking services for small and medium-sized enterprises'. Ellwood reacted with fury and disappointment, dismissing the report as unfair and factually wrong. But the failure of the Abbey National bid effectively marked the end of his banking career. He was fifty-eight, several years away from retirement, but from now on he would be a lonely figure at the top, largely ignored by the City and effectively irrelevant inside the bank. Given the importance he had attached to winning his battle, the press that day wanted to know if he would be staying on or doing the honourable thing and resigning. Would he be looking for another job?

'That's absolute rubbish,' he snapped angrily. 'No way! I am getting on with running a very successful bank, as I have over the past four years. We are absolutely committed to finding a transforming deal, which we always admitted Abbey National wasn't, in Europe or America.' Even that went down badly with the City, weary of Lloyds's European forays which went nowhere. 'To make that a key strategy when it was almost undeliverable was not smart,' remarked one anonymous senior investment banker.

Ellwood's reputation was further damaged a year after the bid when Abbey National announced a loss of nearly £1 billion and cut the dividend. Unknown to Ellwood, unable to do due diligence because his bid was hostile, Abbey had been investing heavily in junk bonds, including those issued by Enron, and had to write off £500 million as a result. Diversification into wholesale banking, aircraft leasing, railway companies and corporate bond investing had all turned sour, and analysts reckoned that all of Abbey's acquisitions were losing money – 'they just weren't properly managed,' said one. Abbey's wholesale division was woefully under-provisioned and its life assurance arm, Scottish Mutual, needed an injection of fresh capital. The shares collapsed and Harley resigned, leaving with a pay-off of £1 million. In 2004 Spain's biggest bank, Banco Santander Central Hispano (Santander), bought Abbey for £8 billion, less than half the value of the Lloyds bid. Although Ellwood would never acknowledge it, Denise Kingsmill had actually done Lloyds TSB a big favour.

.   .   .

Ellwood finally shuffled off the scene in May 2003 at a low point in Lloyds's fortunes, with the shares down two-thirds from their peak. Scottish Widows by then had turned into what one commentator referred to as a 'black hole down which the Lloyds share price has disappeared'. Profits after tax barely covered the dividend and there was serious conjecture in the City about Lloyds's ability to maintain it. At the bank's annual meeting in April 2003, Van den Bergh spooked investors by warning that 'no board of directors could guarantee future dividend payments in the current stock market', causing the shares to drop to 388p, a level they had not seen since the mid-1990s. 'Cutting the dividend would be the ultimate indignity for a bank which had ambitions to call the shots in pan-European banking,' wrote one commentator. 'It's now far more likely that, should any truly pan-European banks emerge, Lloyds will be taken over.'

Ellwood took a much more sanguine view right to the end. 'If I have a regret,' he said in his final interview with Grant Ringshaw of the *Telegraph*, 'I would like to have done another major deal. In a sense we were ahead of the game. We have been there talking, putting our bread on the water. The great European deal will be done. It will not be done by me, but by my successor. It is inevitable.'

Not for the first time, history was to prove him wrong.

CHAPTER 6

ENTER ERIC DANIELS

CHOOSING A SUCCESSOR to Ellwood was the job of the Lloyds chairman, Maarten van den Bergh, and he devoted a lot of time and thought to it. He cast the net widely, interviewing and rejecting candidates from other British banks, as well as from the US and Europe. There were some strong internal candidates: Philip Hampton, the fifty-year-old finance director; Mike Fairey, a veteran banker who Ellwood had appointed as his deputy chief executive shortly after he took over; and Eric Daniels, a 51-year-old American who for the past year had been running the core retail banking side, and making an impressive job of it. All three were interviewed, along with half a dozen outside candidates. Daniels got the job.

If Eric Daniels had been a Scot, like Peter Burt or Ian Harley, he would probably have been described by the financial press as 'dour'. As it was, his soft Midwestern drawl and reflective manner earned him the sobriquet 'the quiet American' – or, because he was a heavy smoker, 'Marlboro Man'. Taciturn and reserved, when his appointment was announced he himself joked that 'Invisible Man' might be more appropriate as he had spent the past twelve months 'quite purposely' staying away from the public controversy which increasingly surrounded the poorly performing Lloyds. 'I have tried to refocus the retail bank around the customer,' he said in one of the early interviews he gave. 'I don't think I will find the chief executive's job hard, but it is a tremendously challenging environment in world markets. I am used to challenges.'

Daniels had originally been recruited by Peter Ellwood who wanted to bring fresh blood into the retail side of the bank which still accounted for the bulk of profits but was increasingly underperforming its peers. He was also looking for his potential successor and was not over-impressed with the talent inside the bank. When the headhunters approached Daniels he was between jobs, eighteen months out of banking and sufficiently well-off to be contemplating semi-retirement. 'I wasn't even sure if I wanted to go back into banking,' he said.

Born in Montana, the son of a German professor and a Chinese mother, he studied history at Cornell University followed by an MBA at the academic hothouse MIT, before joining Citibank in 1975. He stayed there for twenty-four years, starting in Panama, moving on to Argentina and finally Chile where he arrived in the early 1980s when the country was in financial turmoil, deep recession and political chaos. Chile survived and as the economy recovered, so did Citibank's fortunes, and by the time he moved on Daniels had built its business into the country's second biggest bank. In total he spent thirteen years in Latin America where he witnessed a series of financial crises as well as some boom times.

Daniels was no stranger to London, where he had done a three-year stint in the mid-1980s running Citibank's private banking business before returning to increasingly senior management roles in the US. In 1999, bored with banking, he decided on a career change and tried his hand at running a dot-com start-up, the Washington-based Zona Financiera, which had a good idea but, like most of the new generation of internet companies, it was ahead of its time. When it was clear it wasn't going to work, he folded it and returned the money to shareholders.

On his arrival in London to meet Ellwood and Maarten van den Bergh, Daniels dropped in on some of the Lloyds branches, and quickly concluded that it was a retail bank ten years behind the times in terms of customer care and electronic systems. Pitman's unrelenting chase for shareholder return had starved Lloyds's branches of capital, and Daniels was appalled to see chewing gum on the carpets (he later discovered the cleaning contract did not include its removal) and shocked by the general level of uncleanliness and disrepair. On the other hand, he decided after his initial recce, there was enormous potential and many of the problems were 'self-inflicted wounds' which could be fixed. Most of them were down to lack of investment and he determined one of the conditions for taking the job would be that Lloyds commit to a major capital expenditure plan to rebuild the branch network.

When Ellwood, who agreed with him about the need for investment, offered him the role as head of retail banking, effectively putting him into pole position for the CEO position (but with no promises), he brought his Panamanian-born wife Eunice over to London which they decided was as good a place as any to put down roots after their nomadic life together. Their twelve-year-old son had been born in London but had moved six times. 'My wife and I would like to get some stability into our lives,' he remarked.

Much had changed in the years he had been away. The first thing that struck him was how attitudes to banks and bankers had deteriorated to the point where they were seen as public villains rather than the friends they used to be. 'When I first got here in 1988,' he remarked wonderingly to a friend, 'bankers were at the top of the pole in terms of respected professions. Now we're right down there at the bottom.' Little did he dream it would get even worse.

Within a few months of taking over the retail operation, Daniels became aware of just how profoundly promises made to the City had driven decision-making inside the bank, putting huge pressure on the executive teams to deliver on them. When TSB was acquired in 1997, Pitman promised to take £350 million out of costs by Year Three of the merger, but Daniels found the process well behind schedule. The most urgent issue was the IT system: originally it was intended to integrate TSB into the Lloyds system but it couldn't handle it. So they tried the TSB network instead, which was far from perfect, and the decision on a new, fully integrated system was put off for years. When the two teams, Lloyds and TSB, got bogged down in trying to integrate the systems, Ellwood gave the job to Archie Kane, one of his senior executives at TSB. It almost wore him down. 'It was a real balls-busting task,' he said later, 'with lots of vested interests and people fighting from the shadows.' It would take the best part of five years to bring it even close to the standard that Daniels demanded.

Daniels was also astonished to find that, three years after the merger, there were still two distinct factions in the bank, the 'blues' (TSB) and the 'greens' (Lloyds), named after the colour of their liveries. The 'greens' tended to be life-long Lloyds employees who had joined the bank straight from school, whereas the 'blues' were much more what he called 'guns for hire' whom TSB had picked up along the way. It sometimes made meetings a fractious process.

For the most part, Ellwood, increasingly under siege from disillusioned shareholders, left him to it, concentrating on sorting out the problems of Scottish Widows, which refused to make even a token attempt at assimilating itself into the culture of its new owner. The stock market crash had wreaked havoc with the insurer's profits and, far from contributing to group profit, the requirements of the Widows (as it was called inside the bank) for new capital in the first few years was eating up Lloyds's precious cash reserve. Board strategy sessions, Daniels found, were mostly taken up with discussing the elusive European acquisition which stubbornly refused to offer itself, and Ellwood's increasing desperation to pull something off before he finally retired.

In his first year Daniels kept his head down, intent on repairing what he called the 'people fabric', which meant persuading the bank's employees to pay more attention to the customer rather than rely on the much-hated call centres. He found a willing staff, eager to respond, but they were demoralised by a decade of branch closures and retrenchments. 'If you want to know how your customers feel about you, ask your staff,' he told his senior executives. 'I grew up at Citibank in a culture which served clients well and that ethos pervaded the bank. We have to change the ethos here.'

. . .

By the time he finally moved into Ellwood's office in May 2003, Daniels had developed a clear strategy which he immediately began to implement. His priority would be to fix what he'd got, invest in the branches, rebuild the customer relationship and upgrade the IT, all to be accomplished against the need to cut costs. It was also imperative that he got profits moving up again and the share price with it. Acquisitions, which had so obsessed his predecessors, would be put on hold.

A few months into his new role, Daniels invited Brian Pitman and Jeremy Morse to lunch in his office, expecting to gain some insight into the problems he was inheriting. He was to be disappointed: although they became a quarterly event, he never got much from the lunches. The financial world had long accepted that Pitman, great a banker though he was in his day, had left Lloyds in a disadvantageous position in the new world of banking, and finding a way out was going to be a long and difficult haul. Daniels was surprised by Pitman's resolute refusal to accept he had got anything wrong or that the genesis of Lloyds's problems in 2003 had anything to do with him. Pitman stoutly defended his decision to sell Lloyds's extensive overseas operation – more than eighty businesses in total – and focus on the UK domestic market where he still argued the returns were better. Morse was more thoughtful, observing that he thought Lloyds should have kept at least some of its overseas businesses, but he defended Pitman who he believed had got most things right.

Privately, Daniels saw it differently. Lloyds was a medium-sized bank, operating on a small island where there was intense competition and a fierce set of interventionist regulators – there were to be five separate competition or regulatory inquiries into the banking industry in his first four years as CEO – in a sector which had gone ex-growth several years before. He was never a great believer in the bancassurance model which Pitman had espoused with such passion – Daniels could see it worked well in European countries, particularly France, where there were tax advantages for savers, but he had long been convinced that its potential was more limited in the UK. He was deeply disturbed by the dependence on acquisitions for growth and the effort that had gone into seeking a continental partner at the expense of the domestic operation. Leaner, nimbler or more specialist institutions – or giants such as his former employer Citigroup – had moved into Lloyds's traditional markets and HBOS, Northern Rock and a host of smaller banks, driven by aggressive and ambitious managers, were chasing market share by cutting margins and offering mortgages on terms that the cautious Daniels had no intention of matching. The Lloyds dividend was barely covered, its revenues were challenged, its margins were being squeezed and, with acquisitions in the UK basically ruled out after the Abbey National debacle, the scope for cost-cutting was limited. It was going to be a long way back.

Lloyds, the new chief executive concluded after just a few months in the job, had entered a classic 'revenue stall' which in his darker moments Daniels feared could lead to a 'death spiral', a cataclysmic cycle in which revenue growth stops, profits fall, costs have to be cut which in turn leads to a decline in service, which leads to a further drop in revenues, more cost cuts – and so on. 'Only one-third of companies which enter a death spiral ever pull out,' he gloomily warned his senior managers, citing an academic study he had read. For years Lloyds had been disinvesting in its mature and virtually static core business and his fear was it might have gone past the point of no return.

For all that, Lloyds was still a large and profitable concern. It was Britain's tenth biggest company, making profits of £70 million a week, owned the largest branch network, several of the best brand names in the industry, and still enjoyed one of the highest returns on equity in the industry. It was not a bad platform to build from.

One of Daniels's immediate priorities was to tackle the underperforming Scottish Widows which the City half-expected him to sell. He was tempted, but there was a big problem: a quirk in the accounting rules allowed Lloyds to double-count the Widows' capital for regulatory purposes, and a sale would have a disproportionate impact on its capital ratios. Lloyds would also have to sell at a substantial loss and Daniels had no wish to start his new job with a whacking great write-off. When he was asked about the Widows at his first City roadshow in August, he replied that he intended to keep it and restructure it.

That meant changing the management. The Widows was run by Mike Ross, a veteran insurance executive who had joined the company when he was sixteen and stayed there for the next thirty-nine years. Despite Ellwood's attentions, Scottish Widows had stubbornly refused to assimilate into the Lloyds structure, retaining its own headquarters in Edinburgh – and also its old mutual culture, which really meant it wasn't terribly interested in Pitman's 'shareholder value' principle. Ross, although Ellwood made him his joint deputy CEO, ran the insurance business as an independent fiefdom into which Lloyds TSB executives ventured only by invitation. Ellwood had never got much in the way of cross-selling or synergies out of it, and by the time Daniels arrived it had become a drain on Lloyds TSB's profits to the point where the dividend was threatened.

It wasn't all the fault of the hard-working Ross, who Daniels regarded as a sound if unimaginative manager, but nonetheless decided the only way to change the culture was to replace him. He summoned Ross down to London, told him what he had in mind, and afterwards issued a short statement announcing Ross's contract had been terminated. 'We believe it is time to have a new person. This is about putting in place a strategy for Scottish Widows that is going to last for the next five years. Mike Ross is fifty-seven.' The parting, Lloyds insiders insist, was 'more amicable than this implied', but whatever the truth Ross was gone within a week with compensation of £430,000 plus a share of that year's profits.

His replacement was another Scot, Archie Kane, the former head of strategy at TSB under Ellwood, who Pitman had cleverly appointed as his integration director. At fifty-one, Kane had been around: from a modest working-class background in Hamilton he studied accountancy at Glasgow University, got an MBA from Cass Business School in London, spent three months at Harvard and then joined Price Waterhouse. At TSB he had worked his way up to the position of financial controller before Ellwood took him under his wing and put him in charge of operations at both the retail banking and insurance businesses. It was Kane who spearheaded the merger negotiations with Lloyds after a detailed analysis of all the other players, including Abbey National.

Daniels liked Kane and set him the task of using his integration skills and experience to bring the Widows inside the group and get it focused on bancassurance. Before Ross departed he had presented Daniels with a five-year plan which he now wanted beefed up and accelerated: Lloyds TSB had 16 million customers, Scottish Widows had 4 million policyholders and there were clearly opportunities for cross-selling.

When the change was announced, Kane's fellow directors teased him with having drawn the short straw. At one of the long, intense executive meetings which Daniels liked to hold, Philip Hampton, the acerbic finance director who had made no secret of his belief that Scottish Widows should be sold, suggested that Kane should go up to Scotland, spend three months preparing Widows for sale and then they would put it on the market. Daniels was irritated but Kane could stand up for himself.

'If I'm going to go up there, I'm going to need all the support I can get from everyone down here,' he said calmly. 'And this is not a three-month job – there's no point in me going up there for three months.' Finally, at the end of a bad-tempered session, Hampton broke the tension with his ironical humour.

'In that case, all I can say is that I feel very sorry for poor Archie!' he said and the room burst into laughter.

Kane set off for Edinburgh with a spring in his step: 'I am tickled pink to be coming back to Scotland,' he told a reporter on *The Scotsman*. When he was asked did he see Scottish Widows as Lloyds TSB's 'problem child', he responded cheerily: 'I don't see it as a problem at all – it's a great opportunity. That's why I've taken the job.'

Almost from the moment he arrived, Scottish Widows began to improve and within five years, after what one Lloyds executive called 'a massive overhaul', it became the most profitable part of the bank. Ellwood had possibly been right after all. He just hadn't been able to make it work.

.   .   .

Six months into the job, Daniels presented his strategy to the Lloyds board at its annual two-day strategy session in October 2003. The first phase, which he reckoned he was already some way down the road to achieving, was to 'reduce earnings volatility and restore profitability';

after that he planned to get some sustainable growth into the business, which would get the share price moving in the right direction; and finally, probably two years down the road, he would use the bank's stronger base as a platform for overseas expansion.

At a City presentation to investors and City editors a few days later he admitted just how tough he was finding it. One slide set out his analysis of the bank's predicament with five 'key messages':

1. We have underperformed;
2. Markets will not get any easier;
3. We have under-exploited opportunities;
4. We have not executed;
5. Progress will not be quick or easy.

Shareholder return, he confessed, had been 'mediocre' since 2000 (in fact it had been terrible), but he ended on what he hoped was a positive note: the bank, he believed, could grow profits while simultaneously resisting intense price pressure on the high street, overhaul the service it was providing to companies and rebuild the battered insurance and investments business. Commentators, used to hearing similar sentiments from the panglossian Ellwood, were unimpressed: '*Bonne chance!*' wrote Robert Peston, then City editor of the *Sunday Telegraph*.

More pressingly, Daniels had another problem, which was also a legacy of Pitman's time: the dividend. In the late 1990s, when Lloyds was spinning off far more cash than it needed, it had come under pressure from the City to return it to shareholders. First Pitman and then Ellwood wanted to keep it for acquisitions, and their compromise was to raise the dividend and keep raising it, with the result that Lloyds shares, which shareholders bought as an income stock, became a high-yielding, non-growth investment ideally suited to widows and pensioners who, not surprisingly, made up a large proportion of stockholders. In many cases, their Lloyds dividend was their main income.

A more cautious bank might have built up its reserves, but clearing banks at that time didn't need large reserves and in any case it would have reduced Pitman's mission of maximising shareholder value. The cash went on piling up until Ellwood spent it all, £6 billion of it, on Scottish Widows – which itself required a further cash injection of another £1 billion. So the bank remained capital 'thin', paid handsome dividends, sold off its overseas assets, spent its spare cash on a non-strategic acquisition and, when the cash began running down, disinvested in its core business.

In 1996, the year before the TSB deal, the dividend was covered twice by net earnings, but as the benefits of the acquisition began to come through, Pitman raised the pay-out to shareholders by 30 per cent in 1998, by 20 per cent the year after and by 16 per cent in 2000, by which stage the cover was down to 1.6, very low by bank standards. By 2002 it wasn't covered at all and the shares were yielding nearly 9 per cent, twice that of the other big banks, reflecting the market's expectation that the dividend would be cut.

Philip Hampton was one director who certainly thought the dividend, by then costing £1.9 billion a year, should be reduced. Hampton had been a surprising choice for finance director of Lloyds when Ellwood recruited him in 2002, ostensibly because he was a deal-maker and could handle the European acquisition Lloyds was always about to make but never did. His background was the City – he worked at Lazards for nine years where he specialised in mergers and acquisitions, after which he spent the 1990s in increasingly senior finance director roles (British Steel, British Gas and British Telecom), and saw himself as a front-runner for the top job at Lloyds when Ellwood retired a year later. He made no secret of his disappointment when Van den Bergh chose Daniels and the two men never hit it off. From the start, Hampton tried to persuade Daniels to take the plunge and do what his predecessors should have done years before: slash the dividend (the Prudential had just done so and its shares had risen), improve the capital ratios and free up £1 billion for the necessary repairs to the retail division. Daniels, backed by Van den Bergh, preferred a policy which he described as 'growing back into the dividend' – in other words, the dividend would be held while earnings caught up and pushed the cover back above the minimum target of 1.5.

In an interview he gave a few years later, Daniels set out his reasoning at the time: 'In 2003 our growth had stalled and our investors saw earnings as volatile and our dividend at risk.' The share price had fallen as a result but his assessment, arrived at after his first serious strategic review with his executive team and board, was that the bank's organic growth potential was better than perceived by the market. 'A dividend cut at that time would have depressed our value further' potentially leading to a takeover bid at less than the real value of the shares. There were, he knew, plenty of overseas banks waiting to pounce at the first opportunity.

Most Lloyds shareholders sided with Daniels but the independent analysts were mostly against him. So were some of the commentators: Robert Peston dubbed Lloyds 'the bank that really ought to pay less', and urged Daniels to 'use the knife', adding, 'as and when his board forces him to make a dividend reduction (as I suspect it will), investors' opprobrium may well be heaped on Daniels, not on the previous team'.

Hampton had a dry, cutting wit and a habit, not lost on the analysts, of throwing in the odd barbed comment at City presentations which managed to indicate he wasn't in total agreement with a particular point made by his CEO. In executive meetings he was often outspoken, making it clear he had his own – often different – opinions and was not going to compromise them. 'In my view of the situation,' says one of the other directors, 'Philip and Eric were never going to get on. Philip was very much his own man and he wasn't interested in toeing the party line, particularly at shareholder presentations. There were open disagreements at executive meetings and Eric didn't regard him as a team player.'

Nine months after Daniels took over, Hampton was gone, his contract terminated 'with immediate effect', although he was allowed to keep his salary of £500,000 a year until he found another job. Lloyds's spokesman tried to spin it that since Hampton joined in 2002 the bank had undergone 'a change in strategic direction ... resulting in a focus on organic growth within the core businesses'. This, he added, 'has meant a move away from the merger, acquisition and restructuring activity that was the strategic focus at the time of his appointment'. Few believed him. 'The problem was that Hampton was probably too combative and quite possibly too ambitious,' commented one observer. Grant Ringshaw in the *Sunday Telegraph* put it more strongly: 'When Philip Hampton was ousted as finance director of Lloyds TSB, the bank lost one of the most respected and creative numbers men in the City.' Within six months Hampton had been recruited by J Sainsbury as its chairman and he would later, by then as Sir Philip, emerge as chairman of RBS, a role he held until 2015.

After that, there was no more discussion about cutting the dividend. In 2001 Lloyds paid a dividend of 34.2p a share, and seven years later it was still paying 34.2p. It was only in 2008, with the banking crisis looming, that Daniels persuaded the board to increase it (by a modest 5 per cent). Its interim dividend for the first half of 2008 was the last it would pay for another seven years.

. . .

As a replacement for Hampton, Daniels surprised the markets by bringing in a high-flying retailer who wasn't a chartered accountant – and a woman at that. Helen Weir came with an impressive pedigree:

still only forty, she had started as a management consultant at Unilever, got her MBA from Stanford and was then recruited by McKinsey, where she specialised in retailing. She joined B&Q, the DIY-chain subsidiary of Kingfisher, a FTSE 100 company (which Victor Blank had helped found), as finance director and later moved up to become the chief financial officer of the holding company. Her appointment to Lloyds raised eyebrows and, according to the *Financial Times*, 'was greeted with some trepidation in the City, given her background in retailing'. But it didn't take her long to win the respect of her colleagues in the bank as she handled the tricky issues with skill and tact and set about preparing for the Basel II capital requirements, a new international regulatory environment under which banks exposed to greater risk would be required to hold a larger amount of capital. In 2004, when Weir arrived at Lloyds, Basel II was still only at the discussion stage but it was looming on the horizon and every bank was going to have to adjust their capital structures to conform with it. At the time it seemed to many bankers to be the product of an over-cautious, even stifling, regulatory regime. In the event it turned out to be hopelessly inadequate.

In October 2003 Daniels appointed a second woman to the executive team: Carol Sergeant had worked at both the Financial Services Authority and the Bank of England, two of the three arms of the regulatory system. She would head up Lloyds's growing risk division, a crucial role in the events that lay ahead.

Within a year the number of women on the top executive team had expanded to three, the third addition a serious star in the banking firmament. Terri Dial was older than Weir or Sergeant – fifty-six when Daniels recruited her – and a banker to her fingertips. She had started out as a humble bank teller in a Wells Fargo branch in San Francisco and rose to become the bank's executive vice president by 1989. In the mid-1990s she caught the attention of the American banking industry when she pioneered the use of direct-mail marketing to take the bank's struggling small business retail operation coast-to-coast, establishing Wells Fargo as one of the US's top business banks. Her fierce work rate and limitless energy earned her the nickname 'the human cyclone', and one of her American colleagues told Daniels: 'Terri has two speeds – fast and faster.' Her recruitment was widely seen in banking circles as quite a coup for Daniels.

The final addition to the Lloyds executive team was another American, Truett Tate, who Daniels knew from his Citibank days when the two men ran into each other at the regular conferences of global executives. Tate and his wife were in Bermuda when Daniels called to ask him if he was interested in running Lloyds's corporate bank under Steve Targett, the head of the wholesale division. After a brief interview with Van den Bergh (legendary in the bank for his taciturnity, Van den Bergh interviews sometimes lasted no more than two or three minutes), he took the job. Within four months, when Steve Targett decided to go back to Australia where his son had been selected for the Olympic squad (butterfly and breast stroke), Daniels promoted Tate to the role on an acting basis.

Daniels was increasingly convinced that, in an environment where demand for mortgages and consumer loans was slowing and bad debts were rising, the wholesale bank was going to have to pick up the slack. In contrast to the tight controls he imposed on the rest of the bank, Daniels gave Truett carte blanche to hire who he wanted, and Truett did, bringing in 1,000 new executives. By 2005 the total number of people employed by Lloyds's wholesale business was 20,000 and it was generating a third of group profits, fast overtaking the core retail side.

The other key members of the team were performing well too. Away from the City goldfish bowl, Archie Kane was playing a blinder in Edinburgh where he had become the darling of the local press and a fully paid-up member of the Edinburgh Mafia. Scottish Widows had an excellent year in 2005, increasing pre-tax profits by 12 per cent to a respectable £683 million, well ahead of the 4 per cent managed by the rest of the bank. Kane had taken out costs, rejuvenated the sales force, restructured the management and was now confounding all those who believed Widows was a dog when Ellwood bought it four years before. In 2005 alone, new business rose 21 per cent and market shares of life insurance, pensions and long-term savings were all up. It was doing so well that Daniels decided he would take some of his – or rather Ellwood's – money back and Widows paid its parent its first dividend since it was acquired, £200 million, plus another £800 million in excess capital. It was a life-saver in what otherwise was a tough year.

Terri Dial's retail arm was not growing but no one blamed her for that. 'She was doing her job really well and the board was impressed by her,' says one of her former colleagues. 'She was an incredible woman, with an intuitive feel for retail and what would work and what wouldn't. She just had to look at a sheet of figures to tell you what was wrong with them.'

There would be testing times in the days ahead, but Daniels was at least convinced his team was up to it.

CHAPTER 7

IMPASSE

IN OCTOBER 2005 Daniels gave the Lloyds TSB board an upbeat assessment of his performance after two years as CEO. The first two phases of his three-part strategy, he said, were now more or less complete: the bank had been stabilised, the quality of earnings improved, growth restarted and customer relations rebuilt. He was now ready for phase three: takeovers were back on the table.

Daniels had convinced the board that unless Lloyds made a major acquisition it would soon become a target itself – in the past six months alone, he told the directors, he had received at least four approaches, some of them less serious than others, but it was an indication of gathering interest in the group. He had chosen this meeting to make sure the directors fully grasped the stark nature of the choices the bank now faced. Lloyds, he said, remained 'strategically disadvantaged' relative to its peers, basically because it was the most exposed to a single economy, with low-to-zero growth markets, and therefore had less room for organic growth. It was also retaining less capital than any of its peers, a factor which would inevitably have to be dealt with at some stage – although not, he emphasised, by cutting the dividend, which would open the door to the predators.

On Daniel's instructions, Patrick Foley, the bank's director of strategy and corporate development, had opened the two-day session with a sobering analysis of the UK banking market which showed that the five-year period of strong growth had come to an end, and progress for Lloyds from now on would depend on cutting costs, increasing charges (which were already causing a major political and public backlash) and outperforming its rivals – all of them difficult.

Foley laboured the 'increasing benefits of international expansion and size' for Lloyds, making the point that, in the new world of international banking, size and 'scalable' IT systems really mattered. 'The upside available to us as a pure "national focused" bank is likely to be capped,' he said.

For nearly two hours Daniels meticulously took the Lloyds directors and executive team through the various options now open to the bank. There were six of them, and he and the strategy team had already rejected five: turning Lloyds into a multi-country 'universal' bank, which meant building a serious investment bank along the lines of Barclays, needed prohibitively high levels of investment and there were no synergies with existing operations; a multi-country bancassurer, which Daniels had never been a fan of, had been turned down on the grounds that it offered 'low and volatile' returns; the next alternative, focusing solely on the domestic market, was rejected too: Terri Dial was highly dubious about future growth, arguing that revenue and profit growth had 'stalled' and the overall market would remain flat at best – she emphasised the '*at best*' – and would stay that way over the next few years.

Daniels also ruled out two other alternatives on his list: developing into a 'multi-country consumer lending business', a bit like the American giant GE, and, finally, building an emerging markets portfolio – Lloyds had missed the boat on that one when Pitman let Standard Chartered slip through his fingers more than a decade before and there were few pickings left for new entrants. 'There are currently no viable paths to deliver this strategy,' Daniels told the board.

That left just one: 'Building a multi-country relationship bank', which involved creating closer relationships with retail, commercial and local corporate customers 'across multiple geographies'. The economics of these 'deep' relationships, Daniels pointed out, were attractive: 'We make more money from selling five products to one customer than one product to five customers.'

Daniels had come to the conclusion, not all that dissimilar to Pitman's early thinking, that the best way to create shareholder value was by attracting and retaining customers, and then winning a greater share of their financial services business. Lloyds had done a great deal of work to build that relationship model in the past four years, but was not there yet and 'maximising' the value of the UK franchise would require investment of maybe £500 million, which would depress earnings, leave the dividend exposed and probably hit the share price. That might make the bank more vulnerable to a takeover, he told the board, but it would have to be done if the final stage of his strategy was to work: expanding into new markets through a cross-border merger. 'Banking products tend to be similar across countries', he said, adding that there would be considerable savings from sharing platforms if they could find the right partner.

This led back to the same old problem which had haunted Lloyds for a decade: 'Progressing by acquisition will be challenging,' he warned. There were, he added, a few suitable banks – and he had, he confided, been talking to a couple of potential targets, 'but this route is not entirely within our control'. Financing an acquisition would probably require disposals, probably of Scottish Widows, the most obvious non-core part of the group. Given Lloyds's capital constraints and its lacklustre share price, Daniels was focusing on a 'merger of equals', rather than an outright takeover, with a similar-sized bank with roughly the same strategy and ethos.

Finally, before opening up the room for discussion, Daniels addressed the unthinkable: seeking a buyer for Lloyds TSB. Even that, however, would not be easy. Of the potential bidders, Bank of America had just paid $35 billion for the credit card company MBNA, JP Morgan Chase was still digesting its $58 billion acquisition of Bank One and Citigroup was ruled out of further mergers or acquisitions by the US Federal Reserve authorities until it got its internal practices, which had been widely criticised, in order. In August there had been rumours that Wells Fargo was about to make an offer for Lloyds, but it never came to anything and the shares fell when it issued a denial.

In any case, as Daniels pointed out, Lloyds wasn't all that attractive to a bidder because of its dependence on a single economy with 'low/zero growth markets'. It would therefore not command a decent premium on the share price, which had sunk back to a two-year low of 440p, and shareholders would almost certainly reject it.

The Lloyds directors left the session in a sombre, thoughtful mood. Several felt that Daniels had given them conflicting messages – did he want to manage the business out of its difficulties or did he want to sell it? One director even voiced the concern that senior managers were running the business in anticipation of future pay-offs.

Adding to the uncertainty, Maarten van den Bergh announced his intention to step down as chairman as soon as the bank could find a successor. There was some speculation, both inside and outside the bank, that the reason for his withdrawal was because he was not getting along with Daniels, but the truth was different. Van den Bergh's last year at Lloyds was over-shadowed by the disclosure of Shell, where he still had an executive role, in early 2004 that it had greatly overstated its oil reserves, a closely watched indicator of an energy company's health. The shares collapsed, the chief executive resigned and the age-old Anglo-Dutch dual corporate structure was consolidated into a single parent company overseen by one board. Van den Bergh found himself right in the middle of it.

'Maarten was literally shell-shocked by those events,' says one of the Lloyds directors.

> The Shell thing and all the corporate governance stuff really got to him and he felt he had to concentrate all his efforts on that. It had nothing to do with Eric – in fact he had this kind of paternalistic relationship with Eric who he encouraged to look beyond Lloyds. It was Maarten who got Eric onto the BT board for instance.

Daniels appeared genuinely sorry to lose him and later made an untypically emotional speech at his farewell party. 'We gave him a good send-off,' says one of the directors there.

Although he left no lasting impression on Lloyds, Van den Bergh's departure did leave a vacuum at the top which urgently needed to be filled.

CHAPTER 8

DRAWING BLANK

IN THE AUTUMN of 2005, Sir Victor Blank and Eric Daniels were introduced to each other at a charity event in Buckingham Palace. It was the first time they had met although obviously they had heard of one another. They chatted amiably and went their separate ways. But a few weeks later Blank got a call from Ashley Summerfield of the headhunters Egon Zehnder. Maarten van den Bergh, said Summerfield, was retiring as chairman of Lloyds TSB after five years in the job. Would Victor be interested in being considered as his replacement? As all good headhunters do, he left the impression there were no other serious candidates in the running, although in fact there were.

Blank was flattered but did not immediately rush to commit himself. Banks were deeply unpopular at the time, both with the public and with the Blair government, and new and complex regulations were making it uncomfortable even for ordinary non-executive directors to sit on a bank board. Taking on the chairmanship of Britain's fifth biggest bank, which was struggling to make progress against more agile and stronger competitors, was a decision not to be taken lightly.

'It is getting more difficult to find a suitable and available candidate for a FTSE 100 company,' remarked the Lombard column in the *Financial Times* that week. 'It is of course taboo to chair more than one. Those who are approached ... may be deterred by the time they would have to devote to compliance as opposed to strategy.'

Blank was already chairman of two listed companies, Great Universal Stores (GUS) and the Trinity Mirror newspapers group, a merger of the Mirror Group and the regional newspaper company Trinity which Blank had orchestrated. They were demanding roles but as it happened he was coming to the end of his term at both and, at the age of sixty-five, he was looking forward to taking things easier. He had been offered other directorships and even a couple of chairmanships, but he and his wife Sylvia had agreed they should spend more time at their sixteenth-century home near Oxford, where Blank had built his own cricket pitch. But he was intrigued by the Lloyds role and decided it was at least worth exploring.

After meeting several of the non-executive directors, who took him through the strategic issues the bank was wrestling with, he then met Van den Bergh who was clearly disappointed at the bank's failure to make an acquisition in Europe on his watch – and, Blank could not help feeling, pleased to be out of it all.

After that, Blank had two long sessions with Eric Daniels who, he learned later, had interviewed a shortlist of four candidates, only two of which he intended to put forward to the board after agreement with Van den Bergh and the nominations committee. By that stage Blank had emerged as the favourite.

Their first meeting was in the Dorchester where Daniels surprised him by proposing he meet the executive directors, Helen Weir, Terri Dial, Truett Tate and Archie Kane, before going to the next stage. 'I was not quite sure if it was with a view to them having a veto or whether it was just part of the process,' he remarked afterwards. In fact it was simpler than that: 'It was a typical Eric thing,' says a member of his team. 'He wanted the others to get a feel for Victor – he didn't like to run these things as an autocrat.'

The meetings went well enough but Blank remained unsure about Lloyds, a bank he didn't know very well despite half a lifetime in the banking industry. He had served on the board of the Royal Bank of Scotland for eight years and had also run the Charterhouse merchant bank in the City, so he knew the banking world better than most non-bankers. And he could claim Pitman as a friend who he had talked to about banking – and Lloyds – for years. But that was not enough for him to make a decision as important as this one.

Ostensibly the chairmanship of Lloyds TSB was a part-time role, involving, he was told, about two days a week. But Blank knew better. GUS and Trinity Mirror, both much smaller companies, were absorbing a working week between them and he always seemed to be involved in either a crisis – frequent at the Mirror Group – or in major restructuring or capital events. Lloyds was very much in the public gaze, its every action perused by critical customers, baleful government ministers and a hostile press, not to mention a regulatory regime which was getting more unfriendly by the day. Shareholders too were disgruntled after seeing their shares almost halve in six years, and it would be a major job to regain their loyalty. There would be nothing part-time about it.

He was still pondering his decision when, in the dying days of 2005, there was a flurry of disturbing headlines around the bank. A trade union survey accused Lloyds TSB of pressuring staff to sell products they knew customers did not need or couldn't afford, particularly the controversial payment protection insurance, or PPI, policies. Lloyds was the leader in the PPI field and Terri Dial indignantly responded that the product was sold to standards set by the FSA, was fully approved by them and the bank had elaborate procedures to prevent mis-selling. The unions of course had their own axe to grind but the accusations, based on a poll of Lloyds staff, were eagerly seized on by a press which was increasingly anti-bank. 'Lloyds staff fear mis-selling pressure,' said the *Telegraph*, while *The Guardian* warned: 'If you bank at Lloyds, watch out.' There was much more along the same lines.

The Citizens' Advice Bureau felt so strongly about the survey that it made a 'super-complaint' – something a bit stronger than a common-or-garden 'complaint' – to the Office of Fair Trading. That in turn led to an investigation by the FSA which solemnly pronounced that its chairman, Callum McCarthy, had warned the banks 'to be careful with their incentive structures. Where there is too much commission targeting, there can be mis-selling.'

This was serious stuff for Lloyds. Just a few months earlier, Morgan Stanley had published a report which estimated that 17 per cent of Lloyds's profits came from PPI and growth had become dependent on it. Inside the bank the reaction was more of indignation than remorse: to this day many of the former Lloyds directors insist there was nothing basically wrong with the PPI product as originally designed and sold and in a different political climate the big banks would have got together and defended their position, much as they had done with overdraft charges, avoiding – or at least reducing – the enormous penalties. 'The FSA was as complicit as the banks in this,' says one former director. 'They knew everything that was going on, saw the figures, approved the products, heard the complaints – there was nothing we knew that they didn't.' No one at this point, inside or outside the bank, had any inkling of how controversial PPI was to prove – or how damaging for the bank.

Blank read the flurry of press comment with interest but there was nothing there to put him off. Then, in December 2005, Lloyds issued a profits update which didn't make encouraging reading. It portrayed a picture of slow transformation with little sign that Dial's aggressive marketing was working – the bank still only had 9 per cent of the mortgage market compared with over 20 per cent of current accounts, which was a mature and non-growth market. Bad debt, particularly on its credit card business (essentially unsecured loans with a high rate of defaults) was also becoming a serious worry, rates of provisioning were rising and Lloyds confirmed it had a £3 billion hole in its pension fund. Profit growth in 2006, the bank warned, would be slow, causing the *Financial Times* to remark dryly that the Black Horse bank, despite Daniels's best efforts, was 'progressing at a trot, not a gallop'.

The lacklustre results led to another round of takeover rumours, again naming Wells Fargo as a potential bidder (it denied it), and Banco Bilbao Vizcaya Argentaria (BBVA) of Spain, one of the banks Lloyds had been talking to for years. Other market stories described Lloyds as an 'attractive target' for a US bidder such as Bank of America or Citigroup. The hunter was becoming the hunted.

. . .

Blank had still not made his mind up when he had lunch with Carol Leonard, a former *Times* journalist who had become one of the most successful headhunters in the country. She was an old friend of Blank's and he told her in confidence about the Lloyds offer and his dilemma. What would she advise him to do? Leonard's response was immediate and unequivocal: 'Victor, if you're asked to be chairman of a clearing bank, that's an honour you can't refuse.' Even Lloyds? Yes – *particularly* Lloyds, where he could make a real difference. When he bounced it off a couple of other friends whose views he respected, he got the same response. His wife Sylvia also gave her approval. He called Summerfield to say he would accept.

He was still negotiating the terms of his contract when the news of his appointment leaked towards the end of January 2006. The response was positive, with commentators more surprised that Blank had agreed to take the job than they were at the bank for offering it to him.

'Sir Victor Blank looms large in the UK financial world,' wrote the *Financial Times*.

> So if the reports are correct and it took Lloyds 18 months to alight on him as the bank's next chairman, then the headhunters cannot have been looking very carefully. Either that, or it takes time to persuade a candidate of his calibre that the prospect of chairing a perennial bid candidate with an over-dependence on indebted British customers is an attractive one.

Shareholders liked it too: M&G and Schroders offered the view that it was a 'positive appointment', while another institution ventured the opinion that 'Eric Daniels is doing all the right things but it is a long haul – and we see Victor as accelerating the value-creation timetable. But please maintain the dividend!'

. . .

In many ways Blank was the ideal chairman for Lloyds TSB at this particular moment in its history – and in his career. There were very few available people with a financial background as broad and varied as his, and even fewer with his experience of chairing major public companies. A gregarious and popular man, he was completely at home in the City and had a wide range of friends and acquaintances in the world of business, media, politics, sport and even show business. He was a well-regarded chairman of large public companies and had served on countless boards, many of them charitable. For years he had chaired Wellbeing of

Women, a charity that researched obstetrical and gynaecological issues of great importance to women and their ability to give safe delivery to their babies.

His annual cricket matches, played on his own ground, were attended by a wide range of prominent City figures, politicians, show business figures and the elite of the cricket world who regarded it as one of the highlights of their social season. Guest players, who took their cricket seriously, could find themselves facing the spin of Shane Warne or bowling at Sunil Gavaskar, probably the best batsman in the world in his day. Blank captained one team and for years his great friend, the late Sir David Frost, captained the other, each team composed of a mixture of businessmen, who paid up to £20,000 to play – Sir Martin Sorrell, a cricket enthusiast, liked to open the batting – and some of the world's finest professional cricketers, only slightly past their best. The one-day cricket matches raised an average of £200,000 in aid of Wellbeing of Women, and over more than twenty-five years the total raised by Blank and Frost for the charity exceeded £6 million – just from cricket.

The news of his appointment brought forth a flurry of profiles of the man about to step into one of the hottest seats in the British business world and Blank found himself described variously as 'groomed and polished, in both appearance and manner' or 'a sleek, elegant and courteous man'. Another writer commented on his 'rumpled face that can't hide emotion', adding that there was 'an endearing directness and openness to Blank'. Words such as 'charming' and 'clever' cropped up frequently, although no profile was complete without a reference to the hidden side of his character, which concluded that he was either 'tough' or 'incredibly tough' – some people, commented one profile writer, 'call him ruthless, suggesting he revels in an intoxicating mix of power and wealth'. Just about every interview or profile referred to him as 'well-connected', with his 'finger on the pulse of the Square Mile' – which was true.

Blank had been around long enough to let the commentary, good and bad, pass over his head. In a long innings in the City he had seen far too many people come to believe their own publicity, inevitably inviting their nemesis, and he was determined not to be one of them. He had established his reputation originally as a shrewd lawyer and adviser in often delicate corporate situations, and that was a pretty good background from which to handle his most prominent role yet.

Difficult to ruffle or provoke, he was slow to anger and few of the many managers and fellow directors he worked with remembered tantrums or raised voices. Instead they recalled his refusal to be rushed into an opinion or decision, whatever the crisis, without proper thought and deliberation. But his record also showed a willingness to act and an ability to take hard decisions when he was required to: he had been responsible for – or at least had an involvement in – removing half a dozen chief executives and one editor and he made no apology for it.

Blank was descended from Ukrainian immigrants who were driven out of the Pale of Settlement, the only region of Czarist Russia where Jews were allowed to live, by the pogroms of the 1880s – Blank liked to describe this as a 'real-life *Fiddler on the Roof* story'. His grandfather arrived in Liverpool with no possessions and no English, just an address which enabled him to track down his brother who had made the trip a few years earlier. He got a job in Stockport, just outside Manchester, working in a textile factory, a sweat shop where the wages were low and conditions grim. He must have been tempted to follow his more adventurous brother when he moved on again, this time to Saskatchewan under a Canadian Pacific Railway scheme, where he established a small community just outside the town of Saskatoon. Two sisters emigrated to Argentina and a fifth member of the family went back to Russia where he served as a Cossack, fighting for the Czar against the Bolsheviks in the 1917 Revolution.

One of the family legends was that the Blanks were related to Lenin, whose maternal grandmother, Maria Alexandrovna Blank, converted to Christianity when she married Ilya Ulyanov. Vladimir Ilich Lenin was born Vladimir Ilich Ulyanov in 1870, and in the 1920s and 1930s his quarter-Jewish heritage was regularly referred to by the anti-Semitic Bolshevik conspiracy theorists who liked to link Zionism with Communism (Soviet historians, on the other hand, always denied that Lenin had any Jewish ancestry). Nobody really knew the truth of the relationship, but Blank was always seriously entertained by the notion he might be a distant cousin of Lenin.

Grandfather Blank settled in Stockport where there was a significant Jewish community and lived in Bann Street in the town centre, just behind the railway station. In the 1930s he set up his own business as a tailor and gents' outfitter in Princes Street, even becoming head of the local Drapers' Union, which years later his grandson, only half-jokingly, liked to cite as 'proof of my working-class credentials'. His son Joseph eventually took over the shop where he spent the rest of his working life.

Blank, born in 1942, served behind the shop counter in his school holidays and always said he learned many of his most important lessons working in his father's shop. 'It gave me an idea of how a small business should be run,' he said many years later, 'and taught me the principle that the customer is key in the retail business and must be looked after.' One of Blank's earliest memories is of his father, cutting and sewing cloth, sitting cross-legged on the sewing machine table with a cigarette dangling from his mouth and ash falling on the table. That was a happy memory in a childhood tragically overshadowed by the death of his mother from ovarian cancer when he was twelve, the origin of Blank's life-long commitment to raising money for women's health organisations.

Typically for a first generation Jewish immigrant, his father's ambition was for his son to get a good education and then join one of the professions. Blank did both. He went to Stockport Grammar and then got a place at St Catherine's College, Oxford, 'where I not only studied, but imbibed, English history'. However successful he became in later life, he never deserted his Manchester background or his boyhood teams, remaining a fervent fan of Manchester United and Lancashire County Cricket Club. 'If you say: where are your real roots, where did you get your values, where were you brought up, where did you get all your formative experiences? … It was there, and that's all pre-business.'

Even from his early days at university, Victor was interested in the law and, coming up to his final exams, he began looking for a job as an articled clerk with a firm of solicitors. Someone effected an introduction to Clifford-Turner in London and in 1963 he caught the train for an interview which turned out to be the most important one of his life.

He arrived at the offices of Clifford-Turner (it later merged with Coward Chance to become Clifford Chance, one of the largest multinational law firms in the world today) in Old Jewry, near the Bank of England, to be told that the partners he was due to meet were both in the Law Courts in the Strand. He was taken there by an office messenger on the bus and interviewed in one of the busy passageways at the back of the huge building. It was a pretty casual interview, the understanding being that if Blank was good enough to get a decent Oxford degree then he would be very suitable as an articled clerk – in those days there were more vacancies than applicants.

Clifford-Turner, although he wasn't aware of it at the time, was one of the few City law firms enlightened enough to take on Jewish articled clerks – although as yet there was no Jewish partner. Blank's religion didn't even come up in the interview and his principal questioner seemed to be more interested in sport: 'Do you play golf?' he asked earnestly. Blank for a moment was tempted to give the flippant reply, 'No, I am not old enough', but some instinct warned him that was not the right answer. He simply responded 'No'. He discovered later that the partner took his golf very seriously, played off scratch (he later became chairman of the Rules Committee at the Royal and Ancient Golf Club) and an irreverent reply might have lost Blank the job. 'I genuinely believe that the angels smiled on me that day,' he said years later.

It was a story he often related in later life as an important illustration of the lack of prejudice he encountered throughout his career. 'It's less important what it says about me – I am no brighter or more gifted, no more ambitious or insightful than countless of my other countrymen or women – than what it says about Britain,' he told Chris Blackhurst in a *Management Today* interview in 2009. 'It's about tolerance and freedom and opportunity, which to a sceptical 21st-century ear sound like empty clichés. Not for me. They are precisely the things which have allowed me to become what I am.'

Five years after he joined the law firm he became the youngest and the first Jewish partner and by 1980 he was one of the most successful corporate lawyers in the City, specialising in the booming business of mergers and acquisitions. With his friend Mark Weinberg, the South African who founded the Abbey Life insurance business (later bought by Lloyds), he co-authored the definitive guide to takeovers which, updated and reprinted countless times, has been the bible for corporate bankers and lawyers ever since.

Then, in 1981, he moved on, abandoning the law profession to become a banker. When it first approached him to run its corporate finance division, Charterhouse Japhet was a relatively unknown merchant bank which had recently bought the rump of Keyser Ullman, one of the many banks rescued by the Bank of England 'lifeboat' operation. But under its ambitious new chairman, John Hyde, it was rapidly making a name for itself as a mergers and acquisitions specialist, a sector which was booming in the frenetic takeover boom getting under way at the time. Blank was happy where he was, a senior and influential partner in a top City law firm with a secure future and a growing reputation – everything his father could have hoped for him. But he accepted Hyde's offer, much to the dismay of some of his clients. The senior partner of one New York law firm lamented the fact that 'the best lawyer in the United Kingdom' had abandoned the profession to go into merchant banking. Blank, however, never regretted it. As he said later, 'I would have kicked myself if I didn't give it a try.'

His big break came a year later when he engineered one of the most innovative takeovers of its day, the leveraged buy-out of Woolworth which was still, despite many years of decline, one of the most iconic names on Britain's high streets. Although it was quoted on the London Stock Exchange and was run as an independent company under British management, it was actually 52 per cent-owned by the American Woolworth company. Blank, in his capacity as a lawyer, had acted for the American parent and knew it would be receptive to an offer, but only from the 'right' people – it had turned down approaches from bidders whom it dismissed as asset-strippers and opportunists.

Under Blank's leadership, Charterhouse formed a new company called Paternoster Stores, named after its office in Paternoster Row, near St Paul's, and then quietly put together a consortium, largely of British institutions, to back a group of former British Sugar managers led by John Beckett, Geoff Mulcahy and Nigel Whitaker (the man who pioneered Sunday opening). They then launched one of the more audacious offers of the day, going over the heads of the local Woolworth board who were completely caught off guard. After a brief, ineffectual fight, they gave in.

By modern standards, although it was called a 'leveraged buy-out', it was remarkably un-leveraged – the total cost of £310 million was split 50/50 between debt and equity, whereas today the debt component would probably be at least 80 per cent. And the assets being acquired, including hundreds of freehold stores in the centre of towns across the country, were valued in the Woolworth's balance sheet at a fraction of their worth. Blank risked a lot on the deal, putting in virtually all the capital he had accumulated and borrowing even more. 'I believed in it and I backed it with everything I'd got,' he said later.

It was the biggest deal of its kind done up to that time and the first leveraged buy-out of a quoted company – and it was a big success. Mulcahy and his team changed the name to Kingfisher, sold off many of the stores and focused their resources and energies on its main subsidiary, the B&Q home improvement stores (where Helen Weir would later cut her management teeth) and the Comet electrical retail chain. Over the next decade it was transformed into Europe's biggest home improvements company and the third biggest in the world. The Woolworth chain itself was demerged, continued its long decline and closed down in 2009, but the rest of the business boomed and Kingfisher's market value in 2015 was nearly £9 billion.

It turned Blank into a serious player on the corporate stage and more deals followed along the same pattern, propelling Charterhouse into the senior league in the takeover world. Its development capital arm became more and more involved in buy-outs into which its senior management, including Blank, invested alongside the bank. Most of them did well and, on top of the Woolworth deal, and these investments were the principal sources of his wealth. 'It wasn't millions and millions of pounds,' he said later, 'but it was wealth. I was one of the lucky ones.'

In 1985, the Royal Bank of Scotland bought Charterhouse with the idea of building a serious corporate banking operation in the City. It worked well for a while but RBS became increasingly uncomfortable with the City investment banking culture, proving yet again that clearing banks and investment banks didn't – and still don't – belong together. Blank and RBS eventually agreed a new strategy which involved the creation of a cross-border investment banking business. In 1993 RBS sold

90 per cent of Charterhouse to Crédit Commercial of France and BHF Bank of Germany in equal proportions. The concept was that the three banks would merge their interests into a single, well-capitalised investment bank capable of handling some of the big European mergers which were beginning to happen with particular emphasis on the middle market where all three banks were strong. It never worked, or at least not well. 'Each had different businesses and they were disinclined to mould them into the same pattern,' he remarked later.

He finally moved on from Charterhouse in 1996, after eleven years as chairman and chief executive, to take on a portfolio of non-executive directorships, his abiding regret being that he never managed to turn Charterhouse into a major-league international investment bank. 'It would have been nice to get to the top of the hill.'

His biggest non-executive role was at Great Universal Stores (GUS), one of the country's largest retailers which had been founded by Sir Isaac Wolfson, the son of a Russian Jewish immigrant, in Glasgow in the 1930s. In its heyday, GUS had been one of the most aggressive acquirers of companies in the country but by the time Blank arrived it was almost dormant, basically the asset pot for the Wolfson family which still controlled it through an archaic voting – or non-voting – structure. Much of the family wealth was in the Wolfson Foundation, and several years after he joined the board as deputy chairman in 1993, Blank attended a dinner at the Royal Society to mark £1 billion that the foundation had donated to charities, including colleges at both Oxford and Cambridge (Isaac Wolfson, who originally endowed the foundation with £6 million worth of GUS shares in 1955, liked to joke that he was the only man since Jesus to have a college named after him at both universities).

Blank had known Isaac, who died in 1991, slightly and when his son Leonard invited him to join the board in 1993 he willingly accepted. But it was a stultifying place, managed by the ultra-cautious Leonard who ran it as a private, family company where the board played no mean-ingful role. At his first board meeting, Blank found there were no board papers whatsoever, just a list of transactions that required the company's seal and ratification by the board. And even that had to be handed back at the end of the meeting.

That all changed a few years later when Leonard was shouldered aside by his more ambitious cousin David, Margaret Thatcher's former chief of staff, who set about reinvigorating the company. One of his early decisions was to appoint Blank as his deputy chairman and give him an office in the GUS building which he used as his base, in return providing advice to the group. The younger Wolfson, determined to inject some growth into the company, made a rapid series of acquisitions including the Experian credit-checking business, which he bought for £1.7 billion and merged it with GUS's own smaller credit-checking operation, producing a dominant player in a rapidly expanding international industry. After a bitterly contested takeover bid, he also bought the Argos retail group.

Wolfson's most inspired decision was to persuade Rose Marie Bravo, one of the US's hottest retailers – she was president of Saks Fifth Ave-nue – to move from her plush Manhattan offices to a shabby building in London's East End above a coat factory to take over Burberry, which Sir Isaac had acquired many years before and never done anything with. When Bravo became CEO in 1997, Burberry was best known for its iconic trench coats with plaid lining – and for outfitting both Roald Amundsen and Robert Scott on their polar expeditions a century before and Mallory and Irving on their Everest expedition in the 1930s. But it was a nonentity in the fashion world.

Bravo's transformation of Burberry over the next five years became the stuff of legend, one of the most successful retail success stories of the 1990s. 'It was necessary to convince the board that being the first British brand to compete on an international level in the luxury goods market was a good thing,' she said later. Blank, for one, didn't need much convincing and the GUS board gave Bravo its full backing as she set about hiring some of the best creative, financial and marketing brains in the business. Perhaps her biggest coups were poaching the up-and-coming designer Christopher Bailey (now CEO) from Gucci, and hiring the supermodel Kate Moss to redefine Burberry's image, even launching plaid bikinis which quickly became cult items.

Yet, for all its successes, the GUS boardroom was an unhappy place, with the directors increasingly uncomfortable with their autocratic chairman. Wolfson, a brilliant strategist and visionary businessman, lacked management skills and had fallen out with most of his executive team who found it hard to cope with his unorthodox methods of running the company – for instance, it was said that he had never written a memo to any of his staff. The City institutions, aware of the internal tensions, and his own board pressed him to split his role as chairman and chief executive but he flatly refused.

The simmering situation came to a head in 2000 when GUS had to issue a profits warning, the first in its history, and the board decided it was time to act. Blank got the job of taking Wolfson aside and telling him he could either be chairman or chief executive but he couldn't be both. 'David was a better chairman than he was a CEO,' said Blank later. Blank proposed that John Peace, a long-time GUS stalwart who ran Experian, should be promoted to the group CEO role and Wolfson initially agreed. It was an uncomfortable situation however for everyone concerned, particularly Wolfson who eventually resigned from a company which he had transformed and which had been run by the Wolfson family for sixty-six years.

Blank was the obvious choice to take over as chairman and over the next six years he and Peace worked closely together to accelerate the process of getting out of low-growth businesses, such as credit mail order, the core of the old Wolfson empire (later bought by the Barclay brothers, owners of the *Telegraph*), and a big property portfolio. By 2004 the slimmed-down and highly profitable GUS consisted of Burberry (which that year made profits of £138 million), Experian (an even bigger success story), a merged Argos and Homebase which they called Home Retail and a furnishing retail chain (Lewis's) in South Africa.

The big strategic question was what to do next? The individual parts were worth more than the whole, and over the next two years all the major subsidiaries were either sold or floated off. In March 2000, when Blank took over, GUS's market capitalisation was just under £7 billion. In 2015 the constituent parts were worth more than £25 billion (Burberry alone was capitalised at £7 billion, Home Retail at £1.6 billion and Experian, floated in 2006, had a market value of £12 billion).

．　．　．

For most of his time at GUS, Blank was also chairman of Trinity Mirror Newspapers, a challenging and sometimes exhilarating experience from which he emerged both scarred and wiser while managing to retain his standing in the City. During his eight years as chairman there was scarcely a month when he wasn't involved in a drama of some kind, many of them highly contentious issues which were acted out in the full glare of public scrutiny. The *Daily Mirror*, the flagship of the company's national titles (*Sunday Mirror* and *People*, as well as *Sporting Life*) was the only left-of-centre mass circulation newspaper in Britain and had traditionally supported the Labour Party and the trade union movement since its creation almost a century before. At its peak in the 1960s, before Rupert Murdoch launched the more down-market *Sun*, it sold over 5 million copies a day and, together with other group titles, was read by nearly two-thirds of all the voters in Britain. Its then chairman, Cecil

King, claimed that it was the *Mirror* which had elected Harold Wilson's Labour government in 1964 and threatened that if it insisted on increasing taxes, it would un-elect him again (King himself was un-elected a year later, unceremoniously dumped by his horrified board).

The *Mirror*, although pushed into second place by the brasher and often outrageous *Sun*, was still a proud and profitable newspaper group when Robert Maxwell got hold of it in 1984. By the time he fell off his boat seven years later, it had been looted, its pension fund plundered and its reputation seriously damaged. In 1992 the company, staggering under a weight of debt and with circulations and advertising revenues in free-fall, recruited the 43-year-old David Montgomery, the former editor of the *News of the World* and *Today* (both Murdoch papers) as chief executive and he set about restoring it to health in the only way he knew how – through savage cost-cutting.

Six years after Maxwell's departure from this world, Montgomery invited Victor Blank to take over as chairman, replacing another former banker, Sir Robert Clark (chairman of Hill Samuel when TSB bought it in 1987 for £777 million). Blank had met Montgomery a few times and respected him, and the idea of being involved with a major media company, particularly a left-of-centre one, appealed to him. He soon realised it opened up unexpected doors. Shortly after he arrived he got a call from Roy Greenslade, the *Mirror's* former editor and a media commentator (and professor of journalism), asking him if he would take a call from Alastair Campbell, the former *Mirror* journalist and spin-doctor for the Prime Minister Tony Blair. Campbell called shortly afterwards and said that the Prime Minister didn't really know him and wondered if Blank would like to come in for a chat in Downing Street?

Blank, although he had been around the edges of the political world for some time, was both surprised and flattered. Prime Ministers didn't call GUS chairmen or bank executives, however august, and invite them to No. 10 simply to discuss the weather – but newspaper chairmen were clearly more sought after. A few days later he turned up in Downing Street where Blair greeted him warmly and ushered him into the private sitting room which Margaret Thatcher and other prime ministers often used for one-on-one meetings. Blair, it soon became apparent, was concerned that the *Mirror*, under Blank's leadership, would take a turn to the right and change sides in the next election which was then less than a year away. 'He wanted to see me because he had heard I was a closet Tory,' Blank explained afterwards. Blair had heard he was friendly with John Major and wanted to get the feel of his man, grilling him on how well he knew Major (fairly well) and where his political beliefs lay. When Blair pressed him on where the Mirror newspapers stood politically, Blank pointed out that their readership consisted predominantly of working-class Labour voters and to try to change that would be 'commercial suicide'.

In fact Blank was only mildly political, pretty much centre-of-the-road, although leaning more towards the left than the right. When someone asked him what his political views were, he answered 'somewhere between Roy Jenkins and Iain Macleod – and if you can find any space between them, I'm probably sitting in it'. These were his two political heroes, whose liberal views he shared. He admired Margaret Thatcher, but more for her leadership qualities than her political beliefs and he was never a fan. His background, he always said, made that difficult, although friends who came from similar backgrounds, such as (Lord) David Young, were big Thatcher supporters.

After the meeting in Downing Street he saw a lot more of Blair, often meeting him at dinners or receptions and if he needed to talk about something, which occasionally he did, he could always get through. Every September he hosted the Prime Minister at the Labour Party conference where there was a tradition, on the middle day of the conference, of the

Mirror chairman hosting a lunch for the party leader, who in Blank's time was always Blair. In turn he was invited to events in Downing Street or, occasionally, to lunch at Chequers at the weekends.

During this period he got to know Gordon Brown rather better, visiting him at No. 11 Downing Street or the Treasury where the Chancellor liked to talk about what was happening in the City and banking worlds. But he became disenchanted with the Labour government's failure to get a grip on the management of the big public service departments which, in Blank's judgment, wasted vast quantities of taxpayers' money through inefficient management. However at a personal level he remained friendly with both Blair and Brown.

Moving in high political circles was one of the pleasanter and more interesting aspects of chairing a newspaper group. The rest was mostly keeping the peace between warring editors and management, or fire-fighting crises when an editor stepped out of line – at which the imperturbable Blank was expert. When he arrived on the scene, the *Daily Mirror*'s circulation was down to 2.3 million, well behind Murdoch's *Sun* and in third place to the *Daily Mail*. Like all newspaper groups it was facing not just declining readership but advertising revenues that were falling annually in double-digits. Montgomery, a dour, introverted and abrasive Ulsterman, had spent £400 million on acquisitions, including a 50 per cent stake in the loss-making *Independent*, and had seen the share price halve. His hands-on style of management, in the words of one commentator (Peter Preston, former editor of the *Guardian*), 'often seemed to mean clenched fists'. Widely known as 'Monty' – although Rupert Murdoch, when Montgomery worked for him, referred to him as 'Rommel' on the basis that 'Monty was on *our* side' – he had hired and fired a dozen editors at the Mirror Group tabloids since 1992, and, in the four years during which he managed the two *Independent* titles, he got through another seven. The opposition papers were filled with critical analyses written by bitter former editors (mostly of the more sensitive *Independent*) who had suffered at his hands. 'When the skeletal, domineering Montgomery smiles, you can almost hear ice splintering,' one former *Mirror* editor, Bill Hagerty, wrote. By 1999, press comments invariably referred to the 'crisis-stricken' Mirror Group, while Montgomery was variously described as either 'embattled' or 'besieged'.

Within months of his arrival, Blank, backed by the rest of the board, concluded that the group was too dependent on its deteriorating national titles and needed to use its cash flow, still considerable, to diversify. Regional newspapers were enjoying a boom on the back of strong local classified advertising and efficiencies resulting from modern presses, slimmer workforces and competent management. The most successful was Trinity International, owner of the *Liverpool Post*, *Western Mail*, *Belfast Telegraph* and a string of other highly profitable regional titles (many of which have now disappeared or been merged), which was looking for a national newspaper group to add to its stable. It seemed a perfect match and when Trinity proposed a merger, Blank immediately agreed to open discussions. They soon hit a problem, however: Trinity, much the more successful – but smaller – company, was adamant it would not accept Montgomery as the CEO and Montgomery refused to have anything to do with a merger if he wasn't. The talks broke down.

Blank discovered that both before and during his time, there were a number of other acquisition proposals aimed at reducing the dependence of the Mirror on its national titles, some of which he hadn't even known about. They had never got anywhere for the same reason: Montgomery's uncompromising approach to his own role. It was a disturbing situation for the chairman, particularly as in operational terms Montgomery was effective, at least when it came to controlling costs.

A few months later, Blank, wholly by chance, bumped into Peter Birch, the Trinity chairman, in the lobby of the Park Hyatt hotel in Sydney. Over

a cup of coffee, Birch told him that Trinity was still keen on putting the
two companies together but they found Montgomery an 'impediment'.
Blank had come to the same conclusion and back in London, he called
the board together, without Montgomery, and suggested they push ahead
with the Trinity deal – and if Montgomery didn't go along with it, he
should go. Montgomery tried to rally support from the big institutional
shareholders to stop the deal but in January 1999, when Blank threatened
to call for a no-confidence vote at a board meeting, he resigned. 'Monty
was down to me,' Blank, who had been at the Mirror only six months
before the ousting, admitted.

> I was the chairman of the company, and if you think the chief execu-
> tive isn't doing a good job, or is standing in the way of a group's strategic
> needs and progress, you've got to tackle it. There's no point just turning
> up at board meetings, smiling and going away.

Montgomery's departure smoothed the way for Trinity to make an agreed
£1.3 billion offer for Mirror Group, creating Britain's largest newspaper
publisher.

A year later, Blank, who stayed on as chairman of the new group, found
himself deeply embroiled in another controversy which ran, on and off,
for the rest of his time at Trinity Mirror. This time it involved Piers Morgan, the brash and often reckless editor of the *Daily Mirror*, who unwisely
bought £63,000 worth of shares in a computer company called Viglen
just a day before it was tipped in his own newspaper as a 'screaming buy'.

The result of the share recommendation, in a column called City Slick-
ers written by two financial journalists, Anil Bhoyrul and James Hipwell,
was that the price of Viglen immediately doubled. It later emerged that
the two tipsters had also bought shares in Viglen, a company run by Sir
Alan Sugar, just before they wrote about it.

When the *Daily Telegraph* broke the story, which became known as 'Slickergate', it came as a bombshell to the Mirror board, including its chairman. It also caught Piers Morgan by complete surprise. 'I woke up, I saw all the papers,' he wrote later. 'They said I was a scoundrel, blah, blah, blah. I realised then it was going to be a long day.'

Blank ordered an immediate independent investigation by outside law-yers which revealed that Bhoyrul (nineteen times) and Hipwell (twenty-five times) had made a habit of buying shares in advance of tipping them in the *Mirror*. Both men were sacked but Morgan, who claimed he had no advance knowledge of the Viglen article, could not be convicted of wrong-doing. It was a difficult time for Blank who stood by his editor despite the circumstantial evidence against him. The two tipsters categorically denied that Morgan knew what they were going to write about (they later changed their story) and in the absence of anything more conclusive, Blank judi-ciously ruled that 'we can't hang him without evidence'.

That was far from the end of the matter however. The Press Coun-cil, which carried out its own inquiry, found Morgan guilty of a breach of the Code of Practice for financial journalism and delivered one of its harshest censures ever, criticising him for a 'lack of leadership and moral responsibility'. But, as with Blank's inquiry, it couldn't find any evidence of wrongdoing and Morgan hung on. More serious was a Department of Trade investigation which lasted for two years but, once again, while it was highly critical of Morgan's behaviour, did not judge him guilty of any criminal offence. Not so Bhoyrul and Hipwell, who were both charged, tried and found guilty – Bhoyrul did 180 hours of community service and Hipwell served two months in jail.

Morgan was soon in the wars again – in fact he was seldom out of them – this time for publishing photographs purporting to show British soldiers from the Queen's Lancashire Regiment abusing Iraqi prisoners after the Gulf War which the *Mirror*, to Tony Blair's discomfort and anger, had opposed. Within days the photographs were shown to be crude fakes and at Blank's insistence Morgan apologised under the banner headline 'SORRY – WE WERE HOAXED'.

But Blank and the Mirror board had had enough. The problem was that by trying to bluff his way through the issue, Morgan had put the whole reputation of the *Mirror* at risk and was damaging the brand. Morgan was fired but, rubber-man that he was, re-emerged as a television personality, presenting shows on the BBC and Channel 4, becoming a judge on America's Got Talent and even replacing Larry King's evening line-up on CNN with his own *Piers Morgan Live* programme (it was eventually taken off the air because of low ratings in 2014). Morgan was back in the news in 2012 when the official findings of the Leveson Inquiry into phone-hacking were released, showing that Morgan, whose flippant comments irritated Lord Justice Leveson, 'was aware that [phone-hacking] was taking place in the press as a whole and that he was sufficiently unembarrassed by what was criminal behaviour that he was prepared to joke about it'. He was later interviewed under caution by police officers investigating phone-hacking during his tenure as editor and in September 2014, Trinity Mirror admitted for the first time that some of its journalists had been involved in the practice and agreed to pay compensation to some of the victims. The matter was still rumbling on in May 2015.

Besides Morgan, Blank had other problems at Trinity Mirror where, having got rid of one chief executive and an editor, he was at loggerheads with another chief executive, Philip Graf, whose lacklustre performance was increasingly criticised by the group's shareholders. As he had done before, he found himself in the unenviable position of asking him to stand down in favour of a new chief executive, Sly Bailey.

When he left in 2006 to concentrate full-time on Lloyds, Bailey remarked that 'Victor's wealth of experience and deep understanding of the challenges faced by public companies has been of immeasurable help'. Bailey herself felt compelled to resign after a fight with the board over her remuneration package in May 2012.

CHAPTER 9

THE TAKEOVER GAME

ALTHOUGH VICTOR BLANK accepted the chairmanship of Lloyds in January 2006, it would be May before he actually took over – four months during which, in the prevailing conditions of the time, the whole structure of the bank could change, as it nearly did. For several years the federal-minded European Commission officials in Brussels had been doing their best to encourage cross-border mergers between the big European banks with the aim of consolidating what they regarded as a fragmented, localised national industry. But while the banks were happy to talk to each other about mergers, and did so endlessly, that was as far as they went, 'For all the constant rumours of bids and mergers between European retail banks,' wrote *The Economist* in the middle of 2005, 'there has been disappointingly little progress towards the creation of a single, continent-wide market in financial services … So far, most of the mooted cross-border banking tie-ups have faltered in their early stages.'

In fact, by the end of 2005 only two had been consummated:

Unicredito's €25 billion acquisition of the German bank Bayerische Hypo; and Banco Santander's acquisition of Abbey National, which had not been a startling success (a study by the consultants A. T. Kearney later concluded that it had created no value even at half the price Lloyds had originally offered). Eric Daniels, with the approval of the board following his October 2005 strategy session, was determined to be one of the first to change that.

In the past year Daniels had held tentative merger talks with half a dozen European banks, but found he was on pretty much the same circuit as everyone else, clutching the same list of potential targets – on which Lloyds itself often appeared. Everyone seemed to be targeting everyone else and several times he had politely but firmly turned down approaches from banks offering to take Lloyds off his hands at a large discount on its true value. On the other hand, when Lloyds made an approach, the same banks often demanded a hefty premium.

Besides price, the most obvious obstacle to cross-border mergers was cultural difference, which no European bank had yet been able to find a way around. The big Spanish banks, notably Santander and its major rival BBVA, had made a series of largely successful acquisitions across Latin America where they found the political and regulatory climate more comfortable than they did in, say, Italy or France. Similarly, HSBC was more at home in the Far East and the developing markets where it had grown up. On the whole, Italian banks bought other Italian banks and the French bought French (although Crédit Agricole did buy a Greek bank, Emporiki, for €3.4 billion – and lived to regret it).

But activity was speeding up, spurred on by the Commission which in December 2005 began legal proceedings against Italy for obstructing foreigners from buying up its banks – the Italian central bank governor, Antonio Fazio, had almost unlimited power to approve or block acquisitions and was prepared to use it. In the end Fazio relented to the point of grudgingly allowing ABN Amro and BNP Paribas to buy two small Italian banks each.

ABN Amro however, had much bigger ambitions than the Italian market. In Washington at the IMF annual meeting in September 2005, Daniels was approached by Rijkman Groenink, ABN Amro's executive chairman, who suggested they might sit down for a cup of coffee and talk about the possibility of putting their two banks together. IMF meetings, attended by just about every bank chief in the world, were a seething circuit of meetings, lunches and endless cocktail parties where gossip and rumours were freely exchanged and occasionally – just occasionally – some business got done. Daniels didn't much care for the event but religiously attended and did his fair share of shaking hands, making contacts and staying in touch with his fellow bankers. Two days into the week-long meeting, he had already held (very) tentative talks with half a dozen banks before he sat down with Groenink.

Partly because the approach had originated from his Dutch chairman, Maarten van den Bergh, Daniels was prepared to take Groenink more seriously than any of the others he met. He knew him slightly, often running into him at the round of bankers' meetings they both attended, and admired what he had achieved in the twenty years he had been with the bank, the last seven as chairman. ABN Amro, formed in 1990 by the merger of two bitter high street rivals, ABN and Amro, was Holland's leading international bank, the heart of its financial network with over 100,000 employees. Under Groenink, profits had grown strongly – an average of 16 per cent a year for the last fifteen years – as it expanded into the US, Brazil and Asia, and the ABN chairman was looking for another, even more ambitious, merger.

Daniels had done his research on the Dutch bank and was happy to talk. On the face of it, ABN Amro seemed a reasonable fit with Lloyds: its market capitalisation at €43 billion was about the same as Lloyds, which suggested they might arrive at a true 'merger of equals', and so were its profits – €4.2 billion that year. It was certainly worth taking a closer look at. Back in London he put together a small team to begin doing due diligence.

The talks dragged into 2006, by which stage they were they were getting serious, and Daniels, as he always did, convened a lengthy strategic session of his executive team and advisers to review progress. The reaction was not what he expected. 'Some of us were strongly against doing a deal,' says one of the former directors. 'Eric, as he always did, listened to us but he liked to keep his thoughts to himself. We didn't know which way he was going.' In fact, Daniels was open to going to the next stage.

Groenink's erratic management style and his insistence that he should run the enlarged group from Amsterdam was a serious problem. But there were plenty of others, not least a criminal investigation by the US justice department into its involvement in transfers of Libyan and Iranian money, brushed off by Groenink as a technicality but taken seriously by the authorities. Nor did the Lloyds team like the quality of earnings and wondered if growth hadn't stalled. They also learned they were far from the only bank Groenink was talking to: ING was in the frame too, as was Santander, and they heard rumours he was also talking to John Varley of Barclays and Fred Goodwin at RBS. Daniels had no appetite for a shoot-out which Lloyds would inevitably lose.

'Of all the deals we looked at, we probably went the furthest with ABN,' says a former Lloyds executive,

> and we got close to doing a trade-off on who would be chairman and the social side. But then we thought it was going to be a bidding war, with Barclays and Fred known to be interested, and we didn't have the deep pockets. There were some at the table who felt that if we went down

that path and then couldn't keep pace, potentially we would put ourselves into play.

Daniels was on the verge of ending the talks when they came to an end anyway. In his prize-winning history of ABN Amro, *The Perfect Prey*, the Dutch journalist Jeroen Smit described how, early in 2006, Groenink enthusiastically presented a proposal to take over Lloyds to his supervisory board where he 'encountered only incomprehension. [The chairman] Arthur Martinez said that Lloyds was primarily a retail bank and that they wouldn't be able to sell the merger to the shareholders. What would be the profit?'

Martinez, according to Smit, told Groenink that he was disappointed in him and he shouldn't bother looking into it any further. 'To Martinez, this was further proof that Rijkman Groenink lacked strategic insight. Their discussions weren't followed up seriously.'

．　．　．

In March Daniels held discussions with two other banks at the top of his takeover list, who, he told Blank (by now chairman-elect), were potentially the 'right' partners. Asked to define 'right', he elaborated: similar strategy and market capitalisation, focused on relationship businesses, under-exploited growth opportunities and 'share our commitment to the best possible execution of the strategy'. The advisers had created codenames for them both: Matisse and Texas.

First up was the Paris-based bank Crédit Agricole (Matisse), a sprawling financial institution with over 9,000 branches and 20 million customers in France alone (it traded mostly as Crédit Lyonnais). It was France's third biggest bank with a market value slightly smaller than Lloyds's £30 billion in early 2006.

Crédit Agricole made the first move, sending a message through Van den Bergh that it wanted to talk, and Daniels and Helen Weir flew to Paris to meet their French counterparts, Georges Pauget and Gilles de Margerie. They could see a lot of synergies and cost savings in a merger, but they were concerned by the complexity of Crédit Agricole's ownership structure and the mysterious manner in which it translated into board control. Crédit Agricole, although it was a listed company, operated more like a co-operative than a properly listed bank, with its central operation providing services to its regional associates which owned the branch networks – and which were also shareholders in the top company. More importantly, the regional banks, although effectively subsidiaries, had a majority on the board of the parent. Pauget, fresh from his two Italian acquisitions for which he had paid the best part of €10 billion, indicated he was interested in a deal with Lloyds but felt obliged to point out the political complications. There would be an election for a new general secretary for the Casse Regional, the regional banks' organisation, in the autumn and there were two candidates, he explained, one a conservative whom he reckoned would back the direction he was taking the bank in, while the other was 'change oriented' – and might go the other way. Daniels didn't like the sound of that. In any case, the Casse Regional, Pauget added gravely, would 'not be able to imagine' giving up their control of the board.

That caused Helen Weir to remark that, from the point of view of Lloyds's shareholders, this would look like a 'nil-premium' takeover and they would never wear it. She and Daniels could not envisage telling their board that Lloyds would in future be controlled by a group of local French officials probably with left-wing leanings. Both sides politely agreed they had reached an impasse but would stay in touch.

A few weeks later Daniels received a visit at the Lloyds headquarters in Gresham Street, in the City, from his best prospect, José Ignacio Goirigolzarri, second-in-command of BBVA, Spain's second-largest bank (Texas, under Lloyds's coding system). BBVA was on a takeover roll and had recently acquired Laredo National Bank of Texas, followed in quick succession by two other Texan banks, making it the fourth biggest bank in the Lone Star state (after Wells Fargo, Bank of America and JP Morgan Chase). BBVA's ambition (which it later accomplished) was to become one of the biggest banks across America's 'sunbelt'. It was also involved in talks with China's CITIC Bank about a joint venture into which, later in the year, it would plough €3 billion, the biggest outlay by a Spanish company in mainland China and Hong Kong so far. In 2005 it had failed in a bad-tempered bid to acquire Banca Nazionale del Lavoro in Italy but hadn't given up on it and Daniels had heard it was preparing to have another go.

Daniels had high hopes of Goirigolzarri, who he already knew and whom he respected. Lloyds had been trying to do a deal with BBVA for years, and Ellwood had discussions in 1999 which ran, on and off, for two years. Daniels and Goirigolzarri first talked in November 2005 and both banks agreed to set up teams to look at the merger potential. They were wrestling with problems regarding information sharing when the news leaked in February 2006 and Lloyds shares moved up. BBVA issued a denial and the two teams agreed to put the talks on hold. Now, six weeks later, they were back on again.

There was no doubt that Goirigolzarri was serious, regarding Lloyds as the best value and cultural fit of all the big European banks. Just a week before he turned up in Gresham Street, the Spaniard was quoted as saying that BBVA was on the lookout for fresh acquisitions in Europe, and that included Britain. Despite operating in a market with total banking assets a quarter the size of the UK or France, BBVA, like its major competitor Banco Santander, had performed spectacularly well under Goirigolzarri and his chairman Francisco González, and now had a market value of just over €50 billion, marginally bigger than Lloyds. More to the point, it was growing faster on the back of its Latin American interests which remained its main engines of growth. Buoyant demand for consumer credits, home loans, credit cards, remittance services, corporate financing and investment and insurance products had driven its Mexican and South American profits up by 88 per cent in the previous six months, a performance Daniels could only envy while pondering the wisdom of Pitman's scramble out of Latin America two decades before.

Goirigolzarri stayed in Daniels's office for just ninety minutes, long enough for the Lloyds chief executive to reaffirm his view of him, as he later told Blank, as 'not only a very capable CEO but also a straightforward and extremely affable individual'. The Spaniard was open and frank, explaining that he was coming off a couple of years of particularly strong growth during which everything had gone right for BBVA, including the strengthening of the Mexican peso against the euro, and he expected another two years of good growth – but he was far from certain what would happen after that. The European banking industry was consolidating rapidly and Spanish analysts were already saying that unless BBVA took a leading role it would become the hunted rather than the hunter. His main aim, he said, was to become 'a truly global player' – Daniels at this stage caught a hint of BBVA's well-known rivalry with Santander, still marginally bigger but with a much higher profile in Spain.

Finally they got down to the crux of the meeting: Goirigolzarri was interested in a merger with Lloyds – but only if the Spanish bank retained a majority on the board. Francisco González, he insisted, would be executive chairman of the merged group. It would be presented as a merger of equals, but Daniels, wearily, knew exactly what it was – a thinly disguised takeover. First of all, he said, Lloyds was not for sale; and secondly, any deal it might discuss 'must not be perceived as a low or no-premium takeover', which was precisely what the Spaniard was offering. 'If we are in a minority on the board, then *de facto* this is a no-premium takeover,' he said.

Daniels was still attracted to a deal with BBVA but only, he reported back to Blank, if the 'social issues', the make-up of the top management on which so many bids faltered, could be resolved in a balanced way. Without that, there was no point in pursuing the discussions – Lloyds's shareholders would never accept it and he didn't intend to recommend it to the board.

A few days later, Daniels, after again discussing it with Blank and Van den Bergh (now in his final months as chairman), called Goirigolzarri to say that his requirement that BBVA have a board majority 'would not be acceptable to our shareholders'. The Spanish banker was philosophical, confiding that for his part his investors were worried about Scottish Widows and were urging him to bid for ABN Amro or one of the others rather than Lloyds 'because you are too well run'. Although Daniels didn't know it at the time, Goirigolzarri had also approached HBOS, which remained on his list of targets right up to the end of 2007. In the event, BBVA made another string of acquisitions in the US and Latin America and survived the Spanish banking crisis in remarkably good shape (in 2013 Goirigolzarri took early retirement with a pension pot that gave him €3 million a year, putting Fred Goodwin in the shade, and was appointed to run the state-owned Bankia, responsible for sorting out the Spanish financial crisis after the property collapse).

Then word reached the Lloyds team that BNP wanted to engage in discussions, but this time Daniels wasn't interested: its market capitalisation of €78 billion put it into a different league and it would never agree to a merger of equals. The Lloyds team held brief talks with the Italian group Unicredit but it indicated it was too busy absorbing its recent German and Austrian acquisitions to consider another deal. Van den Bergh had yet another chat with Mervyn Davies, chief executive of Standard Chartered, but it was being wooed by just about everyone.

They kept on coming. The City merchant bankers were almost queuing up with marriage proposals, some real, others which even they cheekily described as 'provocative': Morgan Stanley proffered four 'provocatives', including a swap of Scottish Widows for the South African-based

Nedbank, owned by Old Mutual, and a takeover of Investec, another South African bank which specialised in wealth management.

In April Patrick Foley presented Daniels with a paper on a Hungarian bank called OTP which he sent on to Blank with the comment that it seemed to be 'an attractive target' and worth a conversation with the chairman. But as always there was a catch, in this case the fact that the Hungarian state controlled it through a 'golden share' which it was unwilling to relinquish, and in the end that came to nothing too. Daniels was also looking at beefing up the investment banking side, neglected since Pitman's day, with a few 'bolt-on' acquisitions and held talks with several stockbrokers, including Numis (market cap: £275 million) and Collins Stewart (£1.6 billion) and the asset management company Mellon Financial.

Maarten van den Bergh finally departed at the end of May 2006 without landing the European deal he had so earnestly sought – and which was the particular reason why Pitman chose him in the first place. He left that bit of unfinished business for his successor.

Lloyds TSB's Absolute Share Price Performance in 2006

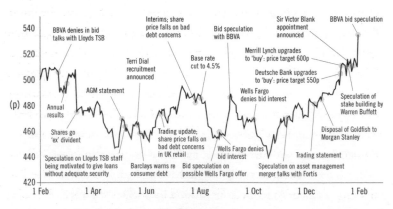

A busy year for Lloyds (for comparison with today's adjusted share price, divide by two)

CHAPTER 10

CHAIRMAN VICTOR

FROM THE MOMENT he accepted the job as chairman of Lloyds TSB in early 2006, Victor Blank was drawn into the bank's strategic discussions. He was fully briefed by Daniels, other senior managers and by one of the bank's brokers, Citigroup, who took him through the wider picture. His first surprise was to discover just how far Lloyds TSB had slipped down the banking league table in only ten years. In 1996, immediately after the Cheltenham & Gloucester and TSB acquisitions, it ranked as number three in the world with a market value of €34 billion (for ease of international comparison, the league tables were presented in euros). Only HSBC and Mitsubishi were bigger – and Lloyds even overtook them over the next three years as Pitman doubled both the dividend and the share price. In 1996 Citibank, as it was then called, was only two-thirds the size of Lloyds, as were Barclays and Bank of America (both around the €25 billion mark), NatWest was half its size and Credit Suisse, UBS and JP Morgan were all grouped at around €15 billion. Back then even Abbey National was bigger than JP

Morgan, which most observers always regarded as one of the Wall Street giants (as it is now). But in 1996, there were no Wall Street giants – the biggest American bank was Bank of America, based in Charlotte, North Carolina, and it was only half the size of HSBC.

Fast forward to 2006 and the situation was dramatically different. Citigroup and Bank of America, on the back of their huge mergers, now vied for the world's top spot, followed closely by HSBC, which had gone about its business of expansion brilliantly in this period (under its legendary chairman Willie Purves, its market value had grown from €51 billion to €168 billion). JP Morgan, after absorbing Chase Manhattan in 2000, was up to fourth place with a value of €128 billion, the Swiss banks had both increased four-fold and even Barclays had tripled. The biggest British bank, other than HSBC, was now RBS with a value of €88 billion and HBOS, number four, made it (just) into the top twenty global banks list with a market capitalisation of €61 billion.

And Lloyds? Its shares had risen more than forty-fold in Pitman's reign, halved under Ellwood and had clawed back 30 per cent under Daniels as the markets realised that success in the franchises was coming through. From its number one position in 1998, now it did not even get into the list. At just €47 billion it was a poor fifth in the UK, just over half the size of RBS, and it ranked sixteenth in Europe. Banco Santander, a quarter of its size in 1996, was now twice as large – and even that was after a sharp improvement in the Lloyds share price, from 440p in October 2005 to 530p, on the back of market upgrades, a dividend yield of 6.5 per cent, twice that of its rivals, rumours that Warren Buffett was building a stake (he wasn't) and speculation that BBVA was still snooping around (it was).

Citibank's presentation ended: 'What could re-rate Lloyds TSB? It's earnings, earnings, earnings – driven by revenue, revenue, revenue.'

Unfortunately revenue growth was still not there. The 2006 results season highlighted the extent to which the gap between Lloyds and the other banks had opened up. For the calendar year 2005, HSBC announced pre-tax profits of nearly £15 billion; Royal Bank of Scotland was second with £8 billion; then came Barclays with £5.2 billion and HBOS, in fourth place, with £4.74 billion. Lloyds was last of the Big Five with a lacklustre £3.4 billion, at the bottom end of market expectations. Lloyds had once again maintained its high dividend pay out, but that was in danger of becoming more of a problem than a benefit. 'Bank analysts have made the point that the company is committed to paying out a high level of dividend, the highest in the UK banking sector, which some fear could leave the bank capital-constrained,' commented the *Financial Times*.

The end-year results also starkly exposed the task Terri Dial was still struggling with: retail profits that year were down 7 per cent, even worse than she had warned the board about back in October. Lloyds had to write off £1 billion on credit card debts, causing Daniels to reduce the bank's commitment to that difficult business. At Dial's suggestion, he agreed to sell the Goldfish credit card subsidiary to Morgan Stanley for £1 billion, a small profit on what it had paid for it a few years before. It kept its own profitable, less risky, credit card business.

There were other sobering facts for Blank to digest. He was aware that Lloyds was dependent on the UK market, but not the extent of it – in fact the UK accounted for 94 per cent of profits (85 per cent for HBOS which was the nearest) whereas Barclays and RBS had both built up size-able operations in the US and Europe. Barclays in particular had cleverly diversified its income streams as well as geographical spread to the point where UK retail banking, where admittedly it was performing worse than any of the others, accounted for only 19 per cent of profits, smaller than Barclays Capital which was growing rapidly under Bob Diamond's management.

Chairing Lloyds, Blank concluded, was not a job for the faint-hearted but he had known worse and set off full of hope and optimism. 'Lloyds is a super bank, with tremendous potential to grow even though it's a tough and competitive market,' he told Margareta Pagano of *The Sunday Times*. 'People don't see all the fantastic things going on behind the scenes. But what I see is that Eric Daniels has put together a superb team, which has perhaps not been appreciated by the outside world.'

He also picked up on Pitman's comment to him: 'Customer service is critical for all banks,' he said. 'Call centres have gone too far and I can see a swing back to more face-to-face service. Lloyds has one of the best reputations for customer service.'

As a gesture of his commitment, he invested the equivalent of his first year's salary (£575,000) in buying Lloyds shares. The price was 515p.

The Changing European Environment

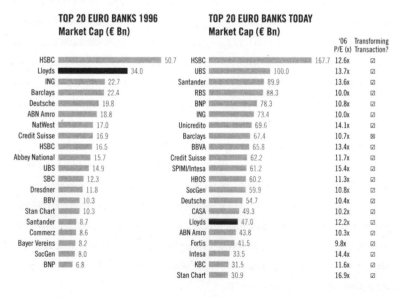

TOP 20 EURO BANKS 1996 Market Cap (€ Bn)		TOP 20 EURO BANKS TODAY Market Cap (€ Bn)		'06 P/E (x)	Transforming Transaction?
HSBC	50.7	HSBC	167.7	12.6x	☑
Lloyds	34.0	UBS	100.0	13.7x	☑
ING	22.7	Santander	89.9	13.6x	☑
Barclays	22.4	RBS	88.3	10.0x	☑
Deutsche	19.8	BNP	78.3	10.8x	☑
ABN Amro	18.8	ING	73.4	10.0x	☑
NatWest	17.0	Unicredito	69.6	14.1x	☑
Credit Suisse	16.9	Barclays	67.4	10.7x	☒
HSBC	16.5	BBVA	65.8	13.4x	☑
Abbey National	15.7	Credit Suisse	62.2	11.7x	☑
UBS	14.9	SPIMI/Intesa	61.2	15.4x	☑
SBC	12.3	HBOS	60.2	11.3x	☑
Dresdner	11.8	SocGen	59.9	10.8x	☑
BBV	10.3	Deutsche	54.7	10.4x	☑
Stan Chart	10.3	CASA	49.3	10.2x	☑
Santander	8.7	Lloyds	47.0	12.2x	☑
Commerz	8.6	ABN Amro	43.8	10.3x	☑
Bayer Vereins	8.2	Fortis	41.5	9.8x	☑
SocGen	8.0	Intesa	33.5	14.4x	☑
BNP	6.8	KBC	31.5	11.6x	☑
		Stan Chart	30.9	16.9x	☑

Lloyds, in second place in Europe in 1996, had dropped to sixteenth a decade later

. . .

Shortly after Blank arrived, Bain & Company produced a strategic review of Lloyds's position in the markets, which Patrick Foley and Daniels were dismissive of, but which the chairman-elect, who had requested it, found useful. On the whole, Bain concluded that Lloyds, despite its obvious issues, had a lot going for it: it was still rated (in a *Marketing* 2005 survey) Britain's most trusted bank; it had a loyal customer base – 73 per cent of its customers had always banked with it against 62 per cent for HBOS; it had twice as many branches (1,924) as HBOS, but HBOS branches did almost as twice as much revenue per branch, and Bain calculated that if Lloyds could get up to the same level it would be worth an extra £3.9 billion of profit, more than double the existing figure.

According to Bain's research, HBOS was outperforming Lloyds because of clever advertising, better customer service and a superior range of consumer products marketed through a greater variety of brands and channels, including online. It was, they said, now regarded by bank customers as the 'consumer champion – perceived by consumers as low-cost'. Daniels, resentful of the £700,000 Bain had charged for the survey, was scathing: 'They are just doing higher risk. They are doing things we won't do – everything they do is higher risk.'

Bain's overall conclusion was hardly original: 'To achieve greatness in the next five to ten years,' said the consultants, Lloyds would have to link with a partner. Lloyds had known that for ten years.

Daniels was right about HBOS whose growth was driven overwhelmingly by its corporate banking division, including its Integrated Finance arm which was rapidly gaining a reputation as one of the most aggressive, gravity-defying private equity houses in Britain. Run by Graeme Shankland, who reported to Peter Cummings, the head of HBOS's corporate bank, it invested alongside some of the biggest tycoons of the day, all of them loyal HBOS customers, including Sir Philip Green, Sir Tom Hunter, Robert Tchenguiz and the Icelandic raider Jón Ásgeir Jóhannesson. From 2000 to 2006, Integrated Finance doubled its profits every year by which stage it was making over £1 billion a year, 20 per cent of HBOS's group profits. Lloyds's equivalent business division was, by comparison, much smaller and more risk adverse, and Daniels had no ambition to change it.

HBOS was increasingly going head-to-head with some of the world's biggest private equity companies, including KKR, Blackstone, TPG and Permira, financing deals which Lloyds had no appetite for. Shankland came up with a formula which appealed to Hornby's keen mathematical mind and gave HBOS an advantage over the competition, provided it was prepared to take more risk. 'We would back management teams in the mid-market to acquire the companies that they worked for, using what we called an integrated model,' Shankland told the *Sunday Times* in 2013. 'We put up all the capital – senior debt, mezzanine capital and we invested equity alongside management teams.' Most private equity companies offered management a 20–30 per cent stake in their business as part of the deal. HBOS offered them 70–80 per cent but required them to pay huge interest rates to the bank before the management saw a penny.

'It was something we just didn't want to do,' says a former Lloyds executive.

> Our model was very different, much more conservative. We never co-invested, were always minority investors and our favourite place was an MBO with a conservative profile. Ideally we looked for smallish, £5–15 million direct investment, and up to a 49 per cent interest, and while everyone else was moving up in the big stuff, we stayed down with the smaller transactions. We would always be happy with an exit of two or three times, five was exceptional, and HBOS were looking for ten and

that's where you get higher risk situations. And our corporate bank stayed profitable right through the crisis.

By 2007 HBOS's corporate banking division, including Integrated Finance, was contributing £2.3 billion to profits and had passed the retail bank as the bank's most profitable division. Later its losses would be enormous.

In 2006 James Crosby unexpectedly resigned as HBOS CEO and Andy Hornby, his anointed successor, inherited much the same problems as Daniels had three years before. HBOS's retail division, although it was Britain's biggest mortgage lender with a 15 per cent share of personal accounts, had, like everybody else's, gone ex-growth. The competition for mortgage business had reached ever more ferocious levels and HBOS, partly in response to the super-aggressive Northern Rock, was offering more and more risky 'self-certified' mortgages which were based on borrowers' own declarations of their earnings.

House prices in Britain doubled between 2000 and 2007 and the highly profitable mortgage business was seen as a major source of growth for stagnating retail banks – as long as house prices continued rising and people had jobs. In fact lending over the past few frenetic years had got completely out of hand and some of the mortgage terms were insane. A BBC investigation revealed that about a third of borrowers, encouraged by unscrupulous brokers, were exaggerating their salaries to secure mortgages and the magazine *Mortgage Strategy* estimated that nearly two-thirds of new mortgages, £200 billion in 2006, were done through brokers who seldom asked for proof of earnings. The BBC investigative team, posing as potential borrowers, visited three HBOS branches where three out of three advisers offered them self-certified mortgages at six times their declared income. One of the advisers even boasted he had got a client a mortgage of ten times his earnings by inflating his salary to £100,000.

Other banks, particularly Northern Rock, were doing much the same thing but Daniels, despite Dial's urgings and a market share which was under threat, refused to join in, arguing – correctly – that Lloyds's brand name and reputation was so strong that it didn't need to sweeten its terms. It never lost market share.

The conservative approach wasn't popular with the analysts, increasingly critical of Lloyds's unexciting performance. When James Eden of Dresdner Kleinwort labelled Lloyds's retail performance as 'very weak', the Lloyds CEO was incensed. 'James had a big downer on Lloyds,' said a Lloyds executive later. 'His big tips were HBOS and RBS. Why do people never hold the analysts to account?'

Daniels stood his ground, concerned by the rising levels of bad debts all the banks were experiencing which, he argued, could only get worse. 'In our parents' generation, a debt was something … that you would repay,' he remarked. 'Today, advice is being given to students that when you graduate it's a smart thing to default. That's a huge societal change.'

CHAPTER 11

MERGERS OF EQUALS

IN 2003 LLOYDS TSB ended more than 200 years of history when it became the last major bank to move out of Lombard Street, the historic heart of British banking where as late as the 1980s runners donned top hats to deliver bills of exchange to the Bank of England every afternoon. HSBC (Midland) and Barclays had already gone, moving into iconic towers emblazoned with their conspicuous logos in Canary Wharf. NatWest had moved in the 1960s into what was at the time the tallest building in Britain, before being taken over by RBS – which a few years later would itself migrate from its temple-like building in Edinburgh's St Andrew's Square to a vast new complex on the fringe of the city. The headquarters of HBOS was technically in the old Bank of Scotland building on The Mound where it had dominated the Edinburgh skyline for more than a century, but after the merger the real power shifted south to Halifax and the senior staff who stayed behind complained their building was no more than 'a shell adorned with a brass plate'.

Lloyds was the only one of the big clearing banks to stay in the City,

migrating the short distance from its historic head office, with its imposing marble banking hall and paneled offices, to a modern, glass and steel
structure on Gresham Street, the other side of the Bank of England. The
move, carried out in Ellwood's final days at the bank, threw up a hefty
one-off gain which filled a hole in that year's profits.

It was there that Victor Blank arrived for his first day as chairman
in May 2006. The bank had given him a new Lexus and a driver, but
that morning (and many other mornings) he drove himself in to the
office in a G-Wiz, just about the smallest car in the world. It appealed
to Blank because it was electric and pollution-free and therefore exempt
from London's congestion charge, could be parked and powered for
free in parts of Westminster (and in Canary Wharf), and had a zero-
rate car tax. Against that, it was tiny, barely big enough for Blank to
squeeze his 6ft 3in. frame into, and it had a range of only forty miles –
just enough for the trip between Blank's Hampstead home and back.
But at a time when bankers' huge remuneration packages were under
fire, he felt it was an important statement: Brian Pitman liked to use
the London Underground and the new chairman didn't intend to be
flashy either.

On his first morning he toured the building, chatting to the senior
people in the bank he already knew, and, gregarious by nature, soon
found his way around the corridors and floors, memorising the names
of most of the doormen, messengers and the PAs and secretaries. He was
also getting to know all of the directors but even so he felt a slight nerv-
ousness at the prospect of his first board meeting, sitting at the top of
the imposing board table. Little did he realise how much time he would
spend there over the next three years.

Daniels had already taken him through the strategic issues, the merger
discussions and the progress he had made on restructuring the bank,
but warned they were close to the limit to which cost savings could be

pulled out of the retail side. Although customer engagement ratings had improved, the publicity around the banks, particularly Lloyds, had not and it needed to tread carefully in terms of both charging customers and cutting further costs. Daniels, along with all the other bank CEOs, had appeared several times before MPs where he had robustly defended the bank's decision to increase its fee for unauthorised overdrafts to £25 and also raise the amount it charged customers for unpaid cheques and standing orders.

In an era of free banking, Daniels led the fight-back against charges of profiteering and unfairness. Overdrafts by their nature were higher risk, he insisted, and carried a high loss rate, and there was every reason why the banks should be able to charge more for them. The fight eventually went to the courts and the banks won – and Daniels always reckoned in a healthier political climate, they could have done the same with PPI, substantially reducing the enormous charges for mis-selling which would be levied on the banks in the years ahead. He won his case, but it was to prove a Pyrrhic victory – MPs and the public would have their revenge.

The Chancellor, Gordon Brown, had become the most strident of the banks' critics, regularly accusing them of making 'huge profits' from the charges they imposed on small and medium-sized businesses, where Lloyds TSB was the third biggest player. The big clearing banks made profits of £34 billion between them in 2005, a sum, one MP pointed out, which was bigger than the national output of Croatia – which made it sound enormous but was actually only 3 per cent of British GDP. MPs were increasingly complaining that the big banks were operating a complex cartel that guaranteed them huge profits, and therefore huge bonuses, which were widely described as 'grotesque'.

The public attitude was aptly summed up by the *Daily Mail* in May 2006, just as Blank was settling in:

We're led to believe bank charges are fair, or at worse a deterrent, but in reality they're all about making money. There is rarely any attempt at personal contact, such as a call from the bank manager suggesting you come in to sort out the problem. Instead the letters and fines are dished out by computer, while personal contact is reserved for attempts to flog us overpriced insurance.

The fact is that banks positively revel in us going overdrawn because it's a massive money-spinner. So long as our overdrafts remain within reason, they can pile on the charges secure in the knowledge they're on to an easy profit for very little work.

The big problem – or one of them – for Daniels was that the retail side was still more than half the group and unless he could get more profits out of it his options for growth were limited. Truett Tate, now into his third year of building up the wholesale side of the bank, was proving a success, but he had started from a long way behind and it would be another year before he caught up with, and passed, Dial. Scottish Widows, after its disappointing first few years, had turned the corner under Archie Kane's ministrations but was never going to make up the gap.

Soon after Blank arrived, Daniels brought him and the board up to speed on his takeover activity. The strategy team, he said, had looked at a wide variety of options, including developing economies in Africa, the Far East and South America, and rejected them – 'It's pretty obvious they're not for us,' he said. HSBC, Citibank and even Barclays (which had acquired Absa in South Africa in 2005) were already way ahead of them and Lloyds had nothing special to offer in the way of expertise or operations on the ground.

Daniels had also considered acquiring a string of regional banks in the US, as BBVA had done, or in Europe, but that had problems too. 'What would we be bringing to the party that added value?' he asked rhetorically.

If distribution is an advantage, we have nothing. Technology? We're now reasonably good at that but no better than BNP or any of the others and we're very UK-oriented. It's not easy to translate what we've got into a French context where the language, regulations, culture and everything else are different.

Nonetheless he had narrowed down the search to Europe where he was convinced Lloyds would find the right partner. By now he had held discussions, with different levels of interest, with most of the European banks but he had become even more sceptical of the kind of 'mergers of equals' he was offered, arguing there was no such thing. One bank or the other was always going to be dominant. He chuckled when someone quoted the robust chairman of HSBC, Willie Purves, at the time of his so-called 'marriage of equals' with Midland Bank: 'In every marriage there is a fucker and a fuckee – and he knew which one he was.' In its weak state, Lloyds could all too easily find itself in the more passive role.

'I don't mind talking to people but I've made it very clear that I'm not going to run with them if I don't like them,' he concluded.

In the meantime, there was more than enough to keep the tireless Daniels occupied on the home front. His cautious approach was coming in for more and more criticism from the analysts and even some of the bank's own shareholders including M&G and Legal & General who wanted him to move faster, take more risks and copy the growth strategies of RBS and HBOS, both of which were galloping away from Lloyds.

'Shareholders are saying "you're dull" but at the same time they're saying "what are you doing to increase the dividend?",' he complained to Blank. 'We can't move them off the dividend. Although we're increasing the share price, we're unsexy.' He was clearly frustrated but refused to be rushed, arguing that the right acquisition would come along if they were just patient enough to wait.

Shortly after Blank arrived, Daniels and his chairman Maarten van den Bergh thought they had found an answer. One of the banks Lloyds had been talking to, on and off, since Ellwood's day was Fortis, a Belgian-Dutch bank and insurer put together in the 1990s by Count Maurice Lippens, an autocratic Belgian with ambitions to build the biggest bank in the world. Its market value in mid-2006 was £26 billion, slightly smaller than Lloyds, and profits were £3.1 billion, also slightly smaller than Lloyds (£3.4 billion that year). Over the past five years Lippens had talked to half the banks of Europe and its name was repeatedly linked to BNP Paribas and BBVA, as well as its less-than-friendly neighbour ABN Amro. Rumours that it was looking at Lloyds, strangely, never surfaced.

Pitman and Ellwood had wasted hours talking to Lippens and never got anywhere. But things changed in 2005 when Fortis spun off its US insurance division, widely seen as the first stage towards making itself more attractive to a European bank, and brought in a new chief executive, the 53-year-old Belgian, Jean-Paul Votron, who had been responsible for Citigroup's retail banking interests in Europe, the Middle East and Africa – and knew Eric Daniels.

Daniels and Van den Bergh were impressed when Votron began applying the well-tried Citi formula to Fortis, combining the bank's regional operations and breaking down the barriers between its semi-autonomous divisions. Fortis had long held a reputation for being one of the most complacent banks on the Continent, content with its dominance of the Benelux market to the point where analysts often referred to it as 'Belgium's Sleeping Beauty'. Votron, who had learned his trade in the US market, set out to change all that, and he immediately began to reduce its dependence on the Benelux countries, which accounted for over 80 per cent of profits, by expanding into neighbouring countries. 'What I am trying to do in Fortis is to say the company is very good at a lot of things,' he said in early 2006. 'Why would it not do more of that, because it has the expertise? Why would it not do more on a global basis?'

His first significant acquisition was in Turkey where he bought Disbank, the country's seventh largest privately owned lender, for €1 billion. Then he made a bid for the much bigger French-Belgian bank, Dexia, and when that was rejected he turned to Lloyds. Van den Bergh, already on the way out, happily bequeathed the issue to his successor.

The talks were well down the road when Blank arrived, with Daniels and Weir almost ready to bring it to the board. There were certainly attractions to a deal: Fortis, after a long period in the doldrums, was now growing rapidly and operated in markets that Lloyds was interested in. The Lloyds strategic team could see advantages from cross-selling each other's products across the two branch networks as well as savings on the IT systems and central services. Wary of the 'social' issues, the Lloyds board was assured that this time the top jobs would be split, with either Daniels or Blank stepping down in favour of their Dutch counterparts. Initially it looked as if Lippens would retire, in which case Blank would head up what would be Europe's third biggest bank, just behind UBS and Banco Santander but ahead of RBS.

The talks were advancing nicely when Lippens suddenly changed his mind and insisted on staying on as chairman of the enlarged bank. He also wanted Votron to be given preference over Daniels for the chief executive position, which meant they were back to square one. In effect this meant transferring control of the 240-year-old Lloyds bank to an upstart Belgian financial conglomerate with grandiose ambitions and a mediocre record, at no premium.

When this had happened with ABN Amro, Crédit Agricole and BBVA, Daniels had walked away. The more pragmatic Blank, as the new man in the job, decided it was worth having another go and got the train to Brussels to have lunch with Lippens. The Belgian was said to possess a considerable ego which was matched by an equally large ambition but Blank found him a charming and urbane man, with a wide knowledge of banking and European politics. They chatted amiably for a few hours but it was clear to Blank that this man was not going to give up the top position easily. Blank tried to point out that it was customary in a 'marriage of equals' for one side to provide the chairman and the other the chief executive, with a board which would have an equal representation from each side and a number of 'quality' independent directors. Where they were now, he said, was that Fortis was proposing a no-premium merger which would be perceived as a takeover, and it would never fly. Lloyds had been here too many times before.

If it would help, he suggested, he was prepared to stand down, or take a lesser position, in favour of Lippens – 'I have no problem with that whatsoever, if it's the right thing to do and it creates shareholder value', which was one of his mantras. But in that case, Daniels would have to be appointed as chief executive. When Lippens still demurred, the resourceful Blank proposed a way of breaking the impasse: they would appoint independent consultants who would examine in detail the merits of the two chief executives and recommend which one would be best suited to drive the enlarged group. If they chose Votron, then Blank would stay as chairman. If Daniels came out top, then it would be Lippens. The Belgian readily agreed.

Anna Mann of the headhunters MWM was duly brought in to do the analysis and after a series of interviews concluded that Votron, with his more flamboyant style and wider experience, should get the job. Blank didn't agree with her and nor did Daniels who felt the tests had been designed to produce the desired result. But for the sake of the merger both men were prepared to abide by it, with Daniels getting the choice of a handsome pay-off or becoming deputy to Votron. They thought the issue was settled when Lippens changed his mind again. Blank, he said, knew nothing about the Belgian banking market or the complexities of Fortis and instead of stepping down, he proposed they shared the chairmanship.

Blank flatly rejected that. 'If a so-called merger of equals is going to work,' he told Lippens, 'there has to be a very clear strategy and strong leadership to drive through the benefits both on the revenue and costs sides. Clarity and effectiveness of leadership is impossible with joint chairmen. It's just a recipe for conflict in a company with no unified strategy.' In any case, he added, the management structure proposed by Lippens didn't even qualify as a merger of equals.

By that stage Blank realised that Fortis, like all the other banks Lloyds had talked to, was basically only interested in taking over Lloyds TSB without paying a premium – which is where all merger talks with European banks seemed to lead. Daniels, when he consulted him, wearily agreed: they had both had enough and Blank politely called off the talks.

They were well out of it. A few months later Votron gave a widely reported address to his managers where he said: 'We are all of us in a comfort zone. We know what we do today … What I am asking is really to think of what we want to be in 2009?'

In fact Fortis, one of the trio of banks Fred Goodwin led to buy ABN Amro, was basically bust in 2009, its core business nationalised by the Belgian government and the ashes of the rest cast across Europe – and Votron was sacked.

CHAPTER 12

THE ROAD TO HBOS

VICTOR BLANK FIRST met Andy Hornby in 2004, a couple of years before he joined Lloyds, when he was looking for a new non-executive director, preferably with some retail experience, to strengthen the GUS board. He engaged Carol Leonard and she duly came up with a shortlist; Hornby, then running the retail banking division of HBOS under James Crosby, was on it. He came with excellent credentials: Allan Leighton, the widely respected retailer whom Blank admired, said he was 'super-bright but also likeable', and 'very good at strategy'. Analysts in the City were equally complimentary: 'His overall record in the retail industry has been exemplary,' one responded, while another described him as a 'superstar'. Dennis Stevenson and the board of HBOS were said to regard him as a potential successor to Crosby, who was still only forty-six and showing no signs of retiring.

As it happened, Hornby, seeking to widen his experience, was also looking for a couple of FTSE 100 non-executive roles and was being courted by Sir Martin Sorrell to join the board of WPP, the biggest advertising company in the world. Hornby was intrigued when Leonard mentioned GUS, which was attracting considerable City interest for its rejuvenated Burberry and Experian subsidiaries. Blank liked him at first sight, responding to his easy charm and also his extensive knowledge of the GUS business which he had taken the trouble to analyse in depth. He had ideas on what could be done with the Home Retail Group and was fascinated by the Burberry story. Blank recommendèd him to his board and made him chairman of the remuneration committee.

Hornby proved to be a model non-exec: collaborative, critically constructive and with a shrewdness beyond his years. All the board liked him and Blank developed a respect for his keen analytical mind, reckoning here was a man who could achieve great things – so long as circumstances allowed him.

When Blank's appointment as chairman of Lloyds was announced, Hornby was one of the first to congratulate him and a few months later it was Blank's turn to congratulate Hornby when Crosby astonished his fan club in the City by suddenly announcing his early retirement. Hornby, after just a year as chief operating officer, was appointed CEO at the remarkably young age of thirty-nine.

In the summer of 2006 Hornby invited Blank to breakfast over which he raised the subject on his mind: 'Have you thought about the possibility of a combination of HBOS and Lloyds? Because we would be interested in exploring it if you thought it was possible. Do you think you would be interested? At least enough to look at it?'

Blank knew there had been talks some years before when Peter Ellwood had exchanged letters with Peter Burt, the Bank of Scotland CEO, in 2000 with a view to merging the two banks. Nothing came of it then but for Lloyds it would have made a lot more sense than Abbey National. Now, in his habitual manner, Blank didn't commit himself and agreed to consider it and discuss it with Daniels. But he was aware of the immense opportunities: the two businesses were highly complementary and a merger would produce cost savings running into the billions, with one head office, fewer branches and a single IT system. It would also catapult the merged banks into the number one position in Britain, if you didn't count HSBC, with the largest retail network, mortgage business and savings base in the country – around 30 per cent in all of them. There would also be considerable synergies and revenue opportunities – at this stage he had no idea how much – from cross-selling products.

But would it ever be allowed by the competition people, he wondered? Hornby agreed that was the biggest obstacle but, if Lloyds thought there was merit in a merger, then he was prepared to explore the possibility of getting it through the competition authorities. Dennis Stevenson, Hornby pointed out, was well connected in government and, given his friendship with Peter Mandelson, would know where to pull strings. The banking landscape had changed since the Abbey National bid, with Santander now a serious player and new internet banks and stores groups encroaching into the traditional market of the big clearers. The European Commission's determination to consolidate the banking industry was also worth considering, particularly if market shares were measured on a Europe-wide basis. Blank agreed to think about it and get back to Hornby.

Back in Gresham Street, he found Daniels interested but dubious. The Lloyds CEO, as he always did, sat silently listening to Blank, all the time making notes on his yellow pad. He had considered a bid for HBOS himself on a number of occasions but had always rejected it for the obvious reasons. He had even done the rough sums, reckoning cost savings would be at least £1.5 billion, more than could be achieved by merging with any other bank in the world by a factor of two or three. They might have to offer the Commission something in mitigation – sell off the TSB network, for instance, which Ellwood had proposed five years before. Unlike Lloyds, HBOS was not strong in small business lending so the monopoly considerations were less in that area. Blank and Hornby had not got as far as discussing who would run the business, Hornby or Daniels, or who would be chairman – that could come later if the principle could be made to work.

Daniels was impressed that the approach had come from Hornby. An agreed merger stood much more chance than a hostile takeover, as in the case of Abbey, of getting through the competition authorities. If there was even an outside chance, he concluded, it was worth exploring. Blank arranged for him to meet Hornby to 'see if there is any way we can push this along'. Hornby offered to seek a legal opinion and Daniels agreed that he should brief a competition lawyer. It was some weeks before the answer came back and it was unequivocally negative. The OFT, the lawyers pointed out, was under a duty to refer a merger to the Competition Commission if it brought about 'a substantial lessening of competition' – as a Lloyds-HBOS merger undoubtedly would. The Abbey National precedent was critical here: an inquiry would be long and messy, and its conclusion entirely predictable. It would not be worth it.

But there was a small chink in the legal opinion, not important then but critical later, which briefly referred to a 'failing company'. If one of the parties was in deep financial trouble and looked likely to fail, then the OFT had a degree of discretion to let a bid go through without a reference. In the case of a bank, the lawyers pointed out, any proposal would have to be backed by the Treasury, the FSA and the Bank of England and the parties would have to show they had explored all other rescue avenues. Even then it would probably not be permitted under the existing rules but the government was considering extending the current exceptions, which currently included only newspapers and the defence industry, to include banks if there was a threat to 'confidence in the financial system'. In other words, the two banks might be allowed to merge if one or other of them was about to go under and threaten the stability of the financial system. In the autumn of 2006, no one at either bank was contemplating that possibility. But Blank filed the information away for possible future reference.

Although their discussions had got nowhere, the ice had been broken and Daniels and Hornby agreed to meet regularly and watch events unfold.

·   ·   ·

When the Lloyds board and executive met for their annual strategy conference in November 2006, the prospects for the bank were looking up. The shares were approaching 600p for the first time in more than five years and a number of the analysts had again upgraded their forecasts. This was Blank's first strategy session as chairman and he was impressed by the detail and thoroughness of the presentations, as well as by an underlying confidence in the executive team. Daniels's rigidly risk-averse approach – or over-caution as his critics would have it – underlay all the assumptions, yet Helen Weir's three-year forecast projected group income rising at 8 per cent a year up to 2010 but costs at only half that. If that were achieved, profits, relatively flat in the past two years, would rise by 21 per cent in 2008 and 14 per cent the year after. By 2010, pre-tax profits were projected to expand from £3.4 billion in 2005 to £6.3 billion, by which stage the dividend, assuming it stayed unchanged, would be covered 2.2 times by earnings against the current 1.3 times. Scottish Widows alone was forecast to raise its profits from £840 million in 2005 to £1.4 billion by 2010.

However, the lack of strategic options and the even greater dependence on the non-growth domestic retail market was still the dominant theme of the session. Patrick Foley again reviewed the merger landscape which, as more and more of the prospects were ruled out – or ruled themselves out – was getting narrower with every month. European bank shares had moved up sharply in the past year, many of them outperforming Lloyds as the sector was re-rated, making potential equity splits increasingly unattractive. For instance, a merger with the Dutch bank ING, which had taken over what remained of Barings when it went bust, would give Lloyds just 40 per cent of the equity, assuming a straight no-premium swap, and pretty much the same for Credit Suisse and BBVA. Lloyds was more or less level-pegging with Deutsche Bank and ABN Amro, marginally ahead of Fortis and twice the size of Standard Chartered, which stayed stubbornly on the list even though its chief executive Mervyn Davies, who had recently become chairman, remained as uninterested as ever.

Over the past year Daniels had become deeply pessimistic about the prospects of finding a suitable partner, and related how he had pulled out of one set of negotiations with a bank which had recorded five years of spectacular growth but which now was 'just scraping the gutter'. Every single prospect the Lloyds team had examined, he said, would have resulted in earnings dilution, a reduction in the level of dividend for Lloyds's shareholders (and an increase for the other side), and a loss of management control. 'I am determined not to do something stupid,' Daniels asserted. Lloyds shares yielded 5.7 per cent, whereas the average yield for the big European banks was 2.6 per cent, indicating just what a hit Lloyds shareholders would have to take in the event of a merger. HBOS, Daniels noted, yielded less than 4 per cent and RBS and Barclays not much more. Lloyds was still an underrated income stock.

At the end of the session they had run through – and dismissed – most of the names on Foley's list. HBOS of course was not on it, although several directors reckoned it should have been. 'There we were, planning for the next three years, and you've got two companies, HBOS and Lloyds, who are saying if the situation were different, we'd like to combine,' said one director later. 'You've got management teams at CEO level saying they'd like to do it, and you've got a Lloyds strategy conclusion which said that the main opportunity for our shareholders would be to combine with a major UK institution and HBOS would seem to be the one.'

Another director recalled that 'there weren't many negatives about HBOS – just could you do it? And that really sat there as the best option for the next two years.'

After the meeting Blank was delighted to receive a letter, on House of Lords notepaper, from (Lord) Sandy Leitch, one of the senior non-executive directors, who wanted to tell him how well he thought the strategy session had gone. 'We have a clear way forward and much greater alignment. Your chairmanship was outstanding. Good job!' Blank wrote back to thank him, adding, 'we are all now moving together in the right direction. Let's hope we get full delivery'.

. . .

It was around this time that Washington Mutual, or WaMu as it was usually known, came on to the scene. In early 2007, WaMu was the seventh largest bank in the US and the biggest originator of mortgage-backed securities, much of it sub-prime, in the world. Catering mostly for consumers who had been turned away by other banks, WaMu offered complex mortgage packages and credit cards on easy terms to borrowers who often didn't understand what they were committing to – or much care. WaMu didn't much care either: it paid real estate agents juicy fees to bring in borrowers often without even checking their income or assets. These mortgages were then bundled, securitised and sold into the hungry market for sub-prime, high-yielding securities. That way WaMu didn't have to worry too much about defaults – they were someone else's problem.

It wasn't Daniels's kind of business but when he was approached by an intermediary he was intrigued enough to send his fellow-American Terri Dial to Seattle to take a look at it. Dial, sceptical at first, was impressed with the speed of its extraordinary growth and the slick machine which drove it, and reported back that that it would resolve some of Lloyds's strategic issues although there were many aspects Daniels was not going to like. Daniels mentioned it to his chairman as a potential prospect – no more than that – and was taken aback by the strength of the reaction.

Blank hated it. 'It would be an uphill battle to get that through the board!' he told Daniels grimly. He was keenly aware of the history of failed acquisitions by British companies in the US, particularly in the areas of retailing and banking, and saw only risk in this one.

Daniels, taken aback by his chairman's vehemence, pointed out that he was talking to two or three other banks but they were just 'first conversations' and WaMu came into that category. Blank on the other hand was concerned that it had got to the due diligence stage and remained convinced it was more serious than that.

It was one of the rare rifts between them. Blank, like all the Lloyds executives and board, respected Daniels and admired his banking skills, work ethic and the loyalty he produced in his executive team, and for his part, Daniels developed a healthy respect for his chairman's shrewdness and judgement and his wide network of contacts in the City and government. After the first few months they settled into a working routine which suited both of them just fine. During the week the two men were in almost continual contact in the office or by phone and Daniels was meticulous about keeping his chairman up to date on the bigger issues in the bank. They would discuss and debate matters in private, sometimes with challenging conversations, but they always went into board meetings with an agreed position.

That was as far as it went. They were never friends and, although they regularly had breakfast or a working lunch together, there were no social dinners, either on their own or with their wives. Blank wasn't alone in that: none of the other executives could remember dining with Daniels other than at banking events and few of them had been to his home on anything other than business. 'He was more respected than liked,' says a director. 'He was not a warm man but he did inspire loyalty among his executives. Archie [Kane] would do anything for him after he supported him through a serious battle with cancer. And he and Terri saw eye to eye, and not just because they shared American citizenship.' Blank loved his cricket and football, sports which Daniels had no interest in, and Blank didn't shoot or fish, Daniels's preferred activities at the weekend. Few of the executives ever penetrated what Kane called 'Eric's carapace', a protective shell he used to hide the more human side of his nature.

There was a reason for it. He was devoted to his son Christopher and, regardless of what was happening at the bank, tried to make sure he was home in time to see him before bedtime when they were in London. It meant he was less visible at evening events, but that took second place. For a whole year, when Christopher couldn't be moved out of Washington, Daniels commuted every weekend, leaving London late on Friday and returning in time to be at his desk, fresh and ready to go, by eight o'clock on Monday morning. In one 52-week period, he made the return journey forty-four times – and very few people in the bank, including Blank, even knew he'd been away. During the week he worked hours which others thought were 'insane' – if his wife and son weren't in town, he often stayed at the office until eight or even ten in the evening and then would put in another couple of hours at home. It was the side of him he never revealed to anyone in the bank other than his immediate office team. It didn't leave him much time for socialising, which didn't appeal to him anyway.

In the office he drilled down into what one executive called 'incredible detail', trying to keep on top of every aspect of a complex business. 'I only have one speed,' he liked to tell his executives, 'and that's flat out.' He expected the same from them and on the whole he got it.

'Eric had a very good way of having us bond,' says one of the team.

> He created an executive committee environment which was really healthy and challenging. One of his strengths was that he produced a balance between accepting that you were going to make mistakes and the need to get new ideas and be innovative. People are often afraid to challenge and be wrong. Eric encouraged it, usually not saying very much – he didn't talk a lot, even in committee meetings – and he usually liked to hear you out and then ask questions but not try to force his view on you.

On the other hand, most of the executives agree, he was 'not the warm and fuzzy type and he didn't have a warm way of talking to the masses. He was really good one-on-one and it worked in a committee environment when it might be ten-to-one. But he was not at home socialising.'

Blank was the polar opposite. 'He was personable, he was engaged, he was involved and he spoke to the troops with no pretence,' says one of the senior executives.

> My staff loved Victor. He walked the floors, he talked to people, he remembered their names, asked them about the photo on their desks – 'what a darling child' – and it really worked. Eric wasn't good at walking the floor like that so he didn't mind Victor doing it. I think Eric saw that Victor could supply some of that warmth that he didn't have.

Others weren't so sure. 'Victor was more involved in the bank than you would expect most chairmen to be,' says another former executive. 'And

Eric felt he sometimes crossed the line when he was championing particular agendas.' Blank's response was that Daniels was brought up in the American culture of executive chairmen – Jamie Dimon, for instance, was chairman, president and chief executive of JP Morgan Chase – and never quite got used to the British governance model where roles of chairman and chief executive are distinct and split.

In a private moment Blank remarked to friends that Daniels was 'an odd bloke' and, for his part, Daniels described Blank as 'a leaner', which he explained was a basketball term used to describe a player who seeks to gain advantage by leaning a bit too heavily on his opponents at a critical moment.

But it worked for both of them. In the months and years ahead, they would spend many tense, testing days in each other's company and undergo trials and tribulations which would strain any relationship. Yet no one ever saw them fall out, raise their voices or undermine each other's position, even at the worst points of the crisis. 'I kind of detected they had different views on things but I never saw any issues between them,' says one of the executive team. 'Eric probably had a better relationship with Maarten van den Bergh but Victor supported him and I think Eric appreciated he was there in the really bad times.'

CHAPTER 13

SUB-PRIME TIME

THERE IS A widespread myth that nobody foresaw the American sub-prime financial crisis of 2007–08. That is not entirely true. Robert Shiller, the Yale economist and author of the 2000 bestseller *Irrational Exuberance*, told *Barron's* in 2005: 'The home-price bubble feels like the stock market mania in the fall of 1999.' In June 2005 *The Economist* warned: 'The worldwide rise in house prices is the biggest bubble in history. Prepare for the economic pain when it pops.' And Warren Buffett later testified to a congressional committee that he too had forecast 'the greatest bubble I've ever seen in my life ... The entire American public eventually was caught up in a belief that housing prices could not fall dramatically.'

But it is certainly true that no economist and very few bankers saw – or at least understood – what was coming. That included even the great Alan Greenspan, in his day possibly the most revered chairman the US Federal Reserve ever had, later a sad and discredited figure who had to bear his share of the blame for the biggest financial crash in his long life-term.

In early 2007 Greenspan was still brushing aside warnings, dismissing the concept of a bubble, arguing that American house prices, which had doubled in less than a decade, had never endured a nationwide decline and that a bust was highly unlikely. He later repented, admitting that he had put too much faith in the self-correcting power of free markets, failing to anticipate the self-destructive impact of wanton mortgage lending. 'Those of us who have looked to the self-interest of lending institutions to protect shareholders' equity, myself included, are in a state of shocked disbelief,' he told the US House Committee on Oversight and Government Reform in October 2008, shortly after Lehman Brothers went down. But for him the real culprits would be the big Wall Street banks who had bundled sub-prime mortgages into pools and then sold them as mortgage-backed securities. Global demand for the securities was so high, he said, that Wall Street companies pressured lenders to lower their standards and produce more 'paper'.

In the spring of 2007, when Eric Daniels attended a banking conference in Paris with the heads of most of the top European banks, Greenspan still reigned supreme and no one seemed too worried about the economic situation. The US property boom had peaked six months before and the implications for the values on the trillions of dollars of bonds and securities based on sub-prime mortgages was, at least in Daniels's view, ominous. Just about every bank present – Lloyds was a rare exception – had bought, sold and invested in sub-prime securities and most of them had hefty exposures to them (Citigroup alone later admitted to $55 billion).

There were already some indications of what was on the way. Ownit Mortgage Solutions, an aggressive Californian sub-prime lender, was the first to go when it filed for bankruptcy in December 2006. Just a few weeks later (February) the chairman of the mighty HSBC, the highly regarded lay preacher Stephen Green, shocked the banking world by disclosing the bank was writing off $10.6 billion on its US sub-prime book which it had acquired just three years earlier when, in an uncharacteristic bout of madness, it bought Household Financial, one of the biggest sub-prime lenders in the country (it would end up with losses of $30 billion in total, more than it paid for it). Freddie Mac, the quasi-government-backed supplier of mortgages and a last line of defence for mortgage lenders, announced it could no longer stand behind riskier sub-prime mortgages; then New Century Financial, another mortgage lender, filed for Chapter 11 bankruptcy. All of a sudden, America's house-builders were warning of huge losses from the collapse of new developments yet few people made the connection with the health of the banks which had financed them.

Daniels had kept Lloyds clear of sub-prime securities and of the riskier and wilder investments embraced by most of the other British banks (Standard Chartered, even more cautious than Lloyds, was an exception), and was feeling pleased he had. But in Paris he found himself listening in amazement as one after another the heads of the big banks dismissed what was happening in the sub-prime market as little more than a minor setback in a banking boom which most of them expected to resume after a bit of a shake-out. This was several months before the famous *Financial Times* interview with Chuck Prince, the CEO of Citigroup, in which he said, 'When the music stops, in terms of liquidity, things will be complicated. But as long as the music is playing, you've got to get up and dance. We're still dancing.'

Despite the flashing warning signals everyone at the Paris conference still seemed to be dancing and Daniels felt increasingly out of step. All the big European bank chiefs were there: Stephen Green of course; Josef Ackermann, the Swiss-born CEO of Deutsche Bank; Francisco Gonzalez of BBVA; Marcus Agius of Barclays; Fred Goodwin of RBS; and a couple of dozen others, most of them seeming remarkably optimistic. Bank profits were up, share prices were at record levels, economies were growing across the globe and everyone was making stacks of money, particularly bankers. The French banks were riding high, the Spanish banks even higher, and the Icelandic and Irish banks, there in force, were experiencing a boom to end all booms. American financial groups were making billions out of complicated, little-understood financial products, most of which were based on collaterised mortgage-backed securities, which in turn were based on the American house-price boom – which had already cracked. Everybody other than Lloyds seemed to be having a gay old time.

'The consensus was that this can't go on forever,' Daniels reported back to his executive committee, 'but they can't see what's going to derail it. All the banks feel it's going swimmingly.' Some of his fellow bankers, in Daniels's view, didn't properly understand risk and believed that by spreading it around the system in the form of re-packaged collaterised debt they were actually de-risking the system. In his opinion the opposite was true. 'They don't understand what they are doing, even the financial experts,' he argued. 'What started out being a very efficient allocation of risk in 2000 to 2003, where the risk/reward was where it belonged, has now got out of control.' The big banks, he added, were focusing on the wrong issues: Would Asia slow down? Was the US deficit getting so big it would tip the world into recession? And then there was terrorism, which all the banks were worried about and which was a major subject of discussion at the conference. Sub-prime and collateralised debt, which for Daniels was the real problem, was way down the list.

Daniels came back more convinced than ever that caution was the right course and his task should be to position Lloyds to take advantage of the opportunities which even a modest crash would throw up. Being cautious of course meant foregoing potentially profitable business and growth opportunities and in the short term that made Daniels unpopular, not just with the City and Lloyds's shareholders, but with some of his staff who felt they were missing out on the huge bonuses being paid at

Barclays – Bob Diamond earned £20 million in 2007 and total bonuses in BarCap, the investment banking division of Barclays, totalled almost £500 million. The Lloyds team weren't in that league, but they weren't doing too badly. In 2007 Daniels's bonus was £1.8 million taking his total package to £2.8 million and the other senior executives earned between £1.4 million and £1.6 million.

Daniels's orders to his executives were that the bank would have nothing to do with the sub-prime derivatives and financial instruments being spawned by some of the best mathematical minds on Wall Street. The City had now basically accepted that Lloyds was a dull, dull income stock, and if you wanted sex and fun you went for the banks which were dabbling merrily in the more fashionable but higher-risk instruments.

That essentially meant RBS, the City's favourite among the big British banks, and HBOS, which were both in the thick of it. In 2005 and 2006 the two biggest issuers of sub-prime mortgage securities, according to *Inside Mortgage Finance*, were Lehman Brothers at $106 billion, and RBS Greenwich Capital, a wholly owned subsidiary of RBS, at $99.3 billion. These two were well ahead of the next three: Countrywide Financial ($74.5 billion), Morgan Stanley ($74.3 billion) and Credit Suisse First Boston ($73.4 billion). And HBOS, through its little-known Jersey-registered subsidiary Grampian Funding, was raising billions in short-term credit – ninety to 270 days – and investing it in packages of long-term American mortgages, earning a handsome margin in the process. In August 2007, when HBOS unexpectedly had to provide credit for its wayward subsidiary, it emerged that Grampian held assets of $36 billion, of which $30 billion was invested in the US mortgage market.

Barclays was heavily into the sub-prime and other high risk/reward markets too and later disclosed that BarCap had a £5 billion exposure to collaterised debt obligations (CDOs), another £5.4 billion on its loans and trading book, and a £7.3 billion exposure from unsold leveraged

finance underwriting positions. By the end of 2007 its most risky residential mortgage-backed securities, including all those where Barclays
did not have first call on the mortgaged property, were worthless.

.   .   .

Alone among the Big Five British banks, Lloyds stayed largely clear of
the sub-prime market, although even for the careful Daniels it must
have been very tempting. There was an almost insatiable world demand
for high-yielding investments and the main source of supply was securities
based on US mortgages, basically thousands of individual loans bundled
together into a single security, awarded a rating by an obliging ratings agency,
and sold to one of the hedge funds, investment companies, or kept on a
bank's own balance sheet. It was later estimated that in the early part of
the decade there was some $70 trillion worth of worldwide fixed income
funds seeking yields higher than those offered by US Treasury bonds. And
they found them in the mortgage-backed securities based on the biggest
housing boom – or bubble – in American history. The big trick pulled off
by Lehman Brothers and other Wall Street banks was to connect the two,
with enormous fees accruing to everyone down the supply chain, from the
mortgage broker selling the loans, to the small banks that funded the brokers and on to the giant investment banks that bought them.

The first serious attempt to get Lloyds to join in came in late 2006
when a team from Lehman Brothers, led by its European chairman Jeremy Isaacs, arrived in his office touting for business. Isaacs at the time
was a star, the youngest head of an investment bank in Europe who had
made a fortune for his parent company in New York – and for himself – from the sub-prime market. 'You only have to see Jeremy Isaacs's
triangular-shaped office – which comfortably fits a boardroom-size conference table – at Lehman Brothers' Broadgate headquarters in London

to realise that this is a man who's doing well,' wrote *Euromoney* in a 2005 profile. In a decision which had divided opinion on the Lloyds executive, Lehman had only recently been appointed as Lloyds's corporate broker, replacing ABN Amro Hoare Govett. JP Morgan Cazenove, UBS and Merrill Lynch all pitched for the mandate when Helen Weir put it out for tender. Daniels had favoured Cazenove, but Blank, who served on the selection committee, and several others thought Lehman would do a better job and carried the day.

After their appointment as brokers, Lehman lost no time in taking advantage of the relationship and Isaacs brought in his 'structured finance' team, which handled sub-prime mortgages, to present to Daniels and Helen Weir. Their proposal was that Lloyds would originate sub-prime mortgages that Lehmans would then package, get Standard & Poor's to give them a rating and sell them as high-yielding bonds. 'What they really wanted was volume,' says one of the Lloyds people who dealt with Lehman. 'They had a machine and the more they put into it the more they could package and sell it on and take huge fees. They wanted us to take customers that normally we wouldn't give mortgages to – anything that could generate fees.'

The supposed benefit for Lloyds was that it would receive a hefty commission running into hundreds of millions for doing next to nothing. 'We will take 100 per cent of the credit risk,' said one of the Lehman team to Daniels, 'all the stuff you don't want.' The effect on the bank's profits and balance sheet, Lehman argued (and they had done the sums), would be immediate and huge, de-gearing it by removing liabilities and replacing them with bonds, allowing Lloyds to raise its dividend which would in turn lift the share price.

Daniels listened to Lehman's elaborate presentation before he growled: 'This is going to involve the livelihoods of people we have built relationships with over years, maybe threatening to put them out of their houses.'

Lloyds was quite happy with its existing book, he said, and was getting a decent income off it. He refused to have anything to do with the proposal and sent Lehman packing. 'They just wanted us to originate more fodder for their machine,' Daniels reported to Blank afterwards, who vehemently agreed.

The second opportunity came when a senior executive in the Lloyds mortgage division presented a plan at one of Daniels's quarterly business reviews. His proposal basically was that Lloyds copy the Northern Rock model, then widely praised in the City, as the way for a modern, profit-oriented bank to go. 'He was basically urging us to go into more sub-prime because of the margin,' says a former Lloyds executive. It was not dissimilar to the Lehman pitch but this time it was Terri Dial who led the way in turning him down. When the manager tried again, complaining that competition in the money markets was killing profit margins and Lloyds could make much more money by securitising its mortgages like everybody else, Dial, backed by Daniels, told him firmly he was not the person they wanted running their mortgage book and he should find himself another job. He left shortly afterwards.

The third opportunity was perhaps the most bizarre – but also the most memorable. In the summer of 2007 Victor Blank got a call from a lady he knew by reputation only. Up to 2003, when things went wrong for her, Robin Saunders was one of the most successful and best-known – and certainly most glamorous – deal-makers in the City. An elegant, blonde American, Saunders was seldom out of the financial headlines in the late 1990s for the audacious and high-profile deals she pulled off: assisting Philip Green's acquisition of BHS which helped make him Britain's richest man (and in 2016 would plunge him into controversy); brokering a bond issue that saved Bernie Ecclestone's Formula One empire; raising the pivotal £1.5 billion refinancing for Wembley Stadium, and so on. In five years she completed at least thirty transactions worth £15 billion.

A trained dancer, the newspapers called her 'Rockin' Robin', or 'the City's Claudia Schiffer', and revelled in gossip about her, including the £400,000 fortieth birthday party which she threw in Florence for her 180 closest friends. 'In City parlance, she is a player – someone who brings in the business and earns millions both for her employer, in commissions and for herself,' said one profile writer. *The Economist* referred to her as 'queen of the City of London – or princess at least'.

Blank had read enough about her to know that her speciality was not investment banking but securitisation, the subject on everyone's lips. The height of her career was as head of the securitisation division of WestLB, an agressive bank partly owned by the state of North Rhine-Westphalia, where her speciality was to lend companies (or management buy-out teams) cash from a €3 billion pot and then issue bonds against future income streams generated by her latest acquisition. 'She likes to dream up new ways of making the assets sweat, of using them as backing in return for an injection of capital,' wrote the *Financial Times* admiringly.

At first, getting the money was easy: with its state backing, WestLB was able to undercut other private banks by a whole percentage point or more. Then it all unravelled. In 2002, WestLB became the first Landesbank (traditional state-owned regional banks, unique to German) to be forced by the EU to give up its state guarantees and its access to quick and cheap money dried up. At the same time, some of Saunders's long-term loans started to go wrong and WestLB posted a €1.7 billion loss for 2002. By late 2003, she was gone, her passing marked in *The Economist* by the heading: 'A star falls – Robin Saunders, a case-study in the dangers of burning brightly'. (After losses of €7.21 billion, WestLB ceased to exist in 2012, 'its demise a lesson in hubris', remarked Bloomberg.)

But she was not finished yet – not by a long way. After leaving WestLB, Saunders launched her own company, Clearbrook, and in 2007, casting around for a way back into the big time, she settled on Lloyds. Its reputation as a boring, conservative, low-growth bank was exactly what appealed to her. So she put her fine, analytical mind to work on finding a way to ginger it up, eventually developing a plan which she believed could make a lot of money for everyone, including Lloyds shareholders, and for herself of course.

Her concept basically was to create a fund which would take a stake, around 10 per cent, in Lloyds which then had a value of about £30 billion, by persuading it to issue new shares which she would buy. She would politely request a place on the board and, if she didn't get it, she would become an activist shareholder, asking for other shareholders to back her in demanding that Lloyds beef up its returns by adopting some of the more aggressive strategies she proposed, including securitisation of the mortgage book. Early soundings among some of Lloyds's institutional shareholders, too timid to take any initiative by themselves, suggested she would find ready support.

First of all, however, she had to raise a fund of £3 billion and she spent the first half of 2007 working on it. A brilliant presenter, she set out her case in a slick slideshow which showed Lloyds to be a 'land-locked' (a phrase she used all the time) bank which needed to be 'forced out of its rut'. The shares were undervalued and, she argued, if a group of shareholders presented a new and coherent strategy for change, which would involve raising both profits and the dividend substantially, they would be sharply re-rated. 'Everyone loved the Lloyds story,' she said later.

Her first big break came when she wangled an introduction to Sheikh Hamad bin Jassim who, in addition to being Prime Minister and Foreign Minister of Qatar, was also chief executive of the Qatar Investment Authority (QIA), among the richest sovereign wealth funds in the world (estimated assets of $100 billion). Under the control of 'HBJ', as he was known, the QIA had bought big stakes in the German automakers Volkswagen and Porsche, the Anglo-Swiss mining giant Xstrata, and the

French football team Paris Saint-Germain. HBJ had also invested billions in the UK, which ruled Qatar as a protectorate until its independence in 1971, including Harrods, the London Stock Exchange and other large property developments (one of them was the Shard, the tallest building in Europe, another was Canary Wharf), leading *The Independent* to call him the 'man who bought London'. He was known to be a multi-billionaire in his own right.

When Saunders approached him with her blossoming Lloyds project, HBJ liked it. He knew about Lloyds and its reputation as an over-conservative bank and had profited considerably from his participation in the banking boom on Wall Street where he had done well out of the billions of dollars he had invested in bank shares and mortgage-backed securities. He listened to her attentively and then agreed to give her £1 billion.

With the Qataris on board, Saunders was able to assemble a group of other Middle Eastern and Israeli investors into a sizeable fund, but was still one investor short when she flew to the Bahamas to tackle a player she had encountered socially as part of Philip Green's circle. Joe Lewis was Britain's ninth richest man as measured by the *Sunday Times* Rich List, with a fortune of £4.2 billion, mostly made from currency dealing, including a big bet against the pound in 1992 when, it was said, he made more money than his partner, George Soros, who admitted to netting a £1 billion profit (for which he became known as 'the man who broke the Bank of England').

When Saunders contacted Lewis he was on board his 68-metre super-yacht *Aviva*, from which he often directed his worldwide empire and deals, and he invited her to join him there. Lewis knew a lot about the banking scene and was a long-time client and friend of Jimmy Cayne, CEO of Bear Stearns, one of the Wall Street banks most involved in securitised mortgage loans and derivatives. After she had finished her presentation, Lewis politely asked her to wait in an adjoining cabin while he discussed the Lloyds proposition with his advisers. Finally he emerged to say he liked it but didn't want to do it at this stage – he had, he said, another banking project which he was working on and two bank investments would be too high a risk. But she should stay in touch and let him know how it was progressing – he might be able to help later.

Disappointed, Saunders returned to London where she read a few weeks later that Lewis had invested almost $1 billion, the funds she was after, in Bear Stearns, making him the bank's largest shareholder. He would have done better giving the money to Saunders. In May 2007, after months of growing instability in the US sub-prime mortgage market, Bear Stearns desperately tried to reassure the increasingly spooked markets that all was well: 'the sub-prime (issue) has been blown completely out of proportion,' it said. A month later it clearly wasn't. In October 2007 Federal prosecutors launched an investigation into the collapse of its hedge funds, and in January Lewis's friend Cayne stepped down as CEO. Lewis lost most of his $1 billion.

Back in London, Saunders soon replaced Lewis's money and, with pledges of £3 billion of 'soft' finance under her belt, called Victor Blank who, she reminded him (he had forgotten) she had met at a *Sunday Times* drinks party. The Lloyds chairman had been around long enough to know exactly where she was coming from and in any case rumours of what she was up to had already reached him. Over the years Blank had acquired a healthy respect for 'activist' shareholders and was determined not to underestimate the trouble Saunders could stir up if she really put her mind to it. She was also well known to the financial press and had engaged Rory Godson, a leading financial PR man and former business editor of the *Sunday Times*, to advise her on a publicity campaign. Despite the WestLB denouement, Saunders was credible, particularly with Qatari money behind her.

Blank listened to her politely, asking a few guarded questions here and there. When she told him she could set up a deal with a European bank, he asked her who that might be? Count Lippens of Fortis, she replied, who she said was interested in a tie-up with Lloyds. Blank had wrestled with his Belgian counterpart for the best part of a year and knew that this was never going to fly, but he kept his thoughts to himself. He couldn't see what she could bring to the bank in the way of novel ideas they hadn't thought of already, but he could also see that a hostile shareholder group could cause immense conflict with the management, consuming precious energy and time not to mention bad PR for the bank. He decided to tread warily. A 10 per cent stake, he told her, would not automatically justify a place on the board and basically she and her group would be treated like any other shareholder, no more and no less. But he agreed to call Eric Daniels and suggest he see her. She was at least worth a hearing.

A few days later Saunders met the Lloyds CEO and Helen Weir at the Lloyds headquarters in Gresham Street. As he always did, Daniels listened impassively, taking notes on his pad, as she announced she wanted to take a strategic stake in Lloyds by investing £3 billion in new shares. 'We think Lloyds is very much a sleeping giant and we can help you boost your performance,' she told him. 'Think what you can do for shareholders if you bundle up your portfolio of mortgages. You can increase your return dramatically, increase the dividend and you wouldn't even have to use your capital.'

Daniels cut her short when she went to roll out her slides. If she wanted to invest £3 billion to take a strategic stake in Lloyds, he asked, why didn't she buy shares in the market?

'Because we want you to expand your capital base,' she replied, 'and do more deals.'

Daniels, with the support of his chairman, turned her down flat. The bank, he said, had its own clearly worked-out strategy which was working and this wasn't right for it. He was not prepared to increase the level of risk by taking a more aggressive approach to securitisation at a time when the sub-prime market had turned toxic and investors were increasingly attracted to Lloyds as one of the few banks not exposed to it. He had also set out Lloyds's plans for mergers many times over the past two years and did not need help on that front either.

In other circumstances Saunders might not have been so easy to brush off. But by the autumn of 2007, the banking world had changed forever.

CHAPTER 14

FALLING ROCK

THE BIGGEST FINANCIAL crisis for eighty years effectively began on 9 August 2007 when the French investment bank BNP Paribas, citing 'the evaporation of liquidity in certain segments of the US securitisation market', froze withdrawals from three of its funds which had substantial holdings of American mortgage-backed securities. The funds were relatively small – €1.6 billion out of the €600 billion BNP had under management – but it was the French bank's accompanying statement that it found it 'impossible to value certain assets fairly, regardless of their quality or credit rating' which sent shudders through the world's markets. If BNP Paribas couldn't work out the value of its own funds, how could any other bank know the value of the trillions of mortgage-backed securities, particularly sub-prime assets, which they held on their balance sheets?

The BNP announcement was instantly seen for what it was: an acknowledgement that the pricing system, on which all free market economies depend, had broken down. The implications of that were horrific and

the reaction of the global credit markets recognised it. Share prices plummeted, with the Dow Jones leading the way, down 387 points, or 3 per
cent, on the day. Bank shares were worst hit, but the real carnage was in
the global credit markets where investors rushed for the safety of government bonds, sending yields, already at record lows, falling precipitously.
The interbank lending market, where banks extend credit to each other on
a daily basis, dried up overnight – something that had not happened since
the emerging markets crisis of 1998. Mortgage securities hardly moved
at all – the market had simply frozen, with trading in many securities
halted, causing consternation among the banks, investment companies,
hedge funds, mutual funds, pension funds and every other kind of fund
which held trillions of them in their portfolios.

The European Central Bank reacted first and pumped an initial €95 billion of emergency credits into the system, followed by a further injection of
€61 billion a few days later – vast sums which even then were not enough.
The Fed went even further, assuring the big American banks it would supply
them with as much short-term credit as they needed to keep on lending.

Alone among the big central banks, the Bank of England stood aloof,
its Governor, Mervyn King, arguing that the markets would soon correct
themselves, valuations of most asset-backed securities would be re-estab-
lished and 'liquidity in these markets will build up'. When the chief
executives of the big British banks, who did not share his faith in the effi-
ciency of markets, pleaded with him to inject liquidity into the system,
he flatly refused. King cited his famous principle of 'moral hazard', arguing that if the Bank provided extra liquidity, with little or no penalty, it
would encourage even more risk-taking by the banks 'and the next crisis
will consequently be greater than it would otherwise have been'. There were,
he added, circumstances in which action might be necessary by the Bank
to prevent a major shock to the system – but this was not one of them.

King would later change his mind, but at this stage most of the City's senior bankers and commentators found him out of touch and not terribly interested in the banking industry that he was supposed to be regulating. More to the point, they believed he was just plain wrong. An analysis by Goldman Sachs later showed that in thirty-four speeches in the period 2000–06 as Governor and deputy governor, King used the word 'banks' or 'banking' only twenty-four times. But the most damning criticism of him was his lack of concern for financial stability ahead of the crisis, something which was apparently widely discussed inside the Bank and for which he was responsible. Insiders accused him of being obsessed with inflation targets, which was his true speciality and passion, causing the Bank's financial stability role to take a back seat until it was almost too late. As far as King was concerned, the Financial Services Authority was responsible for regulating the banks and other financial institutions, with the result that financial stability became a backwater in the Bank. He would later come to the party and perform creditably in the crucial weeks of the crisis, but he had to be dragged there and was always a beat behind the music. As his deputy Sir John Gieve later admitted ruefully: 'The Bank's footwork owed more to John Sergeant than Fred Astaire.'

In these early days, the view in London's regulatory circles was that the crisis was largely an American one, brought on by the bursting of the property bubble, and the impact outside the US would be temporary and limited. It was August and many people, including the new Chancellor Alistair Darling (he had been in the job for less than two months), were on holiday. At the FSA, the non-executive chairman Callum McCarthy, who had already indicated his intention to retire within a year, was at his holiday home in France, and of the heads of the three bodies which made up the so-called Tripartite structure of bank regulation, the Treasury, the Bank and the FSA, only the Governor was at his desk in the Bank of England. The inadequacy of Britain's regulatory regime was about to be exposed in the most brutal manner imaginable.

The chief executive of the FSA, Hector Sants, had only been in his job a matter of days when the financial tsunami swept towards him. Sants officially took over on 20 July but for various reasons, including a holiday with his young family, it was early August before he actually moved into his new office. His experience of dealing with banking crises was, to say the least, limited. Up to that time he hadn't even been involved in banking supervision and had never met the chairmen or chief executives of most of the banks he was about to supervise. His closest contact with Lloyds was when, as an analyst at the stockbrokers Phillips & Drew, he met Brian Pitman at a City function some years before. His speciality then was food manufacturing.

Sants joined the FSA in 2004 with responsibility for the equity markets side, which meant liaising with the London Stock Exchange and overseeing the investment banks – but only if they were standalone entities such as Rothschild or Lazards. If they were part of one of the bigger banks, as for instance in the case of Bob Diamond's BarCap operation at Barclays, then they were looked after by someone else. Sants had nothing to do with the big British banks at all. The FSA ran what it called a 'unitary' system – Sants preferred the word 'silo' – whereby a small team in the retail division, usually two or three people, had sole responsibility for supervising a big bank such as Lloyds. Later, in evidence to the various parliamentary inquiries into the banking crisis, Sants admitted that 'we didn't really talk to each other – the style of management was independent units and I didn't ever discuss the state of the British banking sector with the others'.

'The Treasury and the regulators', said Alistair Darling, 'tended to focus on the financial health of each individual bank, rather than on how much the banks depended on each other and the extent to which, if anything went wrong with one of them, it would infect the others.'

Until the crisis arrived that August, no one gave much thought to the flaws in the widely hailed Tripartite system of bank supervision which had been set up by Gordon Brown when he gave the Bank of England its independence in 1997 and transferred its responsibilities for regulating and supervising the banks to the newly formed FSA. The City and the banks loved it and for a decade, Britain's 'light-touch' regulatory structure was much admired around the world. But even by 2007 professional bankers were arguing its focus was wrong. 'The banks were supervised with political oversight and the regulators were looking at the wrong things,' says one former CEO.

> They were looking at what they perceived as the oligopoly position of the big banks and how we were out to take advantage of the public, which is really all they were concerned about. They never understood wholesale banking, investment banking, securitisation and the whole area of derivatives and so on, which was where the real problems lay. They just didn't get it.

Hector Sants laboured under another handicap. The FSA's first chairman in 1997, Howard Davies, was the executive chairman and, under the Act which set up the Tripartite, the role of CEO of the FSA didn't formally exist. When Callum McCarthy replaced Davies as chairman in 2003, he split the roles but the Tripartite committee still officially consisted of the Chancellor, the Governor of the Bank of England and the chairman of the FSA. The result was that Sants was not included in any of the Tripartite meetings. He met with more junior officials of course, mostly with Clive Maxwell, the young man overseeing banking at the Treasury at the time, but it was McCarthy who attended the Tripartite meetings, such as they were, which Brown officially chaired until he became Prime Minister in June 2007. McCarthy, a classic hands-off chairman approaching retirement, saw his role at the FSA as carrying out what he called 'high-level financial diplomacy', which meant attending meetings of other European regulators, or handling calls from Alan Greenspan or one of the other international figures if they wanted to talk to the UK regulator – which, he admitted wryly, they seldom did.

McCarthy did propose including Sants in the Tripartite meetings but that would have meant each of the other members adding on another person to their teams, a move stifled by the Bank of England. The rumour among the officials was that King didn't want to invite his deputy, Sir John Gieve, the ex-Home Office official who was responsible for financial stability, because he didn't much care for him.

Communication between the heads of the Tripartite was almost non-existent. In his five years at the FSA, McCarthy later reckoned he met Gordon Brown about once every two months – 'mostly by accident'. He later recalled only two 'what I would call meaningful' discussions with him. Before the banking crisis broke he barely knew Alistair Darling either and in five years the Treasury was represented on the Tripartite by five different civil servants, an average of one a year. He saw more of the Governor, who he had known for some years, but as the crisis wore on they were to find themselves at odds – 'The relationship between Callum McCarthy and Mervyn King was often strained, at times prickly,' Darling remarked later.

'The FSA was not really talking to the Treasury,' says a former FSA official, 'and the Bank and the FSA, who might have been expected to liaise more closely, didn't talk very much at all.' No one seemed to want to take responsibility for the crisis that was looming, with each Tripartite member looking to the other to take charge – which no one did. It should have been no surprise, therefore, that this dysfunctional group that made up the Tripartite system in charge of overseeing Britain's financial system failed so lamentably when crisis came its way. It was some time before any of them even realised there was a crisis, at least on the scale which was about to overwhelm them.

At the Bank of England, the one institution which should have known better, the view was positively myopic as the minutes of the Court of Directors' meetings over the period of the crisis reveal. In July 2007, just a month before the crisis broke, Andy Haldane, later the Bank's chief economist, presented a paper on the bank's system for assessing risks to financial stability which, he told the Court of Directors, 'had improved through a better dialogue with risk managers'. He had, he concluded, 'not identified any looming gaps'.

Even after the gaps became gaping, King stubbornly refused to accept there was anything wrong, advising the Court that events 'had proven the sense and strength of the Tripartite system'. When he invited Callum McCarthy to a board meeting to give the Bank directors his assessment of the situation (which by that stage was critical), the FSA chairman insisted the UK banking system was 'sound' and in a position to cope with any fall-out from the sub-prime crisis. Directors, according to the published minutes, 'congratulated the Governor for setting out a rigorous intellectual underpinning of his position'.

They were not alone in being blindsided of course. The chairman of the US Federal Reserve Ben Bernanke later admitted, in an interview with the journalist John Cassidy, that he and others 'were mistaken early on in saying that the sub-prime crisis would be contained. The causal relationship between the housing problem and the broad financial system was very complex and difficult to predict.' Alistair Darling, in his book *Back from the Brink*, confessed to sharing that view: 'It was still thought on both sides of the Atlantic that this was little more than a temporary squeeze and, even at the beginning of August 2007, the Treasury believed there were no serious implications for the British banks.'

But from the middle of August some of the officials in London were becoming concerned, although they were slow to do anything about it. On 10 August, the day after the BNP bombshell, the FSA and the Bank of England began building a list of the UK banks most at risk if the sub-prime crisis got worse, although no one had yet considered what they would do if one or more of the banks ran into problems. 'There was a set of banks using the wholesale market who were going to have problems in the autumn if the wholesale market didn't reopen,' said Hector Sants later. 'That was obvious.' But at that stage the regulators – and most of the banks – thought that was no more than a remote possibility.

The vulnerable banks were easily enough identified: the four former building societies, Northern Rock, Bradford & Bingley, Alliance & Leicester and HBOS. All of them had long outgrown their deposit bases and had financed their rapid expansion by raising money in the wholesale market or, particularly in the case of Northern Rock, by bundling their mortgage loans together and selling them as securities, the market for which had just dried up. These four were also the most exposed to the UK housing market which, if it followed the US downwards, would put pressure on their balance sheets.

On both counts, Northern Rock, which raised about 75 per cent of its funding from the wholesale and capital markets (more than any other bank in Europe), stood out as the institution most at risk. Of the bigger banks, a senior FSA official later recalled, Fred Goodwin at RBS was seen

as a very successful CEO who had an image of being a very good man-ager, very close to government, a very dominant person whose influence with the top people the FSA supervisors were afraid of. We also proba-bly thought he was a better manager than events proved, but in August 2007 that was the view of him.

None of the officials liked Barclays and didn't understand Bob Diamond's investment banking money-making machine, but it was well diversified with a smaller exposure to the UK market and they were less concerned about it. They didn't much like HBOS either, but for different reasons. 'We saw Dennis Stevenson as a very aggressive, assertive and arrogant chairman who very much took the view that the bank was very well run and wouldn't talk to the FSA, or spoke only to the chairman of the FSA,' says the former official. 'Both he and Goodwin were assertive that their banks were in very good shape. But right from the beginning we could see that HBOS had vulnerabilities because of the funding model. We were more worried about HBOS than about RBS at this stage.'

One of the ironies, which muddied the waters even more, was the presence on the FSA board of James Crosby, who had been appointed as deputy chairman by Gordon Brown three years earlier while he was still chief executive of HBOS. Of all the bank chiefs, he had arguably been the most aggressive, and HBOS's vulnerability, which the FSA should have been panicking about, had largely been created on his watch.

In the judgement of the FSA, Lloyds came out best – the cautious approach that was much criticised by the analysts and its shareholders earning it high marks with the authorities. 'Lloyds was seen as a strong bank at that point and the general perception was that it was well run,' said the FSA official. 'Eric Daniels was regarded as a good manager running a good bank which we had no real concerns about.'

The first indication that the crisis had arrived in the UK came on Monday 13 August when Hector Sants took a call from Adam Applegarth, the chief executive of Northern Rock, who told him he had a 'liquidity' problem and might need support if the market freeze continued. But the picture he painted was far from catastrophic. Northern Rock's loan book, Applegarth insisted, was good, defaults were half the industry average (which turned out not to be true), assets more than covered liabilities, his business model was intact but with the markets closed to him he might have a short-term funding shortfall, particularly if depositors continued to withdraw funds. He had been planning on another funding in September by selling a further batch of securitised mortgages, but if the current market conditions continued he was not sure he could get it away. He was therefore requesting a 'backstop' support facility from the Bank of England in its capacity as lender of last resort, only to be used in the unlikely event that the markets didn't return to normal. He was, he added, already looking for a bigger bank to help him out if things got really bad.

Even to McCarthy and Sants, Applegarth seemed remote from the pending crisis and acted resentfully when they probed him for details. That morning the Northern Rock CEO put the blame solidly on the unprecedented change in markets which had come at the worst possible moment, catching him mid-way between his funding rounds. 'The world has stopped,' he complained to Sants. 'It's been astonishing.' Northern Rock had been diversifying its funding platform, he explained, with programmes to raise money in the US, Europe, the Far East, Canada and Australia. But these markets had all dried up simultaneously. 'I did not see this coming,' he admitted. 'No one did.' It was, he kept repeating, 'unprecedented'.

In fact, problems for Northern Rock had been looming for some time. Inexplicably, they had been missed – or ignored – by a board of directors which included experienced bankers and financiers (Sir Derek Wanless had been chief executive of NatWest, Nichola Pease, wife of the hedge fund manager Crispin Odey and sister-in-law of John Varley, was one of the best connected bankers in the City and Rosemary Radcliffe had worked for the FSA) who should have done better, and would later be roasted when they were grilled by MPs. The first public signs of trouble had emerged just six weeks earlier when the bank shocked the City by issuing its first profits warning, saying it had been 'caught out' by the impact of higher funding costs created by rising interest rates. 'If anyone had forecast a 70-basis point increase in two-year swap rates and a

40 per cent increase in Libor, we'd all be in Monte Carlo driving Ferraris,' Applegarth defiantly told journalists. 'Events have changed' – a mantra he would repeat again and again in the weeks that followed.

As a sign of his confidence that Northern Rock would soon resume its spectacular growth, he announced a 30 per cent increase in the dividend and fiercely defended his funding model, which he said had allowed him to accelerate growth in the first half and would go on doing so. 'The medium-term outlook for the company is very positive,' asserted Applegarth.

The analysts went away disappointed but, in the light of his confidence, revised their profit forecasts down only marginally, from an average 17 per cent increase on the previous year to only 15 per cent. That still left the consensus profit forecast at a respectable £420 million, and the market value of the bank, even with the shares down 40 per cent from the peak at 834p (12 per cent down on the day as a result of the profits warning), at £3.5 billion.

By the beginning of August, however, the shares dropped through 700p and were still heading south. More seriously for Applegarth, depositors were beginning to move their money to safer havens (including Lloyds), suggesting that shareholders and depositors were ahead of the regulators in anticipating trouble. In the City, views were divided on which way it was going to go: 'The management has lost all credibility,' one analyst told the *Financial Times*, although another opined that it was just a short-term problem and 'does not indicate the business model is not working'.

In fact, by mid-August the business model was hopelessly broken. In the late 1990s, Northern Rock had been the first UK lender to embrace mortgage securitisation, financing its growth through an ingenious method which seemed safe enough – until the financial crisis closed the markets. By 2007, less than a quarter of its funds came from deposits, compared to 43 per cent for Alliance & Leicester, 44 per cent for HBOS and 49 per cent for Bradford & Bingley. It filled the gap, which widened spectacularly in the 2005–07 housing boom, by what was called the 'originate to distribute' model. Instead of waiting for mortgages to be repaid, which could take up to twenty years, it packaged them into bonds, or securities, and sold them to international investors who were looking for higher yields than were available from government bonds or other instruments – which is pretty much what Robin Saunders proposed that Lloyds did. The funds raised were then lent to new homeowners at a healthy margin and the cycle was repeated, getting bigger each time. The FSA approved the bonds, agreeing that 'the structure of the [Northern Rock] securitisation meets industry norms and there is nothing to suggest that [it] is not functioning as intended'. By 2007 securitised mortgages accounted for nearly half of total funds raised with another 25 per cent coming from the wholesale market, relatively short-term loans which would normally be 'rolled over' or replaced as they fell due.

Under Applegarth, who took over as CEO in 2001, the Rock became the first company in Britain to offer mortgages worth the full value of a home; it then went even further by adding on another 25 per cent loan for improvements in what it advertised as its 'Together' policy. It also offered some of the lowest interest rates in the market and heavily incentivised the independent advisers and mortgage brokers to favour it with their business. Daniels had refused to allow Lloyds to follow, even when HBOS and others did, and he had been proved right. Borrowers on the whole still preferred to deal with old-fashioned Lloyds rather than the flashier models and it lost no market share. 'The analysts and investors all wanted us to go down that road,' says a former Lloyds executive. 'That was where the growth in revenues was coming from. But Eric wouldn't go there.'

To manage its spectacular growth, Northern Rock created what was generally regarded as the best IT system and technology in the industry, with a highly professional staff who responded instantly to requests from customers. Mortgages, many of them buy-to-let, were made at the click of a mouse, often based on self-certified statements of earnings and assets, in what was the slickest operation in the industry.

The tragedy of Northern Rock was that, despite its reckless, suicidal rush for growth under Applegarth, it was fundamentally a decent company with deep roots in its community where it was much loved. Based in Newcastle, it was yet another of the old building societies which had demutualised in the late 1990s and thrived in the private sector. It was also one of only two north-eastern companies in the FTSE 100, employing nearly 6,000 people in its native city where, through the charitable Northern Rock Foundation, which owned 15 per cent of the quoted company, it had distributed £175 million in grants to local people and enterprises in the past decade. *The Economist* described it as 'a financial institution which underpinned for years the economy and self-image of one of England's poorest regions'. Its failure would not just threaten the financial system – it would be a tragedy for north-east England and for a group of employees who were loyal to a fault and firmly believed they were doing the right thing.

Daniels and his team at Lloyds had always been highly sceptical of the Northern Rock funding model, which in many ways was the polar opposite to theirs, but until the early summer of 2007 it seemed to be functioning well enough. In January the Rock raised £6.1 billion by issuing securitised bonds, and in May it sold a further £10.7 billion batch to Lehman Brothers, which regarded the bonds as a cut above the sub-prime rubbish it was being offered – and was accepting – from less scrupulous institutions in the US. 'By tapping global wholesale markets, securitisation worked a treat,' remarked *The Economist*. 'Northern Rock was able to raise money more cheaply than its home-bound rivals, price its mortgages more keenly and carry on its hectic expansion.'

In the first six months of 2007, when even HBOS was starting to rein back, Northern Rock's growth actually accelerated and its lending soared by 31 per cent which, net of redemptions, came to a 47 per increase on the year before. Its share of new lending in that six-month period grew to 19 per cent, making it the biggest lender of new mortgages in the country, twice as large as HBOS which was traditionally the giant of the industry. It was wild, reckless lending which could only have one ending. Daniels instructed Terri Dial not even to try to compete.

On 14 August, the day after he was first formally notified of Northern Rock's problems, Sants met with his Tripartite peers, Gieve from the Bank of England and Maxwell from the Treasury. They were the second team but they were all that was available. Their big concern that day was the contagious, or 'systemic', effect of a Northern Rock failure on the weaker banks. If it went down, then so probably would Alliance & Leicester and Bradford & Bingley, with HBOS next in the firing line – and goodness knows who after that. Mervyn King was alerted that day by the FSA and told about Northern Rock's request for a 'backstop' facility, and Alistair Darling, still on holiday, was informed a day later. Matt Ridley, the chairman of Northern Rock, called King personally to discuss the 'backstop' support operation and received a lecture on reckless behaviour. King indicated he was not sympathetic to bailing out every institution which got itself into trouble through its bad lending practices. This was effectively King's often-quoted principle of 'moral hazard', which he later expanded on in a letter to MPs: 'The provision of large liquidity penalises those institutions which sit out the dance, encourages herd behaviour and increases the intensity of future crises.'

King's advice to Ridley was to look somewhere else for help and pursue a 'safe haven' solution, which basically meant finding a stronger bank to rescue him. And that's when Lloyds entered the picture.

Northern Rock had actually been looking for a 'safe haven' since it first realised it was in trouble. On the day following the BNP Paribas bombshell announcement, Matt Ridley called Matthew Greenburgh, head of Merrill Lynch's financial institutions group, to seek his urgent help on the crisis developing around the bank. Greenburgh was something of a legend in the City, probably the leading corporate financier specialising in banking, with close links to the heads of all the big banks who regarded him with a mixture of fear and respect. His role as adviser to Fred Goodwin in RBS's year-long, epoch-making battle for NatWest in 2000 had firmly established him as the corporate banker you wanted on your side, and he had done all Fred Goodwin's big deals since. His relationship with Lloyds went all the way back to the TSB acquisition on which he advised Ellwood in the 1990s, and he and Eric Daniels were friendly, sometimes shooting together at weekends. Although he was not formally a Lloyds adviser, he was one of the people in the City whom Daniels held in high regard and the feeling was mutual.

When Ridley called, Greenburgh was still enmeshed in RBS's complicated, three-party acquisition of ABN Amro, which was the biggest bank takeover ever done up to that point and which dragged on for almost a year. He was simultaneously advising Clara Furse, the first woman chief executive of the London Stock Exchange, to fight off a hostile takeover bid and was also, by an odd coincidence, handling the sale of the shrunken ICI group, which was chaired by Peter Ellwood, another old friend from his days of acting for TSB. These were three hefty deals, even by Greenburgh's busy standards, but when Ridley asked him for help he didn't hesitate. How he found the time for a fourth deal was always a mystery to his colleagues, but Greenburgh had a serious deal-making machine behind him at Merrill's where he was the star earner – his personal bonus that year was £11 million, causing great controversy when it was announced a year later. In fact only part of it was related to Northern Rock, and he earned many times that in fees for Merrill.

The board of Northern Rock was now meeting in more or less continuous session, nervously debating what they should do in a situation which was spiralling out of control. It was clear they needed help, either from another bank or from the government, and the FSA – and maybe the Stock Exchange – had to be alerted as soon as possible. Greenburgh's advice was crystal clear: 'You need a liquidity line – and you need a partner. Fast.' The first would probably have to come from the Bank of England and the other he would get to work on at once. He immediately began to pull together a basic information pack, which would be needed for the meetings with the FSA and the Bank of England, and also with interested banks.

Once Sants was brought into the picture, Greenburgh drew up a list of potential bidders, which he and the FSA, whose approval would be required, then cut back to five names, the maximum they could approach simultaneously under the Takeover Panel rules. Lloyds was at the top, followed by the usual suspects, RBS, Barclays and HSBC. To round it out Greenburgh threw in Santander, although he didn't think he would find much interest there – it had been stung by the Abbey National aftermath which it was still trying to sort out. Lloyds, he believed from the beginning, was his best bet. So he called Eric Daniels.

Northern Rock, Greenburgh told the Lloyds CEO, had 'liquidity problems', was in discussions with the Bank of England and the FSA about support but had concluded that its best plan was to merge with a stronger bank. At this stage, he said, he was basically assessing the level of interest among possible buyers and he was not yet in a position to talk about price. 'Obviously, it's not going to be at market,' he emphasised, 'the current price (over 600p) is irrelevant. Certainty rather than price is the main consideration.'

But it would have to be done at great speed. Northern Rock, Greenburgh went on, was due to provide the markets with a trading update in early October and that would now have to be brought forward and its liquidity problems disclosed. Daniels could guess the rest of that scenario – additional pressure on funding, mass withdrawal of deposits and, unless it was bailed out, a death spiral in the business, possibly even a run, although he didn't let his imagination go that far.

Daniels's instinct was to say 'no' to Greenburgh. He didn't like Northern Rock's aggressive selling tactics and was even less keen on its funding model, and he could sense all sorts of complications, including competition problems (although the FSA offered to help on that front) if he mounted a rescue operation.

'Matthew, you ought to be ashamed of yourself,' he told Greenburgh jocularly. 'I'm not going to touch that.'

'I am doing it out of a sense of loyalty,' Greenburgh replied defensively. But within minutes he was selling the deal hard. 'There's significant value here at the right price – and we're talking a fraction of market,' he urged. 'Northern Rock is a really strong player in the mortgage market and, combined with Lloyds, you'd have the biggest distribution reach in the industry.'

When Daniels still hesitated, Greenburgh said: 'Why don't you meet Adam Applegarth and see what you think?'

Largely as a favour to his old friend, Daniels agreed, but he was still chuckling as he got off the phone. 'Matthew was really sheepish,' he remarked to his team as he briefed them on the conversation. 'He doesn't do sheepish. He knows darned well this is a pig. But let's take a look.' That, he felt, was the least he could do.

The following evening he met Applegarth for dinner at the offices of Merrill Lynch, near what used to be the old Newgate Prison on the edge of the City. Such was the need for security that the two men were instructed to enter through separate entrances and were escorted through the huge, rambling building up to the private dining rooms where Merrill liked to entertain important clients. Both men, used as they were to lav-ish dining, were impressed. 'I love the way these investment bankers live,' Daniels remarked, breaking the ice.

He had never met Applegarth before, but as a professional banker him-self he had a grudging respect for his record and what he had done for his bank in what had been, up to that point, a stellar career. A lifetime 'North-ern Rocker', Applegarth had started as a graduate trainee and worked his way up to become the first person to get to the top of the bank on merit. Even in the new millennium the bank still liked to fill its upper echelons with the local gentry and the chairman was a case in point: Matt Ridley, a former journalist, was the nephew of the former Cabinet minister Nick Ridley and son of the 4th Viscount Ridley (he is a widely read author and scientist and now writes an excellent column for *The Times*).

As the Merrill butler served the first course, Daniels, who didn't do small-talk, got straight down to business.

'Tell me why we're having dinner,' he said. 'Let's hear about your com-pany and what's going on that's so urgent.'

Applegarth explained his problem, blaming again the unforeseen clo-sure of the wholesale markets at his most vulnerable time. The Northern Rock business, he said, was actually in good shape, with a good brand and a growing market share. 'I love this company,' he repeated several times. 'The quality of the loan book is very good but the wholesale market has dried up on us. We just need help on the liquidity front.' Northern Rock, he said, was 'still funding' and had some weeks of liquidity left, but it needed to act now before the rumours got out. He was, he added, under some pressure to make a Stock Exchange announcement.

At the end of dinner Daniels agreed to send in a team to do some basic due diligence before committing himself. As he was leaving, Applegarth startled him again by saying: 'If Lloyds bought the Rock, would there be a role for me?' Daniels pretended he hadn't heard.

Later that evening, Daniels began to have second thoughts about Northern Rock. It didn't fit into the cross-border merger strategy which he had been telling the City and press about for two years, but then that wasn't working anyway and he was becoming thoroughly disillusioned with traipsing around Europe pandering to egotistic bankers who had no intention of surrendering their sovereignty in the first place. What if he reversed the strategy, seized the opportunity to get through the competition rules and grabbed Northern Rock when it was being offered to him on an exclusive basis at a knock-down price? He would never get the chance again. It might be difficult to explain to the City and might threaten Lloyds's reputation as a low-risk bank. But, on the other hand, it could be presented as a return to the Pitman strategy, still much admired in the City, of expanding UK market share through acquisitions, stripping out large chunks of costs along the way, and injecting growth back into the retail side of the business. It might kill any chance of going for HBOS, the really big prize, but he didn't think that would ever be available anyway. The more he thought about it, the more interesting it became.

Early the following morning, when Greenburgh called looking for his feedback on the Applegarth dinner, Daniels told him he was prepared to go to the next stage. In that case, Greenburgh said, they would have to move fast, and they set a deadline for an announcement by the middle of September, leaving Lloyds just three weeks to perform its due diligence, get to understand the Northern Rock business model, form a judgment on the IT systems, the asset quality and potential impairment levels if house prices fell further and arrange the resources to cover it (it would be an all-share deal). The most critical question, which Daniels set out in a briefing note to the board, was 'would we be able to fund their business, and would the impact on our own funding requirements (including the cost of that funding) be acceptable?'

Northern Rock's crisis was still a tightly kept secret when Daniels, keeping his views to himself, asked Helen Weir to drop everything and take charge of the due diligence process. Some of the directors were surprised he gave the job to the relatively inexperienced Weir rather than to Terri Dial, the person who best understood the mortgage business, but he had his reasons. 'Eric reckoned heading up the due diligence would be important for Helen's development and reputation in the bank,' says one of his former confidantes. 'He also wanted her to form her own view on it and then commit herself fully to it – which was not something she always liked to do.'

Astonishingly, even while Weir built her model of the Rock's funding needs, bank shares briefly staged a recovery. On 24 August the *Financial Times* carried a market report headlined 'Private investors snap up bank stocks' and quoted one broker, Alison Cashmere of TD Waterhouse, enthusing, 'last week and the end of the week before were the busiest time we've seen since March', with volumes up some 50 per cent. Clients, she said, were focusing particularly on the big banking stocks and four of the five big banks, Barclays, RBS, Lloyds and Northern Rock, were among the top performing stocks bought that month.

It was the last spasm of the dying bull market and within days sentiment had reversed as the implications of the developing sub-prime crisis began to become apparent. Bank shares went into freefall and by the end of August the big UK banks had between them lost £23 billion in market value in six months. Lloyds alone had shed £5 billion.

By the beginning of September Greenburgh was down to just one potential buyer: Lloyds. He and Sants had talked to the chief executives of all the other potential bidders, but only RBS, probably out of respect for Greenburgh, expressed more than a desultory interest before Goodwin came back to reality. Goodwin was still wrestling with his huge ABN Amro deal, and Northern Rock was a distraction for a man with ambitions to build the biggest bank in the world (in balance sheet terms he was already there). All the other banks, such as HSBC, cited long-term strategies which did not include increasing their exposure to the UK mortgage market when house prices were starting to tumble. Standard Chartered wasn't interested and HBOS ruled itself out on the basis that it was already too focused on domestic mortgages and, even in crisis circumstances, would inevitably run into competition issues. Barclays never even responded.

Northern Rock shares were still holding above £6 when the Lloyds team completed their basic due diligence, or as much of it as they had time for, in the first week in September. Despite his misgivings, Daniels was impressed with Northern Rock's disciplined sales machine which he grudgingly concluded could probably teach the Cheltenham & Gloucester subsidiary a thing or two about processing mortgages. The IT system was also much superior to the system at Lloyds which was still causing problems. 'We believe their capabilities would improve our own performance in this channel and might also have some benefits for our branch mortgage sales,' he told Blank and the board. He was particularly impressed with the service experience it offered customers and it could be the 'exemplar' for the Lloyds group, which, he readily accepted, had something to learn from it. There was a relatively small exposure to sub-prime, and the loan book, despite the aggressive salesmanship, was also better than he had expected, although clearly that might change if the housing market fell further. Ironically, Northern Rock was one of the best-capitalised of all the banks but its Achilles heel was its enormous funding gap which was getting bigger by the day. Even the Lloyds balance sheet might not be strong enough to support it if the markets deteriorated further. If that could be de-risked, he was prepared to have a go.

Weir's assessment was cautious but positive and Daniels called his executives together to review the options. There were, he reckoned, four main issues: competition, which didn't seem insuperable if the FSA and

Treasury went in to bat for them; the familiar 'strategic factor' – Northern Rock, which was basically a one-product, one-geography bank, would make Lloyds even more land-locked; the bad debts which the 'Together' product might throw up; and the funding model. The first three, his executive agreed, they could deal with. But funding was a different matter – unless they could get reassurance on that, the deal was dead. And there was only one source of reassurance available.

Daniels called Greenburgh to say he was willing to enter into discussions with Northern Rock but only on the condition that Lloyds could get a two-year funding package from the Bank of England. They could discuss price later, but he would be looking at a 'fraction' of the existing price, something nominal. Daniels knew that Northern Rock was already talking to the Bank about emergency funding, and he now proposed that Lloyds, with Northern Rock's permission, should approach the Bank with its own proposal. He would be seeking a £30 billion facility, a sum which even the Bank of England could not take on its own balance sheet without a guarantee from the Treasury. This would not have been a cash injection or recapitalisation, which is what occurred more than a year later – simply a guaranteed line of liquidity which could be used to repay the Northern Rock loans as and when they fell due. The Bank would lend money at normal commercial rates and take securitised mortgages on its books as collateral, fully covering itself in the event Lloyds defaulted. There would be no risk and the facility would not rank as government debt – it would sit on the Bank's balance sheet, matched by at least an equal amount of securities. If the markets re-opened, the strength of the Lloyds reputation and balance sheet might mean not all – or even none – of it would be needed, but Daniels was not going to take any chances on that. 'Eric was demanding certainty,' says a Lloyds director, 'and he was right.'

Later there would be questions asked as to what exactly Lloyds's intentions were towards Northern Rock and just how serious it was about taking it over. 'I felt they were merely sniffing around for a bargain,' Alistair Darling said dismissively. Mervyn King was equally scathing, remarking later that at no stage did Lloyds table a firm offer, and Gordon Brown repeated that message in the House of Commons.

In fact Daniels and Blank were serious enough to call a board meeting for Monday 10 September to approve a deal they expected to be agreed by the weekend and announced the following Tuesday. 'They were pretty keen to go ahead and they knew it had to be done quickly,' says one of the advisers. 'And if they'd got their line of credit from the Bank of England, they would have bought it.' Callum McCarthy later reinforced that. 'In my view they were very serious.' Daniels's colleagues had no doubt: 'It would have been a smart thing for Lloyds to do,' says one board member. 'It is rubbish to say we were not interested.' For his part, Blank was prepared to support his chief executive but only if Mervyn King provided the necessary guarantee.

Daniels had driven his team hard in the last three weeks, hammering out the bones of a structure in which Northern Rock would be merged with Cheltenham & Gloucester, with the Lloyds mortgage business moved on to its more sophisticated systems with considerable benefit in both cost savings and cross-selling. One of the critical components of the model was the forecast for house prices over the next few years, and the Lloyds economics team was remarkably sanguine (and wrong) about that, estimating they would remain level during 2008 and experience 'a mild pick-up' after that. On that basis the model threw up some juicy figures. Even if house prices remained flat for the next three years – the most pessimistic assumption – the team concluded that the business value of Northern Rock to Lloyds would be £2.5–3 billion. At the right price, it could be one of the great bargains of its day and would sort out Lloyds's growth issues for the next few years at least.

Daniels, after subjecting the figures to a further series of stress tests, took Blank through the funding issues, setting out clearly the degree of Bank of England support he was asking for. Truett Tate and his Lloyds team, working with Merrill's, had meticulously valued the Northern Rock securities and loans which fell due over the next two years, working on the most pessimistic assumption that none of them would be rolled over and nothing new could be raised from the markets. On that basis, Northern Rock needed £10 billion of funding in the first three months alone, £20 billion within six months and £30 billion in the first year. The comparative tables prepared by his team starkly highlighted the vulnerability of the Northern Rock funding model: deposits from savers accounted for only 24 per cent of total funds compared to a healthier 56 per cent for Lloyds and 71 per cent for Nationwide which had remained as a building society and was the most conservatively funded of all the UK banks. Even HBOS, for all its wholesale dependency, still raised 44 per cent of its funding requirements from its depositors, a legacy of its building society days.

If Lloyds absorbed Northern Rock, the total funding required over two years would be nearly £60 billion, including a 'shock' amount, estimated at £9 billion, which Lloyds reckoned could be withdrawn by savers once the news of Northern Rock's problems became public knowledge. As what he called a 'sweetener', Daniels offered to fund half of that if the Bank of England would guarantee the other half. 'I don't know where the markets are going to go,' he told Greenburgh, 'but if everything closes I need to have cash and liquidity from somewhere. I want a line of £30 billion for the first year and £15 billion for the second, although I don't think I'll need it in year two. We're not entirely happy about the book, but we can work with that – but we can't get our heads around the funding issue.'

'What happens if we don't get the funding?' asked Greenburgh.

'Then it's a non-starter,' Daniels replied firmly. Greenburgh said he would talk to Paul Tucker, the Bank's executive director responsible for markets, and get back to him.

At this stage Daniels had not actually committed to a deal or even made an offer, and no detailed papers had been prepared for the board. He had kept Blank fully up to speed but both men were agreed there was no point in proceeding to the next stage unless the Bank of England came to the party. Lloyds had cautiously committed to 'enter into discussions' – a phrase that cropped up in the conversation several times – but there had still been no serious negotiation about price and no proposal had been made to Northern Rock shareholders who were still in the dark.

Meanwhile inside the Bank of England a clear division of opinion was arising over a possible bailout. Paul Tucker (who was seen as the most likely successor to King but who got passed over for Mark Carney), had come to the conclusion that the Lloyds proposal, even with all its demands on the Bank, was the best solution available and in a heated debate with the Governor argued that they should provide the liquidity it was asking for. He was supported by his fellow deputy governor, John Gieve, who carried less weight in the Bank but was nonetheless influential. 'Paul was pretty shocked by Mervyn's stubbornness and his "moral hazard" stance,' says a City banker who he confided in at the time. 'If necessary, Mervyn was prepared to let Northern Rock go bust and he had no idea – none of us did – how serious this was.' Tucker's call, he reckoned, was 'pragmatic', seeing a Bank-supported rescue by Lloyds as the best way of restoring stability to a market which was perilously fragile. 'Both Gieve and Tucker believed that something should be done rather than there being a banking crisis,' says the banker, 'and they saw that as the Bank's job, but Mervyn saw his job as being to teach the banks and the markets a lesson.'

No one could move him. 'I don't think Mervyn would have listened to anyone,' says one of the bankers most involved.

Fred and the people at Barclays used to look down on him and give him a really hard time and now he could get his own back. The whole

thing about providing liquidity to the market is that it is the Bank of
England's primary duty but he didn't want to do it at all because of the
moral hazard business. He was the only one in the world talking about
moral hazard by then.

Even Alan Greenspan, who had just stepped down as chairman of the
Fed, had changed his mind on that subject and now accepted that 'in
financial panics you should not worry about punishing the egregious
and the greedy'.

Later, even King's friends and admirers – and he had plenty – concluded that this was not his finest moment. 'He was conceptual, sort of
indignant and judgemental, but didn't actually do anything,' says a leading City banker who advised HBOS at this time. 'I admired his intellect
hugely, but he just wasn't market-based or practical.'

Around the City there was much muttering by senior bankers of how
much they missed the skilled and experienced hand of Eddie George,
King's predecessor, who had been much loved by the banking community, which he intuitively understood in a way the more academic
King never did. Known affectionately as 'Steady Eddie' or 'the banker's
banker', George once asked a startled journalist over lunch: 'What d'you
think turns me on? The answer is: stability!' If ever there was a time for
a steadying hand and 'stability', this was it. Later a member of the Bank
of England's monetary policy committee, DeAnne Julius remarked that,
'the first duty of a central bank is to retain confidence in the banking
system, especially at a time of illiquidity, and our central bank didn't.'

At the Treasury, Alistair Darling, increasingly worried by the speed at
which the crisis was escalating, was still swayed by King's certainty and
the didactic way he presented a case that brooked no argument. King was
the master of the withering *bon mot* which Darling had not yet got the
measure of and which he was slightly cowed by. 'King liked to display

his intellectual superiority – and let's face it he was *very* bright in an academic sense – but it often simply obscured the issue,' says one former bank CEO. In this case the issue, which Darling had not yet fully grasped, was that Lloyds was not asking for equity or even a loan – just a guarantee of 'back-stop' liquidity, or 'bridging finance' as Daniels preferred to call it, in much the same way an individual might arrange an overdraft facility to tide him over a cash-flow shortage. It would even hold collateral in the shape of Northern Rock's loan book with a face value well in excess of the facility.

But Darling, influenced by King, was uneasy about providing aid to a healthy bank, giving Lloyds an advantage over other banks who might well have taken a different attitude if they thought state guarantees were available. In evidence to the Treasury Committee a few weeks later, King argued that 'were such lending to be made available to one high street bank, a matching facility would also have to be offered to other potential bidders' and Darling, in these early days, could see the logic of that.

The immediate problem however was there *were* no other potential bidders and by Friday 7 September there were no bidders at all. Daniels called a meeting of his executive that day and went over all the issues again. Opinion on his own team had now become more divided. 'When we started, Helen was fairly positive,' says one of the committee. 'But she later became ambivalent, not because of the price or anything but because if it didn't go right we would look bad in the markets.' Her point was that it was not a matter of price but of 'risk profile' – Lloyds had adopted a low risk position right through the crisis which was increasingly appreciated by the market and a Northern Rock deal did not fit into it. Several of the executive team took their cue from her and the meeting was a negative one.

At the end of Friday Daniels called Greenburgh to say that without Bank of England support, the funding risks were too great and Lloyds was withdrawing. He also called a disappointed Sants, who was standing by ready to speak to the OFT about the competition issues, and Blank cancelled the board meeting set for Monday morning.

But the deal was not yet dead. On Saturday morning the indefatigable and infinitely inventive Greenburgh called with a new proposal. The Stock Exchange, he told Daniels, had told Northern Rock it had to make an announcement by Tuesday morning at the latest, informing shareholders of its approach to the Bank and its urgent need of liquidity. Once the news was out its share price would go through the floor and the bank would probably not survive another week. The Northern Rock board therefore had to agree a deal over the weekend and was basically prepared to accept even a nominal sum. 'We are talking £1 to £2 a share here,' he said.

That got Daniels's attention. At that price – and Daniels was already mentally working on the lower figure – he could acquire Northern Rock at between £500 million and £1 billion, a small bite for Lloyds which had a market value of £35 billion. The value-creation, based on Helen Weir and Patrick Foley's sums, would be at least three times that. Greenburgh, who had been talking with Paul Tucker, went on to tell Daniels that he had received indications from the Bank of England that it would provide 'some support for your funding requirements'. That wasn't very solid but it was enough to revive Daniels's interest and he went back to work, spending the rest of the day on the phone to Tucker at the Bank, to Sants and David Strachan, head of financial stability at the FSA, to Greenburgh and to Blank. The Treasury and the FSA had now hired Goldman Sachs who joined an already crowded group of advisers, regulators, Treasury officials and bankers trying to put together an eleventh hour deal, which on Saturday afternoon still seemed possible.

The discussions that mattered were with the Bank and that took some time as bank officials insisted on getting details of the collateral it would be offered in return for the facility. They were also unclear on the amount Daniels was seeking – where did that figure come from? Daniels, however, was crystal clear on what he needed in order to go ahead with the deal – 'access' to a liquidity facility of £30 billion on 'commercial' terms, not on the 'penal' terms Mervyn King was now insisting on, to cover the Northern Rock funding gap.

'I don't know if we'll fund this without a penalty,' Tucker told him, adding that a penalty rate was 'normal' for the Bank in these kinds of circumstances. King was insisting on 150 points over Bank rate, which he justified as minimising the risk to the taxpayer, and Tucker didn't believe he would move off it. 'We are stepping in here with mixed feelings and we don't want this extended to others,' he said. But he would talk to the Governor again and try to find what he called a 'bridge with a footpath'. The Bank, he added, had to be very careful about being seen to set a precedent.

'There is no way we are going to do this with a penalty,' Daniels warned him.

As the day wore on the Lloyds team, working closely with the FSA, were convinced they were getting somewhere. Discussions increasingly focused on the message sent to the markets – both the Bank and the FSA were keen to present the deal as a 'normal' transaction with no preferential terms offered, while Lloyds needed to reassure its shareholders it was not taking on any undue risk or paying more than market rate for its liquidity facility. The offer to Northern Rock shareholders, they had now decided, should be all-cash, funded by a placing of Lloyds shares, and the lawyers were at work on the mounds of paperwork required.

By Sunday morning Daniels, with Blank's approval, was confident enough to send an email to the board setting out the state of play and seeking its approval to go ahead. The Tripartite would be meeting later that day in the Treasury and McCallum and Sants from the FSA had undertaken to urge the Bank and the Treasury to back the Lloyds proposal. All they were looking for that weekend was an agreement in principle, just enough to support an announcement before the markets opened on Monday morning. 'We wouldn't have had to do the deal,' said an FSA official afterwards, 'just say we were in serious discussions with Lloyds and the Bank of England was supporting it with a guaranteed credit line. That's all it would have taken – the other details could then have been sorted out afterwards.' King later took a different view arguing that a 'covert' rescue of a quoted bank could not be achieved in the way the Bank of England had done in the past (in the case of Slater Walker in 1975 for example), arguing that 'it could not be managed except through a long and prolonged timetable set out in the Takeover Code'. There were very few who agreed with him that weekend, with Applegarth arguing that 'an announceable offer over the weekend with a major high street brand … would have provided sufficient confidence so a run did not happen'. In fact the Treasury had the powers to override the Panel's procedures, as it did a year later, and if the Governor had really put his mind to it there is little doubt he could have found a way around.

Blank alerted the board to the possibility of the Monday board meeting being back on, and the City PR firm Finsbury drafted a press release which would be issued to the markets and the financial press. All now hinged on Mervyn King, and on Sunday morning discouraging signals began to emerge from that quarter. Greenburgh, still acting for Northern Rock, called Tucker at home to assess the Governor's mood. Had he softened at all as the crisis deepened? 'He's not going to change his mind,' said the deputy governor gloomily. Greenburgh decided not to pass that message back to Daniels.

As it happened, none of the three Tripartite heads were physically present in the Treasury for the hastily scheduled meeting that Sunday afternoon. Mervyn King and Callum McCarthy were both at (different) meetings in

Basel and Darling was in his constituency in Edinburgh. When McCarthy's plane was diverted to Brussels, he called Hector Sants and asked him to substitute for him and argue the FSA case – he would join the meeting by phone as soon as he landed. Sants was not in the Treasury either and dialled into the conference call from his home in Oxford, the first time he would speak to the Chancellor (whom he had still not met) or the Governor. It now fell to Sants, not the most self-confident or prepossessing of men at the best of times, to present the case for a Northern Rock bailout.

It was a bad-tempered and unsatisfactory discussion from the beginning. Sants, hopelessly outgunned by an intransigent Governor and an unsympathetic Chancellor, made a hesitant and unconvincing argument for intervention at Northern Rock which, he said, was going to fail within a matter of days without support. The FSA had received a conditional commitment from Lloyds that it would 'enter into discussions' – he emphasised that at this stage it was only that, there was no formal offer – but it had said it would not go ahead without a liquidity guarantee. He was careful not to mention a figure, although everyone knew he was talking about £30 billion.

He had barely finished when the Governor interjected. 'No,' he said decisively and abruptly, 'I could not in any way support that. It is not our job to support commercial takeovers. And I'm not prepared to provide any liquidity on that basis.' Nor, he added, was he prepared to give one bank an unfair advantage over any other – that was not the Bank's job.

Sants spluttered that he thought that was a mistake and it was the only private sector solution they were going to find. McCarthy, joining the conversation from Brussels airport, was in time to hear King become even more vehement. 'This is a remarkable idea,' he said. 'If any of us were to say we wanted to buy IBM provided you give me the money to buy IBM, we would dismiss the idea out of hand. Why are we even contemplating it?'

No one ever knew why he picked on IBM, but Darling had had enough. 'Well, we've heard the Governor so the matter is closed,' he said resignedly. 'Let's move on.'

The Chancellor, although deeply concerned about Northern Rock, was even more worried by the wider problems looming in the markets. 'If we could sell Northern Rock, that would be desirable,' he wrote later, 'but most urgent was the need to get more money into the system to keep it afloat and to prevent further imminent collapses.' He was coming under pressure, not just from the chairmen of the big banks, but by his fellow finance ministers and by the Prime Minister to persuade the Bank to act. King still flatly refused, citing once again his moral hazard argument which everyone had heard too many times already.

Darling was furious as he put down the phone. 'My frustration,' he recorded in his account of the crisis, 'was that I could not in practice order the Bank to do what I wanted.' Only the Bank could put the necessary funds into the system – indeed, that was its core purpose in life – and the Chancellor, nominally King's boss, had no power to overrule him. Still fuming at King's obstinacy, he called the Treasury officials to ask them was there 'any way I can force his hand'. There wasn't of course, although the markets would soon do it for him. 'The fact that we had given the Bank independence had a downside as well as an upside,' Darling remarked sourly. Hurriedly he packed his bags and set off for London, intent on wrenching control of the situation back to where it rightfully belonged, which was the Treasury.

From his home in Oxford, Sants disconsolately called Daniels to give him the news.

'I'm very sorry but I've put your proposal to the Tripartite and it hasn't been supported,' he reported. Daniels, who had begun to expect as much, took it philosophically and called Blank. The board meeting the next day was cancelled for the second time.

In his evidence to the Treasury Committee a few weeks later, King gave his own version of this 9 September meeting. The Lloyds proposal, he said, was in the form of 'one pretty vague telephone call which came to Bank officials and then passed to me, originating in the FSA'. He himself had not been party to the discussions between the FSA and Lloyds and the request, as he understood it, was 'to borrow about £30 billion without a penalty rate for two years'. Both he and the Chancellor, he added, had an 'instinctive reluctance' for the Bank to act as a commercial lender to a going concern. King's preferred solution, he said, was to provide, 'if necessary', support directly to Northern Rock through its 'lender of last resort' function.

He remained scathing about the FSA/Lloyds plan, telling MPs: 'The idea that if [the Chancellor] stood up and said, "I am willing to lend £30 billion to any bank that will take over Northern Rock" – that is not the kind of statement that would have helped Northern Rock one jot or tittle. It would have been a disaster for Northern Rock to have said that.'

It was a disaster for Northern Rock in any case. Monday and Tuesday were dire days for the world's big banks with the inter-banking market almost seizing up. Libor, the rate at which banks lend to one another, rose sharply, shares fell further and rumours began to circulate of all sorts of problems among the big American banks. Funds flowed out of Northern Rock, its shares tumbled and by Wednesday it was clear that it was not even going to make the weekend without help.

King, by now under siege from all quarters, including his own Court of Directors, called an emergency meeting at the Bank on the evening of Thursday 13 September. He and Callum McCarthy, he told them, had just advised the Chancellor to authorise a liquidity facility to the stricken bank which would carry the same penalty rate he had demanded from Lloyds. There was, he agreed, 'the potential for some commentators to suggest we are doing a U-turn' by comparing his recent statements with what he was proposing now. The minutes of the meeting indicate he remained defiant on that front: 'There was a clear distinction to be drawn between moral hazard of a general bailout to banks ... and the type of collateralised assistance considered here.' That distinction would be lost on the City, on Darling, on MPs and on the commentators who would roast him over the coming weeks and months for his intransigence and lack of foresight when it was needed.

King signed off the meeting by giving the Court another ringing endorsement of the success of the Tripartite system, which he himself had done much to undermine. 'The episode had provided the evidence of the virtue of the new framework,' the minutes noted. In fact it had done the opposite. As Chris Giles, economics editor of the *FT* (and, overall, a supporter of King) later commented: 'Court directors were never told of serious dissent among senior staff, including Sir John Gieve, over the delayed and feeble response by the BoE to the run on Northern Rock. "The Court was largely out of the loop," Sir John told the *FT* in 2012.' Nor were they told anything – not a mention anywhere – of the even more serious dissent going on between the Bank and the FSA, whose managing director King had just humiliated in front of the Chancellor.

Whatever the level of debate in the Court that evening, the Governor had gone through the motions, got the approval he technically needed for what he called 'the most significant lender of last resort facility since the lifeboat episode in the seventies', and had his Court-approved statement ready to go. His intention was that the Northern Rock facility would be announced after the weekend, but Darling, fearing the story would not keep that long, insisted it should go out the next morning, Friday 14 September. They never got that far. The meeting at the Bank broke up at seven on Thursday evening and within minutes details of the bailout were running live on prime-time television. The BBC's economics editor, Robert Peston, who was to have scoop after scoop during the events that followed, revealed that Northern Rock was in trouble and had been forced to seek support from the Bank of England. 'But,' he added disingenuously, 'no one should panic.'

Of course that's precisely what everyone did, including the government and officials. The national newspapers hastily remade their front pages to lead with the story which dominated the late news bulletins and the early morning news. By seven the next morning, just twelve hours after the meeting in the Bank, Darling was forced to announce that he had authorised the Bank of England to provide a liquidity support facility 'to help Northern Rock to fund its operations during the current period of turbulence'. The FSA, he added, 'judges that Northern Rock is solvent, exceeds its regulatory capital requirement and has a good-quality loan book'.

The statement simply fanned the flames. By eight o'clock queues began building outside Northern Rock's branches and by nine they were stretching around the block. There were only two branches in London with two tills each to handle depositors, and dealing with each customer took time. At first the bank staff tried to persuade customers their money was safe and they didn't need to panic, but that caused the queues to get even longer. By mid-morning TV footage of lines of depositors, bearing flasks of tea and deckchairs, were flashing around the world, and by lunchtime it had turned into a full-scale bank run, which for any financial regulator – or government – was the stuff of nightmares. No self-respecting banker could watch the scenes on TV without a shiver of terror as the relentless 24-hour news programmes beamed it onto their office screens. As King and Darling both later admitted, depositors were merely doing the logical thing: protecting their savings, and no one could blame them for that. It was the officials and the board of Northern Rock who had to bear the blame.

From his office in the New York Fed, the president, Tim Geithner, watched the snaking queues on TV with growing astonishment. The US banks had made all the running in the crisis up to that point and suddenly, out of the blue, the UK had put itself in the front line. He could barely believe the ease with which depositors in a regulated bank in a modern economy could panic, and that was a scary thought – if a British bank could go like this, why not a much shakier New York bank, several of which were in much bigger trouble than their British counterparts? Later he remarked (to Martin Wolf in the *FT*) that 'panics are different. I think the hardest thing to understand is that runs in a panic require a different response – a much more counterintuitive response – than in a normal financial crisis.' There had been nothing counterintuitive about the Bank of England's response in this particular crisis.

A sample of the newspaper reports gives a flavour of the frenzy that gripped Northern Rock depositors that week: Chris Robertson, a 67-year-old pensioner, said he was 'doing what everybody else is doing and panicking. I'm joining the herd.' Another depositor said she was in the queue because the bank wouldn't answer the phone 'and when you go to the website, it just crashes'. A woman leaving a branch in Liverpool clutched a handbag packed with £3,000 and told a TV reporter: 'It is not much but it's all I have in the world.' In Cheltenham the police had to be called in when two joint account holders barricaded the bank manager in her office after she refused to let them withdraw £1 million from their internet-only account, which they were unable to access. And so it went on all through Friday and into the weekend, with no one knowing where it was going to go – or how to end it.

In Downing Street, Gordon Brown watched in growing disbelief the first bank run on a British bank in 141 years (Overend, Gurney & Company collapsed in 1866). He later remarked, 'It was like a scene in a film or a picture in a text book, but not something I had ever expected to see in my lifetime or under our watch.' It was, he added, 'the first sign the

British people had of the global banking problems that would eventually overwhelm our largest banks'. And in a swipe at the Bank Governor,
he added: 'It was a disastrous outcome after what should have been a
straightforward bank rescue.'

Next door in No. 11, an equally shaken Alistair Darling determined
he would no longer be pushed around by the Governor. 'I was damned
if our reputation was going to be destroyed over the failure of a small,
reckless bank,' he said later. 'We had to stop this run and regain control
of events, no matter what it took.'

That day Brown and Darling, who were barely on speaking terms after a
series of slights and policy disagreements, decided to take the momentous
step of guaranteeing that every penny of savers' money in Northern Rock
was safe, a desperate measure which they hoped would stem the immediate panic. But there still remained the problem of what to do with the
stricken bank. 'I had concluded that we would have to offer a guarantee
to savers in Northern Rock,' wrote Darling, 'but if we could link it to a
purchase by Lloyds ... that might do the trick. I was reluctant to provide
an open-ended guarantee to depositors without being able to say that the
bank had been purchased and thus ending the crisis.' The Bank of England, rather than the FSA, was given the task of trying to re-open talks
with Lloyds, the only major bank which might be remotely interested,
even if the Bank of England made a credit facility generally available.

Eric Daniels was in Paris on a shareholders' roadshow on Monday
morning when he got a call from Sir John Gieve. 'Where do you think
this is all going to go?' asked the deputy governor.

'Think £10 billion a day,' replied Daniels laconically.

Gieve then indicated there had been a change of mind over the weekend and asked would Lloyds still be interested in Northern Rock if the
Bank supported a rescue. 'What would it take for you to do it?'

A week earlier, Daniels would have done the deal. But the situation had changed dramatically with the run and the Lloyds CEO reckoned Northern Rock had now gone past the point of no return. A rescue would only focus attention on Lloyds – no one knew how the Northern Rock contagion might spread and if ever there was a time to be cautious, this was it. Politely but firmly he told Gieve that, even with a guaranteed line of liquidity, it was too late. Lloyds could not enter into discussions to rescue a bank that was in the middle of a run.

When the message was passed back to the Treasury, a disconsolate Darling trooped next door to No. 10 to give the Prime Minister the news, adding that not only would there be no rescue, but they would now have to guarantee not just savers' deposits but also funds, amounting to billions, deposited with Northern Rock by local councils and commercial bodies. The Chancellor announced the blanket guarantee a few hours later at a press conference in the Treasury, standing beside Hank Paulson, the US Treasury Secretary who happened to be visiting London for routine talks. Watching the scene in bemusement, Paulson shook his head and remarked to Darling: 'Your guy Mervyn sure does have a high pain threshold.'

. . .

For his part, Hector Sants still burns with anger at the way things worked out.

> I believe to this day that the Bank of England's decision was one of the biggest mistakes made in the UK in this period. If we had stopped Northern Rock failing in a disorderly fashion, we would have been seen as the leader by the rest of the world and in control of the situation. Lloyds, with a liquidity guarantee, could easily have absorbed Northern Rock whose balance sheet actually wasn't that bad.

The run on Northern Rock also dealt a severe blow to the Labour government's reputation for economic competence which would hurt it badly in the general election two-and-a-half years later – and may even have determined the result. Several political historians point to that fateful Friday (14 September 2007) as Labour's equivalent of John Major's 'Black Wednesday' moment in 1992 when sterling fell out of the European Exchange Rate Mechanism.

Above all, the failure of Northern Rock exposed the fatal flaws in Brown's Tripartite structure of bank regulation and Darling, who recovered rapidly from a bad start, made no secret of his view that the rescue operation had been a monumental cock-up from beginning to end. 'The only good thing to be said about the entire episode was that it was a valuable preparation for what was to come a year later,' he remarked in his memoirs.

CHAPTER 15

RIDING THE STORM

O N **18 NOVEMBER** 2007, two months after the run on Northern Rock, Victor Blank and his wife Sylvia drove to Chequers for Sunday lunch with Gordon Brown. They had often attended dinners or lunches there during John Major's and Tony Blair's time, but this was their first invitation from Brown, still only six months into his premiership. They were enjoyable occasions and gave Blank the opportunity to talk informally to the Prime Minister amid varied and interesting company.

After the traumatic events of the Northern Rock run, the financial and banking scene had calmed down, although Blank was far from convinced the worst had passed. In recent weeks, almost all the big Wall Street banks had announced massive write-offs on mortgage-backed securities and share prices had crashed again – in four months the share price of the mighty Citigroup had more than halved. The US economy was grinding to a halt, unemployment had risen past 7 per cent and the National Bureau of Economic Research later fixed December 2007, just a month away, as the date the recession formally began.

Despite the shock of Northern Rock, the UK economy appeared to be holding up reasonably well (GDP rose 3.7 per cent in 2007, 0.7 per cent of it in the final quarter) and most forecasters were still forecasting GDP growth of 2–3 per cent for 2008. There were some ominous signs however: house prices had peaked in the summer and were now falling faster than at any time since the 1930s and companies were reining back on investment, beginning to hoard their available cash.

Brown was cheerful enough as he greeted his guests but Blank was conscious the Prime Minister looked tired and had visibly aged since he moved into No. 10 in June. He had been through a savage autumn, largely the result of what became known as 'the non-election' when he bottled out of calling a snap election in September when Labour was well ahead in the polls, which he would probably have won. The party was now 13 per cent behind the Tories, a figure it had not seen since Mrs Thatcher's days.

Northern Rock, heavily propped up by Bank of England funds, was not high on Brown's agenda, but Blank was determined to raise it with him. The stricken bank continued to trade but was having to borrow more and more money each day just to stay open as depositors continued to withdraw their savings. With no solution in sight, it had used up nearly £20 billion of the £30 billion advanced by the Bank of England. Blank wanted to remind the Prime Minister that Lloyds had been a much more serious bidder than he believed and that the guarantee it had asked for had been provided by the Bank just a week later, by which stage the run had happened and confidence in the system had been eroded. If it happened again, the government needed to have a plan in place to deal with it, he reckoned, and he wasn't convinced it did.

With Lloyds out of the picture, Alistair Darling and Hector Sants were still looking frantically for a buyer of the 'good' bank and had hired three of the City's heavyweight deal-makers, Matthew Greenburgh of Merrill's,

John Studzinski, acting for the private equity specialists Blackstone, and David Wormsley of Citibank, to find one. The bankers had sent out an information memorandum to more than fifty potential buyers, depicting the Rock in glowing terms as 'the UK's fastest growing mortgage company' with underlying profits of £588 million, which was true up to a point. There had been no lack of interest but so far no acceptable offer had materialised.

Blank's concerns were not with Northern Rock itself but with the wider banking scene, which looked very shaky. The September bank run had exposed the vulnerability of banks with similar funding models and, as Blank feared, the rumours had now spread to Alliance & Leicester and Bradford & Bingley, which were also experiencing heavy withdrawals of deposits. HBOS, another former building society dependent on the wholesale markets which had never re-opened to them, was also coming under pressure. The short-term problems may have been resolved but the underlying issues had not gone away.

Brown, as he later recorded in his memoirs, was still fuming over Northern Rock, which had occurred at what was probably the most critical moment in his political career. The bank was still owned by its shareholders, many of whom had acquired their smallholdings when it went public in October 1997 and had seen their investment basically wiped out. In Newcastle, where Northern Rock bizarrely was still completing a grandiose new headquarters, loyal staff were being laid off and no one knew what the future of the others would be. In the Sunday newspapers that morning there was speculation that, in the absence of a credible buyer, the only remaining solution was to take Northern Rock into public ownership, which Brown was determined to avoid at all costs.

'The search [for a buyer] was Brown's obsession,' wrote the political commentator Steve Richards in his book *Whatever It Takes: The Real Story of Gordon Brown and New Labour*, 'shared by no one else in the Cabinet including Darling.' Richards, who saw a lot of Brown over this period and knew him well, described his 'relentless quest' for a private sector solution, driven by his fear of 'being associated with Labour's past' and its predilection for nationalisation. 'He had made strenuous efforts to prove that he was not an Old Labour figure,' wrote Richards, 'and now he was suddenly under pressure to nationalise a bank. Not even Old Labour had nationalised a bank.'

Brown himself later confirmed this. 'I was against nationalisation, especially of a failed bank, and at that stage I would not let it be considered,' he wrote. 'I favoured a private-sector buy-out of the bank, partly because I believed we could isolate Northern Rock's problems, and partly because, ever since the 1970s the Labour Party had been losing elections on the question of economic competence.' Nor did he want to be recorded as the only Labour Prime Minister who had ever presided over the repossession of people's homes.

Blank had come to Chequers expecting to be quizzed about why Lloyds had pulled out of the Northern Rock deal at the last moment, or at least to be asked for an opinion on the present state of the banking sector. Besides the very public efforts of Greenburgh and the others, he was also aware that Darling had approached Stephen Green, chairman of HSBC, and asked him to sound out the other big banks about the possibility of forming a consortium to buy it. None of them, including Lloyds, was remotely interested, and Blank never even put it to his board.

The advisers were now down to three potential bidders, all of whom wanted the same kind of Bank of England support that Lloyds had asked for in the first place. Two of the bids were from private equity funds looking for a quick bargain, but on the face of it the third should have been more promising. A bid from Richard Branson's Virgin Money, chaired ironically by the 75-year-old Brian Pitman, had emerged as the front-runner but required the injection of large amounts of government money upfront with little chance of the British taxpayer sharing in the upside if the bank recovered. On the other hand, the taxpayer would have to bear most of the losses if things went wrong – or, as Brown sourly remarked, Branson's proposal would 'nationalise the losses and privatise the gains'.

Blank was concerned that the longer uncertainty over the future of Northern Rock lingered on, the greater the threat to the stability of the other banks, and when he had the chance he made that point to the Prime Minister. 'You obviously have your views on the different consortiums and which one you prefer,' he told Brown. 'But it actually doesn't matter what the Northern Rock solution is. The important thing is that you urgently provide a degree of certainty to the markets.'

Brown respected Blank, listened attentively without responding, then the conversation moved on down the table and the moment passed. But Brown would remember it when they met again in the summer.

.   .   .

In the event it took another three months to resolve Northern Rock's fate and Brown never did get the result he wanted. By early 2008 the shares had fallen to 50p, the Bank of England had pumped in £25 billion and the taxpayers' exposure was up to £55 billion. Applegarth, Ridley and most of the board had gone by then and a new man, Bryan Sanderson, was doing what he could to keep the bank afloat. Only Virgin was still in the bidding race but was refusing to move off demands that were unacceptable to Darling. On Friday 15 February 2008 the talks finally broke down, the shares were suspended and over the weekend Darling, after consulting the Prime Minister, did the unthinkable and announced its nationalisation. Even then Brown insisted on inserting the words 'taken into temporary public ownership' instead of 'nationalised' into the press release. It was a big personal blow for him, made worse the next morning when David Cameron and George Osborne gleefully called a press conference to proclaim the death of New Labour.

Northern Rock was eventually broken up into a 'good' and 'bad' bank, the 'good' bit bought by Virgin Money, the 'bad' bit held by UK Asset Resolution (UKAR), the taxpayer-funded body which managed the toxic debts of various other banks nationalised since 2007 at a cost of £47.5 billion. Virgin ended up paying £1 billion for the branch network and took on 1,800 Northern Rock employees – and the government, after liquidating the old mortgage business (where defaults were only 4 per cent), will probably emerge with a small loss. But most objective observers have long agreed that a Lloyds rescue, backed by the Bank of England, would have been infinitely preferable to what happened. And, in their eyes, there was only one man to blame for that.

. . .

Towards the end of 2007, Eric Daniels bumped into (Baroness) Shriti Vadera at a drinks party in the City. They knew each other slightly but had never really talked much before. The Oxford-educated Vadera, born in Uganda and brought up in India, was a former City banker who turned politician when Gordon Brown made her a minister earlier in the year and put her in the House of Lords. She had recently been promoted again, this time to the Department for Business where she was known – among other things – as 'Gordon Brown's representative on earth', his eyes and ears on the banking and financial world which he wanted to keep tabs on. For his part, Brown referred to her as 'our brilliant business minister' whom he increasingly relied on for advice and support at a time when he was becoming suspicious and estranged from his own ministers, particularly his next-door neighbour Alistair Darling.

Northern Rock was still a big talking point that evening and several senior bankers complained to Vadera about the remoteness of the Bank of England and their inability to pick up the phone and talk to anyone, as they used to in the beloved Eddie George's day. Daniels asked her did she know of Lloyds's interest in Northern Rock? She didn't in fact – she had been in the Department of International Development at the time – but she was intrigued to hear about it. 'We would have done Northern Rock,' said Daniels, 'but we got no support from government.' The Treasury, he added, had backed Mervyn King and the thing had died.

After that they talked from time to time or had lunch, as she did with other senior bankers, and she pumped him for his views on the stability of the banks and what the government should be doing to keep them lending, information she fed back to Brown in their frequent conversations. Daniels, concerned by what was happening in the housing market, was highly critical of some of the reckless lending that was still going on, arguing that mortgages should be restricted to 80 per cent of the value of a house, which was the Lloyds policy. Others, including HBOS, were still offering much more.

He also opened up to her about the criticism Lloyds had been subjected to over the past five years because of its caution. Lloyds's shares, he said, had been consistently undervalued because it refused to follow everyone else into mortgage-backed securities, investment banking and high-risk corporate lending and it had been punished for not 'playing these exciting games'. But now he reckoned its time had come and Lloyds was one of the very few banks in a position to take advantage of the looming crisis to pick up assets cheaply. If there was another Northern Rock-type situation – and there would be – he would like the government to come to him rather than reject him as they had previously done. Vadera promised she would do that.

In many ways the Northern Rock episode was a watershed for Lloyds, the moment when Daniels was prepared to abandon the cross-European model for an even greater share of the domestic market. Although Lloyds would pursue its European strategy for another six months with a final frenzied round of fruitless takeover discussions, its moment had passed. The unthinkable had been thought and a UK acquisition was back on the table. The events of September 2007 were a rehearsal for the HBOS deal, with which it would have close parallels, almost exactly a year later. Lloyds had made an opportunistic bid, an attempt to take advantage of a financial crisis to get through the competition process – just as they would for HBOS, with the same objective: increase market share and take out costs, which is what Pitman had done when the regulators let him.

Across the Atlantic, the American banking system was now in melt-down, with some of the most illustrious figures on Wall Street paying the penalty for a decade of excessive expansion and involvement in the sub-prime market. Early in December, Chuck Prince, amid taunts that 'the music has finally stopped', abruptly quit Citigroup after revealing an $11 billion loss on mortgage-related securities. He followed Stan O'Neal, chief executive of Merrill Lynch, the 'thundering herd' of Wall Street, who announced a loss of $7.9 billion, also on mortgage-backed securities, and then departed with a package worth $160 million. In January 2008 it was the turn of Bear Stearns's 73-year-old chief executive Jimmy Cayne to go after announcing fourth quarter losses of $850 million and a $1.9 billion write-off on sub-prime loans. Bear Stearns itself soon followed, sold for a knock-down price to JP Morgan which demanded – and got – a $29 billion guarantee from the Fed to cover a large hole in its balance sheet. A year earlier Bear Stearns had enjoyed a market value of $18 billion. JP Morgan paid $240 million for it.

The collapse of Bear Stearns took the total capital hit taken by US investment banks and brokers to $175 billion on mortgage and credit-related securities, with more to follow. America's two biggest mortgage finance houses, Fannie Mae and Freddie Mac, were in trouble, savaged by an unprecedented surge in defaults in the housing market. In London the share prices of both Alliance & Leicester and Bradford & Bingley halved, sending rumours through the markets that Lloyds would buy one or both of them. Alex Potter, an analyst at Collins Stewart, speculated that Lloyds could 'rip out' annual cost savings of £280 million from A&L's cost base – 'but the question is whether strategically it is the right thing for Lloyds to do'. Blank and Daniels had already decided it wasn't – the Lloyds team had no appetite for getting embroiled in another Northern Rock-type situation and it was too small for them. There would be better targets. The financial crisis was already bringing down unrealistic expectations of values, and they could bide their time.

Compared with all but a handful of world banks Lloyds TSB was in relatively good financial shape in the spring of 2008. The benefits of Daniels's three-phase plan were coming through and the markets had grudgingly accepted that the bank's cautious approach wasn't so bad after all. Headlines such as 'Lloyds gets plaudits for sound business model' and 'Why an unambitious strategy paid off for Lloyds TSB' were appearing in the financial press, reflecting the changed views of the analysts and financial commentators who were grudgingly warming to Daniels even if the feeling wasn't reciprocated.

Daniels's confidence in the bank's prospects had now risen to the point where, at the February board meeting, he proposed that the dividend should be raised for the first time in five years. The Lloyds directors had grown used to discussions about *cutting* the dividend and just maintaining it had been one of the issues (among others) which had caused Philip Hampton to leave. The CEO's suggestion therefore that it actually be increased, at a time when the FSA and the Bank were demanding that all the banks strengthen their capital bases, seemed like heresy. Daniels, however, argued that an increase, even a very small one, would be an important, symbolic gesture, a reward for the patience of shareholders who had stuck by the bank all this time. A higher dividend should also increase the share price, an important factor if they were going to use the shares as currency in a takeover situation. Helen Weir put up slides showing that the dividend cover was rising and the bank could afford a higher pay-out, and eventually Daniels, against some opposition – Blank for one was initially not so enthusiastic about it but came around – carried the day.

It received a mixed reaction in the City, distracting attention from the strong message Daniels wanted to give the markets. In February, Lloyds reported profits of £3.9 billion for the 2007 financial year, up a healthy 11 per cent and at the analysts' briefing following the results, Daniels ticked off the bank's positive points: a strong balance sheet, a huge deposit base, great brands and no exposure to toxic assets. Some of the analysts welcomed the dividend increase but there were some critics. 'The high dividend pay-out means the growth cannot be self-funded,' commented the brokers Cazenove, adding, 'our analysis suggests … the market will fret until it can see a path for Lloyds to build a stronger capital base'. The Cazenove analyst, Simon Wilkinson, estimated that Lloyds would need to make an equity issue of £3 billion over the next few years simply to meet the tougher demands of the regulators. Even that figure, he added, assumed 'a relatively benign economy' – which even then seemed unlikely. And no one knew about the PPI problem coming down the road.

Lloyds continued to trade strongly through the first quarter of 2008, when the UK economy was still growing, and Helen Weir's presentation to the board in April seemed to confirm Daniels's confidence. Income, she said, was running almost 7 per cent ahead of the previous year and her forecast for the whole of 2008 showed a profit of £4.3 billion which, after allowing for 'market dislocation' costs of £500 million caused by the international banking situation, left a net pre-tax figure of £3.8 billion, more or less unchanged from the previous year. That, in her view, wasn't great, but it wasn't bad either – she preferred the word 'acceptable'. Others thought it was a lot better than that, even if Weir did add the warning that 'there are significant risks in terms of the economic environment and further market dislocation'.

It was Weir's last board meeting as finance director. In April, Terri Dial, one of the highest-paid executives in the bank – her salary and bonus in 2007 was over £2 million and share options and other incentives lifted that figure above £3 million – informed Daniels that she had been offered a job as chief executive of Citigroup's consumer banking division and would be returning to the US. Daniels was disappointed to lose her but he took the opportunity to move Helen Weir to the operational role she had been pressing for since she joined the bank. She would replace Dial as head of the retail division, still the biggest part of the group. The appointment sparked suggestions in the City that, as the *Financial Times* commented, 'she is being groomed as a possible successor to Daniels'.

There was an obvious internal candidate for the chief financial officer job, whom Blank and the other executives expected Daniels to recommend to the board for approval. Tim Tookey had originally joined Lloyds from Prudential in early 2006, just a few months before Victor Blank, in the new role of deputy group finance director. When she interviewed him for the job, Weir made it clear that she did not see herself staying in the CFO role forever and gave Tookey to understand that he was hired on the clear ticket that he should get himself into a position where he could succeed her.

Tookey did just that over the next two years, running the group finance functions under Weir, which at Lloyds, with its minimal exposure to the wholesale markets, was not as exacting as at other banks. Soon after he arrived he was given the task of handling Lloyds's first – and only – significant securitisation issue, a £13 billion residential mortgage-backed security (RMBS), which was the largest single transaction the bank had ever done. The RMBS was issued through a vehicle called Cancara, which Lloyds stressed to the analysts was 'Rolls-Royce' in nature, with 100 per cent-rated securities and no sub-prime asset-backed (ABS) exposure.

Although Daniels had his doubts about it, it was a classic banking instrument, a superior version of the securities that Northern Rock had used so widely, but which in the end it couldn't finance, consisting basically of bundled mortgages put into a special purpose vehicle (SPV), which was then used as security for a loan which would be repaid as the mortgages were redeemed. The issue was well received in the securitisation market which welcomed Lloyds as a new entrant and hoped for more.

Tookey's handling of it impressed even Daniels, who asked him to accompany him on some of the investor roadshows when Weir wasn't available. Lloyds was still unfashionable because of its well-known aversion to risk, and Tookey watched in astonishment as a fund manager in Boston tried to persuade Daniels to relax Lloyds's strict banking covenants and lend more money at a higher risk – or 'covenant light' in the jargon used. Several times Tookey found himself stepping in to defend the Lloyds model against vociferous objections from American investors, used to their more aggressive domestic banks, while Daniels stood fast.

In May 2008, almost two years to the day after he joined, Tookey took a call from Daniels's office asking to see him first thing the next morning. As it happened, he was about to move house and had booked the day off, but when he tried to explain that he couldn't make the meeting, one of Daniels's assistants told him icily: 'No, you don't understand – *Eric wants to see you in the morning*!' Reluctantly, Tookey drove up to the City from his home in Kent, and went up to the eighth floor, where Daniels explained that Dial was leaving, Weir was taking over her job and he wanted Tookey to move into Weir's office immediately. He would be appointed 'acting' chief financial officer, without a place on the board, although of course he would attend all board meetings and present the financials. Daniels explained that the bank would still go through the process of appointing a headhunter to interview other candidates, Tookey among them. There was no guarantee he would get the job.

'Tim saw himself as the obvious candidate but Eric liked to survey the whole market before settling on someone,' says a former Lloyds executive.

> He liked Tim but he also had some reservations. He had very little investor or City experience and up to that time he was basically an internal numbers man. Eric wanted to bench-mark him against other candidates which is why he used headhunters – he had done the same for Truett when he was made acting head of the wholesale division.

It meant that over the next seven months, when he found himself at the epicentre of the biggest crisis in Lloyds's – and Britain's – financial history, Tookey was still not formally confirmed in the CFO role. Nor was he on the main board. While the financial world was falling apart, the acting CFO of Lloyds had to go through the humiliating process of being interviewed for what all his colleagues regarded as his own job. At one point the headhunter said to him: 'Tell me, if you were to get the job, what would you do in the first 100 days?' She seemed blissfully unaware that Tookey had already been doing the job for months and shadowing it for two years. Furiously, he began listing the hundred things he had *already* done in 100 days before he stalked off in a rage to complain to Daniels, swearing he would never deal with that particular headhunter again.

Meanwhile Daniels was spreading his net wide, talking to a range of other potential candidates for arguably the most critical role in the bank. When Weir was moved, Daniels told Victor Blank that his priority was to have a CFO beside him who was skilled in mergers and acquisitions and who could present credibly to shareholders. These, he added, were not Tookey's strengths, although he was developing them and he wanted to give him the chance to grow into the job. Blank on the other hand had great confidence in Tookey who, he believed, had a fine track record and had done well at Lloyds. But at the end of the day it had to be Daniels's decision.

Eventually Daniels came down to three names, including Tookey and John Cryan, a City high-flier who was then CFO of UBS where he was highly regarded (he is now CEO of Deutsche Bank). The third candidate on the list was a surprise: Matthew Greenburgh, the high-rolling investment banker from Merrill Lynch and the same man who had tried to sell Northern Rock to Lloyds. When Daniels showed him the list, an astonished Blank told him bluntly that, much as he admired Greenburgh as a practitioner, he felt he was 'wholly inappropriate' for the job.

Daniels retorted that Greenburgh was a 'sharp tool' who would be brilliant at communicating with the City, but the Lloyds chairman refused even to consider it. 'This is a very big institution where you have to be on top of a vast array of financial controls and disciplines, including treasury, budgets, capital requirements, regulations and all the rest,' he told Daniels. It required specialist, technical skills and practical experience, particularly of financial and management accounting, which Greenburgh, who had grown up as an investment banker and deal-maker, simply did not have. 'You must have someone who gives you accurate and balanced information, who you can trust completely to be on top of very detailed figures. Matthew has different skills.'

Blank never knew how Daniels broke the news to Greenburgh and was left wondering why the Merrill Lynch executive, with his huge bonuses and his love of deals, would even consider it. In fact, the idea had come from Greenburgh himself who, over breakfast one day, told Daniels he wanted to get out of investment banking and 'do something more substantial'. He had already made his fortune – several times over – and didn't much care for where the profession was heading. Daniels reluctantly crossed him off the list but still didn't formally appoint Tookey, who got on with the job. Even Daniels seemed to forget he was not on the board and the non-execs simply assumed he was.

.   .   .

In the middle of March HBOS became the victim of one of the most brutal bear raids the London market had ever seen. The trigger was the announcement that it was forced to pay a crippling 9.5 per cent for a new £750 million ten-year bond, which was a full 300 basis points more than it was charging for its mortgages. The high interest rate meant the issue was twice oversubscribed but within hours the rumours were spreading across the markets that HBOS was in talks with the Bank of England for lender-of-last-resort financing, a potential re-run of Northern Rock. The story was given some dubious credence after someone was said to have seen an email recording HBOS's discussions with the Bank which had cancelled all staff leave over the weekend. It was entirely fictitious but in the febrile atmosphere it was enough to send HBOS shares plummeting 17 per cent in just a few hours when the markets opened on 19 March.

Stevenson stormed off to see Darling at the Treasury while Hornby called Hector Sants, both furiously insisting they do something immediately or there would be another bank run by the end of the day. Fortunately, by that stage the authorities had learned something about runs, and first Sants and then the Bank issued statements of support, condemning the 'market abuse' and threatening to track down and punish the perpetrators (they never did of course). Sants and the Bank officials were concerned enough to call the City editors of the major newspapers to assure them there was no truth in the email story, the first time that had happened since the height of the fringe banking crisis in 1974 when the potential target was NatWest.

The rumours subsided but they left their mark, particularly on Andy Hornby, who appeared seriously rattled by the ferocity of the attack and the readiness of markets to believe the worst. Stevenson dismissed any suggestion of his vulnerability by describing Hornby as a 'hell of a tough guy', but in fact he wasn't. In contrast to the bullying, overbearing Goodwin at RBS, Hornby was more collegial and less assertive, preferring to manage by persuasion and consensus than by diktat. He was well liked, both inside the bank and in the City, and up to the spring of 2008 had never encountered adversity in his glittering career. When it came, it found him far more fragile than the other, more robust bank chiefs. Gordon Brown picked up on this when he called all the bank chief executives to a meeting in 10 Downing Street on 15 April. Hornby, he recorded afterwards, 'sounded very worried' while the others 'appeared to be suffering a quiet anxiety'.

He had reason to be. In February HBOS again shocked the market by disclosing it had £63 billion of higher risk assets on its balance sheet, some of which were backed by US sub-prime mortgages. That was about 10 per cent of its £667 billion balance sheet and the markets speculated it was just the tip of the iceberg. The shares fell again.

Brown's intention at the Downing Street meeting was to berate the banks for not lending, which he admitted 'was rapidly becoming my obsession', but instead found himself the subject of a coordinated attack from the bankers demanding that 'liquidity be provided to the whole system'. Getting nowhere with the banks, he called a meeting of his ministers and advisers and asked Sir James Crosby, Hornby's predecessor and now deputy chairman of the FSA, to investigate ways to get the mortgage market moving again. Bank lending to British industry, in the Prime Minister's view in April 2008, took precedence over the stability of the banks.

But the Bank of England did react a few days later by belatedly launching its special liquidity scheme, designed to allow banks to swap illiquid and untradeable assets, particularly mortgage-backed debt, for more secure and easily tradable UK Treasury Bills. Lloyds participated in the scheme like everyone else, but only marginally – it had very few mortgage-backed securities to swap and in any case it was not experiencing any great difficulty in financing itself at cheaper rates. HBOS by contrast grasped the lifeline and hung on for its life.

As Hornby's self-confidence waned, Stevenson's more forceful personality came to dominate the bank more and more. It was he who now mostly dealt with the FSA and the Bank, seething when he was criticised and hitting back bitingly at real or imagined slights. He had long felt aggrieved at the attitude of the FSA, accusing it of 'a continual paranoia about HBOS's position on the ladder of vulnerability'. The management of HBOS, he wrote to the FSA in an email on November 2007, 'has done a superb job' and had taken tough decisions to ration assets growth, starting immediately after the Northern Rock affair. It had demonstrated its 'responsibility and competence' and, in return, he demanded, 'there could be some release of the FSA paranoia button'.

After the collapse of Bear Stearns in March, Callum McCarthy emailed him to ask politely how he was 'feeling about things', and got back the bullish reply:

> I and we are feeling about as robust as it is possible to feel in a worrying environment which we would rather did not exist! As I said to you, we have faced into the need to be boringly boring for the next year or two and we are setting out our stall to do that...

HBOS, he added, was having no problems in financing itself 'even on the hairiest of days and weeks'.

A few days later he emailed McCarthy again: 'Without wishing to be the slightest bit complacent, we feel that HBOS in this particular storm and given its business characteristics, is in as safe a harbour as is possible while at the same time feeling commercially rather frustrated.'

It fact, as events were to prove, HBOS was sailing into a tropical storm and Hornby and his team were concerned enough to meet with Simon Robey, head of corporate finance at Morgan Stanley, to discuss ways of riding it out. It turned into a gloomy session. 'After the Northern Rock thing, Andy and the crew at HBOS became very thoughtful about life,' says one of the advisers. 'And that was the moment when Morgan Stanley started asking more probing questions about its financial robustness and how it should respond to the regulator's demand for more capital. It was clear that, if you looked around the corner, a rights issue was the sensible thing to do.'

Any hope the authorities had of restoring stability to the markets disappeared on 22 April when RBS, the worst capitalised of all the big banks, announced a rights issue of £12 billion, the biggest in British financial history, and said it planned to raise another £8 billion from disposals – £20 billion in total, more than the market value of HBOS. Just two months earlier Fred Goodwin had publicly ruled out the need for a capital raising and whatever reputation he still had disappeared overnight. RBS's losses now were enormous, £5.9 billion on sub-prime and other investments and its takeover of ABN Amro, in a lop-sided partnership with Santander and Fortis, was already turning sour as the Dutch bank racked up losses on its sub-prime portfolio.

On 28 April, four days after RBS, HBOS announced it was raising £4 billion at 275p a share, a whopping 45 per cent discount on the prevailing price of 495p. It also revealed it was writing down its portfolio of complex debt securities, many of them sub-prime related, by a further £2.84 billion. The reaction in the City was one of anger and shock. 'This is a massive U-turn,' said one big shareholder. 'They have just recently raised the dividend by 18 per cent and told us they had a strong capital base. You have to question whether this is poor judgement, weak management information – or worse.' Another opined that 'this is a bigger *volte face* than RBS'.

Hornby now joined Fred Goodwin in the public's 'discredited banker' stable, another from-hero-to-zero figure whose reputation was savaged in the week that followed. He tried his best to spin it, pointing out that the rights issue would raise the bank's core Tier 1 capital from 5.7 per cent to between 6 and 7 per cent, closer to the pan-European banks which were around 6.5 per cent, and would deliver the stronger capital base the FSA was asking for from all the banks. It was, he asserted, a 'prudent step-change in our capital strength and our target ratios. We need to be prepared for all macroeconomic events. Banks that do not have strong capital ratios will find it harder.'

No one wanted to hear it. Several disillusioned shareholders pointed out that just a year ago HBOS had been buying back its own shares at between 855p and £10.70, and now it was issuing them at a quarter of that. It seemed like madness.

HBOS was not alone in finding life going from tough to awful. In May, Alliance & Leicester also issued a profit warning and a day later Bradford & Bingley (B&B) followed with an even more dismal statement and a rights issue at a 48 per cent discount to the market price. Worse still, on orders from the FSA, the big banks, including Lloyds, were forced to subscribe to B&B's £400 million issue, knowing they had little chance of any return.

'Eric, we should account for this as a charitable donation,' Tim Tookey said to his chief executive, only half-jokingly, 'because we'll never get our money back.'

He was right: it turned into a fiasco a few days later when B&B's debt was downgraded, the shares collapsed and the chief executive resigned.

Tookey wrote off the £35 million investment which he hadn't wanted to make in the first place.

By 14 June it was Barclays' turn to announce a £4 billion rights issue, underwritten by Qatar's Investment Authority. In less than two months, more than £20 billion of new capital had been raised by British banks, a figure which Gordon Brown called 'mind-boggling'. And yet it was to prove far from enough.

From their eyrie in Gresham Street, Blank and Daniels watched these events unfold with a mixture of wonder, fear and *schadenfreude*. Lloyds was still on target for profits of £3.8 billion and was also financing itself relatively comfortably. It was the only big bank (other than the well-capitalised HSBC, which raised £14 billion a year later, and Standard Chartered) not to do a capital fundraising at this time. In May it was able to tell the markets it had no direct exposure to US sub-prime asset-backed securities, very limited exposure to asset-backed security CDOs and only a modest exposure to other risky instruments. Its funding gap was £67 billion, a fraction of HBOS's, and its funding needs from the wholesale market were no more than £10 billion a year. In a time of growing banking failures, it was one of the strongest banks in the world.

At the board meeting on 7 May Tim Tookey described the group's capital position as 'robust and satisfactory and we enjoy a strong liquid-ity position'. On the existing rules (Basel II), Lloyds's core Tier 1 ratio was 7.4 per cent compared to 5.1 per cent for Barclays, 5.7 per cent for HBOS and 4.5 per cent for RBS. Even on the new targets set by the FSA of a minimum of 6 per cent for core Tier 1 – basically equity capital – Lloyds was still fine.

But he still cautioned that Lloyds would need to raise money at some point. Recent developments, Tookey said, 'are leading us to reflect on our position'. The bank faced a proposed regulatory change in the way insurance subsidiaries were treated on a bank's balance sheet, and unless it sold Scottish Widows, Lloyds's Tier 1 capital would drop below 6 per cent (HBOS, which also had substantial insurance interests, would fall to 5.2 per cent on the same basis, even after the rights issue). At the same time, UK house prices and share prices were falling, pension deficits were rising and Lloyds TSB needed to prepare for an increased level of bad debts and one-off shocks. To meet the new capital rules, Tookey concluded, Lloyds would need to boost equity capital before 2009. Its advisers Citibank were urging it to raise around £4 billion, partly to fund further acquisitions, but it should move quickly to avoid 'last mover disadvantage'.

A few days later on 15 May, Tookey took advantage of a window in the market to raise over £1 billion of Tier 1 capital in a mixture of dollars and euros, a token amount in terms of the overall long-term capital needs but welcome for all that. Daniels reported to the board that 'market feedback on this deal was very strong and the transaction was substantially oversubscribed, leading to tight prices being obtained'. Much to Daniels's amazement, *EuroWeek*, part of the Euromoney Institutional Investor stable, considered the operation significant enough to feature it on its front page. It didn't remove the need for an eventual rights issue, but it took some of the pressure off and bought more time. The board concluded, after a lengthy debate, to wait until markets improved and discounts narrowed before going for anything larger.

. . .

Through May and well into June 2008, lawyers, accountants and bankers worked feverishly in offices across the City on the HBOS rights prospectus, which would be signed off by the accountants KPMG and two leading firms of City lawyers, Allen & Overy and Freshfields. It would be fully underwritten by two merchant banks, Morgan Stanley and Dresdner Kleinwort, who guaranteed that HBOS got its money. The finished prospectus, 194 pages long, detailed every aspect of the HBOS business and set out the potential risks – general economic conditions, credit quality in the markets, interest rate changes, funding and liquidity and so on, routine stuff for any bank prospectus. The FSA had swarmed all over it and Bank of England and Treasury officials went through it line by line. Yet there were no danger signals, no red flags and no hint of serious problems – in fact the opposite. Trading, HBOS said, 'continues to be satisfactory', the retail division was 'robust' and the funds raised would equip HBOS for any emergency. The Morgan Stanley team, which included specialists in every aspect of clearing bank operations, uncovered nothing unexpected in their six weeks of due diligence. 'There was no sense that the corporate book was in a particularly fragile state,' said one of the advisers later.

> It is easy to forget now that Peter Cummings was considered to be running a really impressive and important business and he continued to be impressive. I think obviously lots of calls that were made at the time were not the right calls as it turned out. But it didn't feel as if there was a particular piece of the business that was in looming crisis.

As the document went out to shareholders, there seemed no reason why HBOS shouldn't get the rights away.

Inside Lloyds, meanwhile, the focus had switched from the defensive to the offensive. The global crisis might be taking its toll on the weaker banks, but the investment opportunities it had waited the best part of a decade for were beginning to emerge. Some of the big European banks, which had dismissed Lloyds's approaches a year before, including Fortis, were now in trouble themselves and looking for saviours. Daniels passed on most of them but for nearly a year he had been pursuing – amid several other options – an ambitious plan which would solve a number of his strategic issues in one fell swoop: a swap of Scottish Widows for Dresdner Bank, one of the three biggest retail banks in Germany.

Dresdner was owned by Allianz, the largest insurance company in Europe, but it was a loss-maker and Allianz didn't know what to do with it. Daniels had first approached Michael Diekmann, Allianz's chief executive, in May 2007 and after a polite discussion about the general banking scene told him that if Allianz was interested in selling Dresdner, Lloyds would be interested in exchanging it for the Widows. The markets, he added, had never understood why Lloyds owned Scottish Widows and he reckoned a 'pure play' bank would command a higher rating. 'Bancassurance has worked reasonably well for us,' he told Diekmann, 'but the key question is whether we need to be a manufacturer as well as a distributor.' Allianz too would benefit, he pointed out, by offloading its problem child, which was holding back Allianz's share price, and by strengthening its position in insurance with a powerful presence in the UK. They could continue the relationship with Lloyds's retail operations by selling Allianz and Scottish Widows' products across an even bigger network.

The 53-year-old Diekmann was not the typical head of a large financial institution. Apart from his professional accomplishments, he had canoed down the Zambezi, ridden across Argentina and trekked up the K2 mountain in Tibet, writing a string of adventure travel books along the way. He was admired in German business circles for his handling of Allianz but was also under fire for buying Dresdner which, in the words of the *FT*, had 'tottered through a string of crises, with each green shoot of revival almost as quickly withering'. The financial crisis had brought the issue to a head.

Diekmann promised to get back to Daniels after he had discussed Lloyds's approach with the Allianz board at their forthcoming strategic 'away day'. A few weeks later Paul Achleitner, Allianz's finance director, called Helen Weir to say that the board had decided not to pursue the opportunity at that stage and wanted to see what they could do with Dresdner on their own.

The deal went quiet for the best part of a year and Lloyds explored other opportunities, which were now coming thick and fast. In May 2008, China Life, which controlled half the Chinese insurance market with more than $500 billion of revenues, offered to buy a minority stake in Scottish Widows for cash, but by that time Lloyds was pursuing something much more interesting: the German Postbank, Germany's largest retail bank (by number of customers – 14.5 million of them), with 850 branches and representatives in over 6,000 post offices. One of its biggest attractions was its highly sophisticated IT platform which, unlike Lloyds and other big banks that operated a patchwork quilt of legacy systems, it had built from scratch. 'They were able to throw everything out and invest in a single platform,' says one of the Lloyds executives who struggled with the bank's system for years. 'We could have moved everything onto it.'

For a time Daniels saw Postbank as his potential game-changer: its market value was €9.4 billion, which was within reach, and by the end of April negotiations had got to the point where Blank and Daniels were ready to discuss it with the board and Tim Tookey began planning how to finance the acquisition. The strategic attraction of Postbank, as with Dresdner, was in building an international footprint for Lloyds as a retail bank. The Lloyds board, sceptical at the outset, was reassured when Wolfgang Berndt, an eminent German/Austrian businessman who sat on the Lloyds board, gave it his approval. Berndt warned of the danger of union problems but added that after reading the material Daniels had sent him he could see how it could bring growth to the bank. 'I came away with a much more positive view than I had going in.' Blank, however, had his doubts: Lloyds had little management expertise for running a bank in Germany, there would be very few synergies or cost savings and he could not quite see how Daniels and his team could accelerate the growth of Postbank when its own management couldn't do it. Its customers were mostly blue-collar and lower middle-class, a market where Lloyds had little expertise and was not where it strategically wanted to be.

By 7 May 2008 Postbank was off the agenda and Dresdner was back on. Almost exactly a year since they had first talked, Paul Achleitner called Daniels to admit sheepishly that Allianz's attempts to manage Dresdner had not been a success and with the German banking industry about to go through a serious round of concentration, it had decided to sell it. Would Lloyds still be interested in a swap of Scottish Widows for Dresdner?

There were, the Allianz finance director warned, several obvious buyers in the shape of Commerzbank or Deutsche, and the German papers were filled with speculation about a three-way merger between Dresdner, Postbank and Commerzbank to form a second major force in the fragmented German banking market. The German authorities preferred an all-German solution but Allianz feared that any attempt at rationalisation would result in serious trade union action against the whole Allianz group. The board had therefore decided a deal with a non-German bank would be preferable – which was why Achleitner was talking to Lloyds.

Allianz had bought Dresdner for €24 billion in 2001 but the price tag now, the Lloyds team estimated, should be about half that, not that far from the open market value of Scottish Widows. It had its problems of course, including an €8.1 billion exposure to asset-backed securities at the end of 2007, most of which it had written off. But it was well capitalised and the more the teams looked at it, the more Daniels liked it. Lloyds's sums showed a 'value-creation potential' for Lloyds of £6.8 billion, supporting an offer of up to £10 billion. On the same basis, the value of Scottish Widows was £7.4 billion, leaving a £2.6 billion gap. Tookey proposed financing that through a £5.2 billion rights issue which would not only pay for it but would raise Lloyds's core Tier 1 capital ratio above the 6 per cent level and leave £1 billion available for further expansion.

The story leaked in the German press on 16 June and was soon picked up by the *Financial Times*, which reported that Lloyds was considering mounting a bid for 'one of the German banks which are currently up for sale', which included Postbank, Dresdner and Citibank's German retail banking operations (which Daniels, with his Citibank background, had briefly considered). A few days later the reports became more specific, identifying Dresdner as the number one target and a more informed news story in the *FT* on 22 June suggested Lloyds had made a 'tentative' approach to buy Dresdner from Allianz and referred to speculation that Lloyds could exchange Scottish Widows for it, adding 'this option is seen as less likely given that Lloyds has made clear that bancassurance is a core part of its operation'. In fact, the Widows was a crucial part of the deal.

A few days later Daniels called Diekmann to check on progress. They were now deep into due diligence and the management teams were meeting on a daily basis but Allianz was having trouble doing its own due diligence on Scottish Widows. 'We tried to access your data room on Friday but it was not available,' Diekmann complained, before asking Daniels for his reaction to the recent press leaks, which had clearly disturbed him. 'It's uncomfortable not being able to respond,' said Daniels sympathetically. 'But we both have to live with it.' At least, he added, they had moved off the front pages and for his part the leaks added to his desire to move as quickly as possible. He was relieved when Diekmann solemnly agreed.

Within a fortnight however it was all over, partly because of the leaks but also because market conditions had overtaken it. Lloyds shares had hit 586p in the middle of 2007 and opened 2008 just above 400p. But after the Dresdner talks leaked, the shares dropped sharply and by mid-July they were 292p, halving in a twelve-month period and taking the market value below £15 billion. By that stage the landscape had changed and shareholders did not want Lloyds going off on a Continental jaunt when within a few months it might, like every bank in the world, be fighting for its life. The deal no longer made any sense for Lloyds and Daniels called to say it was off.

Two months later Diekmann appeared on a podium in Frankfurt to announce he had found an all-German solution to 'the most intractable problem' of his reign: Commerzbank had agreed to buy Dresdner for €9.8 billion, well below the price the Lloyds advisers had recommended and less than half what Allianz had paid for it. By that stage Daniels and Blank were pleased to be out of it.

It was Lloyds's last attempt to acquire a European bank. From now on, the strategy would be to re-focus on the UK where the financial situation was getting more serious by the day – and where there would be some excellent opportunities for a bank in a strong enough position to take them. Europe was out; the UK was back in. The world had turned full circle.

CHAPTER 16

PUTTING THE
BANKS TO RIGHTS

BY THE EARLY summer of 2008 the plight of HBOS was becoming critical. In February Andy Hornby had predicted that UK house prices that year would be flat but four months later the bank was forecasting a fall of 9 per cent, while the level of housing transactions, which drove the old Halifax business, had almost halved. By June the housing market had deteriorated further and HBOS's profits outlook for the first six months of 2008 had become decidedly grim, threatening its rights issue which was looking precarious. Morgan Stanley and Dresdner Kleinwort, the two underwriters, were on the hook for £1 billion each, a serious risk for two financial institutions which were already reeling from their sub-prime exposure. Through June and July the HBOS share price gyrated wildly, sometimes below the rights price of 275p, sometimes above. In a show of confidence after the bear raid in February, Hornby and Stevenson had invested £6 million of their own money in buying shares at over 500p. They had already lost half of it.

From his office on Broadway, Morgan Stanley's chief executive John Mack watched the HBOS saga unfold with growing unease. A lifetime banker and legendary cost-cutter – for which, unoriginally, he was known as Mack the Knife – Mack had earned $41 million in 2006 when times were good but just six months earlier Morgan had written off $9.4 billion on sub-prime securities and with it his 2007 bonus. Even worse in the eyes of Wall Street, he was forced to seek an equity injection of $5 billion from a Chinese sovereign wealth fund, an unpopular move with the regulators who would have preferred him to shop locally. Morgan's share price was under pressure, as was Mack's job, and every time the HBOS price sank below the rights price, Morgan Stanley's shares fell too. 'I feel as though I've got the fate of two institutions resting on my shoulders,' Simon Robey remarked to Hornby after a particularly nasty day in the market. The normally unflappable Morgan Stanley corporate banker, who had been through many tight situations in his day, later described this time as particularly 'unnerving' and even 'terrifying'.

When the HBOS rights issue began to look really bad, Mack flew to London to check things out for himself and Robey took him along to meet Stevenson and Hornby. He came away grim-faced but determined, remarking to Robey, 'Listen, Simon, you know what you're doing. All I want to ensure is that we are getting good information from the client. We are committed to doing this and we'll do it.' He flew back to New York to battle with his own problems in a climate which was now threatening even the four mighty Wall Street investment houses, Goldman Sachs, Merrill Lynch, Morgan Stanley – and Lehman Brothers. Leaving it all to Robey was a brave thing to do, but Mack was well known for his strong nerves which were needed now.

Morgan Stanley wasn't the only institution watching the HBOS rights issue with growing concern – the FSA and the Bank of England were becoming increasingly nervous and wondering what to do if it went wrong. At a meeting of Bank of England Court non-executive directors on 16 July 2008, Mervyn King reported (according to the board minutes) that the rights issue was being 'monitored' and the FSA strategy was 'to encourage and facilitate mergers with stronger institutions'. There weren't many 'stronger institutions' that HBOS could merge with – other than Lloyds, but if that what was what he had in mind, the minutes don't record it.

Rights issues are long, drawn out affairs and it would be eighty-three days from the announcement to the day HBOS would finally get its money. A lot could happen – and did – in that time. The rights prospectus, after two months of due diligence, was published on 19 June and a few weeks later Dennis Stevenson chaired a general meeting in Edinburgh to seek shareholders' approval. He had lost none of his ebullience, defiantly declaring: 'Armageddon may happen, and we should be prepared for it – and we are.'

In the event, Armageddon did happen and the rights proved a dismal flop. On 19 July the Morgan Stanley and Dresdner teams, after a titanic sales exercise, had to concede defeat. Only 8.3 per cent of the issue was taken up by shareholders and the rest was left with the underwriters, adding to Mack's problems back in New York. Barclays' £4.5 billion rights issue suffered a similar fate, with less than 20 per cent subscribed, leaving the Qatar Investment Authority as Barclays' biggest shareholder with 6 per cent. 'The poor response is ignominious,' commented the *Financial Times*, 'particularly for HBOS which has seen its shares plunge 40 per cent since the bank announced its rights issue almost three months ago.'

Gordon Brown, who had urged the FSA and Bank of England to insist the banks raise more capital, saw the failure as a clear indication 'that the markets did not believe that HBOS had come clean on its toxic assets and future write-offs'. Some 20 million people held savings with HBOS and the possibility of its collapse was too awful even to contemplate. Long

after the event Alistair Darling remarked, 'there was a whiff of death
surrounding the whole operation', but actually there wasn't – there were
signs of serious problems certainly, mainly because the wholesale market
was closed to it, but at this stage it was not terminal, or beyond rescue.

Despite the failure of the rights, HBOS had got its money and for
the moment its capital issues seemed to have been solved. But its liquidity situation was getting worse by the day and from now on Hornby
and his team would be in crisis management mode and HBOS basically
ceased to operate as a bank. Its exposure to US toxic debt, including
£7.1 billion of sub-prime mortgages which it held on its books, was rat-
tling even the panglossian Stevenson. At home, deposits were beginning
to flow out and its customer funding gap, the difference between loans
and deposits, now totalled over £200 billion, more than all the other big
banks put together and double what it had been five years before. Some
of Peter Cummings's big corporate loans to highly geared property companies were also beginning to look shaky as the property market went
into a spin and leveraged buy-outs started to unwind. HBOS was running out of liquidity and unless the wholesale markets opened – which
had become even more unlikely as the crisis in the US deepened – it was
going to need help. It was, in short, the perfect storm. And even the irrepressible Lord Stevenson was humbled by it.

Callum McCarthy called to ask him to come in to the FSA to discuss what next. 'You've had a long and difficult rights issue and it is not
clear if you are out of the wood,' he said. What assets could HBOS sell?

Not much, said Stephenson, running through the alternatives. The
Australian business could go but it would be a fire sale and not big
enough to make much difference. There was the insurance business
which, like Scottish Widows, was holding up well, but a forced sale
would send the wrong signal to the market and could result in the run
they were all trying to avoid. Every other business had a problem too

– there were not many buyers around for troubled assets and it would all take too long.

'He has gotten into a very difficult position,' McCallum told Sants gloomily, 'made more difficult if you've been a man who has been supremely self-confident.'

Watching the HBOS share price continue downwards, Matthew Greenburgh called Daniels in early July. 'Things are not looking good for HBOS,' he said. 'Maybe this is a climate in which the OFT issues get pushed to one side?' Blank had already discussed the possibility with Daniels and they both felt the competition window might be opening. A few days later Andy Hornby, fending off growing calls for his resignation and that of Stevenson, called his friend Victor Blank. The time had come to look for that safe harbour. Would Lloyds be interested in a merger?

. . .

In the last week of July 2008 the top executive teams from the two banks, Lloyds and HBOS, started meeting in secret in a three-bedroom flat in St James's which Bank of Scotland executives had traditionally used as a London pad when they were in town. The Lloyds team was led by Eric Daniels flanked by Tim Tookey and the ubiquitous Matthew Greenburgh as their sole adviser; Truett Tate and Helen Weir dipped in and out as they were needed. HBOS fielded Hornby, Mike Ellis, its chief financial officer, and Simon Robey of Morgan Stanley, its financial adviser. Also present was Harry Baines, HBOS's legal counsel, who impressed the Lloyds team with his grasp of the competition and other legal issues (to the point that he later became company secretary of the enlarged group). 'Harry was pretty influential,' says one of the Lloyds team. Victor Blank and Dennis Stevenson were kept informed of progress but never went to the flat.

As the merger talks began, the atmosphere in the City was more sombre than ever. Just a few days before, Bradford & Bingley's £400 million
rights issue had also proved a dismal failure, with 28 per cent left with
the underwriters, UBS and Citibank, who at that stage needed it like a
hole in the head. The £35 million the FSA had forced Lloyds to subscribe
went down the drain with it.

The agenda for the Lloyds team was a straightforward one: HBOS
needed rescuing and Lloyds had long wanted to take it over. The competition issues were huge but, given the financial circumstances, the
government might be persuaded to help out. Lloyds's balance sheet and
credit rating was strong enough to shoulder the HBOS funding issues
and, with the Bank of England taking a very different attitude than it did
during the Northern Rock debacle, there should be no liquidity issues
this time around. An approach to the Bank was not even raised during
the discussions – no one thought there was any need.

For three intense days the two banks swapped confidential information in a process they called 'high-level due diligence', as the Lloyds team
tried to fathom the scale of HBOS's exposure to sub-prime and corporate debts. There was no opportunity to delve too deeply, but the HBOS
prospectus was still relatively fresh off the presses (although, like all such
documents, the audited figures were historical – nearly six months old)
and both sides had agreed on 'an open and frank exchange' which would
include their best guesses of potential write-downs, sub-prime and other
losses and profit forecasts for the rest of the year. They examined each
other's asset and loan books, made their separate calculations on potential
impairments, and Tookey and Ellis prepared a rough *pro forma* model of
what a joint bank would look like.

'In those early days there were discussions about people's businesses
along the lines: so what's in your retail book? What's in your wholesale
book?' says one of the executives present. 'And Eric or Andy would say,

you look at that and we do this. They were not due diligence meetings – they were: "talk to me about what's in your business, tell me about your customers and your types of lending, talk to me about how your book is performing".'

From the start it was clear that this was not going to be a merger – Lloyds would be taking over HBOS which effectively meant, although no one mentioned it, that Stevenson and Hornby would probably be out of a job. Just a few months before, HBOS still had a larger market value than Lloyds, but the collapse of its shares had changed all that. In the first six months of 2008, HBOS recorded a profit of just £848 million, a 72 per cent fall on the previous year, after taking a £1 billion hit on its US sub-prime mortgages. Those were the latest figures available.

As the talks began, Lloyds shares stood at 305p and a measure of the impact of the financial crisis was illustrated starkly by the fact that the market value of Lloyds TSB, £55 billion at its peak in Pitman's day, was now down to £17.4 billion. HBOS, even after the rights issue, was £5 billion below that whereas only a year before it had been 50 per cent bigger. Even that, as in the case of Northern Rock, was no guide to what price Lloyds would actually pay if they went through with a deal. Greenburgh was keen to get into discussions on price, but Robey argued that the HBOS share price was too volatile for that and it was agreed that it should be parked for the moment. The principal aim was to see whether they could get an agreement in principle before going to the next stage.

By the second day Daniels and his team could see there was a deal to be done, assuming you believed the figures presented by HBOS. And it looked good: Lloyds would grow its share of current accounts from 19 per cent to 30 per cent, mortgages from 8 per cent to 28 per cent, and it would have a 23 per cent share of savings accounts, 24 per cent of small business accounts, 20 per cent of mid–large corporates, 22 per cent of personal loans and 20 per cent of credit cards. It would also become one of the biggest insurance companies in the country with 16 per cent of life insurance and pensions (against 6 per cent) and 14 per cent of home insurance distribution (8 per cent).

Most important of all were the cost savings, which would be a minimum of £1.5 billion, and possibly £2 billion. That would mean losing up to 28,000 jobs out of 125,000, a daunting figure which they agreed not to make public, but they consoled themselves with the argument that if HBOS failed, job losses would be even higher.

By the end of the week the bankers had agreed on the outline of a deal that they reckoned could work for both sets of shareholders. Two issues remained unresolved: price and competition. Price could be negotiated but the competition issue was a tougher one to crack. They would need help from friends in high places for that.

Daniels called Blank to brief him on where they had got to. He wanted to do the deal, he said, and so did the others, but they all agreed they needed a guarantee from government, preferably from Downing Street, that the competition rules would be waived, even if it required special legislation. They would make representations through the proper channels, which meant the OFT, the FSA and the Bank of England, but at the end of the day only Gordon Brown could override the various ministers and regulatory bodies who had a hand in the process and push legislation through Parliament. Without support from No. 10, the risks were too great. Someone with the ear of the Prime Minister needed to talk it to him personally. And the unanimous view was that it should be the Lloyds chairman.

Blank called Downing Street the next day and, after explaining the importance of the situation, arranged to see Brown, which he did a few days later. He started by saying that HBOS looked to be in big trouble, its shares were down 60 per cent in 2008 alone and there were only two solutions to its problems. One was nationalisation, which would be awful for the whole sector as well as the government, and the other was to seek a solution within the industry. Consolidation seemed the best alternative. Lloyds, he added, was interested in acquiring HBOS, as it had tried to do with Northern Rock, but it needed the Prime Minister to push it through the regulatory machine which could clog it up for months – by which stage it would be too late.

Brown, appalled at the prospect of another run or of being forced to take another bank into public ownership, listened attentively and finally replied neutrally that he would 'discuss it with colleagues' and get back as soon as he could. He was due to lead an eighteen-person trade delegation to the Palestinian territories and Israel in a few days' time and he knew that Blank, who sat on the Israel British Business Council, would be joining him in Jerusalem and Ramallah. They would travel together for a few days and Brown suggested they discuss the HBOS situation then.

They got their chance on the return journey, propped up on bar stools in the centre of the plane. Even in the week since they had first talked, the financial horizon had darkened visibly. At home, the Nationwide Building Society reported that UK house prices had recorded an annual decline of 8.1 per cent, the largest fall since statistics began, and mortgage lending had shrunk by 32 per cent in the past year, a fact which, Brown confessed, 'made my blood run cold. I knew what that meant: people and businesses stuck without credit and possibly a bad recession.' The more pessimistic commentators and economists were already warning that the swift withdrawal of credit from the global economy could tip the world into one of the deepest recessions since the 1930s. The Treasury had recently revised down its economic growth forecast for 2008 from 2.5 per cent in January to 1 per cent – not quite a recession yet but getting dangerously close.

Brown wanted to hear Blank's view about the wider banking situation and they discussed the US Fed chairman Ben Bernanke's ideas about quantitative easing, basically pumping money into the markets in unprecedented quantities, and the need to avoid the Japanese banking experience, or as Bernanke called it, 'the wasted decade'. Brown also referred to Northern Rock, which clearly still angered him, and that led Blank into the discussion he was there to have.

'HBOS is getting weaker by the day,' Blank said, finally getting to the nub of the conversation, 'and is going to need rescuing.' Letting it fail was simply not an option – more than £1 in every £5 saved in Britain was held by HBOS and another Northern Rock could not even be contemplated. Taking it into public ownership, with £650 billion of liabilities on its balance sheet, was not very appealing either.

'Consolidation may be your best solution,' Blank urged. 'There are only two possible banks which could buy it: HSBC and us. And from what I hear HSBC doesn't want any more UK exposure, so we're the prime candidate. We are interested in taking them, and, as you know, we've had discussions with them. The principals on both sides are willing to get together.'

But, he added, there was 'an impediment' on which they had taken counsel's advice and on which they needed government help: competition. 'If we had rescued Northern Rock it might still be the subject of a competition inquiry nearly a year later, and that would be crazy,' he reminded Brown. 'If this is reviewed, it will take months, you will have terrible uncertainty in the markets, the full position of HBOS's balance sheet will be exposed – and in our view, it will not survive.'

Blank was aware of the unprecedented step he was asking Brown to take. Prime ministers did not normally get involved in the competition process and to intervene meant entering a minefield of rules, regulations, practice and precedent, involving not just half a dozen of his ministers but the competition authorities in Brussels who loved nothing more than to have a go at the British regulatory system.

'I'm aware of the HBOS situation and we've already had some discussions about this,' he said cautiously, which Blank took to mean with the Treasury and Bank officials. 'I'll take it back to colleagues and think it through.' They landed at Heathrow and Blank, for the only time in his life, found himself exiting through the VIP terminal.

In August, Brown took a holiday in Suffolk where he picked up a copy of Ben Bernanke's essays on the Great Depression that plunged him into a fit of depression himself. Brown read voraciously when he had a chance, and he chose this particular break to read everything he could on past financial crises, particularly the 1929 crash, hoping he could find the key to deal with this one. 'The summer of 2008 was like the summer of 1914,' one of his Downing Street aides was later reported as saying. 'The drums of war were beating.'

Blank didn't try to chase him and heard nothing more, but was aware that talks were going on behind the scenes. What he didn't know was that the Treasury had belatedly realised how close to the edge HBOS actually was, and had discovered it had no real plan in place to do anything about it.

They almost left it too late.

CHAPTER 17

LEHMAN

IN THE LAST few weeks of August 2008, Alistair Darling took his family on holiday to his croft in the Outer Hebrides, as far as he could get away from the financial maelstrom that was building up on both sides of the Atlantic. Although he hated press interviews and seldom agreed to them, on this occasion the Chancellor gave in to the urgings of his press secretary, Catherine MacLeod, a former Scottish journalist, and agreed to let *The Guardian* profile him. But in the hope of putting them off, he insisted the interview should take place at his home in the Western Isles, one of the most inaccessible places in Britain (in bad weather it is barely accessible at all). To his dismay, the offer was accepted 'with alacrity', and a few days later the feature writer Decca Aitkenhead turned up with a photographer in tow to write what she called a 'colour piece'.

The interview, which was not scheduled to appear until the eve of the Labour party conference a month later, ranged over a wide range of topics, personal and political, and finally came to the economy. 'Arguably, this is the worst downturn there has been in sixty years,' Darling unwisely opined. 'And I think it is going to be more profound and long-lasting than people thought.' In the remote Hebrides that sounded harmless enough. In Westminster and Whitehall it was a bombshell.

Two weeks later someone at *The Guardian* discovered that the paper was sitting on a major scoop and the story was elevated to the front page under the headline 'Economy at sixty-year low says Darling'. It was soon running in all the other newspapers and on the ten o'clock news that evening with devastating impact on the markets the next morning. A furious Brown ordered his spin-doctors to brief the press that the Chancellor had been 'ordered' to make a public apology. The worst part of it for Darling was his experience at the hands of what he dubiously referred to as Brown's 'attack dogs', particularly Damian McBride, press secretary in No. 10, who set out to undermine him. They condemned both his gloomy forecast and him personally in such unpleasant terms that Darling later likened it to 'the forces of hell being unleashed on me'. His relationship with Brown, once close, had been strained ever since he moved into No. 11 but after this they spoke only when they had to. 'Clearly he did not trust my advice, and now he appeared indifferent to what I thought,' said Darling.

Although Brown still argued that the recession would be over in six months, with the turning point 'just around the corner', that clearly was not true. The British economy had grown by 2.7 per cent in 2007 but almost all of that was in the first nine months and in the final quarter it just stayed in positive territory. It limped through the first quarter of 2008 with growth of a meagre 0.1 per cent and revised Treasury and Bank of England statistics later showed a fall of nearly 1 per cent in the second quarter. By late summer it was clear, regardless of what Brown thought, that Britain was about to follow the US into recession, in the sense of recording two successive quarters of negative growth. But not even the canniest economists had yet glimpsed quite how serious it would be.

. . . .

After his meeting with Brown in July 2008, Blank called Callum McCarthy at the FSA to bring him up to date with the HBOS discussions and to speculate on how they could speed up the merger process. McCarthy, dismayed by the failure of the banks' rights issues, was becoming increasingly concerned about HBOS and delighted with Blank's interest. 'By that stage we knew HBOS needed rescuing and we were looking for a private sector solution, so we welcomed the fact that Lloyds had reached that view under their own decision-making process,' says a former FSA official.

After Blank put the phone down, McCarthy, breathing a large sigh of relief, walked across the open-plan floor of the FSA office in Canary Wharf to brief his chief executive. 'Victor Blank has just told me that Lloyds are thinking of buying HBOS,' he told Hector Sants. 'It seems to be a Lloyds-originated idea. They're hoping to get the OFT to waive the competition rules and Victor is apparently talking to some people in very high places.' Both of them could guess who that was.

Sants was still smarting at the way he had been brushed aside by the Bank Governor and the Chancellor when he had backed the Lloyds bid for Northern Rock, and was cautious about sticking his neck out again. But the world had changed since then – lessons had been learned, attitudes had changed and he would do his best to ensure Lloyds received a different reception this time around.

The FSA and the Treasury had spent the summer putting contingency plans in place in case the situation deteriorated further in the autumn, and Lloyds's initiative offered it a potential solution to its biggest problem.

It didn't have anything else. 'HBOS was about the biggest bank where there could be a private sector solution,' says the official.

> Anything bigger and no one would buy it. Once the American banks got into trouble, we started looking at plans for all the banks. We thought HSBC and Standard Chartered were broadly safe, Barclays less so and Lloyds as a standalone should be fine. RBS was too big to do anything with other than nationalise it – you were never going to find a buyer for RBS.

Oddly, at that time the FSA was not too worried about RBS – its biggest concern was HBOS which, in the absence of a rescue, could bring down the others. 'If we nationalised HBOS, that would have threatened RBS and Barclays would not be far behind – and even Lloyds would have been affected,' says the official. 'Therefore we had to find a solution to HBOS – and it had to be a private sector one. And the only one available, as it was with Northern Rock, was Lloyds.'

By the beginning of September the US banking crisis was building towards a crescendo, with Fannie Mae and Freddie Mac, with debt securities amounting to over a trillion dollars, facing insolvency, and Citigroup, Merrill's and Lehman Brothers also in serious trouble. AIG, the insurance company which was a massive player in all the financial markets, was desperately seeking a government bailout of mind-boggling proportions and Washington Mutual, America's largest savings and loan institution, which Eric Daniels and Terri Dial had briefly looked at, was downgraded to junk status and then closed by the Office of Thrift Management. It was later sold to JP Morgan Chase for $1.9 billion, a fraction of what it had been worth at its peak.

Tim Geithner, head of the New York Fed, later remarked that he felt he was 'watching a disaster unfold in slow motion, with no ability to prevent it'. The flood 'had already breached the levees', he added, 'and all we could do was pile up more sandbags'. Lehman Brothers was 'on the edge of the abyss' but the Obama campaign had put out the message that the Democratic candidate didn't want it rescued with taxpayers' money, a sentiment emphatically echoed by both parties in Congress. Geithner was now convinced that the American banking system was 'headed for Armageddon' (a phrase widely tossed about that summer and autumn) and the government agencies, the Fed and the Treasury, did not have the weapons to stop it – that would require pushing urgent legislation through Congress which, until Lehman went down, was in no mood to listen. Geithner dreaded what was about to unfold.

On 7 September 2008 the US government finally took Fannie Mae and Freddie Mac into public ownership after huge defaults on house mortgages, and two days later the shares of Lehman Brothers fell almost 45 per cent on reports that a Korean bank had pulled out of a multi-billion dollar investment. Money drained out of the bank and by Friday 12 September, it was almost out of cash. Its last hope of survival was a rescue by Barclays but even though John Varley, the Barclays chief executive, and Bob Diamond – particularly Bob Diamond – were keen to buy it, and had even raised the finance for it, the UK authorities were not. Callum McCarthy, in his last week in office before retiring, told Varley the deal in his view seemed to have been 'cobbled together' in haste and the British government would not stand behind Barclays' balance sheet, which they would be required to do if it all went wrong. The FSA was not prepared to give its approval and without it there was no deal.

With Barclays out of the running, Lehman's situation was now dire and all the major American newspapers, TV stations and newswires, cit-ing 'sources close to the Treasury Secretary Hank Paulson', reported that the government was not going to come to its rescue. 'Paulson Adamant No Money For Lehman', reported Bloomberg. By the final bell on Fri-day, Lehman was down to its last $2 billion in cash and as Geithner later recorded, 'if we couldn't find a solution over the weekend, we'd have a corpse on Monday'.

At the FSA, McCallum and Sants thought they might have a corpse on their hands too. If Lehman went down over the weekend, there would clearly be a massive knock-on effect on all the international markets and they were not convinced HBOS would survive it. The Lloyds solution was looking increasingly attractive but at the last moment another possible alternative emerged out of nowhere. Standard Chartered Bank which, under its canny chairman Mervyn Davies, had been anticipating a crash for more than a year, had a net £40 billion in deposits and zero exposure to any bank on the endangered list. Now, like Lloyds, it was looking for ways to exploit its position and get some return on deposits which were earning it nothing. It had prospered mightily in the booming Far East markets and as its market value soared it had even considered reversing Brian Pitman's overtures by making a bid for Lloyds, which it had comfortably outgrown. Just a few months earlier it had rejected an approach from Morgan Stanley, which sought a full-scale merger as a way out of its own problems.

Watching the HBOS shares collapse that weekend, Davies called Alistair Darling, an old friend of his, to tell him he might be interested in a deal to buy the retail side if the bank collapsed. He had no interest in the whole bank, he said, particularly the corporate side, but if his old chum needed help with the branch network, where most of the staff were employed and which depositors and customers dealt with, he might be able to assist.

Peter Cummings was a real bogeyman for Davies who had a poster of him, with the word WANTED splashed across it, pinned on his office wall as a warning to his executives: 'No one in our bank must behave like this man!' He had looked at HBOS's lending policies and held them up as a prime example to his staff of what not to do. 'Cummings was buying deals and he was starting to pervade our space offering terms that we couldn't compete with. And if you have one bank buying loans like that, everyone says we should be doing it too, but I said we're not going to be that kind of bank,' Davies said later. HBOS, he reckoned, had a great retail business but a 'hopeless corporate bank that didn't know what it was doing'.

Darling called Callum McCarthy to tell him of the Standard Chartered approach and on Friday afternoon Davies and his chief executive Peter Sands, accompanied by their finance director Richard Meddings, arrived at the FSA office to develop their proposal. They had done a high-level analysis of HBOS, Davies said, which they reckoned could not survive another week and would have to be nationalised. No private sector bank, he reckoned, would buy it, and its collapse – or nationalisation – would have the most devastating effect on the banking system and on the whole British economy. However, for a nominal sum Standard Chartered was prepared to take on the retail operation. 'He made it sound as if he was doing us a big favour,' says a former FSA official. 'And he probably thought he was.' In reality, it was completely unrealistic.

Alistair Darling was at a meeting of European finance ministers chaired by the French finance minister, Christine Lagarde, when Hank Paulson called from Washington Airport where he was about to board a plane to attend an emergency meeting in New York. The Treasury Secretary said he needed Darling's help urgently. Barclays wanted to take over Lehman, the US authorities were very keen that it did but it appeared that the FSA was putting up all sorts of obstacles. Could Darling get them to waive some of the rules and smooth the way? Darling, well briefed by his officials, replied that he couldn't – in the first place, the Companies Act required Barclays to get shareholders' approval for such a deal, which would take six weeks, and secondly he did not want the British government ending up supporting an American bank that was on the verge of collapse – particularly as every other American bank had walked away and the US government itself was not prepared to help.

Paulson later claimed that Darling's actual response was, 'We don't want to import your cancer into Britain', but Darling doesn't recall that remark. An exasperated Paulson rang off. He was even more upset when Tim Geithner, after another acrimonious conversation with Callum McCarthy in London, told him the Barclays deal was definitely off – and there was no Plan B. 'We're fucked,' said Geithner.

Paulson, a former Goldman Sachs banker and Christian Scientist, was furious with Darling but later saw his point:

> The British had their own reasons for not wanting this deal done. In truth, I could understand their hesitation. The UK's bank situation was more perilous than ours. Altogether, British banks' assets amounted to more than four times the size of the national GDP; total US banking assets were about the same size as our GDP. Moreover, individual banks, including Barclays, had capital issues of their own. It was understandable that the country's officials might be reluctant to waive normal shareholder procedures for a deal that could have resulted in big losses to one of their largest institutions while carrying no risk to the US government.

The conversations with the US authorities increased the degree of alarm already rapidly spreading through the ranks of the officials and ministers in London. 'Throughout that weekend we got a real sense that the US administration was in a state of panic,' said Darling later, and both Geithner and Paulson freely admitted he was right. 'The Lehman aftermath was absolutely horrifying,' said Geithner, 'transmitting panic through global markets like never before.' Hank Paulson too 'could sense the start of a panic', and Ben Bernanke, the Fed chairman, later wrote a whole treatise on market panics, concluding that 2008–09 was one of the worst in banking history. One of the few bits of good news that weekend was that Bank of America, which had pulled out of a Lehman rescue at the last moment, agreed to buy Merrill Lynch for $50 billion. But the American authorities now had an even bigger problem with AIG, which insured the lives, health, homes, pensions and cars of millions of Americans, as well as 180,000 businesses employing two-thirds of the American work-force. It was in even deeper trouble than any of the banks and a bailout would stretch the mighty US resources to the limit.

In London that weekend there was a surreal air of calm before the storm. Tim Tookey had taken the Friday off to go water-skiing with City friends at his boat club in St Neots in Cambridgeshire, only vaguely aware of what was happening in New York. Victor Blank had driven down to his home in Oxfordshire and Eric Daniels had left the office late to spend the evening at his London house with his wife and son. In Canary Wharf, Win Bis-choff was chairing a board meeting of Citigroup, which was in deep trouble long before Lehman's problems. Alistair Darling was in Nice with his fellow finance ministers and Gordon Brown was in New York addressing the UN.

Darling called Brown on Sunday to brief him about his bad-tempered discussion with Paulson. Brown, accompanied by Shriti Vadera, had just visited George Bush in the White House to urge him to take the lead in persuading the major countries to act together to recapitalise their banks and he told Darling that they should support the Americans 'without risk-ing our own stability'. But he agreed with Darling's stance on the Barclays deal, adding that there was no way a British government could effectively bankroll an American bank that was about to go under. 'For me,' Dar-ling recorded, 'this was one of the most profound decisions made during the course of the entire banking crisis. Lehmans collapsed that night.'

Over what became known as 'the Lehman weekend', Shriti Vadera, remembering Daniels's entreaty after Northern Rock, called him from Washington to ask him how interested he was in HBOS. 'Eric, if you are having any interesting discussions and you want to talk to us about them, talk to us now,' she said.

'So, you're saying yes?' asked Daniels, instantly assuming she was referring to the competition issue.

'I'm most certainly not saying yes,' she retorted. 'I'm simply saying you haven't put any question to us so don't turn around, as you did to me after Northern Rock, and say nobody talked to you. If you want to ask a question, you ask the question – what's the worst that can happen to you?'

Daniels replied that his chairman had already asked the question and he was still waiting for a reply. Unless they got it soon, it would all be academic.

The news that Lehman was filing for Chapter 11 bankruptcy broke in London late on Sunday evening, and Blank called Daniels to get his take on how it would affect Lloyds. Daniels's immediate concern was the bank's direct exposure to Lehman and he was already trying to get a handle on it. The Lloyds dealers reported that on Friday the Lehman parent in New York had done a sweep of cash held in its subsidiaries around the globe, particularly London, where its biggest international operation was based, and brought it back (about $8 billion of it) to the US in a final desperate effort to save itself. Some of that would be Lloyds's money, Daniels told Blank, but he wasn't sure how much. Given the rumours, Lloyds had been keeping its lending to Lehman to a minimum but the nature of global banking meant there was always going to be some exposure. The bigger problem was the potential systemic effect on the whole banking system – who else was going to go down? Where did it leave HBOS? Indeed, where did it leave Lloyds?

It was a sombre executive group that met early on Monday morning in the Lloyds headquarters in Gresham Street. All around them in the City and in Canary Wharf where Lehman's London headquarters was housed, similar groups were meeting to discuss damage control and how best to protect themselves from what promised to be a tidal wave. On Wall Street, not yet officially open for business, bankers had been in

their offices all night trying to make sense of the biggest financial catastrophe in their lifetimes. An article in that morning's *New York Times* by
Joe Nocera encapsulated the mood in the city:

> How can it be possible that we wake up on Monday morning to discover
> that Lehman Brothers, a firm founded in 1850, a firm that has survived
> the Great Depression and every market trauma before and since, is sud-
> denly bankrupt? That Merrill Lynch, the 'Thundering Herd', is sold to
> Bank of America the same weekend? It boggles the mind.

No single event caused so much chaos, uncertainty and turmoil in the
US financial markets since the Crash of 1929 as Lehman did that Monday. The US Federal Reserve rescued AIG by injecting a massive $85
billion into it in return for an 80 per cent stake in the insurance giant.
The shares of Morgan Stanley and Goldman Sachs, the last two surviving Wall Street investment banks, plummeted amid widespread horror
at Paulson's tough stance on bank failures: if he had been prepared to let
Lehman go down, why not them too? Amid a record volume of trading
– 8 trillion shares changed hands that day – the Dow Jones industrial
average opened more than 500 points down and recorded its biggest
decline since 9/11.

In the Treasury, the Bank of England and the FSA's offices in Canary
Wharf, officials frantically worked on plans to shore up the system and
the heads of the Tripartite were in emergency session all day, as were
most bank boards. In Downing Street Brown was briefed every hour by
his permanent secretary, Jeremy Heywood. 'Every time Jeremy said he
wanted to update me on something,' said Brown, 'I expected another bit
of bad news from the markets.'

Tim Tookey's team quickly identified the scale of the Lloyds's exposure to Lehman, which they put at £120 million, a considerable sum

but not huge in the context of the overall business. Its Lehman position was hedged but that didn't help – as Tookey pointed out gloomily, there were obviously two parties to every hedge and if one went down the other had to pick up the loss. The wholesale market had seized up completely and even the biggest banks refused to lend to each other on anything longer than a 24-hour basis, if at all. Securitisations were impossible and inter-bank borrowing rates soared. Every portfolio of loans and mortgage-backed securities, in the absence of any buyers, was technically valueless.

Blank called a board meeting to brief his directors on the Lehman fall-out and discuss the situation of HBOS, whose shares that day fell to 230p compared with 450p before the rights issue just six months before. If it had been in trouble before the weekend, its situation was now parlous. Once again Stevenson called the FSA and the Bank of England demanding support and both issued statements to the effect that the bank was 'sound, strong and well-funded', which they knew was not the case. An HBOS spokesman announced that the bank 'was winning' new deposits and there was 'no evidence of customers withdrawing their money any more than usual'.

It was all untrue of course, but it didn't matter because no one believed a word of it anyway. In fact deposits were flowing out of HBOS at a record rate. Fortunately withdrawals were mostly electronic and not visible – unlike Northern Rock, whose website broke down when depositors began seeking to get their money out, HBOS's stood the test and deposits were withdrawn silently without public queues. But there was no coming back from such a savage beating and the bank was effectively finished – only a friendly takeover or nationalisation could save it.

For Lloyds, it was now or never. Despite the turmoil of the past twenty-four hours, the fundamental case for a merger with HBOS seemed as strong as it had been in July. Blank and Daniels went over the case for going ahead with the board once more: strong franchises, increased market share in all the retailing categories, huge cost savings and synergies, earnings enhancing and the long-sought answer to Lloyds's ten-year strategic problem. There were risks too: falling house prices, unknown exposure in the corporate loan book and to the US sub-prime market and dependence on the wholesale market. Tookey, on the basis of the high-level due diligence done in July, reckoned there would be negative adjustments to the HBOS balance sheet of about £10 billion but that was discounted several times over by the price they could get it at, a fraction of HBOS's value at the peak.

Blank summed up the tone of the meeting: if they wanted to go ahead with the deal they had been trailing for years, he said, it had to be now, that very week – HBOS might not be around by the weekend. There would never be a better – or another – opportunity to persuade the government to relax the competition laws and regulations. The executives were keen to go ahead, he said, and he agreed with them. The board did too. There were no dissenters.

Watching events unfold from No. 10, Gordon Brown was finding the Lloyds solution more attractive by the moment. 'HBOS was most under pressure,' he wrote, and could not survive on its own, 'but there was still a private sector solution. If we were forced to nationalise HBOS there could be a domino effect and the focus would switch to other banks. The chaos in the US was at the forefront of all our minds.' All day long Darling, who had been hoping to go through his Pre-Budget Report with Brown, had been in discussions with officials in the Treasury, the Bank and the FSA about what to do with the banks, particularly HBOS. The Lloyds request for a competition waiver was high on the agenda. No one, particularly the Treasury, liked it, but on the other hand they didn't want nationalisation either. And there was no other alternative.

As he prepared to set out for Spencer House, and his meeting with Victor Blank, Brown made up his mind. He would do what he could to support the Lloyds/HBOS deal.

CHAPTER 18

MERGER

AN EXTRAORDINARY MYTHOLOGY has built up around the Spencer House *tête-à-tête* between Victor Blank and the Prime Minister on the evening after Lehman went down. Newspaper reports over the next few weeks and many of the books on the banking crisis suggest that Brown, in a conversation lasting no more than fifteen minutes, strong-armed his old friend into taking over HBOS in order to save the financial system – and Blank meekly succumbed.

The truth is quite different. No Prime Minister has the power to jam two great financial institutions together over a conversation at a cocktail party – and no bank chairman could ever agree to it. HBOS had been in Lloyds's sights for five years, serious discussions had first taken place two years before and in July the two parties had agreed in principle on almost everything other than price and the final management structure. For weeks the FSA and Treasury officials had been aware of Lloyds's interest and had done their best to encourage it. The Prime Minister had known about it since his meeting with Blank nearly two months before and had discussed the competition implications with officials on several occasions since. The missing piece was the final go-ahead which involved a statutory change to the competition regulations, which no individual minister or official could authorise, and could only come from No. 10.

The conversation that evening between Brown and Blank was watched by half the room, which included many of the leading bankers in the City, and was the subject of considerable speculation as the guests filed into dinner. Digby Jones, the former director general of the CBI who had been brought into the government by Brown a year earlier, had for weeks been privately urging the Prime Minister to be more social and 'work the room' in the way Tony Blair was so good at. He was delighted to see Brown begin to chat to people, then he groaned as the Prime Minister took Blank aside and virtually ignored everyone else for the rest of his time at the party. 'He's at it again,' he remarked resignedly. 'He just can't help himself.' It was only when Jones heard the news of the merger on his car radio a few days later that he understood what was going on.

In fact Brown, knowing the Lloyds chairman would be in Spencer House, had gone there with the explicit intention of giving him his decision personally. He did so succinctly and clearly: if Lloyds still wanted to take over HBOS, he should go ahead immediately and the government would play its part. The Treasury, the Bank of England, the FSA and the whole Whitehall machinery all supported the deal and were standing by ready to do what was necessary. There would be no competition issues – he would personally see to that. Blank should keep him informed if there were any problems. And that was more or less it. The button had now been pressed on the biggest merger in British banking history and within minutes of Brown's departure the process was in motion.

The two teams, led by Eric Daniels and Andy Hornby, met at eight o'clock the following morning, Tuesday 16 September 2008, at the HBOS flat in St James's. They had two days, three at maximum, to reach an agreement in principle which could be announced to the markets before the weekend. The biggest item on the agenda, around which everything else hinged, was price – and the adviser who Daniels relied on to negotiate that for him was not there. Matthew Greenburgh was in Wood Green Crown Court when the Lloyds CEO finally tracked him down. He was on jury service and for the past week, during which time the shares of his employer Merrill Lynch had fallen 40 per cent and it been bailed out by Bank of America, he had fretted through a nasty rape case, desperately trying to stay in touch with his office and the markets during the breaks. Greenburgh was an information junkie and the interminable questioning and cross-questioning in the court was agony for him with so much going on outside. Much to his relief, the jury reached a decision on Monday – they found the accused innocent – but Greenburgh was put down to hear another case starting the next day. He didn't think he could take any more of it.

On Monday evening he equipped himself with an employer's letter and every plausible-sounding excuse he could think of (the fact that his bank had basically gone bust over the weekend should have been excuse enough but it was difficult to explain the intricacies of Wall Street finance to court officials in north London) and turned up on Tuesday morning to present them to the court official, almost begging to be released. He was just leaving the courthouse, after being excused the rest of the week, when Daniels got through. Could he head straight for the flat in St James's, he asked, careful not to give too much away over the mobile phone. There had been a major change in the situation overnight and the teams had gathered there to resume where they left off in July. 'We have to agree a price by tonight, or tomorrow at the latest,' he added. Greenburgh didn't need to hear any more – he knew exactly what was going on.

As he drove in, Greenburgh was already mentally calculating how hard a bargain he could drive. The world had changed utterly since July and the price he and Daniels were thinking about then was irrelevant. From the car he called his office in Merrill Lynch to set his team in motion with instructions to update the July figures ready to brief the Lloyds team later in the day. The reports from the markets were unnerving: the Far Eastern stock exchanges had taken another savage beating and Europe was almost as bad. In London the HBOS share price was fluctuating alarmingly, opening at 232p, then dropping like a stone to 88p, before recovering again. The word was that deposits were flowing out at a frightening rate and with the wholesale markets closed, it was only a matter of time before HBOS followed Lehman into bankruptcy, though how long he couldn't guess. He didn't envy his opposite number, Simon Robey, having to negotiate a price in those circumstances.

And it was not just HBOS: the contagion from Lehman had spread to some of the biggest European banks, including the Swiss bank UBS and several of the smaller German ones, any bank with exposure to the American mortgage market and Lehman. The French and Italian authorities intervened to steady the markets, and the Icelandic and Irish banks were rumoured to be even worse off than HBOS. The sub-prime crisis, which had begun on Wall Street, had become a world event.

'The main problem with sub-prime was its lack of transparency – no one knew where the bodies were or who'd got what,' says a former bank chairman. 'That's why the inter-bank market dried up – no bank wanted to lend to another. There was complete uncertainty in that market and that resulted in liquidity drying up. And without liquidity the banking system just seized.'

A last-minute ring-around the other big banks by Sants established that there was one other bank interested in bidding for HBOS: Standard Chartered was still in the running. Mervyn Davies called Darling personally to tell him he and his team had been working through the weekend and had developed a rescue plan for HBOS. 'We'll take the branch network off your hands,' he said. 'But we'll only pay a nominal sum. We'll give you a pound for it.'

It wasn't much of a deal. HBOS's branch network, with its deposits, mortgages, brands, accounts and properties, was worth many billions if the debts were stripped out, and both men knew it. Davies was in fact suggesting that the government take the rotten bits while it ran away with the crown jewels. Darling listened politely and then calmly trumped him: 'Well, actually we expect to announce over the next few days that there is a bidder for the whole thing. So you can stand down.' After cautioning the Chancellor about the dangers of a 'systemic risk' for the unknown buyer, a stunned Davies rang off.

Meanwhile Tim Tookey was wrestling with a different problem. He had woken up on Monday morning with the news that one of Lloyds's corporate brokers, Lehman, had gone bust and, with markets in turmoil, he urgently had to find a new one. He immediately called David Mayhew at Cazenove and Tim Waddell, global broking head of UBS, two of the most respected figures in the City, who had pitched for the role when Helen Weir had offered it two years earlier (and lost to Lehman), and asked them if they were still interested. Both were, and Mayhew even summoned his colleague Tim Wise back from India to lead the pitch. By the time he arrived, Lloyds was already in deal mode and the pitch had to be cancelled. Tookey eventually appointed UBS but too late to participate in the discussions.

Greenburgh arrived at the flat in St James's to find the meeting well under way with Daniels in charge and Andy Hornby, sitting across from him, looking pale but outwardly calm. Mike Ellis, HBOS's finance director, and Harry Baines, the legal counsel, were working with Tim Tookey on the financial details and Simon Robey popped in and out all day. Back in the offices of Lloyds, HBOS and Merrill Lynch, Truett Tate and Helen

Weir had teams going through the HBOS loan book and the debt book, running sensitivity analyses based on their own current performance which they hoped would not be all that different from that of HBOS.

From the start, the tone of the meeting was very different from that of the July one in this same flat when the financial crisis still seemed distant. Now everyone had an overpowering sense of urgency, of huge pressure from the markets and from government ministers and officials who saw the situation as a national emergency and made it clear that this was a deal that must get done, and done fast. Even the Bank of England was on side, ready to supply whatever liquidity was needed – a complete *volte face* from its attitude to Lloyds in the Northern Rock episode.

Before they settled into the serious part of the day, Daniels was keen to clear up one issue: the nature of the support the government was prepared to provide on the competition issue. Without an assurance that the bid would not be referred to the Competition Commission, there was no point in going any further. So far all they knew was what Blank had heard from Gordon Brown the night before and Daniels wanted official confirmation. After the scheduled meeting in Downing Street with the Prime Minister, the Chancellor and the Governor that morning, Hector Sants called Blank to tell him 'the regulatory issue is in hand', and the banks were free to finalise terms. The Treasury had been asked by the Prime Minister to give the two banks the reassurance they needed.

Later that morning Sir Nicholas Macpherson, permanent secretary to the Treasury and Britain's second most senior civil servant, strolled across the park to join the meeting in the HBOS flat. In his precise, formal manner, Macpherson spelled out the government's position carefully: the Treasury understood the need to avoid a reference to the Competition Commission which could drag on for months and that the banks couldn't survive that. But it was not a simple matter, requiring changes to the regulations which would have to be approved by both Houses of

Parliament and legally the views of a wide number of institutions, including the OFT and all members of the Tripartite, had to be considered. The Treasury was working on that and the government, said Macpherson, was already preparing draft legislation, which would allow the takeover to go through on the grounds of 'the public interest'.

On the question of the European competition authorities, the Lloyds team later vehemently insisted they were left in no doubt. 'Macpherson confirmed that the deal was within UK jurisdiction, and there would be no problems with Brussels,' says a former Lloyds executive.

'He was confirming that the government would look after the competition issues, including Europe,' says another of the advisers who was at the meeting. 'That was totally specific. We were told Europe wasn't involved and there was no reason to believe that Lloyds would have to sell off branches to appease Brussels.' In the hustle and bustle that morning, no one thought to ask Macpherson to put anything in writing and he never did – and nor did anyone else in government. It was an extraordinary lapse on the part of the lawyers and advisers which was to have serious consequences later.

Greenburgh opened the price negotiations by saying that Lloyds could not take the risk of being seen to be over-generous to HBOS shareholders who otherwise would get next to nothing for their shares. HBOS's only alternative to a Lloyds offer was nationalisation at a nominal price and a Lloyds offer therefore had to be well below the market. That morning, Lloyds were 270p and holding steady despite the market jitters but HBOS were all over the place, dipping below 100p at one moment then back up to 182p the next. The balance between the two banks, fairly evenly matched when they had met in July, had swung dramatically and the price, Greenburgh argued, needed to reflect it. Robey argued that the recent price fluctuations should be disregarded and they should work around an average for the previous three months and add a premium

– which came out at 300p. Daniels had edged up to 200p a share when they broke for tea and he called Blank to give him an update.

As the negotiations continued, the Lloyds team were more and more impressed with Andy Hornby who stood his ground when his career – and his bank – was falling apart around him. 'He knew he had to do a deal and he knew the deal would be the end of him, but I grew to have great respect for him that day,' says one of the Lloyds team.

> He always knew that his responsibility was to save the bank, the position of customers and so on, and never once did I hear him mention himself, not once. I had never met Andy before and had no reason either to like or dislike him, but I admired him that day. Later people would say he was like a rabbit in the headlights and that he was panicking. But if he was, he never showed it and negotiated as if he held all the cards.

In fact he didn't hold any cards, as the Merrill and Lloyds teams clinically exposed. Without knowing about the merger talks, one banking analyst summed up HBOS's position that day:

> HBOS has an enormous exposure to the UK mortgage market, where prices are under pressure. The rest of its loans are to small and medium-sized enterprises, which are struggling, and it's been feeding at the trough of private equity, which is also not what it used to be.
>
> The amount of loans it has outstanding is almost twice that of deposits. It has wholesale funding it has to roll over at what are likely to be much higher prices, and it needs the funding just to stand still. So it's either got to shrink rapidly or its margins are going to be hit.

In fact by then it was not getting any funding at all. HBOS's borrowings from the wholesale market were £278 billion, two-thirds of it repayable within a year, and rolling that over was an impossible task. Deposits were £100 billion less than that and rapidly diminishing: it was later estimated that £30 billion was withdrawn by small businesses and individual savers that week, far more than from Northern Rock.

The price negotiations went on for most of the day with each side withdrawing every so often to regroup and consider their strategy. Several times Daniels and Hornby were left on their own for quiet one-on-one discussions while the others found somewhere to perch in what were by now overcrowded quarters. There were in fact two HBOS flats, each with two bedrooms, but the rule in the old Bank of Scotland was that they could only be occupied by one sex at a time, a source of some merriment to the Lloyds team who were now expecting to inherit them. There was some light relief when Tate, Weir, Tookey and several of the Lloyds advisers withdrew to the downstairs lounge where there wasn't room for all of them to sit. Helen Weir suggested Tookey prop himself up on a coffee table, which promptly collapsed, leaving a spluttering finance director sitting on the floor. Very embarrassedly, he had to own up to the HBOS team that he was the culprit.

By the end of the day the two sides had tentatively agreed on a 'pencilled-in' price of 0.90 of a Lloyds share for every HBOS share, or around 250p, subject to the usual raft of conditions, particularly board approval, competition approval and shareholder approval (from both sides). Lloyds insisted on adding a 'material adverse change', or MAC, condition which meant that if they found a glaring hole in the HBOS accounts or something else changed dramatically (market conditions did not count) the terms could be renegotiated – or Lloyds could pull out.

They broke up late in the evening agreeing they would get the teams together the next day to go through the HBOS books, which were now open to them for the first time (with some reservations), and hammer out the details with the intention of making an announcement when the markets opened on Thursday morning. The Lloyds team had now swelled to nearly thirty people and on Wednesday they moved into the City offices of the Lloyds solicitors, Linklaters, which they called 'base camp', occupying every spare meeting room on the first floor of the soulless building near the Barbican. Daniels and Tookey divided the teams into ten separate work-streams, each one focusing on their own specialised areas of the business: treasury, FSA capital requirements, synergies, dividend policy, investor relations, public relations, rating agencies, employees, customers, one on funding and yet another on deal mechanics. They would be there for most of the next twenty-four hours.

Tim Tookey moved between five of the teams, all in different rooms, while Truett Tate and Helen Weir oversaw the areas they knew most about, wholesale and retail, which accounted for about two-thirds of the HBOS activities. The core team – Daniels, Tookey, Tate and Weir – then met every hour or so while each work-stream leader briefed them on where they had got to. They were identifying plenty of problems but no deal-breakers as yet.

Wednesday was not a good day to be a HBOS shareholder. The morning's newspapers were full of gloomy headlines which further destabilised the market: 'HBOS shares hurt by crisis', 'Wholesale jitters take toll on HBOS', 'HBOS shares slump puts the frighteners on 15 million savers' and so on. A Q&A in *The Guardian* started off with the question 'Why is HBOS in trouble?' and went on to remark that: 'HBOS is too important for the government to allow it to go under. The knock-on effect of such a collapse could be seismic, undermining confidence in the rest of the banking sector. Think Northern Rock on a much bigger scale.' That was hardly encouraging for depositors, who continued to withdraw their cash.

By mid-morning the HBOS price had dropped to 120p, driven down by the 'hedgies' who were having a field day, before bouncing back as the bargain-hunters moved in, and the analysts were asking fresh questions about its ability to fund its operations in markets which were paralysed. Standard & Poor's deepened the gloom by downgrading HBOS's credit rating, highlighting its exposure to higher risk specialist and buy-to-let mortgages as well as concerns over the big bets it had taken on the property market. That undermined HBOS's own feeble efforts to protest that it had a large pool of deposits – £180 billion – which accounted for 52 per cent of its funding and had a 'strong capital base'.

The gyrations in bank shares, particularly HBOS, was now topping all the news bulletins and Vince Cable, the Liberal Democrat Treasury spokesman, demanded the FSA stop short selling. 'The hedge funds are betting against the taxpayer, since they know that if a leading British bank were to collapse, the government would have no alternative but to intervene,' he said. The Bank of England and the FSA, like everyone else in the City, were wary about intervening by stopping short selling, which played an essential role in the functioning of markets, but this had got out of hand and, after much debate, the FSA complied by banning short selling – too late to steady the HBOS shares.

Out of the blue Daniels got a surprise call from a banker representing what remained of Lehman, asking would he be interested in buying some of its assets out of Chapter 11. Lehman's highly profitable broker-dealer business was being sold off separately and Lloyds could have it for a fraction of its pre-crisis value. He asked Tim Tookey what he thought and the finance director threw up his hands in horror. 'You've got to be joking,' he said. 'We have enough problems without that.'

'It looks too good to be true,' agreed Daniels, 'which probably means that it is! And we don't want to get into merchant banking.'

In fact they wouldn't have got it anyway. Bob Diamond had already been approached by Bart McDade, Lehman's chief operating officer, asking him if Barclays would be interested in buying the whole of Lehman out of bankruptcy. Diamond, who had spearheaded the takeover discussion over the past weeks, immediately brought his teams back together to crunch the numbers once more. By Tuesday, two days after the Lehman bankruptcy, he had a deal: for less than $2 billion he bought the core business – or, as he preferred it, 'the crown jewels' – of a group which had a value of $45 billion on the stock market just a year before. For his money he got most of the investment banking and broker-dealer businesses, with 10,000 staff, plus three buildings, including Lehman's iconic headquarters near Times Square in New York. He left the toxic assets behind, including Lehman's huge holdings of sub-prime loans and impaired property investments.

It was perhaps the best deal done in the whole banking crisis – or seemed so at the time – and a triumphant Diamond walked out onto the Lehman trading floor to celebrate it. 'You have a new partner.' Later, bank analysts reckoned that Barclays had by far the strongest US business of any European bank. The irony was that Callum McCarthy and Alistair Darling had done Barclays a big favour. When the US authorities were badgering Darling to intervene, the New York Fed as well as potential bidders including Bank of America thought Lehman had a capital deficit in the tens of billions of dollars. But a 2013 study estimated Lehman was in fact 'in the hole' for at least $100 billion, and possibly as much as $200 billion, when it filed for bankruptcy. It was an unsalvageable institution with nothing but overvalued assets and a damaged reputation as a trading house. It would have sunk Barclays – and maybe the British government too.

On Wednesday afternoon, with most of the details agreed, Matthew Greenburgh decided Lloyds was paying too much for HBOS. He had been watching the markets closely and studying the results of the due diligence work done so far, and went across to Daniels's office in Gresham

Street. 'We must re-cut the price,' he said bluntly. The market conditions had worsened dramatically over the day and so had the sentiment
towards bank shares – and it wasn't going to stop there.

He and Daniels discussed it quietly on the pavement outside the building where Daniels retired every couple of hours to grab a cigarette. The
'pencilled-in' price was now twice the market price – if there was such a
thing – and Lloyds could not possibly justify a premium of 100 per cent,
urged Greenburgh. 'The markets will crucify us.'

Both Blank and Daniels, on the basis of the information they had
been receiving all day, had come to the same conclusion. 'This price is
not going to wash, Victor, and we're going to have to reduce it substantially,' Daniels told his chairman.

Blank agreed. 'It's not a sustainable deal as it stands,' he replied, 'and
we can't put it to shareholders.' They would have to renegotiate, even if
it meant losing the deal.

Daniels went back to his office down the hallway where Greenburgh
was waiting to get on with it. He called Simon Robey – and waited for
the eruption. Within minutes Sir John Gieve, the Bank's deputy governor, was on the phone to Daniels angrily demanding to know what
was going on. 'You could hear shouting down the phone,' says one of
the Lloyds team who was with Daniels at the time, 'and they were saying you've agreed a price and you can't renegotiate it. And then Alistair
Darling called him.'

Darling was more measured but also angry, insisting there had to be an
agreed deal that night – or the government would be forced into nation-
alising HBOS. 'It's Dennis you should be calling, not me,' Daniels finally
snapped. 'The price is totally unrealistic.'

'I remember Eric telling me that Wednesday that Gordon Brown was
getting frustrated that nothing had been announced and the window of
opportunity was closing,' says one of the Lloyds team.

And Eric stood fast through the day and of course HBOS were very upset and that's when there was a breakdown in the relationship, which up to that time had been OK. And Hornby was in a terrible state and Dennis was furious, but Eric stuck to his guns and Victor and the board supported him.

Callum McCarthy, equally frustrated with Daniels, called to say there was a meeting in Mervyn King's office in the Bank of England and he would like Daniels to attend. Daniels took the precaution of bringing Truett Tate with him, knowing this was not going to be pleasant.

'Are we all set for an announcement tomorrow morning?' the Governor asked brusquely. Daniels, no fan of King's after the Northern Rock affair, replied they were still discussing terms and were some way off, provoking an angry outburst from McCarthy.

'I'm issuing an ultimatum that unless you announce tomorrow morning, we will nationalise HBOS,' McCarthy told him.

Daniels returned to his office and relayed the message to Blank. 'My God, these guys are desperate,' he remarked.

'Let them nationalise it, if that's what they want to do,' Blank responded. 'We're only going ahead at the right price.'

Daniels was right about the desperation that was creeping into the Tripartite who were watching what was happening in the US with deep foreboding. However bad the news was in London, on the other side of the Atlantic it was even worse. Wednesday 17 September turned out to be one of the worst days in Wall Street's history. Yields on short-term Treasury bills dropped into negative territory, which meant that investors had lost all faith in banks and were actually paying the US government to hold their money. Money market funds, which were effectively cash funds, were suffering unprecedented runs and were in danger of 'breaking the buck', which meant repaying less than $1 for every $1 invested – something which seemed mathematically impossible. In one day panicking investors pulled $32 billion of funds out of Morgan Stanley which the markets now expected to be the next domino to fall after Lehman and Merrill's. Goldman Sachs, traditionally the strongest of the investment banks, would lose half its $120 billion of liquidity in a week. 'Goldman was getting killed,' said Geithner, who at one stage privately called back its chairman, Lloyd Blankfein, after a conference call, to say, 'Lloyd, you cannot talk to anyone outside your firm, or anyone inside your firm, until you get that fear out of your voice.' Geithner later remarked ruefully, 'At that moment, fear was a sign that you were awake and intelligent. Anyone who wasn't scared had no idea how close we were to the abyss.'

In London the Bank of England and the FSA certainly understood that – as did Gordon Brown. 'My colleagues and I thought we were looking at another global depression that would hurt billions of people.' A great deal depended on getting the Lloyds/HBOS deal over the line.

In the offices of Linklaters they were still at it late into the evening, with a frantic Hector Sants calling Daniels and then Hornby, and then Daniels again, urging them to find a compromise. The timing could not have been worse for Simon Robey who had recently taken over as chairman of the Royal Opera House, one of the most prestigious roles in the arts world. He was hosting a dinner in the opera house for all his surviving predecessors, which had taken months to arrange, and had just finished pre-dinner drinks when he was called back to Linklaters. The tireless Greenburgh, he was told, was trying to renegotiate the price.

It was just after nine when Daniels finally called Blank with the terms of the revised deal. They had agreed on a swap of 0.833 of a Lloyds share for every one HBOS share, which at the closing price of Lloyds was equivalent to 232p a share, capitalising HBOS at just over £12 billion. At that level the split between the two sets of shareholders was 56:44 in favour of Lloyds, which Daniels and Hornby, although they weren't going to admit it to each other, both regarded as a good result.

Blank, as he had promised to do, put in a call to Downing Street to pass on the news and received back the message that the Prime Minister was 'pleased with the result' – as indeed he was. 'This seemed to me a good deal for taxpayers because we knew from the United States that contagion was the issue,' Brown revealed later.

It was 9.10 p.m. when Blank put down the phone to Downing Street and fifty minutes later Robert Peston broke the story on the ten o'clock TV news, causing consternation in both camps. There was still a lot of details to be thrashed out before the morning, press releases and analyst briefings to be prepared and conditions to be settled, and Sants, at Lloyds's urging, was just about to agree to let the two sides have until noon before forcing an announcement. 'That leak placed us in a very, very difficult position,' said Sants later. 'It caused us immense problems.'

The most immediate one was that Peston had got the wrong price, and blogged that a deal had been done at £3 a share, which was the opening price Hornby had asked for. One of the advisers called Peston to tell him he was wildly wrong and thirty minutes later Peston blogged again: 'Maybe I've slightly over-egged the price that Lloyds TSB will pay for HBOS. Perhaps it will be nearer £2 than £3.'

The Peston leak caused fury in the Lloyds boardroom, where the directors were either physically present or attending by phone. The leak, they reckoned, had to have come from Downing Street and had therefore been deliberate. 'They're putting pressure on us to do the deal,' commented one director.

There is no evidence that the leaks did come from Downing Street, and Peston – and later Mark Kleinman of Sky News who also broke some highly sensitive stories – never revealed their sources. But many of the bankers and FSA officials believed the leaks were authorised from the top, or somewhere very close to it. Almost all the major decisions affecting the banks over this period leaked within hours, sometimes minutes, and most of them were deadly accurate, often wrecking carefully prepared timetables and rushing people into announcements well before they were ready. 'These leaks became a huge frustration to the FSA and especially Hector [Sants], who found himself severely compromised on many occasions,' says one of the Lloyds directors. 'He found it really difficult to keep the Treasury and Downing Street informed on progress without the BBC getting the full info.'

At midnight the teams began work on the draft announcement which would now have to go out before the London Stock Exchange opened at seven, and Daniels called in the two communications directors for a meeting with Tate, Weir and Tookey to discuss how to position the deal the next morning. It was 4.40 a.m. before Tim Tookey, after working straight through for nearly forty-eight hours, was able to get away to grab a few hours' sleep before the announcement. He had booked a room at a budget hotel near Trafalgar Square but when he arrived it had been given away and there was nothing else available. Disconsolately, he trudged back into the City to grab an hour's rest on a colleague's couch. He was back at work ready to present to the analysts at seven.

It was a tired but euphoric team that trooped into a basement suite in the Dresdner Kleinwort office, the only available room which Tookey, phoning around in the middle of the night, could find at short notice. Tookey had hastily scratched together a ten-page PowerPoint presentation, setting out the bones of the deal, the best he could do in the circumstances; he and Daniels would have to wing the rest. The photographers and TV camera crews were already gathered when Blank arrived to give them their best photo opportunity of the day. Pictures of him winding his long frame out of his tiny red G-Wiz electric car made many of the front pages the next day.

Blank chaired the conference, flanked by Lloyds's top executive team: Eric Daniels, Helen Weir, Truett Tate, Archie Kane and Tim Tookey. Only one HBOS executive was on the podium – a grim-faced Andy Hornby who looked as if he wished to be anywhere other than in that room that morning. Stevenson, about to lose his job, sat in the audience. In his opening remarks Blank emphasised that this was not an opportunistic deal but one which Lloyds had been thinking about for years. 'It marks for Eric and me the culmination of an ambition we have had for some time – and one we know has been shared by Andy Hornby.'

When it came to his turn, Daniels was upbeat: 'Those of you who had heard me before, know that I don't use superlatives often but what I wanted to say is that this is a fantastic deal. This is a great combination and I am very excited about it.' It marked the conclusion of the three-part strategy which he had been telling the analysts about for five years. 'This is a unique opportunity, a unique point in time. We seized that moment.' He paused on one of his slides: 'If you look in retail, you look in wholesale, you look in insurance – any one of the key divisions, we have leading shares and market brands. The power of this franchise is really phenomenal.'

Tookey presented the financials, emphasising the figure which mattered most that morning: a *pro forma* core Tier 1 capital ratio for the combined group of 5.9 per cent which would be raised to 7 per cent through cost savings and earnings retentions, relatively healthy at the time but well short of the ratios the authorities would impose after the crisis. 'Any bank reporting a ratio of 5.9 per cent today would be dead in hours,' says a bank finance director. 'If you haven't got 10 per cent then the markets will kill you.' But in September 2008, before the capital ratios were repeatedly lifted by the FSA, it seemed a very robust figure.

In the Q&A session which followed the main speakers, Hornby only had to field one question, but it was a pertinent one. Richard Buxton, the well-respected head of UK equities at Schroders, asked him how he could explain to HBOS shareholders 'why in the light of some relatively temporary turmoil post the demise of Lehman, you should be prepared to fall so readily into the arms of Lloyds TSB at such a substantial discount to book value?' Could he not have taken advantage of the Bank of England's special liquidity scheme to keep going until he could dispose of assets and manage his book?

Hornby's answer revealed a great deal about his state of mind that day. First of all, he said, he didn't see the current turmoil as 'temporary' – he reckoned the securitisation markets were going to be closed for at least another year. Secondly, he said, 'Eric and I have spoken over the years and always saw this as a very, very powerful combination'. This was a decision 'we had to take' in the interests of long-term stability for shareholders and customers 'as well as to partake in the upturn and the benefit of synergies'. He was still discussing with Daniels his role in the management of the joint company but his demeanour indicated he had no expectation of personally participating in that upturn.

The press was waiting out on the pavement and instead of climbing back into his G-Wiz Blank decided to walk back to his office, just a block away, followed by the camera crews and reporters. Hornby went with him but Daniels and his assistant exited through a side door onto the street where Daniels hoped to grab a quick smoke. They emerged at the back of the cavalcade following Blank and, heads down, walked back to the office a few paces behind Blank. None of the press noticed them.

Back in Gresham Street, the Lloyds team allowed themselves a moment of self-congratulation. Blank, Daniels and the rest of the Lloyds team had finally pulled off the deal which had eluded them for years and which was the logical culmination of the chain of events put in train by Brian Pitman a decade ago. In just two working days, Lloyds had made the biggest acquisition in its history, agreeing to acquire £30 billion of net assets for £12 billion and two of the great brand names in the financial services industry, the Halifax and Bank of Scotland. After a gap of eight years, it would be number one again, a position which probably mattered more in the banking world than in other industries in terms of ratings, confidence and ability to lead the pack. It had moved swiftly and decisively, deploying all its resources to take advantage of the only window in the competition rules it believed would ever come its way. On the wider, public interest front, it had also saved HBOS from immediate bankruptcy and staved off the prospect of financial meltdown – at least for the moment.

Things would look very different in a month's time. But on that particular morning, 18 September 2008, Blank's reputation in the City, and that of his management team, had never been higher.

CHAPTER 19

CRISIS

THE DAY AFTER Lloyds TSB announced its agreed bid for HBOS, world markets staged a recovery. It was as brief as it was unexpected, but it was welcome for all that, lifting for just a moment the mood of deep gloom that had settled over the global financial industry after two traumatic weeks.

London witnessed record gains, with the FTSE 100 index rising 8.8 per cent and on Wall Street the Dow jumping 4.3 per cent. Lloyds emerged as one of the biggest winners, its shares closing at 282p, up 48p on the day. The ban on short selling of financial stocks which came into place that day boosted all the banking shares, with Barclays rising nearly 30 per cent. Astonishingly, in view of what lay just around the corner, RBS shares recorded the biggest gain of all, up 31.9 per cent.

The rally lasted less than twenty-four hours but it was long enough for Lloyds to use its triple A-rating to raise £767 million in fresh capital (about 5 per cent of its equity) at 270p, a modest discount on the prevailing price. Conceived by Tookey overnight, it was a brilliantly executed, opportunist operation conducted at lightning speed by the bank's brokers who completed it by 4 p.m. the same day. Tookey knew all the banks would soon face higher capital requirements and wanted to get the issue away while he could. He was just in time: a few days later Fitch, the ratings agency, put Lloyds on a 'negative watch' rating, reflecting its discomfort over the impact of the HBOS acquisition on its capital ratios. Tookey, trying to limit the downgrade to no more than one notch, argued that the combined group would have an overall 11.4 per cent total capital ratio which was healthy by most standards, was well within the Basel II requirements and met the new, much tougher, FSA rules. He also expanded on his plans for improving on that still further: the 2008 dividend would be paid in scrip and the 2009 dividend would be 'rebased' at no more than 40 per cent of earnings (which would mean a cut); synergies over three years would add up to nearly £5 billion and would also be used to strengthen the capital base; and they had already identified some non-core assets, such as HBOS's Australian subsidiary, which would be sold. He was confident, he said over and over again that week, of achieving his target of a core Tier 1 capital ratio of 7–8 per cent by 2010. Lloyds kept its triple-A rating.

Behind the recovery in the markets was the momentous news that the US Treasury, as part of a concerted plan to prop up the financial system, planned to seek authority from Congress to use $700 billion of taxpayers' money to buy toxic assets from the banks. It would need urgent implementation and Ben Bernanke warned that if Congress and the administration didn't move fast, there wouldn't be an economy left to save. He talked of a potential death spiral developing in the money market funds and the commercial paper market, but was even more concerned by the sustained attacks on the remaining two major investment banks, Morgan Stanley and Goldman Sachs, which were, he said, in danger of 'igniting two more Lehman-type explosions'. The markets could not sustain that.

In the immediate aftermath of the Lehman crash, Hank Paulson, Ben Bernanke and Tim Geithner, the three men responsible for handling the crisis, were hailed by the American Right for their 'courage' in letting Lehman fail, a lesson that the US government was not going to bail out financial institutions that got themselves into trouble no matter how big they were. But within a few days, as the fall-out threatened to pull down the whole system, a more sober assessment was coming to the opposite conclusion: it had been a colossal mistake. The full story only emerged later after all three of them testified that there had been nothing deliberate about it and was never a question of moral hazard. All of them had done their best to prevent the disaster and were horrified when they failed. 'After Lehman, I lost whatever minimal tolerance I might have had for letting moral hazard or political efforts impede our efforts to attack the crisis,' said Geithner.

The Treasury plan, or Troubled Asset Relief Program (TARP), was initially aimed at relieving the pressure on bank balance sheets by swapping highly liquid government bonds for illiquid assets, but it soon became obvious that even a trillion dollars would barely scratch the surface. Although it was the first serious attempt at a systemic, as opposed to a bank-by-bank, approach, it contained serious flaws. 'Unfortunately it was, in my view, expensive, difficult to implement and not going to the heart of the matter quickly,' said Gordon Brown. 'I was not sure it would work, at least not in the UK.'

A much better use of the funds, which Gordon Brown advocated to his American and European counterparts with almost evangelical fervour, was to inject it – or some of it – into the banks as new capital. 'If we were to step into the banks in any way,' wrote Brown, 'I wanted the government to be compensated in full, with ownership of a stake, even if it took a long time for us to be paid back.' In the US, however, that was too radical a concept for congressmen who saw it as a step down the road to nationalisation. However the youthful Geithner in the New York Fed was an early convert to recapitalisation and some of the wiser heads in the Treasury and Fed were coming around to the British view.

The UK plan, still at a nascent stage, was actually based on a three-point strategy developed by Shriti Vadera, Peter Sands, the CEO of Standard Chartered and a team of professional bankers, working well away from the Bank of England. Injecting new capital, most of which would have to come from the taxpayer, into the banks was at the heart of the proposal, but there were two other integral principles without which it could not work: credit guarantees designed to free up the banking system by getting banks to lend to each other again; and liquidity, which the Bank of England would provide in order to restore a degree of stability to the banking system.

The respite following the TARP announcement was brief and the markets were soon on the slide again. Nothing had been resolved and the markets sensed that worse was on the way. AIG might have been saved but at enormous cost and the Fed's concern had now switched back to the banks, particularly Morgan Stanley. John Mack called Hank Paulson at the Treasury to say he was 'under siege from the hedgies', his shares were collapsing and he was desperately seeking an injection of capital from the Japanese who seemed to be getting cold feet. One bit of good news was that Warren Buffett announced he would invest $5 billion in Goldman Sachs through a private placing of preferred stock, a gesture designed as much to inject a bit of confidence as to save Goldman Sachs. But when Goldman shares resumed their slide, giving the Sage of Omaha an immediate loss, the gloom deepened.

By the end of September the crisis began to take its toll of the weaker banks. The independent career of the plucky little Bradford & Bingley, whose origins dated back to 1851, came to an end when Alistair Darling sadly sanctioned its nationalisation, the 'good' part of the bank to be sold to Santander, which had already taken over Abbey National and Alliance & Leicester, and the 'bad' bank put into the same pot as the carcass of Northern Rock. There was a full-blown banking crisis in Iceland, and an even more serious one in Ireland where HBOS had substantial interests. Fortis, which Van den Bergh and Daniels had pursued three years earlier, was nationalised by a coalition of the Belgian, Luxembourg and Dutch governments and 75 per cent of its Belgian operations sold to BNP Paribas. Dexia, which Fortis had been about to merge with, had to be rescued by the Belgian government, as did major banks in Germany and Italy. And so it went on, a growing emergency which was not only closing down the entire banking system but bringing the world economies juddering to a halt, which in turn resulted in still more defaults, collapsing property values and massive loss of household and corporate wealth.

Two weeks after the Lehman crash, the US Congress, against all expectations, rejected Hank Paulson's TARP proposal by 228–205 votes and the Dow plunged 9 per cent, its biggest one-day decline since Black Monday in October 1987, wiping more than $1 trillion off the wealth of Americans. But after two days of market turmoil when Americans citizens protested bitterly about their disappearing life savings and jobs, Congress changed its mind and passed a tweaked version, which allowed part of the funds to be used for capital injections. As Tim Geithner later remarked of the flip-flop: 'The abrupt reversal evoked the Winston Churchill line about Americans always doing the right thing after trying everything else.'

On 30 September Darling called the bank CEOs to the Treasury for an emergency meeting, smuggling them in through the courtyard on Whitehall rather than through the main entrance. When Daniels arrived with the others at six o'clock he found Mervyn King and (Lord) Adair Turner, who had now taken over from Callum McCarthy as FSA chairman, already waiting with the Chancellor. They were joined by the Treasury mandarins Nick Macpherson and John Kingman, the 39-year-old ambitious second permanent secretary with responsibility for banking. Kingman's keen mind and grasp of detail made him a favourite of Brown, Darling and Shriti Vadera, but not of the bankers who resented his aloof manner and obvious disdain for them. He and another bright young Treasury official, Tom Scholar, led the Treasury banking team throughout the crisis.

The first item on Darling's agenda was Ireland's unilateral decision earlier in the day to guarantee the deposits of all its banks, a dangerous and irrational decision which nearly sank the Irish economy – and for which its citizens were still paying eight years later. British banks with Irish interests were not covered by the guarantee and in the Treasury that evening the immediate concern was that there could be a flight of precious deposits into the Bank of Ireland and AIB, both of which had branch networks in the UK. RBS which had substantial interests in Ireland would be most affected but HBOS was also exposed on the corporate front because of Peter Cummings's over-aggressive lending at the top of the market. Darling told the CEOs he had contacted his Irish opposite number, Brian Lenihan, warning him that the FSA was standing by to take immediate action if there was any indication that funds were flowing from British to Irish banks.

That evening however Darling had an even more urgent reason for the meeting which was to find ways of re-opening the banking system by persuading the banks to lend to each other again, something they were refusing to do. 'It was that stark: the banks didn't trust each other anymore. They wanted some form of credit guarantee,' Darling said. They also wanted more liquidity, a particular refrain from Goodwin who still argued that RBS's problems were liquidity-based and he didn't need more capital – or at least not much.

It was another bad-tempered session, ending with no consensus and the bankers arguing among themselves, refusing, in the view of the officials, to face up to the seriousness of their situation. 'As they trooped out of the room, my thought was this had been a less than satisfactory meeting,' Darling, who had little time for most of the bank CEOs, remarked.

Friday 3 October produced yet another surprise: Peter Mandelson returned to government, brought back from Brussels by Gordon Brown who had been his sworn enemy only months before. Threatened with a potential coup from a group of backbenchers who were concerned by Labour's low standing in the polls, Brown forgave all and appointed him Business Secretary, which meant Mandelson was in overall charge of competition policy. One of the first items on his list was the proposed Lloyds/HBOS merger.

Another new figure, who would become central to the fate of the British banks over the next few months, also joined the government that weekend. Brown appointed Paul Myners, a City veteran and former chairman of Marks & Spencer and of the Guardian Media Group, as his 'City minister', or more officially Financial Services Secretary, a new role in government and a reflection of how seriously Brown was taking the financial crisis. He would work under Alistair Darling at the Treasury where his main job, Brown told him, would be to 'stand toe to toe' with the banks in the negotiations to get them to accept the Treasury's developing plan to recapitalise, a task which he expected to be acrimonious. Brown was determined there would be no compromise with the banks: 'At all times we were absolutely clear of one thing: we were going ahead regardless [with the recapitalisation plan]. That is why our bottom line was no funding support without recapitalisation.'

Both Mandelson and Myners were elevated to the House of Lords and appointed to the board of the new National Economic Council, an economic 'council of war' designed to co-ordinate the government response to the emergency. There was already a catastrophic fall-off in lending to small- and medium-sized businesses and the economy was, in Mandelson's words, 'falling off a cliff'. The collapse of one of the major banks could turn the recession into a full-scale depression even worse than the 1930s. If the last two weeks had been bad ones for the financial industry, the next looked like they could be many times worse.

. . .

Lloyds by that stage was well into its due diligence work, with a dozen or more work-stream teams digging as deep into the HBOS books as the legal constraints would allow. Teams working under Helen Weir and Truett Tate methodically worked their way through the loan books and treasury assets, valuing each separate portfolio, and then checked their figures with external advisers. Half of HBOS's loan portfolio was made up of residential mortgages, a business Lloyds knew as much about as any bank on the planet, and segments of it were run through the Cheltenham & Gloucester models to test for 'delinquency' rates, which proved not all that much different from their own. In the wholesale, treasury and corporate banking areas, Tate's team tested the HBOS grading and ratings methodologies and ran the various asset books through different stress scenarios to predict expected losses – all standard stuff.

The HBOS balance sheet reflected a very different culture from the one they were used to. Several years earlier, Paul Moore, head of group regulatory risk at HBOS from 2002 to 2005, had warned the board of the high-risk philosophy which pervaded the bank and then claimed he had been fired by Crosby for his efforts. Later he went public with his allegations, describing the risk-control structure as 'dysfunctional', which Crosby hotly denied. The bank had grown up on the back of what the Parliamentary Commission on Banking Standards would later describe as 'perilously high-risk lending' and a risk-taking management culture which concentrated on commercial real estate, leveraged loans and exposure to individual names, all areas which would suffer most in an economic downturn.

Critics would later condemn what they perceived as Lloyds's failure to identify the poor quality of HBOS's assets and the problems created by the high-risk strategy of Peter Cummings, but it wasn't for lack of people, expertise or effort. The due diligence process involved more than 200 accountants, lawyers, investment bankers and Lloyds's own internal specialists who did their job as professionally as they knew how. Nor was it, as far any of the Lloyds team could tell, for lack of openness on the part of Hornby, Mike Ellis and the HBOS executives they dealt with and who they found cooperative and anxious to please. They had nothing to gain by being evasive or secretive and no one on the Lloyds side complained that they were, although one of the Lloyds directors remarked that: 'The problem wasn't about what they knew – it was about what they didn't know.' That, as things turned out, included the corporate side, which had been left to run itself as long as it delivered its profit targets, and was to show losses of £21.9 billion.

'There is a lot of confusion over the amount of due diligence Lloyds did,' says one of the Merrill Lynch team who advised Lloyds.

> Certainly they did pretty sketchy due diligence first time around because of the legal constraints but after that we had open access to the HBOS books so by the time we came to negotiate the final price, they had done a lot of due diligence, more than on any comparable deal. Merrill helped them value the market instruments but they knew better how to look at a loan book than anybody and their whole team was swamping HBOS.
>
> And they found some crazy stuff being done on the corporate book, not just by Cummings, but in the US, the sort of things you wouldn't expect to find. We had the information on that and we did the valuations, which we thought were on the conservative side but they turned out to be wrong because the markets kept on falling.

Some of the worst 'stuff' they found was actually in the treasury department which, in the chase for higher interest rates, had taken risks Lloyds would never have dreamed of. 'During the due diligence some of the HBOS people were looking very sheepish and they were really embarrassed by what they had to tell us,' says one of the advisers.

The main reason, as we shall see, that the due diligence process underestimated the holes in the HBOS balance sheet was because the basic premise on which the whole exercise was carried out completely underestimated the scale of the recession. Valuations and risks were measured on the forecast that the economic downturn would be the usual two-to-three quarter negative growth period, involving a drop in GDP of about 2–3 per cent, after which the economy would bounce back, as it always did. 'This was the critical assumption which determined everything else,' says one of the Lloyds team. 'Nobody expected the recession to be as severe as it was and assets valued in September had a completely different valuation six months later when the full force hit us.'

The timetable for the takeover meant the due diligence had to be finished by early November for inclusion in the formal document which would be posted to shareholders a few days later. This document had to be done to full Stock Exchange prospectus standards, the most stringent there is, and required the Lloyds directors to make a recommendation as to whether or not shareholders should vote for the deal. All material information available on both Lloyds and HBOS had to be disclosed in the document and the Lloyds directors could always recommend a 'no' vote if the due diligence revealed something significantly adverse. That never happened.

It would be mid-January before Lloyds formally owned HBOS but by the early days of October HBOS's position had become so critical that Stevenson and Hornby had to accept they were not going to make it that far without emergency support from the Bank of England. They found Mervyn King unsympathetic, forcing them almost to plead for help. 'There were days when I'd be with Andy and Dennis, and Andy would have to go around and see whether they could open the bank in the morning and put money in the ATMs,' says one of the HBOS advisers. The discussions with the Bank, he added, seemed to be detached from reality. 'All forms had to be filled in in triplicate and Andy was saying: we need some money or we can't open the bank in the morning and that's not just a problem for us, it's a problem for the whole financial system.'

It came to a head on the morning of Saturday 4 October when Eric Daniels called Victor Blank at his Oxfordshire home to tell him of the latest twist in the HBOS saga.

'I think you should know,' he began, 'that I've just had a call from Andy Hornby and he says they've run out of money and he is having terrible difficulties getting emergency liquidity out of the Bank.' HBOS had a whole slew of deposits which were reaching maturity over the next few weeks, he said, and had no chance of rolling them over. Big corporate customers were withdrawing deposits and HBOS was struggling even to attract overnight money for repayment the next day. Hornby had been to the Bank, which had agreed to provide covert help through a new emergency scheme – Daniels wasn't sure how it worked – and HBOS had first dipped into it in mid-week. Now it needed a lot more, but the Bank was being very bureaucratic, insisting on setting conditions for collateral which HBOS could not meet in the time available.

'The Governor is sticking his toes in,' said Daniels, 'and if this doesn't get agreed by today, HBOS won't get its money and won't be able to open on Monday. Andy's wondering if there's anything we can do to help.'

Lloyds had already lent HBOS £10 billion secured against some of its best quality assets, but that was as far as it was prepared to go. When Daniels rang off, Blank wandered out into his garden pondering what to do next. It was a beautiful, autumn day with the leaves just turning a golden brown, and it seemed a long way from the Bank of England and the City where a life-and-death struggle was taking place at that moment. If HBOS really did close on Monday there would be no question of a Lloyds rescue – there would be nothing left to rescue and every bank in the country would be under threat. He wondered how much Downing Street knew about this latest crisis – he reckoned the Prime Minister, who had just returned from his trip to New York and Washington, would have been so preoccupied with his Cabinet reshuffle and fighting off the attempted coup that he might not be aware of its seriousness. Remembering Northern Rock, Blank had no confidence that, without intervention, King would react fast enough to save the situation.

He went back into the house, remarking to his wife Sylvia, 'What I've just heard is pretty horrifying and I can't just sit here and do nothing – it's like watching two ocean liners heading straight for each other.'

Finally he took the plunge and dialled No. 10 Downing Street and when a voice answered, he diffidently said: 'I'd like to speak to the Prime Minister, please.' He felt rather foolish, not expecting for a moment he would get through on a Saturday morning. The operator replied coolly: 'He's not here, Sir Victor, but hold on.' He waited a few minutes before another voice came on the line. 'Oh, Sir Victor, you're through to Chequers and I understand you want to speak to the Prime Minister? Just hold on please while I see if he's available.'

After another brief wait Blank heard the familiar Scots voice inquiring what was so urgent. Blank explained what he had just heard from Daniels, adding:

'Prime Minister, I don't know what I'm asking of you, but having heard this I feel it's something you should know, if you don't already.' Brown, although he was fully aware of HBOS's problems, didn't seem to be up to speed on this latest turn of events. Blank went on to say that in his opinion the situation was 'pretty critical – the relationship with the Bank of England seems to be difficult'.

'Leave it with me. I'll get back to you within two hours,' said Brown gruffly. He called back twenty minutes later to say: 'I've spoken to some people and it's being sorted out.' Politely he thanked Blank for calling him and bringing it to his attention. 'If there is anything you can do on your side, I'll get someone to talk to you.'

Blank passed the message on to Daniels and the two of them speculated about what Monday morning would bring.

Brown flew to Paris immediately afterwards for a mini-summit hosted by President Sarkozy, whom he had formed an unlikely friendship with when they were both finance ministers. Angela Merkel, Silvio Berlusconi, Jean-Claude Trichet, president of the European Central Bank, and Jean-Claude Juncker, president of the Eurogroup finance ministers, were also there. Brown's purpose that day, supported by a sympathetic Sarkozy who had organised the meeting, was to persuade the other leaders to support a Europe-wide initiative to inject capital into all the banks simultaneously. Britain was working on a plan to do it, he said, and so were the Americans, but for it to work properly it needed the European countries to come to the party. He also raised the prospect, as Darling had done with the UK bankers, of a joint guarantee on bank lending on a Europe-wide basis, which they hoped would free up the markets. Brown found his fellow leaders curiously detached from the crisis which they still saw as largely an American affair which happened to have spilled over into Britain, whose banks were more closely linked to the US. The European problem, they argued, was 'not because of anything they [the banks] had done but because of contagion from the US', wrote Brown afterwards. In fact, as he pointed out, European banks held trillions of dollars of US mortgage-backed securities and they were more highly leveraged than the American banks.

Back in London on Sunday, Brown could not restrain a rare flash of *schadenfreude* when he learned that Hypo Real Estate, the largest lender to the German property sector, had just been bailed out by the Merkel government and all over Europe that week other governments were doing the same thing.

Brown called a meeting in No. 10 that evening with his most senior team, including Darling, Myners, Shriti Vadera and Tom Scholar to discuss the next stage in the implementation of the elaborate rescue plan, which was still not quite ready despite hundreds of man-hours and sleepless nights spent working on it by officials and advisers. Peter Mandelson should have been there too, but earlier in the day Brown had been called out of a meeting to take an emergency call from his Business Secretary who said he was in agonising pain and needed to get to a hospital fast. Mandelson, who was convinced he was having a heart attack, explained that he had done the rounds of the Sunday morning TV programmes but began to feel more and more uncomfortable because of a pain in his stomach. He went home, took some tablets and waited for it to go away. But it got worse, he had been violently sick and he was now writhing on the floor in agony, unwilling to go hospital on his first day in office for fear of embarrassing Brown. What was he to do?

In much the same way as he had said to Blank the day before, Brown calmly told him: 'I'll call you back,' which was the last response the stricken Mandelson wanted. But ten minutes later Brown did call back. 'I've just talked to the minister of health,' he said, 'and he's on his way to you now.'

'No, you don't understand,' said a despairing Mandelson, 'I don't need the minister of health – I need a doctor!'

'He *is* a doctor,' said Brown, 'and he's already in his car.'

The minister, (Lord) Ara Darzi, was not just a doctor but a highly respected physician who quickly identified Mandelson's problem as a kidney stone and took him to the Royal Free hospital via the ambulance entrance. After an uncomfortable night, Mandelson was still dopey in the morning when Brown called to ask after the patient. He was very weak, replied Mandelson, but on the mend. Well then, said the unforgiving Brown, could he attend the first meeting of the National Economic Council, where the banks, and HBOS in particular, would be on the agenda? It would send a bad signal if he was not there.

Mandelson groaned, and got out of his hospital bed. It was not how he had envisaged re-entering government.

.   .   .

To the great relief of Blank and Daniels, the HBOS branches duly opened for business on Monday morning and its cashpoints paid out money as if there had never been a problem. Blank couldn't tell whether his intervention had made any difference or if it would have happened anyway, but at least he felt he had done something. It was only some time later, well after the deal was completed, that Blank and Daniels learned the true nature of the Bank's support of HBOS over that weekend.

Several weeks before, the Bank, on top of the various other measures it used to inject liquidity into the system, had realised that in certain instances it would have to lend covertly to banks which could not access liquidity anywhere else. It had HBOS particularly in mind but RBS was rapidly coming into the frame too. Normal lending by the Bank left a trace which keen-eyed observers in the markets could pick up, creating immediate problems for the particular bank which had borrowed it. So the Bank created a new emergency liquidity assistance (ELA) programme through which it could make loans to a troubled bank without the markets knowing about it. Starting on 1 October, over the next six weeks the Bank lent HBOS £25.4 billion, and another £36.6 billion went into RBS, which came into the scheme on 7 October, a total of £61 billion between the two of them. In return, it took £100 billion of assets from them as collateral. To outsiders that would later seem a huge sum of money but in the context of balance sheets of £750 billion (HBOS) and over £1 trillion (RBS) it wasn't so large. These two were the only banks in the scheme which was essentially, as the Bank's deputy governor Paul Tucker later called it, 'a classic lender of last resort operation', with the Bank fulfilling its primary purpose in life. 'If we hadn't done it,' said Tucker, 'the economic cycle would have been a lot worse.' Mervyn King added that 'this was a dire emergency' and the Bank had provided 'a bridging loan' before the government rescued the two institutions. 'It was very effective in buying time,' he said (Lloyds repaid all the HBOS loans in full at the end of January 2009 after the merger had been completed).

Monday 6 October was another torrid day in a week which would mark the high point of the banking crisis. That afternoon Darling updated MPs, back in Westminster after their long summer recess, on the gravity of the situation, warning them that the government was 'looking at some pretty big steps which we would not take in ordinary times'. Speculation over the weekend, fanned by a mischievous George Osborne, the shadow Chancellor, had led MPs to expect something more definite, and when he didn't produce it, the Chancellor was given a rough time in the House. Darling's frustration was compounded by the markets which, disappointed by his failure to reveal a major new initiative, went into freefall while he was still speaking. The FTSE 100 suffered one of its largest one-day falls on record, down 391.1 points, or 7.85 per cent, with bank shares leading the way. RBS fell more than 20 per cent after Standard & Poor's downgraded it again.

At Lloyds's Gresham Street office that day Blank chaired a board meeting for Daniels to bring the non-executive directors up to date. The situation was changing by the hour and was already quite different from the circumstances in which the board had supported the HBOS deal three weeks before. The due diligence process, Daniels said, was now well advanced and the team had made a first assessment of the strength and weaknesses of the HBOS balance sheet and trading. It was not encouraging but so far there had been no real surprises and there was no reason to expect impairments to be large enough to make the deal unviable.

There were two contrasting scenarios discussed at length by the board that day: the pessimistic one was that RBS and HBOS would go bust and be nationalised, Barclays would be next, no amount of government money could hold the line, the economy would collapse and house prices would fall by 20 30 per cent. On that basis, Lloyds itself would be seriously threatened. The other was that the US TARP would work, the Bank of England would turn on the spigots and flood the market with liquidity (which it was already doing without telling anyone), the Treasury would put together a package of credit guarantees to encourage banks to lend, and the recession would be a steep but short one. By the second half of 2009, the recovery would be well under way, house prices would be turning up again and an integrated Lloyds Banking Group, as they had decided to call it, would become a cash machine.

In the first scenario, they should find a way to get out of the HBOS deal and maybe pick up some of the pieces later at a nominal price. In the second scenario, this was still their best chance to land the prize they had sought for years and if they pulled the plug, the competition window would close and they would be back where they started, except with egg on their faces. 'We'd look like complete idiots,' someone muttered, 'after all we've been through to get this far.'

'Eric's position was, he was trying to analyse what was the worst that could happen if they did the deal and what was the worst that could happen if they didn't,' says one of the advisers.

And Victor and the board looked pretty dispassionately at the pros and cons of going ahead. But psychologically, they realised it was too late to

turn back and if we could get the price down again and get the government to put some capital into HBOS, then it took away the last reasons
not to do it.

The strategy team ran another series of models on what an enlarged
group would look like if the recession deepened, and house prices fell
further. They examined the probable level of default in the HBOS loan
book and possible declines in the market value of assets held in the trading books if the economy fell at various rates, from -1 per cent to -5. But
they stopped at -5 per cent, which would have been the worst recession
since World War Two.

It would be difficult to believe later, but in October 2008 the forecasts
for UK economic growth for 2009 from a dozen professional forecasters
ranged from +2 per cent to -2 per cent with an average of -0.2 per cent. 'At
anything less than a fall of 5 per cent, it still looked fine,' said one of the
Lloyds team later. 'After that everything crumbled but we never expected
the severity of what transpired. Maybe we would have done if we had had
more data, but the big collapse in the economy only really happened in
the fourth quarter and obviously we didn't have that data in October.'

In the end, they decided to go with it. In 2008, Lloyds was set to make a
profit of £3.7 billion, spread fairly evenly across retail, insurance and Truett
Tate's wholesale, corporate and international division. The next year, 2009,
was clearly going to be a tough one with bad debts rising and impairments
well above normal, but even so their best estimate of underlying profits for
the combined group came out at around £7 billion, and that was before
the bulk of the savings kicked in. On that basis, if they could negotiate the
price down, they would be buying HBOS for about two years' operating
profits, creating considerable value for the bank's shareholders. It was also
a pretty good deal for HBOS shareholders who would share in the uplift.
Once again the board unanimously supported the proposed deal.

CHAPTER 20

THE STORM BREAKS

DANIELS, ALONG WITH the other bank chiefs, was back in the Treasury on Monday evening, 6 October, for yet another meeting with Alistair Darling, whose team had now been strengthened by the arrival of (Lord) Paul Myners. This was the first meeting where the officials noted an element of panic beginning to creep in. 'For the first time in their lives the bankers needed HM government and they didn't know what, if anything, we were going to do,' one official remarked afterwards.

There were eight bank CEOs present, their body languages reflecting the differing states of their balance sheets. Andy Hornby was probably the most pressurised and his mobile features showed it – one observer described him as looking 'gaunt and drawn – he had completely lost it'. Fred Goodwin, in more trouble even than Hornby, remained his usual aggressive self but inwardly he must have been panicking. Daniels, seriously concerned about HBOS and the fate of his bid, was tense but impassive. Douglas Flint of HSBC and Peter Sands of Standard

Chartered (who was secretly advising the government) represented two well-capitalised banks and looked relatively relaxed, although Flint was clearly irritated at being there at all, arguing that HSBC was a lender to the markets rather than a borrower. António Horta-Osório of Santander UK was basically an observer, brought along to make up the numbers, although Santander was more an old-fashioned building society than a bank; Graham Beale, CEO of Nationwide, whom Darling was particularly impressed with, had more deposits than he could lend and was therefore the envy of everyone in the room. John Varley of Barclays, Darling's favourite among the bankers for his cool and objective advice, was somewhere in the middle, not quite in the troubled camp but not rock solid either; unknown to the others, Varley was well advanced with his own plans to raise capital from the Middle East, which he was negotiating with Hector Sants at the FSA, and resented being there at all.

For the past week, a tight group of ministers and officials had been working around the clock to develop the government's recapitalisation plan which Gordon Brown proposed to announce on Wednesday, two days away. Myners, Vadera and Tom Scholar formed the heart of the team, which had been strengthened by the addition of two leading investment bankers, Robin Budenberg and David Soanes of UBS. Shriti Vadera had also recruited David Mayhew of JP Morgan Cazenove, the City veteran who commanded a great deal of respect in Whitehall where he had been involved in many of the government privatisations over the years. Gordon Brown had personally approved his addition to the group of City advisers being assembled by the Treasury and other government agencies.

The serious work was done in the Treasury but the team expanded to include the Bank of England and the FSA to produce what Brown insisted should be a full Tripartite scheme. 'Whatever the differences in our approaches, we were at one on this,' said Darling afterwards. In the Bank of England King, fully behind the scheme, warned the Bank's directors that some of the UK's largest banks were facing failure 'and complete seizure of the banking system threatened'. No Governor of the Bank of England had used words like that for a long time.

The result of this intense process was a two-stage plan, the first part of which was the general bailout of the overall banking system, involving capital, guarantees and liquidity across the board; the second stage was to be the recapitalisation of the individual banks which the FSA was working on and which would only be completed by the weekend.

That evening Darling gave the bank chiefs the broad outline of the plan which, he told them, would require every bank in the room, regardless of their financial strength, to raise new capital. The FSA and the Bank of England had done new stress tests which they would be required to meet by the weekend, and the government was standing by to provide capital for those banks which couldn't raise it themselves – which, everyone knew, basically meant RBS and HBOS. Lloyds did not consider itself in that category but had accepted it would have to raise new capital too. The government, said Darling, saw this as a 'once-and-for-all solution' for the whole British banking system, and would, he hoped, be matched by similar schemes in other countries. Just that day European finance ministers had agreed on minimum guarantees for bank deposits and had also stated that systemically relevant banks should be bailed out. The US and Japanese authorities were also advancing similar programmes in a co-ordinated effort which Britain was currently leading.

All the banks would be required to sign up to it, Darling concluded. The bottom line was 'no funding support without recapitalisation'. If the bankers had any other issues, they should raise them now and in the meantime they should not stray far from their London offices as he might have to call them in at very short notice. He ended with a warning that they should keep the meeting strictly confidential – a leak could wreck the timetable, rattle the markets and threaten the whole scheme.

To Brown and Darling's fury, within a few hours of the bankers leaving the Treasury, news of the meeting was running on the BBC's ten o'clock news, the last thing they wanted. Fortunately it was an incomplete and not terribly accurate version, but the damage was done. 'The point of the plan was to reassure markets with a decisive, clear and completed intervention at one stroke,' said Brown. 'If they saw it coming in bits, the impact on market confidence would be blunted.'

The storm broke the next day, Tuesday 7 October, when Robert Peston, clearly briefed by someone at the meeting, revealed that the heads of all the big British banks had been in a crisis session in the Treasury. His headline could not have been worse: 'BANKS ASK CHANCELLOR FOR MORE CAPITAL', and Peston went on to say that three bankers had told Darling 'they'd like to see the colour of the taxpayers' money rather quicker than he might have expected'. Daniels assumed he was not in that little group.

At 8.45 that morning Fred Goodwin stood up to address the annual Merrill Lynch banking conference in the ballroom of the Landmark Hotel in Marylebone. It was a bizarre, surreal moment, which many of the delegates, monitoring the markets on their mobile phones, would never forget. Although his bank by that stage was in terminal trouble, Goodwin painted a picture of RBS as a healthy and well-capitalised bank with a 'strong franchise', great opportunities for growth and asserted that the ABN Amro integration, which the whole room knew was a disaster, was 'ahead of plan'.

By the time he sat down thirty minutes later the shares of RBS had fallen by 35 per cent and had been suspended twice. It was the end – no bank could survive that. 'I knew the bank was finished, in the most spectacular way,' said Darling, who was at a meeting of European finance ministers in Luxembourg, when he was told the news. 'The game was up. If the markets could give up on RBS, one of the biggest banks in the world, all bets on Britain's and the world's financial system were off.'

The flow of funds out of RBS turned into a deluge and the bank's chairman, Sir Tom McKillop, one of Britain's most esteemed industrialists before he unwisely moved from the pharmaceutical industry into banking (he had actually been a director of Lloyds up to 2004), called Darling to admit his bank was on the point of going bust. How long could he keep going, Darling asked? 'A couple of hours maybe,' a shell-shocked McKillop replied dolefully. In the Bank of England at that moment RBS's group treasurer, John Cummins, was sitting across a table from Andrew Bailey, the Bank's Chief Cashier (his signature was on the bank notes), asking him could he borrow £25 billion. Of course, Bailey replied, inquiring politely was he sure that was enough?

Before the crisis, clearing banks were regarded as impregnable monuments of finance, 'rocks of stability' as Gordon Brown called them, with enormous deposits and reserves and a run on one was inconceivable – it had simply never happened. Now a run was starting on RBS and queues were beginning to build at branch counters. Fortunately there were thousands of branches and the queues never stretched out onto the street, and most withdrawals were electronic. But it was a run nonetheless, hundreds of times bigger than the run on Northern Rock which had so shocked the world.

In the Treasury and Downing Street the prospect of a full-scale panic seemed all too possible, particularly if the run spread to HBOS. Two of Britain's biggest and best-known banks, which held the savings of one in every three savers in the country, were dependent on emergency funds from the Bank of England just to stay alive. It was later estimated that the Bank lent £85 billion of new money to the British banks in just two days, most of it to RBS and HBOS.

On Tuesday afternoon Eric Daniels was again summoned to the Treasury to meet Paul Myners, entering the minister's office as Fred Goodwin was leaving after a stormy half-hour session during which he was reported to have said: 'No business ever dies because it's run out of capital. They die because they run out of cash.' Myners's reply was terse and uncompromising: whether he wanted it or not, RBS was going to be recapitalised. Liquidity alone was not going to do it.

Daniels, next up, was treated with more respect but still found the meeting intimidating, with Myners in aggressive, even bullying mode, prepared to take no nonsense from bankers. He was accompanied by John Kingman and David Mayhew, the first meeting the 68-year-old City legend had attended.

Myners had a different agenda for the Lloyds meeting: he needed urgently to establish whether Lloyds was still prepared to go through with the takeover of HBOS whose position had deteriorated considerably since the bid was first mooted. This was probably the one point in this frenetic period when Lloyds could have pulled out: if HBOS accepted new capital from the government, as it was about to do, then the material adverse change, or MAC, clause which Daniels had insisted on in the September negotiations, would trigger and the deal could either be abandoned or renegotiated. At that moment withdrawal would have been a disaster for the whole government plan, forcing it to nationalise HBOS and RBS – and perhaps Barclays and even Lloyds along with them. Ministers and officials were desperate to head it off and Daniels's response over the next five minutes could make or break the whole government rescue package.

Did Lloyds intend to proceed with the bid, Myners asked Daniels bluntly? He wanted an answer there and then or the Treasury would have to go to its contingency plan (he didn't say what it was). Daniels hesitated a moment and from the back of the room Mayhew, although he was advising the government, found himself willing him to insist on conditions, such as a limit to the HBOS losses which Lloyds would take on its balance sheet, with a government guarantee to cover anything above that. Daniels, he reckoned, would never have a better chance, though there would have been a heavy cost to any government support even if it were available.

After a long pause, Daniels finally said, yes, Lloyds was prepared to go ahead – subject to clearance on the competition issues, liquidity being provided by the Bank of England, and to due diligence, shareholder approval and a number of other items, none of them critical. He stopped there. Myners and the other officials breathed a collective sigh of relief. Anything else would have holed their plan below the water line.

'I remember having discussions with John Kingman and others in the Treasury that night,' says an official,

> and the contingency plan was to nationalise HBOS 100 per cent. That was the fall-back plan, there wasn't anything else – and we all really, really hoped we wouldn't have to go there. And I remember in the meetings thinking it was more than possible that might happen. Certainly the FSA thought that was a possibility and so did the Treasury and the Bank, and I don't know how we would have been able to do it in the time available. But Lloyds would have lost their whole strategy of taking over HBOS and they didn't want to do that.

Daniels returned to Gresham Street to brief Blank, relating how he had been ambushed by Myners and Kingman, who had barely given him time to think. But it wouldn't have made much difference – he had given the answer that his chairman and board had already signed up to. Lloyds was going ahead.

Brown had spent the day on the telephone to foreign leaders, officials and his own ministers, trying to complete the final stages of the plan and to contain the damage done by Peston's leak. As the markets crashed and RBS tottered, he called the Governor to check his part of the plan was in place. 'I wanted the recapitalisation package to be backed by liquidity and for Royal Bank of Scotland to get through to the end of the day,' he said.

He also called the Qatari Prime Minister, Sheikh Hamad bin Jassim (HBJ), to urge him to 'consider investment in recapitalisation of our banks'. HBJ, as it happened, was already working on that and was in talks with Barclays. That was as far as he intended to go however. Brown reached another decision that day, which he communicated to Darling and Mervyn King: the rescue package would contain 'specific restraints on excessive risk-taking and therefore remuneration' which were clearly not going to be popular with the overpaid bank chiefs who loved their bonuses. And he would insist on the resignation of the leaders of the banks at the centre of the crisis – which meant RBS and HBOS.

That evening (Tuesday), Daniels and the other bank chiefs were back in the Treasury yet again, several of them for the second time that day. Although it was 7.30 p.m., the building hummed with activity, with law-yers, officials, bankers, advisers and the odd minister huddled in corners or around every spare desk, talking on mobiles in the corridors or tap-ping into laptops. The bank CEOs were ushered up to a meeting room on the second floor where they sat opposite a grim-faced Darling, just back from Luxembourg, flanked by Myners and the Treasury mandarins Nick Macpherson and Tom Scholar. Darling started off by telling them that the government was bringing forward its plans, the central compo-nent of which was, as he had already told them, that they would all be required to raise more capital. On the basis of the stress tests done by the FSA and the Bank of England, and advice taken from City advisers, the Treasury's best estimate was they would need £50 billion between them, and if they couldn't raise it, the government would provide it. He was not yet in a position to tell them how it would be apportioned between the individual banks, but the FSA would let them know by the end of the week, in time for the opening of markets on Monday morning.

The government would also provide a £250 billion credit guarantee to encourage the banks to lend to each other, and the Bank of England was preparing to double the existing special liquidity scheme to £200 billion (it had still not disclosed its covert lending scheme for HBOS and RBS).

It represented a package of £500 billion, a third of the entire UK GNP, a massive commitment by the UK authorities to head off the biggest catastrophe the British economy had faced in a century. The three parts of the plan were interlinked – without recapitalisation there would be no guarantees to underpin their lending and they would have only limited access to the Bank's liquidity scheme. And there would be no negotiation – this was take-it-or-leave-it time and all eight bank CEOs must sign up to the package that evening, even if it meant staying in the Treasury all night. Darling said the government intended to announce the bailout package first thing the next morning and the Prime Minister had scheduled a press conference at nine.

The bank CEOs, particularly Goodwin, erupted and Hornby, according to Darling, 'looked as if he was about to explode'. Daniels, outwardly calm, told Darling he was not addressing the 'real issue', which was the impact of liquidity constraints on the economy, and the government seemed to have no plan 'other than panic'. Like the others, he also objected strongly to the constraints on compensation packages and dividends. Darling left the meeting and called Brown to tell him the banks were 'incredibly unhappy' but they would come round – he had left them in the hands of Myners and the officials who would stay with them until dawn if they had to.

For Brown, Darling and the other ministers and officials involved in the plan, this night was the peak of the crisis, the moment when, if the banks refused to support the package or if the markets reacted badly – or if Lloyds had pulled out of its HBOS bid – the whole edifice could have come tumbling down. The tension in No. 10 was recorded by Damian

McBride, Gordon Brown's press adviser, who was with him that evening. Brown, he said, sat slumped on a couch fretting about the market reaction and the wording of the Treasury statement, warning morosely that if it all went wrong the banks would shut their doors, the cashpoints wouldn't work, cards wouldn't be accepted and 'the whole thing will explode', he said. 'If you can't buy food or petrol or medicine for your kids, people will start breaking windows and helping themselves.' It would, he warned, be anarchy, with curfews and the army on the streets. 'How do we get order back?'

Brown later admitted that he had even considered warning his wife Sarah that they might have to move out of Downing Street the next day and then thought better of it – he would wait until morning.

Back at the Treasury the hours dragged by and the bankers still argued furiously with each other and with Myners, Vadera and the officials with no agreement in sight. By midnight, Darling, a less volatile personality than his excitable chief, was also getting worried. 'It crossed my mind that the banks … might be daft enough to take up the option of suicide – and I simply couldn't afford a row of dead banks in the morning.'

It was past midnight before the bank CEOs grumpily gave in and Daniels left the building in the early hours to grab a few hours' sleep, uncertain of what the morning would bring. Several of the CEOs, including Hornby, stayed behind to help shape the package which would affect them profoundly.

The Treasury statement went out at seven and when the markets opened, share prices initially edged up a little while the wholesale and credit markets thankfully remained calm. A relieved Darling did his best to reassure the British public on BBC Radio 4's *Today* programme that all was well, and then dashed back to Downing Street to join the Prime Minister at his press conference. In the City the Bank of England cut interest rates by half a percentage point to 4.5 per cent and, in a move initiated in a flurry of phone calls by Brown and coordinated by Mervyn King, the US Fed, the European Central Bank, and the Canadian, Swedish, Swiss and Chinese authorities all followed. Central banks had never acted in such unison before – and probably never would again.

But the crisis was far from over and Blank called another board meeting that morning where Daniels took the directors through the events in the Treasury the night before. It had been made clear, he said, that Lloyds, whether it went ahead with the HBOS deal or not, would have to raise new capital from somewhere and with the markets effectively closed, that inevitably meant from the government. Some of the directors suggested looking for alternative sources, maybe a Middle Eastern sovereign wealth fund, but the terms would have been onerous and time was too short. HBOS would also receive state capital, which Tookey believed would lower the risk to Lloyds considerably. Someone suggested they seek legal advice on whether the proposed recapitalisation constituted state aid and would therefore fall foul of the European competition laws, and was told that the Treasury officials had assured the Lloyds team that it fell under a special emergency provision and there would be no problem. Nick Macpherson had been clear on that – the government would 'fix' the competition issues, at home as well as in Europe. That was a critical issue for the bid going ahead – there was no point in acquiring HBOS to gain market share and then have the combined group broken up again.

At the end of the board meeting Lloyds issued a terse statement, as agreed in the Treasury in the early hours, welcoming the government's announcement 'to bring stability and certainty to the UK banking industry', but more significantly confirming it was progressing with the proposed acquisition of HBOS 'and working with HBOS management on all aspects of the transaction'. There was no backing out now, even if they wanted to – and no one did.

For the banks, the single most important item of information was the one they had not yet been given, which was the amount of new capital they would be required to find. There was a good reason for that: the Treasury didn't know either. Strictly this was a question for the FSA, as the bank regulator, but John Kingman had lost faith in its competence and preferred to do his own sums. For that he needed outside advice and on Tuesday evening, even as the bank chiefs were gathering in the Treasury, Kingman called James Leigh-Pemberton, son of a former Bank of England Governor, who was now head of Credit Suisse's UK operations, to explain what he needed. He would be holding a short 'beauty parade' which he hoped Credit Suisse would take part in, he told Leigh-Pemberton, before he appointed an adviser, but the project would have to be done in a great hurry – days rather than weeks.

'Kingman and the Treasury were uncomfortable with all the conflicting voices coming at them from all sides,' says one of the Credit Suisse bankers who was put to work on the project within hours. 'They wanted to work it out in their own heads. And for that they needed independent advice.'

Leigh-Pemberton got the call on Tuesday night, 7 October, pitched on Wednesday afternoon and arrived with his team in the Treasury on Thursday morning to begin preparing a report which had to be completed by the weekend. Kingman succinctly set out the task: there was a run on RBS and £10 billion a day –'and mounting' – was being withdrawn by the British public, he said. The Bank of England was keeping the bank alive by providing liquidity through a special emergency scheme but its view was that unless RBS could be recapitalised by the weekend, its branches would stay closed on Monday. The Treasury was working on a contingency plan to make Monday a bank holiday, an unprecedented event in British peacetime. That morning the government had announced its overall package but now it needed urgently to recommend a figure for each individual bank, and they should concentrate their efforts initially on RBS. The usual rules of the Takeover Code, listing rules and competition regulations, could be ignored – they could worry about them on Monday morning after the deal was done.

'The minute we were told by Kingman that there was a run on RBS, that was enough to make us realise the scale of the problem we were looking at,' said one of the Credit Suisse team. Leigh-Pemberton coolly pointed out that if the situation was as dire as that, it wasn't going to be enough just to save RBS. Everyone would assume that HBOS would be next because of the domino effect and they would have to fix HBOS at the same time. The problem with that, he went on, was that HBOS had announced a merger with Lloyds so effectively there would be three banks at risk, all of which would need new capital from the government. Kingman immediately saw his point. 'We were asked specifically to look at RBS,' one of the Credit Suisse team remarked later, 'but within half an hour we were into three.'

Oddly, the Credit Suisse team was never asked for an opinion on Barclays despite the fact that it too would have to raise capital over the weekend. The Treasury left that one to the FSA.

Credit Suisse was a bank itself, and in its spacious offices in Canary Wharf there were specialists in every class of asset that the big clearing banks held on their balance sheets. By Friday a team of sixty was working on the project, divided into two teams, one concentrating on RBS, the other on HBOS/Lloyds, while a core team of specialists valued the different classes of assets and liabilities. George Maddison, one of the senior executives, got HBOS.

He spent all Friday morning at the FSA offices in Canary Wharf where the bank data was kept, building a model and trying to form a view of its capital needs, however tentative at this stage. The Credit Suisse team were not impressed with the work done by the FSA. 'They didn't seem to comprehend what they were looking at in terms of the seriousness or the magnitude of the problems,' one of them said later. 'They were looking at everything from 40,000 feet and hadn't gone under to look at what was really happening. So when things went wrong, they were very badly caught out.'

Even former FSA officials grudgingly accept that. 'We didn't really have any detailed information on the quality of the balance sheets of the banks,' says one defensively.

> We didn't have the resources to do it, so we made a set of pretty crude macro assumptions about the housing market, and then made some rough estimates and we modelled and we produced numbers. But we didn't have the resources – we only had two supervisors on each bank and the only information we had came from the bank itself – and if the management of HBOS didn't know what was happening inside its own bank, how could we?

Some of the bankers who had dealt with the FSA over the years were actually quite sympathetic to its plight. 'Remember the FSA had little or no modelling expertise,' says one former bank finance director, 'and years of Brown-instigated style of City regulation – which to be fair the City wanted and supported – had not given them the ability to really understand the details of boardroom strategy and then back it up with experts and teams.'

On Friday afternoon the Credit Suisse teams regrouped at their West End office in Pall Mall and then walked over to the Treasury to meet the officials, followed by a session with the bankers themselves. Maddison handed Andy Hornby and Mike Ellis a long list of the information they needed urgently and arranged to see them the next morning.

When they arrived at the HBOS offices, the Credit Suisse team was impressed to find the Bank of England's Andrew Bailey already there, calmly running his own model on a laptop. They found Hornby falling over himself to be helpful, although they were far from convinced he knew what was going on in his own bank, and by Saturday lunchtime they had done as much as they could there. Their colleagues working on RBS reported that Goodwin had refused to engage and they were struggling to get the quality of data they needed.

. . . .

Tim Tookey had started the week believing that Lloyds might need to raise £1.5 billion in new capital, which was the figure the FSA had given him on the basis of their latest stress tests. That didn't worry the Lloyds CFO too much – if the markets improved even slightly, Lloyds could raise that itself, given a little time. But then the Icelandic banks went down, the markets crashed and RBS trembled on the brink, and the FSA doubled the amount of core capital the banks required. Tookey and Merrill Lynch ran the numbers, raised their estimates to £3–4 billion, and once again Tookey checked his calculations with the FSA.

Unfortunately the FSA was no longer making the rules, which by Friday had changed again. The Bank of England's new stress tests concluded that RBS alone required £20 billion, HBOS at least half that and the other banks another £20 billion between them. 'We are not trying to save the banks,' Mervyn King said, 'we are trying to save the economy.' He was now an even bigger advocate for recapitalisation than Gordon Brown, almost obsessively so.

On Friday Tim Tookey was in Edinburgh chairing his monthly finance meeting in the offices of Scottish Widows when Eric Daniels called him on his mobile. 'Tim, we have a meeting in the Treasury at 3.30 this afternoon,' he said without any preliminaries. 'Where are you?'

It was already 11 a.m. and when Tookey explained that he couldn't get back in time, Daniels exploded. 'Tim, you don't understand – we *have* to be at the Treasury this afternoon. Get yourself to the airport *now* and if you can't get a seat on a plane, hire one!'

To his great disappointment, Tookey managed to catch a scheduled flight and just made it back in time for what was to prove the most momentous weekend of his life.

CHAPTER 21

THE QUEEN'S SHILLING

WHEN ERIC DANIELS and Tim Tookey entered HM Treasury in Whitehall on the afternoon of Friday 10 October 2008, the shares of Lloyds TSB stood at 189p, their lowest level in nearly twenty years and 60 per cent down on the price at which they started the year. The market value was £10.7 billion, a fifth of its peak in Brian Pitman's time and down a third since it announced the deal with HBOS a month before.

The reason for the fall was not the HBOS deal, which at that stage the City and investors still regarded as a good one. Many bank shares around the world had fallen by similar percentages, some even more. The American banks had taken a terrible beating post-Lehman, several of the biggest banks in the world, including Citigroup, recording falls of more than 90 per cent. In London, the virtual collapse of

RBS had a catastrophic impact on the rest of the sector and even the shares of the mighty HSBC and the rock solid Standard Chartered, then in very good shape, were down by a quarter in a week. Barclays had done even worse, falling 50 per cent since January and 75 per cent from the 2007 peak of 790p (they were eventually to hit an all-time low of 51p, a fall of 96 per cent). RBS and HBOS of course had dropped off the scale.

No market or country could escape the market collapse that week. The head of the IMF, the libidinous Dominique Strauss-Kahn, warned that the international financial system was on 'the brink of [a] systemic meltdown', resulting in the Nikkei share index suffering its biggest one-day fall for twenty years, down 10 per cent. The share price falls became bigger as they rolled west across other Asian markets and on through Europe, arriving back in London, which lost £90 billion of its stock market value in just seven trading minutes. A seriously alarmed Bank of England informed the Treasury that morning that, even with the huge amount of liquidity it was providing, it was not sure it could keep RBS alive until the weekend. The implications of that were horrifying: RBS had total assets of £2.2 trillion, the biggest of any bank in the world and larger than the entire British GDP, and its failure would bring HBOS down with it, possibly followed by Barclays. In those circumstances it would be touch-and-go whether Lloyds TSB could see out the crisis.

At a board meeting the previous day – someone later calculated that Lloyds held thirty-six board meetings in one twelve-month period, all of them chaired by Blank – the analysis presented by Daniels still showed the bank trading well after a strong first nine months, on target to meet the analysts' expectations of £3 billion before impairments and exceptionals for 2008. Despite everything that had hit it in the past six months, Lloyds was still a fundamentally healthy bank.

A Year of Huge Change

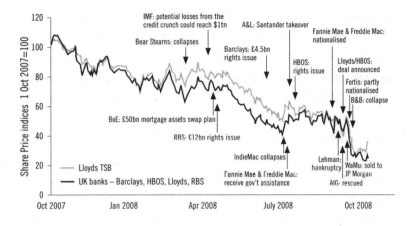

Even before the HBOS deal, Lloyds shares were on the slide – as were all bank shares

Blank's objective at that meeting was to ensure the board fully understood the HBOS deal and the implications of taking state capital, and to have the opportunity to discuss it fully before the weekend, after which it would be too late. Daniels took them through the case for HBOS once more, reiterating the points he had already made several times. 'HBOS has a fantastic franchise with huge long-term value, particularly in savings and mortgages,' he said. It had a 'challenged business model' but most of the issues were short-term and Lloyds had a clear plan to work through them. The government, he had been informed by Myners and Kingman, was about to pump a large amount of new capital into HBOS and was already making even larger amounts of liquidity available to it as well as credit guarantees. On top of the new capital – still unspecified – injected into Lloyds, the combined bank would be well capitalised even if the economic downturn was steeper than expected. If they abandoned HBOS they would never get another chance and years of strategic planning would have to be abandoned.

'This remains a great deal for Lloyds TSB,' Daniels concluded, 'a considerably better outcome than staying on a standalone basis.'

Some of the Lloyds directors later wished they had pressed harder to insist on conditions from the government similar to those offered by the Treasury under its Asset Protection Scheme (APS) a few months later, where the state would bear 90 per cent of losses above a certain figure. When JP Morgan bought both Bear Stearns and Washington Mutual, it limited its exposure by leaving the riskier assets with the US Federal Deposit Insurance Corporation (FDIC) and Citigroup had insisted on a similar condition when it bid for Wachovia. But Britain didn't have an FDIC and there was no time to put one in place, and it was simply not on the government horizon in mid-October. In any case the APS conditions turned out to be so unpalatable for Lloyds that it was prepared to do almost anything to get out of the scheme.

'Guarantees were just not on the table that week – and nor were they going to be,' says a former director.

> That's a myth. We discussed guarantees endlessly but we kept coming back
> to the same issue: we would have run slap into state aid and the government
> could not be seen to be favouring one institution over another. The
> US had the FDIC, which is an independent body, but the UK doesn't
> work that way. Guarantees were just not available.

They also discussed dropping the main deal and just bidding for HBOS's branch network, which would at least have kept the ATMs working and salaries paid. But there were big obstacles there too. In October 2008, HBOS was still an independent entity with its own board and shareholders, and the government could not legally segregate the assets, selling the profitable branch network to Lloyds or Standard Chartered and keeping the bad bits – it didn't own them and would have had to nationalise

HBOS first, a process which would have taken months. Even then the government would have been legally required to hold an auction and there simply wasn't time for that. Later, when they learned about Standard Chartered's proposals to pay a nominal £1 for the HBOS branch network, the Lloyds executives wondered how Mervyn Davies seriously thought he would be able to buy it. It was all so politically, legally and practically unfeasible that the debate moved on.

The possibility of having one final go at raising new capital privately was also debated at the board meetings that week, but that didn't work either: Merrill had already cast the net wide and found no takers. The capital markets were closed and big investors were not terribly interested in a retail bank focused just on the UK market. Barclays, because of its international spread, could perhaps do it, but not Lloyds, which was much less interesting to a Middle East fund.

There was, however, one thing Lloyds could do: renegotiate the price. The terrier-like Matthew Greenburgh was already doing the arithmetic, determined to 're-cut' the price again and relishing another fight with Simon Robey and the Morgan Stanley team. Not for the first time, Daniels was thankful to have him on his side.

. . .

Back in the Treasury once more on Friday afternoon, Daniels and Tookey were shown into a shabby second-floor room – all the rooms in the Treasury, at least to bankers used to the best, looked shabby – on a corner of the huge building overlooking Horse Guards Parade. It was to be their base for the next three days. Their first meeting was with John Kingman from the Treasury, Hector Sants from the FSA and Sir John Gieve from the Bank of England. James Leigh-Pemberton from Credit Suisse, who they all knew but hadn't expected to see there, also joined them. Kingman briefed them on what to expect over the weekend when, he said, they should make themselves available, preferably in the Treasury, at all times, day and night. All the banks, said Kingman, would be involved in the government's recapitalisation plans which they intended to announce before the markets opened on Monday morning. That, he said in answer to a specific question from Daniels, included HSBC and Standard Chartered – there would be no exceptions and therefore no stigma would attach to any individual bank. He did not expect the better capitalised banks to be in the Treasury over the weekend, but all the others would. Did that include Barclays, Daniels asked suspiciously? Yes, that included Barclays, one of the officials assured him.

'Everyone is taking the Queen's shilling,' Gieve chimed in cheerily.

Kingman and Sants then laid out the bare bones of their plan. Credit Suisse, acting for the Treasury, was using the stress tests to determine how much new capital each bank would need. The figures would not be negotiable – each bank would be expected to take state money or raise it themselves and have it underwritten by Sunday evening. Those were the only options. They wanted the banks in the building through most of Saturday and they expected to present the banks with the final figures on Sunday morning.

On that note, the 'quartet', as the Lloyds directors called them, left the room, presumably to brief the next bank, leaving their unwilling guests to contemplate the peeling walls and battered furniture of a meeting room which no doubt had some stories to tell. Other than the HBOS team, they never saw any other bankers that weekend, although rumours reached them from time to time that Myners was sacking Goodwin who was putting up a rearguard fight. Someone popped in to give them the news that HSBC would not be in the building – Stephen Green, at Gordon Brown's personal request, had done his bit and transferred a nominal £700 million from one of HSBC's hidden pots in the Far East to recapitalise its already well-stocked London bank (the former Midland). Standard Chartered's Peter Sands would not be in the Treasury either, and nor would Santander which was regulated in Spain. Nationwide had agreed to raise a token amount of new capital and was also excused. That just left four of them – or so they thought.

'So much for everyone taking the Queen's shilling,' remarked Tookey sourly.

Daniels had a real problem with that. There were now two classes of banks emerging, the rich and the needy, those who would not be forced to take the Queen's shilling and those that would. He hated being in the needy camp, his only consolation being that he believed Barclays was in there too. He was – just about – prepared to share the stigma of a state bailout with Barclays. He was not prepared to be lumped in with two bankrupt banks. Lloyds, he insisted, must be clearly differentiated from the others. 'He could well have walked out if he had known Barclays wasn't there,' says one of his executive team.

> The stigma factor was enormously important to Eric, who had lived through all the 'Plodding Black Horse Bank' jibes and headlines for years and was now being proved right. Lloyds was much stronger than Barclays which was in the high-risk investment banking businesses that Eric had shunned and which were now unravelling. If Lloyds needed state aid then Barclays needed twice as much – and deserved to be in there with the bad boys more than Lloyds ever did. On Friday night, before we got down to the hard stuff, that would have been a deal-breaker for Eric.

When they arrived in the Treasury again the following morning, Daniels and Tookey were particularly anxious to establish that Barclays was there too. They were assured it was. 'We were told absolutely clearly that

Barclays, HBOS and Royal Bank of Scotland were in the building that morning,' says one of the Lloyds executives, 'and that they were having the same conversations. This quartet were in and out of the room at different times, and we believed they were simply moving from one bank to the other.' Treasury staff took great care that the bankers never saw each other, putting them on different floors in different parts of the building.

In fact Barclays was not in the Treasury that weekend at all – and, although Gieve and some of the others seemed to believe it was, it was never going to be. Of all the bank CEOs, John Varley found the concept of 'part-nationalisation' the least palatable, arguing that it would damage the bank's standing in international markets, particularly the US where it had just bought the remains of Lehman, as well as the Middle East. Long before any of the other banks had even thought about tapping the Middle East for fresh capital, Varley had given the job to Roger Jenkins, the highest-paid banker in Barclays – and Britain – in 2005, when he reputedly earned between £40 million and £75 million. Jenkins was renowned for his Middle East connections and in June, when RBS and HBOS were struggling with their rights issues, Barclays had raised £4.5 billion of new capital from sovereign funds, including the Qatar Investment Authority. When Lehman emerged as a serious takeover prospect, Jenkins had gone back to his sources, including the ubiquitous HBJ of Qatar, to arrange the finance for it. In the event, due to Darling and the FSA's opposition, he hadn't needed it, but that money was still on the table. Now, Jenkins, assisted by the glamorous deal-doer Amanda Staveley, was told to go back for a second round and the Qataris and Abu Dhabi had again responded favourably. On Friday, Varley called Sants to tell him Barclays had raised £7 billion in new capital, the figure the FSA required to meet its stress tests, and wouldn't be coming to the Treasury that weekend. On Saturday and Sunday, while Daniels, Hornby and Goodwin were trapped in their uncomfortable government offices, the Barclays CEO remained in

One Churchill Place, the bank's 32-storey headquarters in Canary Wharf, with his lawyers and advisers.

Myners and Kingman already had their hands full with RBS, HBOS and Lloyds, and when Sants told them Barclays had found a private sector solution, they were sceptical but basically left it to him. 'The Treasury officials accepted that, but with some reluctance,' says a former FSA official. 'Hector made that judgement with John Varley and if he had come up with a different answer, I think the Treasury would have been happier.'

One of the Treasury advisers confirms that.

> We always had the impression – although we were never told – that both the Governor and the Treasury wanted Barclays also to receive a capital injection from the state because they wanted all the banks to be in there. The Governor had a very pessimistic view of the amount of capital that was being required and wanted more to be injected than was the case that weekend. It really surprised us when Barclays was allowed to do its own thing.

Gordon Brown, however, took a loftier view. 'The Treasury was worried about Barclays withstanding the pressure,' he wrote. 'In discussion with them it became very clear that taking government money was anathema, and they were prepared to pay the price for capital from elsewhere to avoid that.' Brown was completely relaxed about it. 'As far as I was concerned, the less government money used the better.'

Sants was the only official – or minister – who had any contact with Barclays that weekend and it is possible that Gieve and others believed they were physically in the Treasury negotiating with the FSA. In fact, all the discussions were done over the telephone, mostly from Sants's Oxfordshire home. Unlike Daniels, confronted every hour or so by the quartet or some of the other officials, Varley had no face-to-face meetings with anyone from the Tripartite that entire weekend.

As events turned out, Barclays avoided the stigma of taking state money, but attracted stigma of another kind which arguably has done it far greater damage. In 2012, the Financial Conduct Authority, successor to the FSA, launched an investigation into Barclays over the non-disclosure of the hefty fees paid to Qatari investors – £322 million – which also became the subject of an investigation by the Serious Fraud Office and a legal action brought by Staveley for her share of the fees. It also proved very expensive money, raised at a 40 per cent discount (as opposed to the 8.5 per cent discount the Treasury was prepared to offer). What seemed a smart move at the time came back to bite Barclays later.

.   .   .

The first nasty surprise of this eventful weekend for the Lloyds executives came in mid-morning on Saturday when the 'quartet' arrived in their room, accompanied by several of the advisers, including George Maddison of Credit Suisse. Sants, who had finally driven in from his Oxfordshire home, explained that the new stress tests would require Lloyds to raise more than the £4 billion of new capital they had discussed the day before. They would give them the final figures the next day, he added.

Tookey was perplexed. Lloyds had done its own stress tests, he charged, and had checked them with the FSA just forty-eight hours before. How come the number had increased again? What had changed between Monday and Saturday? Or, indeed, Friday and Saturday?

Back in his office in Gresham Street – they were not continually in the Treasury – Tookey ran the numbers again and then called the FSA demanding to know where this new figure had come from and how it had been arrived at. He got nowhere. 'It's not our figure,' said one of the FSA officials, 'it's coming from the Treasury. But that's the number.'

Tookey stamped into Daniels's office to complain: 'They just won't talk, there's no dialogue – and they say "it's not our number". So the regulators, the people who should know our balance sheet best, are basically saying this is not our number! Well, whose number is it?'

The number had actually originated from the Credit Suisse team in the Treasury who were already arriving at some early, still rough, conclusions. To the Lloyds team it seemed deliberately designed as further pressure to go ahead with the HBOS deal. 'I think it was a put-up job,' says one of the senior Lloyds directors.

> They screwed us – and it was the only point of time when I think we got screwed – and they did it because they wanted us to do the HBOS deal and leave us nowhere else to go. The assumptions behind those stress tests were wrong. If we had only had to raise £1.5 billion, we might well have been able to do it. But we were never going to do five or seven in the markets that week.

Meanwhile back in the Treasury, blood was beginning to flow. Gordon Brown had personally given the order that Goodwin should be sacked, preferably without compensation, but that was not proving such a simple task. In a letter to John McFall, chairman of the Treasury select committee, Tom McKillop said he already warned Myners 'that Sir Fred's pension benefit would be the sensitive issue and that it would be "enormous"' if he was forced to leave. Goodwin, he pointed out, was legally entitled to a pension pot of £15–20 million and an annual pension of £703,000 which he could start drawing at age fifty after only ten years with the bank. On Sunday afternoon, according to McKillop's account, Myners agreed the terms of the pension as a condition for firing Goodwin (Myners, seriously embarrassed by the accusation, denied this version, insisting he had been kept in the dark about the pension arrangements). As for McKillop himself, he accepted he would have to go too but felt he should remain as chairman until things settled down a bit, and Myners reluctantly agreed. Myners also met Dennis Stevenson who, according to the minister, told him that if the government became a shareholder in HBOS he would not tolerate any interference. He too was told he must go. Hornby, also on the defenestration list, would be dealt with separately by Lloyds. So that was the lot – for now.

Early on Sunday morning Andy Hornby called Hector Sants on his mobile phone to ask him what he might look forward to during the day. He expected to catch him in the Treasury but Sants cheerfully confessed he was taking a walk along the river in Oxfordshire to 'clear my head' after too many late-night sessions. 'See you in the Treasury later,' he said, leaving Hornby none the wiser.

At nine o'clock Leigh-Pemberton, Maddison and the Credit Suisse team, after again working through the night, presented their detailed recommendations to Myners and Kingman. Leigh-Pemberton told them they had been so shocked by the state of RBS's finances that they were struggling to arrive at a meaningful figure for new capital. 'We think this is a minimum of £10 billion and maybe £20 billion but we can't tell after just thirty-six hours,' said one of the Credit Suisse team. 'We'll go with the ten and put in the other ten later if we have to,' replied Myners. But, as Credit Suisse went into more detail, he changed his mind – they would need £20 billion after all.

When it came to HBOS, Credit Suisse suggested that in discussions with Lloyds it was important to give the impression that there was a 'standalone' solution available for HBOS, even if there wasn't – or at least a palatable one. They reckoned it gave them just a little bit more leverage in what they expected to be a tough negotiation.

'No one, from Darling down, wanted to go the standalone route for HBOS, which could never have worked,' says one of the advisers. 'But we wanted to persuade Lloyds that it was an option.'

It wasn't much of an option but the government didn't have many that weekend. 'The deck of cards we were all working with,' says the City adviser, 'was that a standalone Lloyds got state capital and HBOS got nationalised. And the second option was that Lloyds and HBOS came together and got less state capital – but they still got state capital. There was no option without state capital.'

Credit Suisse's proposal was that HBOS should be offered £13 billion of new capital if it stayed independent – although they knew there was no chance of that – or £11.5 billion if the two banks merged. Lloyds should be offered the reciprocal of that – £7 billion as a standalone, or £5.5 billion if it merged, giving it a £1.5 billion incentive to go through with the merger. A joint Lloyds-HBOS would therefore get £17 billion of new state capital on terms which would be far more attractive than they could get in the market – if they could get anything at all.

On that basis the government would end up with 43.5 per cent of the shares of Lloyds-HBOS, comfortably below the critical control level which was important to both sides. It would hold 65 per cent of RBS (later raised to 81 per cent).

Despite Daniels's recommitment to the bid just a few days before, Myners and the officials were still half-expecting Lloyds to walk away from the HBOS deal at the last moment, and in the Treasury that Sunday morning they anxiously discussed ways of persuading it to stay in. On Friday, Daniels had presented Myners with a list of points which, he said, he was 'uncomfortable with' and that he wanted resolved. They included government interference in bank policy, executive remuneration and bonuses, the dividend, forced lending to small businesses on uncommercial terms and Brussels. They also included the issue of 'stigma' which Daniels kept coming back to again and again – for the sake of its future reputation (and his own) Lloyds must not be dumped in with the losers. If every bank was in the same boat, there was no stigma. But

if there were just two, RBS and Lloyds/HBOS, it would take a generation to recover from. And for a chief executive of one of the banks, there
might be no way back.

Myners's reaction to the list was unequivocal. 'It was: "I hear you, I
understand you, but let's get this merger done first and then we can deal
with them next week",' says one of the Lloyds executives.

On Sunday morning Daniels brought along Jeremy Parr, one of the
senior partners at Linklaters, to the Treasury to try to formalise some
of the many loose ends. They met with Myners and Tom Scholar and
tried to address the items on Daniels's list. 'You have to give me an
explicit promise that the government is not going to interfere in the
running of the bank, including executive bonuses, and that you will
sort out Brussels,' Daniels said. The Treasury men appeared sympathetic – but insisted the minor issues would have to wait. Liquidity,
they pointed out, was now being offered on a colossal scale to all parties – 'we forced everyone to take liquidity in order not to name and
shame any one particular bank', said a Treasury adviser later. But the
same was not true of state capital.

'By that stage things were so frenetic and the atmosphere in the Treasury was one of "the world is coming to an end", that there was no choice
but to let it go,' says a Lloyds executive. 'On Sunday it was all "we need
your help". By Tuesday it would be "you're the bad boys who caused this
crisis and we're not going to give you another thing". In just two days
the whole attitude changed. And on Sunday morning we didn't expect
that. Nothing happened in between for us to deserve it.'

Before they met the banks Credit Suisse felt obliged to raise the competition issue with the Treasury officials. The government was about
to sign up to the creation of a banking group which would dominate
many sensitive areas of finance for individuals and small businesses. 'Are
you sure you want this to happen?' George Maddison asked. 'Because it

might suit you now but, as our client, we are just pointing out that you will have created something that would not have been created in normal times – and you're going to have to manage it.'

That went down badly. 'Everyone said, no, no, this is going to happen,' said one of the advisers present.

> The Prime Minister, the Chancellor, the Governor and the FSA want this to happen. And in an environment where everything was happening so quickly, that was just taken as a given. It was a matter of national interest that it did – we all felt that, even the bankers. This had gone well past being just another commercial transaction – that was the mood in the Treasury that weekend.

. . .

The meetings with the individual banks got under way on Sunday in mid-morning, starting with RBS. Myners now came into his own, his pugnacious, no-nonsense style cowing even the toughest of the bankers. He made it clear that nothing was for negotiation: this was the government imposing a solution on the banks. When they protested he responded angrily, 'Don't give me any of that banker's crap!' Goodwin emerged from his session to complain: 'It's a drive-by shooting', a phrase which caused great hilarity among the officials (and the press) for months afterwards. HBOS received much the same treatment.

'Paul played a blinder that weekend,' said one of the advisers who didn't like him but came to admire his negotiating strategy. 'And he probably saved Her Majesty's government a lot of money.' The bankers at the receiving end of his behaviour were less generous: 'He was a real bully,' says one of the Lloyds men, 'just throwing his weight around and making promises he could never keep just to get the deal done'.

Blank arrived in Whitehall early and he and Daniels, who desperately needed a cigarette, took a stroll around St James's Park to discuss how to handle the Treasury meeting later in the morning. At that moment they held the fate of HBOS in their hands, and with it, perhaps, the whole banking system which was so close to the edge. If HBOS went down, they were both aware, all the other banks – including Lloyds – were going to suffer from its inevitable nationalisation. That would have done Lloyds shareholders no favours. And neither of them wanted to be remembered as the men who helped trigger the biggest collapse in financial history.

An hour later, joined by Tookey, they were in the Treasury facing Myners and Kingman with other officials and advisers grouped around them. Myners started by reiterating the government's intention to announce 'specific and comprehensive' measures to ensure the stability of the UK financial system and to protect savers, depositors, businesses and borrowers. The FSA, the Bank of England and the Treasury had been working with advisers to produce detailed figures for the new capital required by each bank. He was careful to emphasise that they had the choice either to raise it themselves, in which case it had to be fully underwritten by six that evening, or accept it from the state.

The government, he emphasised, would not be a permanent investor in the banks and intended to sell its shares when markets improved. In the meantime, Lloyds would pay no future dividends without Treasury approval. Executive bonuses for the past year could still be paid but the bulk of them would have to be in scrip form – cash could only be paid where it was unavoidable because of contractual obligations. Bonuses going forward would be strictly limited. There was another nasty pill for the Lloyds team to swallow: 'We cannot take the risk of this deal going off,' said Kingman, 'so the material adverse change condition will have to go.' If Lloyds wanted to renegotiate the price, he could not stop them, but they must do it by close of play. After that there would not be another chance.

George Maddison got the job of taking the Lloyds team through the recapitalisation figures, which he knew they were not going to like. As a standalone bank, he said, Lloyds would be required to raise £7 billion of new capital, but if it merged with HBOS it would need only £5.5 billion, £1 billion of which would be in the form of preference shares. The equity would be provided at a small discount (8.5 per cent) on the closing prices: 173.3p for Lloyds, 113.6p for HBOS. So a joint Lloyds/HBOS would be receiving £17 billion of new Tier 1 capital, £13 billion of it in equity, at terms they could not possibly match in the market. The five-year preference shares would have a coupon of 12 per cent, a penal rate designed to persuade the banks to buy them out as soon as possible.

The result would be that if Lloyds stayed on its own, the government would own 42.5 per cent of it, and slightly more if it merged.

Tookey was the first to break the stunned silence. What was the logic behind making Lloyds take more as a standalone bank, he demanded angrily? 'We buy something more risky and you make us raise *less* capital?' Surely the figures should be the other way around?

He was also incensed by the manner in which the figure kept increasing. On Monday, he charged, Lloyds was told by the FSA it would need £1.5 billion. On Friday the Bank of England said the figure was £3 billion which was increased to £4 billion on Saturday and now, on Sunday, it was £7 billion, or £5.5 billion if they merged with HBOS – 'and we have to find it today when the markets are shut. And not just because it's Sunday!'

From his Oxfordshire home, Sants tried to explain that the government wanted to build a 'confidence premium' into capital ratios with a 'sensible' level of capital going forward as a cushion against a crisis. That would mean all the banks raising more capital than they had previously planned. Tookey continued to press him to justify his figures until Sants finally gave up. 'I don't know,' he replied in answer to a particularly testing question. 'Ask George Maddison, he's done the work.'

Maddison took Tookey down the corridor to explain that the calculations for the joint bank took account of the £1.5 billion a year of synergies
Lloyds had publicly forecast, which, he said, meant it would need less
rather than more capital. 'It takes account of the very significant savings
you will be making if you do this deal.'

Tookey couldn't see it that way and the two argued for most of the
afternoon (and still do). 'Somehow it was always slightly misconstrued,'
Maddison said later. 'He thought we were doing arm-twisting to get him
to do the deal when actually we intended the reduced contribution to
be a helpful gesture.'

When they broke to consider the government proposal, Blank tried
to calm Tookey down. 'As I see it,' he said,

> we are being told there is a bit of capital for us, and a lot of capital for
> HBOS. The sweetener for us, which is a huge stick to do the deal, is that
> if we buy HBOS we will take less money than if we don't. And we can't
> raise that kind of money by six o'clock tonight. So we are almost doubling
> our market cap at an 8.5 per cent discount, whereas out in the market we
> would pay a discount of at least 40 per cent – if we could get it.

Put that way, it didn't seem such a bad deal – and it was the only one
available. They trooped back in to accept the terms.

·   ·   ·

Back in the City, Matthew Greenburgh and William Chalmers of
Morgan Stanley, HBOS's adviser, began the task of renegotiat-
ing the terms for the second time in a month. At the last market price
of 189p per Lloyds share, the value of the existing offer was 158p per
HBOS share, which was well above the 123p level in the market and a

hefty premium on 113.6p, the price at which the government was putting in new money. Greenburgh reckoned a more realistic price, given HBOS's perilous situation, should be around half that. Chalmers's senior colleague from Morgan Stanley, Simon Robey, was still in the Treasury but hurried across to the HBOS office where, for the next six hours, he and Greenburgh slugged it out. 'Matthew and Simon were a long way apart, which is where they should have been if they were doing their jobs,' says one of the other advisers. 'But it was getting pretty late and everyone in the Treasury was getting very twitchy as the discussions dragged on.' Myners asked Leigh-Pemberton and Maddison to get involved but the tenacious Greenburgh was not budging. A furious Robey tried to tell him this was a national emergency and the deal had to get done that night. 'Come on Matthew, let's think of the bigger picture,' he urged. 'I'm negotiating on behalf of my client,' Greenburgh retorted, 'not the national interest.'

As the talks dragged on, Stevenson, Hornby and the Morgan Stanley bankers broke off to consider another possible choice: could they abandon Lloyds and go back to the Treasury to ask for more state money? 'It's surreal to think now that we had that discussion,' says one of the Morgan Stanley team. 'We're not idiots, and I can't believe now that we did that. But everybody was exhausted and I think we were all a bit unnerved by the speed and the seriousness of the situation. And Andy felt he should at least explore it.'

Greenburgh and Robey were still at it at nine when Blank, who had already briefed the Lloyds board, called Daniels to say they had to get an agreement that night and it was getting late. The Chancellor had to be briefed and probably even the Prime Minister who would be flying back late that night from a crisis meeting of European leaders in Paris where he spent the day trying to persuade them of the need for a joint plan to rescue the banks.

Greenburgh and Robey finally settled on 113.6p, the same price the government was injecting its new capital at and probably the price Greenburgh had in mind all the way through. That equated to 0.603 of a Lloyds share, a cut of 25 per cent from the September (already revised) offer. Blank called Downing Street, as promised, to pass on the news and once again it was running on Robert Peston's blog within minutes, and the BBC News half an hour later. 'His source was someone very senior,' says one of the advisers,

> and it was unnerving. People speculated it was the Prime Minister himself and others that it was Shriti. But there were plenty of suspects and we all chatted to him. I learned a lot. We'd say 'Robert, what are you hearing?' and we all shared information. But, my goodness, those leaks were damaging.

The torrid weekend still had some twists left in it. After the deal had been agreed, Simon Robey called Daniels to ask him could he come across to his office to discuss a delicate matter. Daniels, surprised by this request from HBOS's senior adviser, agreed and a few minutes later Robey was in his office. 'I know it's unconventional for advisers to see the principal on the other side,' he said, 'but can you figure out what you want to do with Andy?' Daniels was under no obligation to do anything, he added, 'but I think he'd like to know definitely if there is anything for him'.

Daniels, just leaving to go back to the Treasury where he expected to spend the rest of the night, was not unsympathetic. Originally he had planned a senior role for Hornby in the structure, maybe even deputy CEO, but that had been overtaken by the complete collapse of HBOS and by the Prime Minister's uncompromising stance to the senior managers of both RBS and HBOS. Hornby was a talented young man and could play a part in the integration of the two banks. Daniels told Robey he would try to come up with something and, in between meetings, he managed to raise the question of Hornby with Myners. The minister had just agreed that Fred Goodwin could keep his entitlement to his £700,000 a year pension and was in no mood to be generous to Hornby. Daniels was too tired to argue and realised there could be no job for Hornby in a company where the government was the biggest shareholder. But as he left the Treasury he called Robey to say he might find him a consultancy role once the dust had settled.

It was 10.30 p.m. on Sunday evening before Blank got away, but as he was driving home his mobile rang. It was Myners, still in the Treasury preparing for the announcement which would be made in the morning.

'Victor, you know we said the executives could take part of their bonuses in cash?' he said. 'Well, they can't. Can you please persuade them to take their bonuses in shares only?'

This was not what had been agreed earlier in the day but, after thinking through the consequences of state-controlled (or almost controlled) banks announcing they were paying out cash bonuses in a politically charged, anti-bank climate, the Treasury ministers had changed their minds. They were particularly concerned about RBS, where the bonuses would run into the billions (over £2 billion in fact), a potentially explosive situation when they were announced early in 2009. But they were also worried about the other banks, including Lloyds which had had a good year in 2008 and met the bonus thresholds. After a long day of often bad-tempered wrangling, Myners didn't want to tackle Daniels head-to-head and was appealing to Blank.

'Paul, we've done a deal,' Blank protested.

'Victor, I need you to do this because it's going to be very difficult otherwise and we're all going to have a big problem,' said Myners. Blank agreed to try and called Daniels.

'Eric, you're just going to have to do this. We don't really have a choice,'

Blank told him. Daniels was furious. 'They're reneging on another promise,' he said, 'and we will have two classes of banks on remuneration. We will just lose good people.' But he said he would talk to the other executives and eventually rang back to say they had accepted.

Blank called back Myners, who was effusive in his thanks. 'Victor, I'm so grateful.'

This remarkable weekend was not over yet. At four in the morning, Simon Robey was woken by his bedside phone ringing. It was Matthew Greenburgh, who told him there was a problem. The lawyers were arguing over the interpretation of one of the clauses agreed earlier in the day which was ambiguous and led to two different answers. The difference was slight, a few million pounds, but Greenburgh insisted it still had to be resolved before the deal was signed. 'Matthew was looking after his client, as he had to do,' says one of the Lloyds executives, but Robey was appalled. 'Matthew, we're trying to get these two institutions to open the ATMs tomorrow morning and stop a financial meltdown, and we can't do this – we announce in three hours!'

George Maddison was still in the Treasury when he got an angry call from William Chalmers. 'George, this is outrageous! First of all we've just agreed the offer and we took it lying down, because we had no choice. Now the boards have all gone home and you want to change it again!'

'I'm not changing anything,' Maddison protested. 'I'm just the traffic cop here.' He soon realised that Greenburgh was at the bottom of it and called James Leigh-Pemberton, who had left to walk back to his flat a few minutes before, asking him to come back to the Treasury immediately.

'George, how long is this going to go on for?' a Treasury official asked Maddison.

'We have to let it run,' Maddison replied. 'We can't do anything unless you are prepared to impose the answer.'

As the clock ticked down towards announcement time, Myners began to consider the real possibility that he might have to wake up Darling and tell him the Lloyds deal was off and the whole package was at risk. Instead, he called both Daniels and Hornby, insisting they get their acts together and find a solution.

Hornby rang Daniels. 'Look, it's your call,' he said. 'This is what we thought we'd agreed. Can you give me this one?' Daniels agreed.

At five in the morning, the Treasury team arrived in the study of No. 11 Downing Street to brief the Chancellor, who had just returned that day from an exhausting trip to the IMF in Washington and was already working on the speech he would make in the House of Commons later in the day. Darling felt he should brief the Prime Minister before the markets opened but Brown had arrived back from Paris in the early hours and only got to bed at three. No one wanted to wake him.

That task fell to Shriti Vadera who crept up the stairs to the Browns' small Downing Street flat, trying to rouse Brown without waking his wife Sarah. A few minutes later Brown appeared in his dressing gown, duly signed off on the terms agreed with the banks and went back to bed. The announcement went out a few hours later.

CHAPTER 22

RECESSION

IT WAS MONDAY morning before Eric Daniels learned the grim truth about Barclays. The headlines that day were dominated by the government's £37 billion 'rescue' of three of the country's best-known banks, the biggest in Britain's financial history. But even as that statement went out, Barclays was issuing its own triumphant press release, announcing that it had raised £7 billion from private investors and had turned down the offer of state money. 'We've made the decision,' said John Varley, 'because of the confidence we have in our capital, and we don't need to use the government facility. That view is shared by the UK authorities who have approved our capital status and capital plan.' The Treasury had insisted that Barclays, like the other banks in the bail-out, should scrap its final dividend, but to Varley that was a small price to pay for escaping the state's clutches.

Daniels could barely believe it. He had spent the whole weekend in and out (mostly in) of the Treasury under the impression that Barclays was also taking 'the Queen's shilling', and he now angrily accused ministers and officials of deliberately misleading him. 'It was inconceivable to Eric that Lloyds would need government money and Barclays would need nothing,' says one of his former colleagues. 'Eric was promised on Saturday morning that Barclays were coming in and would be part of the whole funding thing. And if he'd known they weren't, he would have seriously considered walking away.'

Barclays was initially coy about publicly revealing the sources of its funds, but did confirm that the Qataris were in there with a billion or so – the same £1 billion that Robin Saunders had hoped to pump into Lloyds from her friend Sheikh Hamad bin Jassim (HBJ) – and the extortionate terms, including the huge fees involved for Amanda Staveley, would only emerge later. Varley rubbed salt in the wound by remarking disparagingly that the commercial opportunities arising from raising money from the private sector were very different to the 'opportunities – if you can call them that – which might arise if the UK government were on our shareholder register. They are in no way comparable.'

When the Lloyds team, battered and exhausted, assembled in Gresham Street that morning, Daniels was still fuming and it took some time for him to return to his cool, professional self. There was an enormous amount of work to be done and the immediate task was to 'crank up the machine', as Blank phrased it, and let the professionals get on with the job of preparing the mountain of documentation that had to go into the formal HBOS offer document. They had just three weeks to wind up their due diligence and finish – and print – the document, which would run to 286 pages.

In the City and the rest of the country, all anybody wanted to talk about that day was the huge government bailout of the banks. The front pages and TV and radio news were dominated by it, but, in contrast to the friendly reception the original Lloyds announcement had received a month before, the public mood had turned ugly. There was a rising tide of indignation at the perception that the big banks had brought the financial system to the brink, initiating a crisis which was now plunging the economy into deep recession, destroying jobs and savings and leaving huge holes in pension funds. Most of the ire was directed at Fred Goodwin, with Dennis Stevenson and Andy Hornby close behind, and for the moment Lloyds was relatively immune, a saviour rather than a villain. But the public mood, fanned over a period of years by politicians and press – and by some of the bankers' own behaviour and their huge bonuses – had become violently anti-banks and bankers and ultimately no one was immune. It was not a good time to be a banker.

The markets initially liked the Treasury's proposed cash injection and Lloyds's shares rose 12 per cent to 212p, a bit of a recovery after their precipitous 21 per cent collapse the previous week. But the shares were soon falling again, dropping below the price at which the government had agreed to invest. Blank issued a statement assuring investors and customers that the revised deal was still a good one, adding that Lloyds's already robust financial position was 'further enhanced by today's capital raising'. The bank's customers, he added, could feel confident their money was secure: 'Lloyds TSB is and will remain a great place to bank.'

That day the US authorities unveiled their own recapitalisation plan, which Paulson and Geithner publicly acknowledged they had, at least partially, copied and adapted from Gordon Brown's version – but significantly improved on it. The British bailout amounted to about $50 billion but the Americans topped that, injecting $125 billion into nine institutions which held more than half of American banking assets. JP Morgan, Wells Fargo and Citigroup all got $25 billion in new capital; Bank of America received $15 billion; and Morgan Stanley, Goldman Sachs and Merrill Lynch (about to become part of Bank of America) got $10 billion each. They were given no choice. Hank Paulson assembled the CEOs in the US Treasury's historic conference room in Washington and told them the US government was going to take shares in all of them, adding bluntly: 'We're planning to announce that all nine of you will participate.' All of them did – which meant that, unlike the British version, no stigma attached to any individual bank. Germany, France and Italy unveiled similar plans the same day and other countries soon followed, all more or less following the Brown principle.

Blank called another full board meeting for Wednesday 15 October, when he, Daniels and Tookey (who had still not been formally appointed to the Lloyds board) briefed the Lloyds directors on the events of the last momentous week. The directors had been kept in touch hourly but this was their first opportunity for a proper catch-up – and there was a lot to catch up on. Daniels had not forgotten about Barclays and let rip his still smouldering anger. He had been given assurances by the government, he told the board, that they would clearly differentiate Lloyds from the others. Instead, he said, they had been 'lumped in' with the bad banks that had to be bailed out, and the American authorities had handled it much better, imposing fewer penal terms and avoiding stigmatisation of any individual bank.

But he had more pressing concerns. Lloyds branches, Daniels reported, were already fielding calls from bewildered shareholders, employees and customers demanding to know what it all meant for them. Was the bank safe? What about their savings? Why did Lloyds, which they had been assured repeatedly was a strong and well-capitalised bank, need government assistance, and would this mean it would lose its triple-A rating? Staff wanted to know what it meant for their jobs, pay and their bonuses. He was doing his best to reassure both customers and staff but it was not proving easy.

The share price that day dipped to 146p, its lowest level since the 1980s, another blow for shareholders who had also just lost their dividend. Income funds, among Lloyds's biggest shareholders, were turning sellers. Daniels told the board he was in discussions with Myners and Kingman in the Treasury about lifting the dividend constraints and it was agreed that anyone else with government contacts should join in to help. Sandy Leitch was a friend of Darling and offered to take it up with him; Blank agreed to raise it with the Prime Minister as soon as he could get an appointment.

Several directors brought up the issue of competition, and the strength of the assurances the bank had received on that front. Were they cast-iron? Did they have it in writing? The OFT, simply doing its duty under the existing legislation, had already given its view that an inquiry into the merger was warranted; however, Peter Mandelson as Business Secretary had the power to overrule it, which he intended to do, on public interest considerations.

The existing conditions which would allow Mandelson to intervene were restricted by legislation to national security and media mergers (Mrs Thatcher had famously allowed Rupert Murdoch to buy Times Newspapers in 1980 on the grounds that *The Times* would have gone under if he hadn't). There was no public interest condition that covered banks, so the resourceful Treasury officials invented a new one: 'the stability of the UK financial system'. However, that needed parliamentary approval which would have to be rushed through both houses at near-record speed. The task fell to the new Business Secretary.

Although he had brought himself up to date with his usual diligence, Peter Mandelson had taken no part in the original competition discussions and only arrived in government three weeks after the Spencer House evening. He was therefore faced with what he called a 'force majeure' and was basically told that the Prime Minister had already taken the decision and he must get on with piloting it through Parliament. Mandelson had no problem with that – he had already decided it was the right thing to do anyway. 'I never had any doubts about it,' he said later. 'As far as

I was concerned, it was a done deal.' This applied also to the European issue – Mandelson, better versed in the ways of the European Commission than anyone else in the Labour government, saw it as essentially a British matter. There was, he believed, no reason why the Brussels officials should intervene and it never occurred to him until later that they would. He and the Treasury officials were as one on that.

But the creation of a super-bank, which is what a combined Lloyds-HBOS would be, could not just be nodded through without at least a token resistance. Within a few days of taking on his new role, Mandelson got a message from Denise Kingsmill requesting an urgent meeting. They were old friends and Kingsmill, who now acted as an adviser and consultant (RBS was among her clients), was genuinely pleased to see him back in government where, she told him, she heartily approved of the way 'Gordon and Alistair are tackling the banking crisis'. Her main point, however, was to remind him that she had chaired the Competition Commission inquiry into Abbey National which had turned Lloyds down. She gave Mandelson a copy of her report, urging him to read it, particularly the references to Lloyds's large share of current accounts (over 30 per cent). The banks, she pointed out, made no money at all from current accounts but they were their entry point into the market and their business model was based on cross-selling other products which were sometimes inappropriate for customers – particularly PPI. She wasn't against the merger, she said, but she suggested Mandelson seek pre-merger undertakings from Lloyds not to exploit its position. He should also revisit it once the crisis had subsided.

On 15 October the newly ennobled Lord Mandelson stood up in the House of Lords to deliver his maiden speech. Mandelson, in or out of power, was a magnet for press and political attention, and most of the parliamentary sketch writers, who seldom visited the Lords, were in the press gallery to witness his return. 'The business which Lord Mandelson had arrived to transact', remarked the *Daily Telegraph* sketch writer Andrew Gimson the next day, 'did not sound very promising as given on the order paper: Enterprise Act 2002 (Specification of Additional Section 58 Consideration) Order 2008. But this meant giving the government the power to sanction the merger between Lloyds TSB and HBOS, so it is actually very topical.'

In fact the subject of the banking merger was almost submerged in Mandelson rhetoric as he presented the house with a *tour de force* of his family history, reminding their lordships that his grandfather, Herbert Morrison, had made his maiden speech in the Lords fifty years before and that his father 'was not above driving his car into the precincts of Parliament, although not a member'. It was rousing stuff and the peers loved it, particularly his blatant flattery: 'One of the great privileges of being a member of your lordships' house is the richness of the political experience gained from the decades and available for our debates today,' he said. The *Guardian*'s sketch writer, Simon Hoggart, acidly summed it up: 'Nominally [Mandelson] was moving the order that will allow Lloyds to take over HBOS. In reality, he was bailing out his own reputation.'

Lord (Gordon) Borrie, a former director general of Fair Trading, and Denise Kingsmill did manage to tackle him on that issue but no one could finesse him that day. 'Lord Mandelson assured us in his most mellifluous tone that if the merger goes through, "We will not relax our vigilance when it comes to the proper protection of consumers",' wrote the *Telegraph*. 'With his return, we can enjoy once more the pleasure of watching a great spin bowler performing in front of, and indeed on, his home crowd.'

The order, giving him the power to push through the merger, passed seamlessly onto the statute book. There was no mention of Europe.

. . .

L loyds had begun its detailed due diligence work in mid-September when the HBOS deal was first announced, and the renegotiated terms and government injection made little difference to the teams hard at work in the City. The figures in the balance sheet had to be altered to reflect the new capital, but otherwise the numbers were basically unchanged. The big task was to establish just what was in the HBOS loan books, particularly the corporate side run by Peter Cummings, and that led to some interesting debates on the respective audit committees. There was still a limit to what the HBOS team could legally disclose for client confidentiality reasons, and Lloyds had to rely on the opinion of the HBOS audit committee, headed by Tony Hobson (a former finance director of Legal & General and a widely respected City figure), supported by the whole board and by the HBOS auditors KPMG, who of course had full access to all the numbers. The Lloyds team found their HBOS counterparts helpful enough but were careful about what they committed to. 'We didn't know what they knew or what they were worried about,' says a former Lloyds director.

> Dennis clearly didn't have a clue what was going on but whether Andy
> was concerned there were some big real issues, it was hard to tell. He
> might have been, but in that case he would have been wary about giving
> us information which might have allowed us to alter the terms.

'I don't think Andy knew the extent of how bad the book was,' says another member of the due diligence team.

> We did enough work to predict what the corporate losses would be, and
> we shared it with Andy who was really surprised. After just a few weeks,
> we understood the losses better than the CEO of the bank did.

But what they still did not understand was the scale and speed of the recession and its significance for asset values – and nor did anyone else.

Oddly enough, the Lloyds team found themselves developing a grudging respect for Peter Cummings, one of the few professional bankers at the top of HBOS. Although he moved in the company of billionaires, they were customers rather than friends, and he actually lived fairly modestly – by the standards of the very wealthy – in his house in Scotland. 'He had done some brilliant deals for the bank in his day,' says a former Lloyds executive who got to know him during the due diligence process,

> and my impression of him was that he had increasingly been left on his own while he was doing well, and he was allowed to get out of control. But there was nothing fraudulent in what he did. Nor was he ever a wealthy man, at least by the standards of many of his clients, or even colleagues. .

The formal offer document was due to be posted to shareholders in the first week of November, three weeks after the 'drive-by shooting' weekend, and the rush was on to complete the due diligence and the paperwork. There was obviously a great deal to get through by then but there were also plenty of experts to do the job. Truett Tate and Helen Weir had already seconded their best teams who bench-marked HBOS's mortgages and loan books against their own performance; Archie Kane brought a team down from Scotland to comb through HBOS's insurance business. Besides teams from Citigroup, Merrill Lynch and UBS, all of them advisers to Lloyds on the transaction, the auditors Price Waterhouse had a sixty-strong team working on it, HBOS's auditors KPMG had a similar number, and there were countless lawyers working on each individual aspect. All of them signed off. It was later reckoned that 5,100 man-days were spent on the exercise.

The task of coordinating the due diligence exercise was given to Stephen Roughton-Smith, Lloyds's deputy head of risk, reporting to Carol

Sergeant and Tim Tookey. Roughton-Smith very quickly found he was dealing with a moving target. HBOS's half-yearly figures, issued in September, forecast impairments of £1.7 billion for 2008, but a month later that was already out of date and, challenged by the Lloyds team and the auditors KPMG, HBOS raised it to £2.4 billion. A month later they raised that to £6 billion; the eventual figure was £12 billion.

The Lloyds people noticed a worrying divide between the HBOS people and KPMG, which they felt had probably been running for some time. 'The HBOS management were certainly towards the bullish end of the spectrum compared to their own auditors, and compared to where the Lloyds appetite would have been, which tended to be right down the middle or on the conservative side,' says one of the team leaders.

Lloyds's underestimation of the size of the holes in the HBOS balance sheet, particularly in the corporate loans book, would later become the single biggest criticism of the deal. 'Our big problem was that we were always looking at historical figures, which were already out of date by the time we got them,' explains one of the team, 'and we projected them forward on the basis of a pretty gloomy view of what was happening in the economy and what that would do for property values. What we didn't foresee was how fast and how far the economy was actually falling – those figures didn't appear until later.'

Everyone in the bank had heard the stories about Cummings's big bets on property, housebuilding and loans to tycoons, and the corporate book reflected it. It was huge, £120 billion, and Lloyds had already had to lend £7.5 billion against it just to keep HBOS afloat. However, they had insisted on substantial collateral, careful to accept only loans they were comfortable with. The question was: what else was in there? Roughton-Smith and his team sampled £30 billion of it, concentrating on the bigger exposures and grouping them into a mix of 'good', 'high risk' and 'impaired' assets. They then applied the result to the rest of the loan book and checked their figures with the HBOS senior risk managers who, after initially arguing that the impairments were too high, reluctantly agreed. When Blank asked for an update in late October, Roughton-Smith detailed the huge amount of work going on, adding, 'The HBOS people disagreed vociferously with us initially. Only gradually did they smell the coffee.'

Valuing HBOS's £4 billion portfolio of private equity investments provided the first real shock. 'We found they had often put in equity and then geared up on the equity,' says a former Lloyds director. 'The kind of stuff that never should have been done – we had some real stinkers in there.' Appropriately, this became known as the 'crock of shit portfolio'.

Roughton-Smith and the team, working on the economic forecasts made by Patrick Foley, initially did their analysis on the basis of a 1-in-15-year recession, a fall of 2–3 per cent, a pretty average economic cycle over the past fifty years – worse than 1990–91 but not as bad as 1980–81 in the early Thatcher years. Then, on 24 October, the Office of National Statistics announced that the economy had suffered its first contraction in eighteen years, falling by 0.5 per cent in the third quarter (it was later revised to -0.8 per cent). Growth in the second quarter, originally measured at a tiny +0.1 per cent, had been revised down into negative territory. The economy was now officially in a recession.

But to the Treasury, Bank of England and City economists, it still looked like an ordinary recession, a bit steeper maybe than the last one, but not as steep as several other post-war recessions. No one at this time was forecasting anything worse, but to be on the safe side the Lloyds team changed their prediction from a 1-in-15-year recession to a 1-in-25-year recession, or a 4 per cent fall in GDP, which had not happened since the first oil crisis and the three-day week in the early 1970s. On that scenario, potential impairments on the HBOS balance were revised up from £6–8 billion for 2009 to £10–16 billion. It still made the deal worth doing, but the margin was getting tighter.

Daniels, with his almost obsessively tight control of every detail of Lloyds, found great difficulty in getting his head around the degree of autonomy allowed to Cummings, which was beyond anything he had experienced. The corporate division had been the powerhouse of HBOS's growth, increasing profits from £823 million in 2001 to £2.3 billion in 2007. New loans grew at 50 per cent in 2007 and were still growing at 12 per cent up to the middle of 2008 when HBOS finally ran out of money. The faster it grew the more Stevenson, Crosby and Hornby left it alone, letting it basically manage its own risk, happy to take the profits.

Cummings's boast was that HBOS was equally prepared to lend in bad times as in good and was 'never just a fair-weather friend'. The bank's strategy was to lend into a downturn, and after the Northern Rock crash Cummings confidently asserted that 'some people look as though they are losing their nerve, beginning to panic in today's testing property environment; not us'. As the Parliamentary Commission on Banking Standards later remarked, 'The picture that emerges is of a corporate bank that found it hard to say "no".'

One of its specialties was financing management buy-outs, often investing in them alongside its clients, outbidding the big London banks for the business. Lloyds liked management buy-outs too, and they had proved very profitable, but they were much smaller. HBOS preferred more highly leveraged transactions, wonderfully profitable in the good times, but vulnerable to even a modest downturn. In the early days, Cummings had backed successful entrepreneurs who had delivered handsome returns for the bank but, driven by Crosby and later by Hornby who demanded more and more profit, he had lowered his standards and financed all sorts of fly-by-night Irish builders and dubious property developers. The Parliamentary Commission later estimated that the bank had exposure to thirty 'significant single names' of more than £1 billion each, the biggest being £2.9 billion. Several of Cummings's billionaire clients were to become minus-billionaires in the crash that followed and fourteen of the top thirty had their debt restructured. What surprised the Lloyds team, by now becoming used to surprises, was HBOS's appetite for taking these big exposures on its own book. 'Whereas our policy was to syndicate, they would take huge lines, so on some of the HBOS individual lending they were losing hundreds of millions of pounds, which in any normal banking world would have been syndicated,' says a former Lloyds executive.

Lloyds recognised some of the customers and loans as ones they had been offered and turned down – or lost because they couldn't match the terms HBOS offered – and others where they were too exposed.

> There were some risks which Lloyds had a slice of and HBOS had a slice of, and we both got hurt – so I wouldn't say for one minute that everything that Lloyds did was good and everything HBOS did was bad. The difference is that they took bigger risks, and more of them,

says the executive.

Lloyds was unable to drill down as deeply as it would have liked. 'Further work would have required detailed file reviews which were not possible because of client and commercial confidentiality,' Roughton-Smith reported to the board when he was asked for an update. He hit similar problems in valuing the joint venture portfolio which contained £2 billion of equity and £15 billion of debt, and on the international operation which had £73 billion of assets. His best answer was to sample what he could, stress-test it, talk to the auditors, make his impairments – and then take the word of the HBOS team that there was nothing else they should know about.

'We didn't own HBOS,' says one of the Lloyds team, 'so we had no rights to confidential information, and HBOS were pretty careful in their legal analysis of what they could and couldn't share with us.' The

one range of assets the team was able to examine properly was the collateral HBOS offered against Lloyds's loan. 'Our corporate teams did
a huge amount of work looking at the exposures in their corporate
book and saying we can lend on that and we can lend on this, but we
won't lend on that or on the other,' says the director. 'We put together
a package and we really thought seriously about our collateralised exposure. So if the deal didn't happen, we weren't going to be embarrassed
in any way, shape or form, by having lent in a way that would cause
us to take a loss.'

As the due diligence progressed, Daniels found himself more and
more unimpressed with the HBOS management. Stevenson, Crosby
and Hornby, he concluded, were 'talented amateurs' who should never
have been running a bank. 'You need deep professionalism, especially
in today's environment: the sophistication of financial products and the
ways in which things can go wrong are that much greater than in the old
days,' he told the Parliamentary Commission. He had decided from the
early days that very few of the HBOS team would survive into the new
regime: this was going to be a Lloyds-run operation from the beginning,
although he was still trying to find a role for Hornby.

His biggest criticism was the HBOS attitude to risk, which broke all
the banking rules and conventions. 'In HBOS [the group risk role] was
viewed more as a rotational set of assignments to round out people,'
Daniels later told the Parliamentary Commission. 'So rather than getting experts, they would bring in people as development experiences.'
Group risk directors didn't stay long at HBOS: Jo Dawson did the job
for fourteen months before she was promoted to run the insurance side.
Her successor, Dan Watkins, was there for less than a year before he too
was promoted and Peter Hickman, who succeeded him, was still learn-
ing the ropes when Lloyds arrived on the scene. Dawson later admitted
to the Commission that the internal challenge to the divisions was 'quite

low' and she felt she had 'influence rather than authority'. When he was quizzed on the fact that two successive risk directors had no specific experience of managing risk, James Crosby admitted that 'it could be characterised as bizarre'.

Tookey and his team had concluded some weeks before that there would be a 'net negative capital adjustment' of £10 billion to HBOS's financial position and nothing they had seen since had made them want to move away from that figure. That, along with the hefty impairment charges HBOS would take in its 2008 accounts, should be enough, they believed, even in an economy which was all too visibly in deep recession. 'I think we were all a bit shocked by the level and speed of the decline, and what that did to the property market,' says a former Lloyds director.

> But there was no sense from anyone that we shouldn't have done it or that it was a bad thing. There was a feeling that we've seen these things before and that it would come back pretty quickly – and although we might have to provide more, we would get it back when things turned up again.

The formal offer document was finally mailed to shareholders on 3 November 2008 incorporating HBOS's third quarter trading update which disclosed that the bank was now making a loss. Yet Stevenson down to the last remained remarkably sanguine, emphasising HBOS's 'robust capital position' and 'good growth opportunities' once it was part of Lloyds, now only two months away. It was complete pie-in-the-sky.

On 4 November it was time for the Lloyds team to brief the analysts, their first opportunity since the deal was announced. The whole executive team lined up alongside Blank, Daniels and Tookey in front of a packed room in the City. The share price had steadied in the last few weeks and was back above 200p again, and the Lloyds executives were determined to convey some of the confidence they felt in the deal. Daniels again referred to it as a 'compelling transaction' which would transform Lloyds's market position by making it number one in loans, deposits and customers in the UK; it was, he reiterated, 'a great deal for shareholders' who would be acquiring £30 billion of assets for £14 billion.

The collapse of the banking sector, and the catastrophic fall in share values, had taken the analysts as much by surprise as anyone else. Several of them had been recommending HBOS and RBS shares ahead of Lloyds TSB for years, and many millions of shares had been bought by pension and investment funds – and private individuals – on their advice. Some of the analysts in the room that morning were the same people who had raised City expectations of RBS and HBOS to absurd levels and encouraged Fred Goodwin and Andy Hornby to keep expanding long past the point of no return. Now Goodwin and Hornby were gone and Daniels, who they had underrated for years, was having his day – however briefly.

Blank and Daniels concentrated on tackling the particular concerns the analysts – and shareholders – had been raising since the deal was announced: the impact of the HBOS deal on the Lloyds capital ratios, its funding and the level of impairments. Capital was no issue Daniels insisted: following the merger and the injection of state cash, Lloyds would be 'among the best capitalised banks in the world'. On funding, the bank was actually raising money at below Libor and still had access to the Bank of England's special liquidity scheme. On the third issue, Daniels, after listing some of the due diligence work done, concluded: 'We are comfortable on the impairments.'

Tookey devoted much of his presentation to the impairment issue, telling the analysts that in the past two months Lloyds had conducted 'a thorough set of reviews, and as each review has been completed, we have been able to get significantly more comfortable'. In addition to deploying Lloyds's own specialist teams, he added, they had also used external advisers, each one testing the other.

'The bottom line,' the (acting) finance director concluded, 'is that we have conducted thorough and detailed assessments on the HBOS lending portfolios – such that the guys running the programme actually told our board that they would have seen no value in doing anything more – even with twice the number of people and twice the amount of time.' By that he meant that, because HBOS was a public company, commercial restrictions imposed a limit on how deep a due diligence team could drill down – and they had reached it.

What he didn't tell them was that Lloyds had revised the level of savings resulting from the merger to £2 billion by 2011, more than 20 per cent off a base of £9.5 billion. Up to that point the bank had only admitted publicly to 'significantly in excess of £1 billion', which was only 10 per cent, and the analysts had pencilled in £1.5 billion, the figure the Treasury had worked on. The plan involved laying off 22,000 bank employees, a figure regarded as highly sensitive for a bank where the government would be the biggest shareholder. The eventual figure would be more than twice that.

Later that day a barely noticed event took place which was to have a major impact on Victor Blank's future. The Treasury announced that it had set up a new body, to be known as UK Financial Investments Limited, or UKFI, which would hold and manage the government's stakes in the banks, including the shareholdings in Lloyds, HBOS, RBS and the carcasses of Northern Rock and Bradford & Bingley. It would be run by John Kingman, the Treasury official the bankers had got to know very well indeed over the past few weeks. Its chairman would be Philip Hampton, the former finance director of Lloyds.

. . .

t was around this time that a bizarre challenge to the HBOS takeover
appeared out of the blue. On 8 November, Dennis Stevenson received
a letter from two of the more distinguished figures of Scottish banking
in the recent past, Sir Peter Burt and Sir George Mathewson, the former chief executives of Bank of Scotland and Royal Bank of Scotland
respectively. The gist of the letter was that, with the proposed injection
of government money into HBOS, the bank didn't need Lloyds's help
anymore and would be better off on its own. 'The takeover is no longer
necessary to ensure financial stability,' it said, and Stevenson and Andy
Hornby should make way immediately for Mathewson as chairman and
Burt as chief executive. If the HBOS board refused, they added sternly,
they would call a shareholders' meeting and 'seek your and Andy Hornby's removal from the board'.

Burt and Mathewson, or the 'tartan twosome' as the financial press
called them, in their day had been iconic figures in Scotland's financial community, but were scarcely untainted by the disasters which had
overtaken the banking industry by November 2008. Burt was one of the
original architects of HBOS, which had relied heavily on the assumption that he would be chief executive of the enlarged bank; instead, he
had opted out in favour of the non-bankers, James Crosby and Andy
Hornby. As for Mathewson, following the NatWest acquisition in 2001,
he handed the executive reins of RBS to his protégé Fred Goodwin and
remained as chairman until 2006, a period when the bank made some
poor decisions and when its expansionist culture was embedded. Even
before Goodwin's destructive run of acquisitions, Mathewson's reputation was in decline as the RBS performance was subjected to closer
scrutiny. Before it announced its hostile bid for NatWest in November
1999, RBS shares stood at £35. By the time it won the three-cornered
battle three months later, the shares had halved, a level which Goodwin
would later take as his starting point when measuring the success of the

NatWest bid. In fact RBS shares only briefly rose above £21 again during Goodwin's reign, a result of his hype and the willingness of bank analysts to swallow his overly optimistic forecasts. The myth of Goodwin's genius for integration, established under Mathewson and perpetuated by a panegyric in the Harvard Business Review in 2003, only really became apparent when the crash came in 2008 and the flaws in the bank were cruelly exposed – and, much later, when the much-vaunted IT systems broke down very publicly.

From the remoteness of their Scottish fastness, these two old knights lumbered out of retirement to present themselves as saviours of their country's oldest financial institution. They claimed to have plenty of support in Scotland, where there was widespread fear of significant job losses, but in the Treasury and the FSA, who had just moved mountains to deliver the Lloyds bid, there was just bemusement. 'They had no money, no staff, an unrealistic proposal and an inflated idea of their own skills,' says an official. They also had an inflated idea of the value of HBOS whose shareholders, they said, 'should be receiving more than one Lloyds share for every HBOS share rather than the 0.605 to which Lloyds have reduced their offer'. By that stage even 0.605 was beginning to look generous.

.   .   .

It was a sober but still positive group of Lloyds directors and management who gathered for the annual away-day strategy session in the middle of November 2008. Daniels opened the meeting by announcing his top team for the merged bank, all of whom would come from Lloyds. Hornby would be offered the opportunity to stay as a consultant at £60,000 a month. The massive task of putting the two banks together was given to Mark Fisher, a blustery Yorkshireman whom Daniels had pinched from RBS where he had driven the integration of NatWest and the various other banks acquired along Goodwin's journey. A controversial but generally respected figure in the banking industry, he was described by *The Guardian* as 'Sir Fred Goodwin's shredder-in-chief at Royal Bank of Scotland, where he produced the savings from NatWest that earned his boss his nickname'. But he was much more than a cost-cutter and over the next four years he would earn his spurs at Lloyds where he successfully integrated two very different cultures and IT systems.

The 2008 strategy session was probably the most important Lloyds had held. Blank and Daniels were determined to keep the mood upbeat even though, as Daniels said in his opening remarks, in the past year they had all been through 'a full-blown crisis which has threatened the very foundations of our financial system'. But, for a strong bank like Lloyds, that opened up opportunities too, he added, the most obvious being HBOS, which would transform the bank 'and accelerates our thinking'.

The success or failure of the HBOS acquisition, everyone was aware, now hung on the state of the economy and therefore on property and asset prices. Every percentage point fall in GDP meant several billion off the value of HBOS's investments and loans, and Lloyds's balance sheet was being hit hard too. Patrick Foley, in his economics role, had become more pessimistic, but not significantly so – he expected GDP to fall by a further 0.5 per cent in the final three months of 2008 on top of the 0.5 per cent already recorded for the third quarter but the economy, he predicted, should be coming out of recession by mid-2009. That was very much in line with the views of other economic forecasters, very few of whom were predicting anything worse.

Unless the forecasts were wildly out (which of course proved to be the case), Lloyds could ride out the storm comfortably enough. Tookey was still forecasting an underlying profit for 2008 of £3.7 billion for Lloyds, much the same as Helen Weir had predicted six months earlier, off which he took £107 million for losses on Lehman, £170 million for the Icelandic banks and £44 million which they had been obliged to plough into Bradford & Bingley at the behest of the FSA. Then there was a provision for the controversial payment protection insurance (PPI) of £90 million, the first of many (it would eventually cost Lloyds more than £15 billion). The big blows, however, were 'market dislocation', the effect of volatile market conditions on asset prices, which had to be 'marked to market', and the impact of the stock market fall on the value of the Scottish Widows portfolio, which Tookey put at £1.3 billion. That left a 'headline' profit, the figure that would be announced, of £1.4 billion, two-thirds below the 2007 level, but still far from disastrous, particularly as most of the impairments were only paper losses which should come back when markets did.

Given any kind of recovery in 2009, Tookey reckoned Lloyds on its own would make £3 billion, double the headline 2008 figure, and £3.7 billion in 2010. Even on a 1-in-25-year recession, the most pessimistic of Foley's scenarios, profits would still be £1.9 billion in 2009 and recover to £2.8 billion in 2010. In the autumn of 2008, that looked like a very healthy bank.

Then Tookey did the same exercise for HBOS, whose revenues were almost exactly the same as Lloyds – £11.7 billion – and which had declared a profit of £5.5 billion in 2007, well above anything Lloyds had ever delivered. Impairments were obviously going to be much larger and he allowed for nearly £14 billion over the next three years, twice the Lloyds figure. That meant that HBOS would declare a small loss – £660 million – in 2008 but be back in profits in 2009 and by 2010 would be making £3 billion. These forecasts, which were to prove wildly over-optimistic, were based on figures that HBOS had approved and which Tookey had revised sharply downwards. When cost savings of £2 billion a year were added in, the new Lloyds Banking Group should be making profits of £7–8 billion by 2010. That was, as Blank summed up at the end of the meeting, 'a very big prize'.

.   .   .

On 19 November, Lloyds shareholders gathered in the cavernous Scottish Exhibition and Conference Centre on the banks of the Clyde for a meeting to approve the HBOS acquisition. It was scheduled to last only two hours but seriously overshot as Blank and his board came under fire on issues which ranged from the wisdom of the HBOS deal to why there had been no free parking for the meeting.

The timing of the meeting was terrible. Just two days earlier, the banking sector had suffered yet another wave of selling, with Lloyds shares sinking by more than 10 per cent to 149p, well below the rights issue price they were there to approve (all the directors had committed to taking up their rights). The trigger was a bearish research report from Citigroup which analysed the performance of the banking sector during previous periods of financial stress. Its conclusion was grim: 'Applying even the least damaging of these episodes (Hong Kong 1997–2002) would see loan books halve and earnings, equity and operating profit all fall 40 per cent from current forecasts,' the analyst, Simon Samuels, warned.

Some of the Lloyds shareholders had travelled from as far as Devon to question their chairman and board, and Blank, after setting out the case for the merger, wisely let them have their say. These were the same people who used to cheer Pitman as he triumphantly announced yet another hike in the dividend but now they had no dividend at all and they were intent on venting their spleen. 'This board will collectively be putting its head in a noose if this takeover proceeds,' said one man bluntly, while another suggested it was unwise for the board to compromise the bank's success by buying 'a very large failed bank'.

Blank and Daniels did their best to defend the deal but when one shareholder, less polite than the others, alleged that the 'deal was cooked up at a cocktail party – and most of us think that it stinks', Blank couldn't help reacting. 'What you say is just untrue,' he snapped back. 'Discussions have been going on for some years.' It was early afternoon before he wearily called a halt and, with the big institutions comprehensively out-voting the smaller investors, the deal was overwhelmingly approved by shareholders representing 96 per cent of the votes cast.

Three weeks later, on 12 December 2008, Dennis Stevenson had to go through a similar exercise, except his was worse. HBOS shares had fallen another 20 per cent that morning, dragging the whole market down with them, after it revealed that its write-downs for 2008 alone would now be £8 billion, eating into the £12 billion of new capital the government had provided. Mathewson and Burt by then had very quietly folded their tents and retired from the field, congratulating – without irony – Victor Blank for striking what 'may well be the deal of the century'.

For once, Stevenson was contrite: 'I should say how sorry I am about what has happened and in particular the impact on shareholders,' he said. He also reminded the meeting that he himself had invested £1 million in HBOS shares in the past year. 'You might ask what kind of chump is that.' Hornby, sitting beside him, could only manage a wan smile – he had lost even more. 'Andy has put every single cent of his bonuses into the company's shares – not into yachts and grand houses,' Stevenson went on. Neither of them got much sympathy from shareholders, some of whom had inherited their shares from the Halifax flotation and had lost the major part of their nest eggs after a fall of more than 90 per cent in a year. Reluctantly, they approved the Lloyds takeover – what else was there to do? They would have got nothing if the bank had been nationalised.

From November onwards, one of the big issues occupying the Lloyds team was the preference shares the government had insisted on as part of the capital package. Between Lloyds and HBOS there would be

£4 billion of them, which at a penal coupon of 12 per cent meant an annual £480 million of interest payments. 'These prefs were horrible and damaging – and expensive', said one of the finance team, 'and the first thing we decided to do was get rid of them.' Apart from the restrictions they imposed on paying dividends and cash bonuses, the major disadvantage was their impact on Lloyds's capital and thus on the bank's ability to lend, the very issue that was giving Brown and Mandelson nightmares.

The arithmetic was complicated but was set out by Daniels and Tookey in a letter to Alistair Darling and Paul Myners in December. The interest charge of £480 million a year, on the basis of a capital ratio of 10 per cent (which they were now required to hold), would support £4.8 billion of risk-weighted assets, which in turn would support nearly £25 billion of extra mortgage lending, only slightly less than the £30 billion of new mortgages the two banks lent each year. 'So the £480 million the government was bleeding out of us could have supported about a year's worth of mortgages in a normal market,' says the Lloyds director. 'And this bizarre government-chosen instrument was actually hurting the very same measure that they were trying to make the banks increase.'

The Treasury officials, not unsympathetic, had made it clear from the outset that they were perfectly willing for Lloyds to redeem the shares. At the end of October, Kingman wrote to Daniels to say that the Treasury 'will permit (and indeed will encourage) early repayment' of the preference shares, adding 'as soon as the shares are repaid, cash dividends are permitted'. Myners, on the other hand, enjoyed teasing the bankers. 'You have to remember we have mixed feelings about getting rid of the preference shares – think of the schools and hospitals we could build with that,' he said one day.

'And it was like a currency to them,' said a Lloyds man, half-admiringly. 'It was their way of translating for us why our capital problem was also their problem.'

In order to repay the loan, the Lloyds executives, working with the City investment banks, explored various possible disposals, but there had probably never been a worse time since the 1930s to make disposals of banking assets than in the dying months of 2008.

In early December, Blank called Downing Street to ask for a meeting with the Prime Minister, their first since the Citigroup cocktail party in September which to Blank seemed such a long time ago. Oddly enough, the period since had been a halcyon two months for Brown whose reputation had never stood higher – and never would again. This short period, running from early October to February 2009 when the bank crisis was at its height, was later dubbed the 'Brown bounce', which in the space of just a few weeks had become so pronounced that Labour MPs were even suggesting Brown should dash for the polls in the spring of 2009, a year earlier than necessary.

Brown himself had never looked more prime ministerial or confident. 'In recent weeks the British Prime Minister has pulled off a remarkable feat of alchemy: the weaker the economy gets, the stronger he becomes,' wrote the *Financial Times*, quoting a Labour MP saying, 'I was standing behind him the other day and even his hair looked confident.'

There was nothing on the economic front to justify it. Government borrowing was spiralling out of control, forecast to top £100 billion in 2009; unemployment was heading towards 3 million (which it got to); the business community was complaining it could not get credit from the banks, house prices had fallen by 15 per cent in the past year, share prices had halved and the oil price had dropped from $150 a barrel to $47. Yet the worse the crisis got, the better Brown looked. 'This is a man unrecognisable from the shrunken, grey figure in the summer of 2008,' said *The Times*. Brown was even making jokes, particularly if they were at the expense of bankers. Bashing the banks was now almost a national sport and Brown indulged himself when he was speaking at a business dinner and a mobile phone rang. 'That will be another bank going under,' he quipped, bringing the house down. Bankers' bonuses were even fairer game.

As the recession deepened, so did Brown's self-confessed 'obsession' – another of them – with the lending policies of the banks, which he accused of deliberately sabotaging the economic recovery, complaining they were 'not open for business'. The unpopularity of bankers seemed to increase in proportion to the speed at which the economy was collapsing, with the mood, in the words of the *FT*, 'assuming almost the wildness of a lynch mob'. Peter Mandelson accused the banks of 'giving in to fear and cutting themselves off from customers who are viable, growing businesses' but in fact they were finding it increasingly difficult to find businesses to lend to. It was borrowers who were 'not open for business'.

Mervyn King, never a fan of bankers at the best of times, joined in the witch-hunt, warning that 'wholesale nationalisation' of the banks could not be ruled out unless they restarted lending to the credit-starved mortgage and small business sectors. 'Remember the government now has a majority holding of shares in more than one bank,' he told one of the parliamentary committees he appeared before during this period. 'It would be an extremely brave person who ruled anything out. The United States has just acquired a very significant stake in Citibank, the biggest bank in the world.' That provoked Brown, still viscerally opposed to bank nationalisation, to issue a sharp reprimand, insisting the government had no intention of going down that road. The Governor, he said, had been referring to 'an extreme circumstance where banks had ceased to function'. But at Lloyds, Daniels winced at what he perceived as King's support for government interference in the running of the banks where they would soon be the biggest shareholder. That was now only weeks away.

That was the febrile atmosphere in which Blank, about to become chairman of the biggest lender in the country, arrived in Downing Street just before Christmas 2008. He had become a bit wary of the Prime Minister, still puzzling over the speed at which the Spencer House conversation had leaked to the press. There had only been the two of them present, no one had overheard them and the only person he confided in afterwards was the tight-lipped Daniels, who had told no one.

The leak had to have come from No. 10, not necessarily from Brown himself but from his staff who wished to portray the Prime Minister as the man brilliantly orchestrating the rescue of the banks and the financial system. The apocryphal version widely carried in the press presented Brown as a decisive man of action, just the man to lead the country through its moment of crisis. But it didn't do much for Blank's reputation as a bank chairman.

He had come on a mission with a clear agenda and started by addressing Brown's 'not open for business' accusation which everyone at Lloyds found offensive. In the last year, he said, Lloyds had increased mortgages by 11 per cent and lending to small businesses by 19 per cent – a total to those two sectors alone of nearly £14 billion. The bank was currently budgeting to lend even more in 2009 and it would bring HBOS, which had been a dead weight on the economy since May when it stopped lending, back on stream as quickly as possible. That alone would provide a big boost for the economy.

But for the banks to do more they needed help, he told Brown, and there were quick wins to be made if the government was prepared to take action. Even a modest easing of the new capital requirements set by the FSA and Bank of England would have a huge impact on available lending capacity. The penal interest rate of 12 per cent on the £4 billion of preference shares which the Treasury had insisted be included in the recapitalisation package was hurting the capital base of both Lloyds and HBOS, and even if it were halved it would allow them to lend another £4 billion to small businesses, or £12 billion of prime mortgage lending.

That could be done at the stroke of a pen and the banks would still be paying more than market rate. He concluded by emphasising the importance of using the banks to revive the economy which they were handicapped from doing under the new restrictions.

What Blank could not possibly have known was that on that very day the Governor of the Bank of England was addressing the same issue in his monthly meeting with his non-executives. The authorities, he told them, according to the minutes, had now recognised 'that the desire to see banks increase their lending was in conflict with the required de-leveraging that they needed to undertake'. Reconciling that contradiction, he added, was 'the main challenge in the current debate'.

Brown ended the short meeting by asking Blank to put his arguments in writing, which he did a few days after Christmas. He could not resist a dig at Brown's continued bank-bashing: 'It is unhelpful that banks are continually being questioned in the round on their lending policies and practices,' he wrote. Lloyds, he added, felt particularly hard-done-by because its posture had always been conservative 'which is why we are able to bail out (or should I say rescue) HBOS and to continue to grow our lending'.

As the New Year approached, Blank reflected that 2008 had come in on a gloomy note and was going out on an even bleaker one. Britain's economic performance was the worst in the world, well behind the US, France or Japan, which were also in recession, and the final quarter was looking worse than any three-month period since the Great Crash. President Bush had bailed out General Motors and Chrysler and the Irish government had basically nationalised its banks, almost bankrupting itself in the process. This was no longer a 1-in-25 recession but something much, much worse. The Bank of England, in a desperate attempt to head it off, had cut interest rates to record lows and they were still falling, but that was hurting pensioners more than it was stimulating growth. In a desperate drive for revenues the Chancellor brought in a package which included an increase in the top tax rate of 10 per cent to 50 per cent, a dangerous measure going into an election but, as Ed Balls argued, it would fall mostly on the bankers who had caused the crisis in the first place. Bankers, although far from blameless, had become convenient scapegoats for the government's own failures.

The Lloyds share price had started the year at 450p and closed it at 150p, a loss of £15 billion in shareholder value. RBS, HBOS and Barclays had all lost more, but that was no consolation. What, Blank wondered, would 2009 bring?

CHAPTER 23

EXIT VICTOR

THE NEW LLOYDS Banking Group, 43 per cent owned by the British government, got off to an inauspicious start on Monday 19 January 2009. On its first day of trading its shares tumbled 30 per cent on rumours that the HBOS losses were bigger than the market anticipated and it would need more government help. In the House of Commons that day, Alistair Darling announced a series of measures designed to 'secure the two banks in which we have major stakes' and added that he would be pumping another £6 billion into RBS. In addition, and perhaps more importantly for Lloyds, he outlined the bones of a scheme, still being hammered out in the Treasury, to insure the assets of the UK banks, in return for a commercial fee, against losses above an agreed level. It was an acknowledgement that the recapitalisation measures taken in October were not enough – the banks were still in crisis.

Darling provided no figures that day, but the Tories quickly pointed to the huge amounts the scheme might involve: RBS's gross liabilities alone amounted to £1.9 trillion, dwarfing Britain's gross national product of £1.5 trillion. And the new Lloyds group wasn't far behind.

The Chancellor later disclosed that after his challenging session in the House of Commons he went straight back to the Treasury and ordered his officials to draw up contingency plans in case RBS failed – which it was still on the verge of doing, despite the huge capital injections. 'For the first time, we had to consider full nationalisation,' he admitted later. And it didn't stop there. 'What would happen', he speculated, 'if things got worse and we were required to nationalise Lloyds HBOS, or even Barclays?' The answer was that Britain couldn't afford it and international markets were already forming the same judgement, with sterling sinking to an all-time low against the euro.

That evening, in an effort to restore calm to the Lloyds share price, Sir Victor Blank appeared on the *Jeff Randall Live* programme on Sky TV, then widely watched in the business community. Randall, one of the most respected financial journalists in the business, had known Blank for years and getting him on his show on that particular day was a coup. But it didn't mean he intended to pull his punches – and he didn't.

Randall set the scene with a few typically challenging openers: 'The banks have been labelled greedy and reckless,' he said provocatively, and the Prime Minister was furious with them for not coming clean about their losses. Yet, on that very day, he had just given the go ahead to inject another 'deluge of cash' into them, the second in just three months. Finally, turning to Blank, Randall demanded,

'Tell me, Sir Victor, after all we've seen and heard today, it's pretty clear, isn't it, that this country's commercial banks have wrecked the nation's finances?' Blank had not come to the studio to defend the whole British banking community but he could defend Lloyds which, he said, had lent more money in 2008 than it did in 2007 and would lend even more in the coming year. The interview got even tougher as it went along with the critical question coming about halfway through:

'Why don't the banks come clean?' Randall asked. 'Why are they not telling us what's really going on?' As far as HBOS was concerned, was 'everything out there now'? Blank replied that he believed it was.

'They've made three or four statements over the course of the last year explaining exactly what their financial position is.'

In his column in the *Daily Telegraph* a few days later, Randall dwelt on the interview, remarking that 'there was a time when such an assurance from a respected grandee would have calmed City nerves. No more.'

That, he added, was not a reflection on Blank, who he held in high regard – it applied to all bankers, whose popularity had sunk to an all-time low. 'It is difficult to think of more unwelcome guests at a Downing Street party than the bank bosses.' It was the first time the chairman of Lloyds had been lumped in with the failed bankers and it was not a comfortable feeling. After all, Blank felt, Lloyds had done nothing wrong and it was hard to be punished for the misdemeanours of HBOS which it had only owned since that morning.

Mervyn King that week, speaking to a group of businessmen in Nottingham, raised the anti-bank rhetoric an octave higher by warning that the recent regulatory measures were not so much designed to protect the banks from the economy as to 'protect the economy from the banks' who were holding their customers hostage. His audience applauded enthusiastically.

'The anti-bank attitude of Mervyn King coloured the whole history of British banking over this period,' says a former bank CEO.

> Look at what happened in the US and look at what happened in Europe
> – the banks took state money but there was no stigma attached because
> of the even-handed way they did it and there was never the corrosive

anti-bank feeling we have here. There was Olympic mis-management of
the economy by the government, the FSA was dysfunctional, the Bank
of England, where King and Paul Tucker were at war, was just interested
in protecting itself and it was all 'Blame the Yanks, Blame the Banks'.

On 19 January the FSA, stung by the mounting criticism of its lax regulatory regime before the crisis, delivered another blow to the already
tottering banks by announcing a new prescribed stress test regime, by far
the most onerous yet. Tim Tookey and his team were working frantically
to complete the 2008 accounts for both Lloyds and HBOS when they
got them and at first couldn't believe their eyes. They were based on a
real Doomsday scenario: house prices to fall by 45 per cent, commercial
property by 35 per cent, the recession to last for two years, inflation and
unemployment to soar and the pound to collapse. Lloyds Banking Group
held more than a third of all the country's mortgages plus a large slice of
commercial property (someone worked out its portfolio was several times
the size of British Land's, one of the biggest property companies in the
country), and the impact of the new tests would mean massive provisions.

'It demanded a staggering level of asset reduction,' says one of the
finance team, 'and it sure was going to make the banks look weak – particularly HBOS!' A gloomy Tookey began reworking his numbers which
had looked pretty bad before but now looked an awful lot worse.

· · ·

Blank, concentrating on keeping morale up among both the Lloyds
executives and board, was becoming increasingly concerned by the
effects of the pressure on his chief executive. Daniels, hard working in
normal times, now seldom left the office except to drive to the Treasury
or the Bank of England where he spent hours fighting what he perceived

(and Blank and the Lloyds board agreed with him) as increasingly iniq-uitous demands. The new FSA capital requirements, which seemed to change every other week, were playing havoc with the bank, forcing it to shrink its balance sheet by offloading huge chunks of assets at the low-est point of the markets. 'It reminds me of my days in Argentina when they were making it up as they went along,' Daniels reflected after what he regarded as yet another unreasonable requirement from the regulator.

Of all the bank chiefs, he was the most resistant to the demands from the Treasury and refused point-blank to accept any attempt at what he perceived as government interference in the running of the bank. He and Myners were now at loggerheads, with Daniels accusing the Treas-ury minister of reneging on promises made in October when he needed to get the HBOS deal done, while Myners accused Lloyds of damaging the economic recovery (which was still nearly a year away) by not lend-ing to small businesses. 'It's hard to contain Myners's ego in the whole of Whitehall,' one of his colleagues remarked sympathetically.

A particularly nasty new problem for Lloyds reared its head towards the end of January – the Treasury, despite its assurances in the autumn, had not sorted out the European competition issue after all. In late January Neelie Kroes, the uncompromising Competition Commissioner in Brussels, unex-pectedly ruled that the British government's support for HBOS qualified as state aid and therefore came under her jurisdiction, and she announced that the Commission would be investigating the monopoly implications of the merger. Suddenly Lloyds, on top of everything else, was faced with the prospect of having to reduce its market share by selling branches and whole chunks of its business. It whittled away one of the reasons for buy-ing HBOS, although in reality it was to prove not that critical.

But there were other issues too, lots of them. Daniels and the Lloyds team were still, unsuccessfully, trying to find a way out from under the penal terms of the 12 per cent preference shares which were seriously hurting the bank and reducing its ability to lend. Lloyds could not understand how ministers, from Gordon Brown down, could demand that the banks increase their lending to small businesses while at the same time require them to raise their capital ratios – the two were incompatible.

Then there were the dividend and bonus restrictions and veiled threats of nationalisation of Lloyds, which was continually being put into the same basket as RBS where it didn't belong. Almost as aggravating was the lack of confidentiality – details of every meeting with officials and ministers were sometimes running on the blogs of Robert Peston or Mark Kleinman, City editor of Sky News, within hours. More and more leaks referred to Daniels's pay package, his entitlement to a large bonus for 2008 and his lack of gratitude for taking the Queen's shilling. 'They want to put pressure on me so they can force us to accept every new demand they make,' he complained to his executives. The complaints weren't just one way: one Whitehall mandarin was heard to mutter that 'there is an awful lot of whinging from the bankers, particularly Lloyds's'. It was no fun having the government as your main shareholder.

Running into Shriti Vadera one day, Daniels criticised the Treasury's increasingly anti-bank attitude which he said was seriously hurting Lloyds.

'Can't you be a bit more emollient?' she asked him.

'Can't you be a bit more reasonable?' he shot back.

If the relationship with government was bad, it became a lot worse when Lloyds was presented with the details of the Treasury's new asset protection scheme, or APS, which Credit Suisse designed and Myners, Kingman and Tom Scholar developed in the Treasury. RBS had no choice but to accept the terms offered, putting £325 billion of its assets into the scheme on the basis that the government would cover 90 per cent of losses in excess of £20 billion. The fee was to be £6.5 billion, payable in RBS shares.

The terms the Treasury demanded from Lloyds were even more penal, with a massive fee twice as large as the RBS levy for guaranteeing fewer assets. It was also insisting on a commitment from Lloyds to lend an extra £3 billion to the mortgage markets and another £11 billion to businesses. Daniels was even further incensed when he learned that only RBS and Lloyds would be included in the scheme and that Barclays would once again elude the government net, even though its capital position too was rapidly deteriorating. To add insult to injury, the fine print in the documentation contained further curbs on executive pay, which for the Lloyds executives, entitled to hefty bonuses for the 2008 calendar year – Daniels's entitlement was nearly £2 million on top of a salary of £1.1 million – was intolerable. Daniels argued it would make it difficult to keep his best people.

The anti-banker climate was further soured by Fred Goodwin's insistence on taking his full pension – to which he was legally entitled – of £700,000 a year which an exhausted Myners, in the middle of the 'drive-by shooting' weekend, had unwisely agreed to. Andy Hornby had given up his redundancy package but Goodwin refused to budge even in the face of a violent public backlash. 'It was a major political problem for us,' said Darling afterwards. Myners finally persuaded Goodwin to reduce his pension entitlement to £400,000 but it was an episode which did lasting damage to his reputation as a competent minister. The biggest loser however was Goodwin. 'His taciturn stubbornness ensured that he became the pariah of British bankers and the focus of public anger,' wrote Darling in his account of the crisis.

Unfortunately all the other bankers also found themselves forced into membership of the Pariah Club, guilty of bringing the economy to its knees and meriting punishment rather than bonuses. The Lloyds executives felt they didn't deserve it: they played no part in the decline and fall of HBOS, and their bonuses related to the calendar year 2008, a trading period before the government became a shareholder when the bank had enjoyed one of its best-ever trading years. They had already agreed to accept most of their 2008 bonuses in Lloyds shares rather than cash. Now they felt the Whitehall mandarins had found a new lever, in the shape of the APS, to force them into abandoning bonuses to which they were legally entitled just to save the government from political embarrassment.

'If there was discomfort before, then the APS was the killer,' says one of the executive directors.

> We were basically being strong-armed into a scheme which Eric and Tim believed was unworkable and which they were using to punish us. But by that stage it was a one-sided fight – the government owned 43 per cent of Lloyds and the APS was the first time they threatened to use it.

At a board meeting towards the end of January 2009, Daniels, after a particularly rough couple of days at the Treasury, painted such a bleak picture of the poisonous anti-bank atmosphere emanating from White-hall that several of the directors began to wonder how long he could go on. Sandy Leitch was the first to raise the subject.

'Are you going to stay the course?' he asked Daniels in his direct way.

The chief executive was unprepared for the question and paused before answering. Finally he said: 'I will consider my position.'

There was a shocked silence as the directors absorbed the implica-tion of that. Leitch then put the same question to Blank who responded with a positive: 'Of course, as long as the board and shareholders want me.' But the spectre of Daniels's resignation was left hanging in the air as Blank moved the meeting on.

It couldn't rest there and after the board meeting, Blank took Daniels into his office and asked him how serious he was about resignation. In fact, Daniels, although he kept his thoughts to himself even in front of his chair-man, was serious enough to have discussed it with his wife. The constant badgering from the Tripartite and the press criticism were getting on top of him and, although he tried not to show it in the bank, he was tired and fed up with being put in the same corner as the RBS and HBOS managers.

Blank was appalled at the prospect of possibly losing his chief executive at probably the most difficult point in the bank's history. Although it was Blank who had initiated the latest discussions with HBOS, it was Daniels who had led the negotiations, battled his way through days and nights in the Treasury, planned and accounted for the synergies, presented the deal to the City and was now deep into the enormous task of integrating the two businesses. There was no obvious successor – Helen Weir might have wanted the job but she had more than enough on her plate with the addition of the Halifax branches; Tim Tookey had only been confirmed in the CFO role for a matter of weeks; Truett Tate had no experience of retail banking; and Archie Kane had recently recovered from serious cancer and in any case was not a retail banker. There were no other internal candidates and to find an outside replacement for Daniels could take months – and they didn't have weeks, let alone months.

Blank did his best to persuade Daniels to commit to staying on, stressing his obligation to Lloyds and his loyalty to his management team as well as to staff and shareholders; in desperation, when Daniels remained impassive, he even threw in the national interest, the government's reason for allowing the bid in the first place.

After a frustrating day, when he felt he was not making much impression, he called Shriti Vadera who was, he knew, probably the only minister who Daniels, although he was invariably cordial with Myners and Darling, respected and liked (although even that had been severely tested in recent weeks).

'Look, Eric is really wobbly and the Prime Minister has always said you are backing this deal and relying on us to see it through and deliver,' he told her. 'It would be wonderful if Gordon could call him and reassure him of how important he is in the scheme of things.' Vadera, equally concerned, said she would see what she could do.

She obviously did talk to Brown because on the following Saturday morning he called Blank on his mobile phone at his London home. Blank was in the bath and for a moment he considered leaping out and wrapping himself respectfully in a towel but then thought better of it. The Prime Minister couldn't see him, he reasoned, so he stayed in the bath.

Blank quickly reiterated what he had said to Vadera: Daniels felt he was being treated unjustly by Treasury officials who were imposing tougher and tougher terms and restrictions on the bank which was trying to cope with the biggest recession in memory. He was under intolerable strain, was convinced Whitehall was briefing against him, and his resignation at that particular moment would be a disaster, not just for Lloyds but for the Prime Minister who had supported the merger all the way.

Brown could probably detect that Blank himself was pretty fed up and sought to reassure him, fearing he might go 'wobbly' too.

'Look, Victor, the reason we did all this was because we wanted you and Eric to run this business and we've got great confidence in you. You're great operators, you've got the experience and that's why you're the guys we want in charge of Lloyds and Halifax Bank of Scotland,' he said. (Brown had a curious habit of using the full names of the Scottish banks rather than their initials.)

'Now, I hear you'd like me to ring Eric?' he went on.

'I'd love you to ring Eric,' said a relieved Blank, 'and give him the same message.'

A few minutes later Vadera called Daniels to warn him to expect a call from No. 10. It was nine in the morning and for once Daniels, exhausted after a tough week, was still in bed, intending to allow himself the unusual luxury of a lie-in. The No. 10 switchboard called shortly afterwards and Brown came on the line to give him much the same message he had given to Blank. He was, he told Daniels, very appreciative of what he was doing at Lloyds, where he was making great progress; he recognised, he added, what an experienced and able banker he was and the government was relying on him to see it through.

'I'm sorry you've had it very rough in the press,' he went on, surprising Daniels who read it as an acknowledgement of what they had all known for some time: the damaging leaks coming out of Whitehall – and often No. 10 and No. 11 – were sanctioned from the top.

Blank never asked Daniels about the call and Daniels, although he might have suspected it, never knew his chairman was behind it. The subject of resignation was not raised again inside the bank, although the festering issue of bonuses was. In the heat of battle in October, Paul Myners had agreed that the Lloyds executives should receive their 2008 bonuses, to be paid in shares rather than cash. But early in 2009 the Treasury and UKFI changed their minds as public opinion swung against the deal. There would be no bonuses that year. For 2007, Lloyds's top five executives received total remuneration of £7.2 million; for 2008 it was less than half that.

. . .

The next crisis for Lloyds broke, appropriately enough, on Friday 13 February, when its already volatile share price tumbled by 40 per cent to a new all-time low of 61p, a third of the price at which the government had injected its £17 billion. That day Eric Daniels was forced to issue a profit warning indicating HBOS would now lose £10 billion, the biggest loss disclosed by a British bank up to that point (RBS would soon top it). The Lloyds profit warning came at an embarrassing moment for Gordon Brown, who had so publicly associated himself with the HBOS deal and now found himself jeered at by the Tories as the 'midwife' for the merger. The Spencer House cocktail party leak had rebounded on him.

The main culprit behind the losses was Peter Cummings's corporate division, where values were being savaged by the terrifying speed of the economic collapse in the final weeks of 2008 and early 2009, the worst of the recession, pushing its losses up from the £3.3 billion forecast in

December to £7 billion just two months later. With full access to the HBOS books for the first time, Tookey and his team were turning up all sorts of risky investments which, at the bottom of the worst property market in post-war history, the bank's auditors were insisting on making savage provisions against. In a market where there were no buyers and plenty of forced sellers, what had seemed reasonably good assets in September were virtually written off in February. The house-builder Crest Nicholson, into which an HBOS-led consortium had invested £715 million, was rated as basically worthless. The joint acquisition of Britain's biggest retirement homes builder, McCarthy & Stone, into which an HBOS consortium had poured £1.1 billion, was written down to almost nothing. Then there was a £1.7 billion equity and loan investment in the De Vere Hotels group, which looked disastrous at this very low point in the cycle (but, as with many of the other investments, emerged from the recession as a profitable business). Someone calculated that HBOS was actually the fourth biggest house-builder in Britain, an unenviable position when demand for new houses had almost dried up. Cummings had also backed the betting group Gala Coral, which had debts of £1.7 billion and would have to be restructured.

In normal times, Lloyds would have managed these investments through the cycle, as Barclays and HSBC were allowed to do, unwinding them when the recovery came and the property and stock markets improved. But these were not normal times and Lloyds had no flexibility in the way the auditors and regulators required it to handle its provisioning. The new fair value rules which applied to acquisition/merger accounting also meant that Lloyds had to crystallise its losses early, providing for them on a 'mark-to-market' basis. That would not have been disastrous if markets were healthy. But the speed of the downturn and the extraordinary depreciation in property prices, against which the rest of the asset portfolio had to be valued, resulted in much more draconian provisions than other banks were required to make, which in turn adversely affected Lloyds's critical capital ratios, forcing it to dump even more assets. It was a vicious cycle, the perfect storm, its implications for Lloyds not lost on the City analysts who were running the numbers through their own models. 'The worry now is they may have blown up two banks instead of one,' commented one of the analysts, Simon Maughan of MF Global, and that view resonated in the days that followed. Lloyds, wrote *The Economist* that weekend, 'is teetering on the brink of nationalisation'.

The possibility of full-scale nationalisation of both RBS and Lloyds, followed by a 'good bank, bad bank' solution, was certainly on the table that week, apparently urged by Mervyn King who had been impressed with the way Sweden had handled its bank crisis a decade before. The Treasury however had other plans and was almost ready to introduce its asset protection scheme (APS) which ideally should have been in place before the crisis broke.

'The antagonism from Eric and his colleagues towards government was spectacular,' says one the new Lloyds directors who arrived to reinforce the board at around that time.

> They were deeply bitter about promises they said had been broken, the continual leaks that they believed came from the government, and then there was the Brussels thing and God knows what else. They hated the asset protection scheme and the prospect that the government would get a majority stake. There was complete lack of trust and that coloured all sorts of things. I remember Eric saying at one stage he was contemplating taking the government to court. It's not a smart move to take your biggest shareholder to court when you're in trouble.

Another director was equally shocked. 'The view of government around that board table, particularly among the executives, was the worst I ever experienced,' he says.

> I mean, it was really terrible. They were accusing the Treasury of reneging on non-interference with bonuses and pay policies, screwing them with penal interest rates, letting them down on Europe and all sorts of things. The government wanted us to run the place for their health rather than for all the shareholders and the whole board was getting really angry.

By the spring of 2009, board meetings had become tense, gruelling sessions which Blank managed to keep even-tempered and focused. But they were really fire-fighting sessions. 'We weren't dealing with strategy any more – these were scary days,' says one of the directors.

> Things were bloody awful and at the board meetings we were faced with crisis after crisis and there was talk in the markets of even HSBC going bust. We were worrying about how much liquidity we had in the balance sheet and how we could refund it or fund it for longer and all that stuff. And the government kept arbitrarily increasing the capital requirements which made things even more difficult at a time when we needed support.

Carolyn McCall, who joined as a non-executive director in October 2008, was taken aback by the air of tension that gripped the board by the spring of 2009, as well as by the antagonism towards the government. As the chief executive of Guardian Media (where her chairman was Paul Myners) and a former non-executive director of Tesco, she was no stranger to public controversy, but this was something well beyond anything in her experience. There were plenty of seasoned veterans, such as Sandy Leitch, Ewan Brown and Jan du Plessis, on the board, and after her first few meetings she sought out Brown, the senior non-exec.

'What do you think?' she asked him. 'Have you ever seen anything like this? Where is this all going?

'This is new territory for all of us,' replied the phlegmatic Brown. No, he said, he had never seen anything even approaching it. The other non-executives, he added, were shocked by how bad things were – 'but this is their first exposure to a real financial crisis'.

The air of uncertainty was all-pervasive. 'It was like people were under water, very deep, cloudy water, and you couldn't see to the next day,' says one former director. 'That's how it felt.'

Yet the board remained remarkably united, even as the crisis deepened and the level of the HBOS losses deteriorated with the economy. 'I quickly came to the view that the HBOS thing was a collective decision for which everyone in the room took responsibility,' says one of the directors who arrived after the event. 'No one was pointing fingers and saying, "What a mess you've got us into." Everyone was in it together. And that was impressive.'

Other directors credited Blank's ameliorative style and outward calmness for holding the board together at the lowest moments, and he in turn tried to ensure they knew everything he and Daniels did. 'Meetings were full and open,' says a former director,

> and all of us, including management, had ample opportunity to question and comment on any issue on the table. Victor was skilled at this – I guess he must have had plenty of practice on his previous boards – and as the crisis wore on he gained a lot of respect from the directors.

Jan du Plessis, chairman of the audit committee, bore a lot of the board pressure. A trained accountant and former finance director of the luxury goods group Richemont, the 55-year-old Afrikaner from Stellenbosch had previously chaired British American Tobacco, which had a market value bigger than Lloyds, as well as the food group RHM, and had quietly emerged as a powerful and much respected figure in the City. It took a lot to rattle him.

Du Plessis, like all the others, had signed off on the HBOS deal but by late February he was beginning to wish he hadn't. He shocked the other directors when he emerged from an audit committee meeting one day shaking his head in bewilderment at the figures he had just been shown for the first time. 'The depth and speed of this recession has put HBOS into a much worse state than we ever expected,' Du Plessis reported to the others at the board meeting which followed the audit committee. 'And the new accounting rules are going to make it look even worse.' Directors, he added, should brace themselves for further shocks.

The news coming out of Ireland was worse than anyone could have imagined, even in their blackest of moods. 'When the boys from Dublin came over and gave us a figure, or the risk people gave us a new estimate, I would say to Jan "let's add a billion" – and I was never wrong,' says one of the audit committee.

'How can we lose so much money in such a small place?' someone asked plaintively. (Impairments of HBOS's Irish loan book would total £10.9 billion over the next three years.)

The pressure on Daniels might have been intense but it was Tim Tookey who keeled over first – literally. Lloyds was due to announce its full year's results on Wednesday 27 February 2009 and, as usual, the executive had a dry run two days before. The whole executive team as well as the bank's stockbrokers, PR advisers and investors' relations team gathered in one of the meeting rooms in Gresham Street, and Blank, who was to top and tail the meeting, went first, followed by Daniels. Tookey, coming third, was about halfway through his rehearsal when he suddenly collapsed, falling over like a sack. Blank, no mean slip fielder in his day, leapt forward and caught him just as his head was about to crash into an electrical fitting. He was out cold for six minutes and woke up to find a hastily summoned medic crouching over him, with Blank and Daniels looking worried in the background. He was taken to hospital, smuggled out through the basement in case anyone was watching, while Daniels despatched a car to fetch his wife and daughter (Tookey's son was away at university). A

battery of tests and a CT scan found nothing serious, the doctors concluding it was just stress and overwork. After just one day's rest, he was
back in the office in time to present the worst set of figures in Lloyds's
240-year history, much to the relief of Helen Weir who had been hastily
drafted in as a substitute and had been up all night preparing.

The results were truly dreadful, as they were for all the banks. Profits
before tax for Lloyds on its own fell from £4 billion to £800 million, a
drop of 80 per cent, reflecting impairment provisions which, on the basis
of the new stress tests and 'mark-to-market' accounting rules, almost
doubled to £3 billion. The figures for HBOS, which Lloyds presented
separately, had deteriorated even further since the profit warning and a
profit before tax of £5.5 billion in 2007 had become a loss of £10.5 billion
in 2008, which fortunately was not for Lloyds's account.

Lloyds TSB Share Price (adjusted for capital issues)

*The government makes a profit at anything above 74p. A 90p price (May 2015) is
equivalent to 180p in pre-crisis terms*

The real shocker, however, came when Daniels put up a slide headed: 'Understanding the HBOS loan book'. It showed total HBOS loans of £432 billion, of which £165 billion, or 40 per cent, fell into a new class he called 'Outside Lloyds TSB's risk appetite', or loans which Lloyds would not have made even in good times. Of the £116 billion corporate loan book, £80 billion of it had been put into that category, £40 billion of it mostly lent to property, house building and hotel companies which the auditors insisted on rating as seriously high risk. Gordon Brown later held up this chart as an example of the dismal decision-making at HBOS and MPs seized on it too, demanding of Dennis Stevenson, 'Your highest-paid banker, your head of corporate lending, Peter Cummings, was lending £40 billion of your £100 billion loan book to construction and property companies?' Yes, replied Stevenson, only slightly abashed, the corporate lending unit had 'lent too much. We made some mistakes and that is the bottom line.'

.　.　.

Blank did his best to keep negotiations – and relations – with the Treasury on track, but it was getting more and more difficult. Vadera and Myners complained that Daniels was becoming increasingly difficult to deal with and reported to Blank that on one occasion he had stormed out of the Treasury with his whole team in protest on more than one occasion. The truth, as Blank soon ascertained, was less dramatic: Daniels needed a cigarette and persuaded Tookey and the others to join him. Someone saw them shivering in Horse Guards Parade and drew the wrong conclusion. The story ran on the blogs the next day.

On another occasion, Daniels and Tookey were called in for a late-night meeting with Myners who arrived straight from the opera, still wearing his dinner jacket. 'People had been hanging around for hours and tempers soon got frayed,' says one of the Lloyds team, 'and Eric kept pointing out that what they were asking us to do didn't make any sense.'

Finally an increasingly irritated Myners looked around the room and suddenly demanded: 'Where the hell is Victor in all this? Why isn't he in here suffering with the rest of us?'

Blank was home in bed, as he had every right to be in the middle of the night, when Myners called telling him to get down to the Treasury immediately to 'sort Eric out'. He hastily jumped out of bed, pulled some clothes on over his pyjamas and drove in to the Treasury where he spent two uncomfortable hours calming both parties down and getting the talks going again.

Two days later the *Telegraph* carried a story headed: 'Lloyds has bust up with Treasury over asset protection scheme', adding that Lloyds had warned the Treasury that Daniels 'feels so strongly about the issue that he could quit'. A day later the *Financial Times*, citing Whitehall sources, detailed Daniels's fight to keep the government's stake below control. 'They wanted to portray Eric as petulant and obsessed with his bonus,' says one of Daniels's colleagues. 'And they were really making life difficult for him, basically to get him to sign up for the asset protection scheme.'

In March, Daniels finally gave in, or appeared to, and Lloyds issued a statement saying it had agreed to participate in the APS on terms which were still onerous but better than the original ones. The government would insure £260 billion of assets in return for which it extracted a massive fee of £15.6 billion paid in new, non-voting convertible B shares; the bitterest blow was that the preference shares would be replaced with ordinary equity. The result, assuming the government converted everything, meant the state could end up with 75 per cent of Lloyds – which for Daniels was about the worst possible outcome.

But he hadn't given up yet. 'We'll wait for an upturn in the market', he told Tookey, 'and find a way out of it. The scheme is completely unworkable and they'll soon find that out.' By the autumn of 2009, he believed, the worst of the HBOS losses would be behind them, and the results of the integration would be coming through. He would fight another day.

But the prospect of the once mighty Lloyds succumbing to what in effect would be public ownership brought howls of indignation from its long-suffering shareholders: 'Welcome to the Republic of UK Plc', one shareholder posted on his blog, while another complained about 'the biggest bank robbery in history'. Several called for the resignation of Blank or Daniels or both, prompting a No. 10 spokesman to reiterate that the duo had 'the full backing' of the Prime Minister.

Unfortunately, particularly for Blank, Downing Street was not calling the shots any more. That role had effectively passed to UKFI, the government vehicle which held the Lloyds and RBS stakes, and more specifically to its chief executive John Kingman, the Treasury mandarin (and former Lex columnist on the *Financial Times*) who the Lloyds team had seen more of than they cared for during the recapitalisation exercise. Kingman had officially left the Treasury, but not the building, and still operated out of three rooms temporarily assigned to UKFI. When Alistair Darling set it up in October 2008, UKFI's mandate was to manage the government's investments in the two banks with a view to disposing of them 'in an orderly manner' when market conditions permitted, and Kingman was given the job of overseeing it. That, effectively, gave him *carte blanche* to do more or less what he liked on the grounds that he was preparing the way for an eventual sale – including changing the management. Brown might have wanted to keep Blank and Daniels in place but Kingman seemed to have other ideas about that.

After only five months in existence, UKFI was already looking for its third non-executive chairman. Philip Hampton, appointed in October, had barely had time to touch the ground before he was whisked off to become chairman of RBS. His replacement was Glen Moreno, an

American-born former Citigroup investment banker and Fidelity fund manager who, by an odd coincidence, had succeeded Dennis Stevenson as chairman of Pearson Group. He was a seasoned City heavyweight, tipped as a future head of one of the big banks, a role he was said to covet (he eventually became deputy chairman of Lloyds where he hoped – but failed – to be chairman but later did make it as chairman of Virgin Money).

But Moreno had no sooner taken up the job than he was accused by the press of links to a tax avoidance scheme in Liechtenstein, and on 13 February 2009, two months after he had been appointed, he announced he was stepping down, just a day after another Brown appointee, Sir James Crosby, resigned as deputy chairman of the FSA. The Tories had a field day, parodying Oscar Wilde: 'to lose one financial adviser may be regarded as a misfortune; to lose two…' Moreno agreed to stay on until a new chairman was found.

He was still in place when the next part of the Lloyds saga unfolded. The UKFI had the power to appoint two directors to the Lloyds board and, after once again employing the headhunter Carol Leonard, had put forward Tim Ryan, an American lawyer and former JP Morgan banker, and Tony Watson, a former head of the Hermes asset management company. Watson, ironically, had been offered a non-executive directorship of HBOS by his old friend Dennis Stevenson several years before, but, as fortune would have it, was too busy at the time to accept. Both men came with impressive credentials, particularly in the area of corporate governance, and Blank and the Lloyds directors who interviewed them were genuinely pleased to have them aboard. Blank and Watson had known each other for years and there was much mutual respect.

Watson was scheduled to join the Lloyds board on 1 April but asked Blank if he could put it back a day, explaining that the family legend was that he had actually been born, in Belfast, at five to midnight on 1 April, but his superstitious mother registered him a day later. Shortly before his first board meeting, Kingman called him and invited him to the Treasury 'for a cup of tea and a chat'. It turned out to be an awful cup of Civil Service tea in the Treasury canteen, over which Kingman suggested they meet on a regular basis to talk about Lloyds once the new director had found his feet there. The fiercely independent Watson, however, bridled at that.

'John, I'm on the board to represent not just 43 per cent of the shares, but 100 per cent,' he replied firmly. 'I can't possibly have a special line to you and at the same time maintain my legal responsibilities – or indeed my collegiate relationship with the rest of the board.' He would feel highly uncomfortable, he added, 'sitting at one end of the table and they're sitting at the other end and staring at me, thinking "he's representing the government"'.

Kingman, looking put-out, backed down. Watson immediately sought out Blank to report the conversation and they agreed that Watson should see the UKFI chief from time to time, but only with the full knowledge of the other directors and if Tim Ryan went with him. Kingman never invited him for a cup of Treasury tea again.

Unknown to Blank or anyone else at Lloyds, at the end of April Moreno and Kingman began touring the City with the apparent objective of sounding out existing and potential investors about their attitude to a future sale of Lloyds shares. Over and over again they asked the same pointed question: would the sale process be hindered if the existing management was still in place? Did investors want change?

At that stage they didn't. No one had even raised the subject with Blank or any of the other directors and most shareholders seemed to feel they should be left to finish the job. Pressed by Moreno and Kingman, however, as to whether they thought either Blank or Daniels should go, they gave the answer the UKFI duo appeared to be looking for. There should be a victim. And it probably should be Blank.

As luck would have it, Blank was standing for re-election at the forthcoming annual general meeting in June, and as the Lloyds share price continued to touch new lows, rumours began to circulate that he might announce his departure at that time. On 31 March, Moreno wrote a comment piece for the *Financial Times* under the headline: 'Anger must not cloud our vision in banking', which purported to be a defence of bankers, but it had a sting in the tail which seemed to Blank and Daniels to be aimed at them.

In his experience, Moreno wrote, successful bank turnarounds required four basic strategic actions, the first being: 'change the leadership'. That had happened at RBS, he said, and 'the HBOS board and senior management have been largely replaced by a Lloyds team that did a good job managing the risk through the credit bubble'. The UKFI chairman left the question of the future of the existing Lloyds management hanging in the air.

. . .

The Lloyds board meeting on 17 April was Jan du Plessis's last. He had been offered the job of chairman of the mining group Rio Tinto, an enormous role, and in mid-March he called Blank to tender his resignation. Du Plessis had become a close and readily available adviser and supporter, and it was a blow to lose him at such a time, but Blank had other heavyweights on the board and asked Martin Scicluna, the former head of Deloittes, to take over as chairman of the audit committee, an unenviable task even in the best of times. Du Plessis left without rancour, feeling he had done his bit as a non-executive but relieved to be out of it.

All the directors had learned to brace themselves for more bad news at every meeting and they were seldom disappointed. What one director termed 'the twin streams of disaster'– the collapsing economy and the HBOS-specific losses – were almost overwhelming the bank. When Tim Tookey passed around a draft statement in April detailing the enormous impairment provisions about to be announced, someone asked how he was going to present that to the City? Tony Watson drily suggested, in his soft Northern Irish accent: 'Why don't you just tell them what it is we paid, and what we thought we got?'

The answer, Tookey told him, wasn't as simple as that. Basically Lloyds had ended up paying £8 billion for net assets of £28 billion, which they wrote down to £18 billion when the deal was completed. That left a £10 billion buffer, which should have been enough, particularly given the level of savings, to cover any contingency. Unfortunately it wasn't. Impairments in the first half of 2009, Tookey reckoned, would now be of the order of £13 billion, more than 80 per cent of it coming from HBOS. And there was more to come: the collapse in the property market, where some values had halved, had exposed many of the vertically integrated HBOS investments, where loans were made to highly geared entities which invested them in even more highly geared companies – gearing piled on top of gearing. This was an area which the Lloyds's due diligence had been unable to get to, and which was now considerably more exposed because of economic conditions which nobody had envisaged when the deal was being considered six months earlier.

．　．　．

In the first week of May, Victor Blank unexpectedly got a call from John Kingman requesting a meeting with him and Moreno. The two UKFI men came to his office in Gresham Street where Moreno told him about the soundings they had been taking to establish the level of investor appetite for Lloyds's shares when the time came to sell the government's holding. It was the first Blank had heard of it and his immediate reaction was resentment that they had gone behind his back.

Lloyds, said Moreno, was approaching its annual general meeting and the UKFI would have to advise the Treasury on how it should cast its vote on the various resolutions proposed, including the one to re-elect Blank as chairman. Some of the big City institutions, he said, believed that if they were to get proper momentum behind a share sale in due course, then either Blank or Daniels, as the two men on whose watch the share price had fallen so precipitately, should go.

Kingman then produced a sheet on which he had recorded the views of some of Lloyds's institutional shareholders and passed it across the table to Blank. The Lloyds chairman gazed at the list sadly. Many of these same shareholders, most of whom were also shareholders in HBOS, had voted in favour of the HBOS deal only six months before and none of them had since even hinted they wanted him or Daniels to go. He could see how it would be presented to the Treasury and to Gordon Brown: Kingman and UKFI would keep their hands clean while insisting they were just reflecting the opinion of outside shareholders. He was by no means convinced that Kingman might not have encouraged the response he wanted.

Moreno would soon be writing to Darling with a recommendation on how the government should vote its 43 per cent shareholding, he said. Based on their findings, UKFI would be recommending change at the top. UKFI, Moreno indicated, would leave it to the Lloyds board to decide who actually went but their preference was pretty obvious: Daniels was needed to finish the work of integrating the two banks and therefore it probably should be Blank. If he agreed to announce his early retirement at the forthcoming AGM and leave a year later, after his replacement had been identified, then they would advise the Treasury to vote for his re-election. Blank had removed enough senior executives in his life to be familiar with the well-worn process – he was basically being asked to go by Lloyds's biggest shareholder. It left him with a keen sense of injustice – the decision to take over HBOS had been fully supported, and even driven at times, by the Treasury, including Kingman and the Prime Minister. Now he realised he was to be made the scapegoat for it and felt he deserved better.

When he confided in his two most senior non-executives, Sandy Leitch and Ewan Brown, they immediately suggested he and the board make a fight of it. For a brief moment Blank was tempted. He could provoke a full-scale public battle by refusing to go and force the government to sack him at the AGM which would be deeply embarrassing for the Prime Minister. But it would also damage the bank, and maybe the whole banking system, as well as his own reputation. He would not go down that track.

Blank had been around long enough to understand where all this was heading and where it would inevitably end. He resented the way Moreno and Kingman seemed to be engineering his departure but he could also accept their logic: looking forward, it would be preferable for Lloyds, and for the government, if there were new faces at the top when it came to selling the shares. A new chairman would be in a stronger position to reassure potential investors that the integration process was on track and the bank was on the right course back to profitability and, eventually, the dividend list. The process, Blank reasoned, had to start somewhere and that probably had to be with him.

He was still brooding over his decision when Leitch and Brown went off to see Moreno to tell him that not a single Lloyds director supported UKFI's decision and this was a time when Blank's reassuring presence was most needed. Moreno was just about to depart for the US and promised to get back to them later. Despite reminders from Leitch, he never did.

Soon afterwards Tony Watson and Tim Ryan, the two 'Treasury-appointed' directors on the Lloyds board, went to see Kingman in the UKFI offices where they told him that they too were both strongly opposed to the action he was taking. Kingman was unmoved. 'The message from investors is that one of them has to go,' he responded. 'And of the two, it probably should be Victor.'

Later that day Blank called his non-executive directors together and briefed them on his conversation with Moreno and Kingman, adding that they had not directly specified which of the two, he or Daniels, should go. But it was clear to him it should not be Daniels – in the febrile and tense situation prevailing, his departure would destabilise the bank and set the integration process back by a year. He had therefore decided he would announce his retirement before the forthcoming AGM in three weeks' time and leave a year later, by which stage he would be sixty-six.

One of the directors proposed they should tell UKFI how strongly the board felt and threaten that if they proceeded along this course then the whole board would resign. 'We all felt that Victor was a good chairman and the board was very supportive of his continued leadership. And we were not at all sure that he should be the one to go,' said one. 'Everyone has their faults but Victor was very statesmanlike and the executives looked to him for a lot of things. There was a great deal of unhappiness and disappointment at the way it was being handled.'

Blank appeared visibly moved by the show of support but began to feel the situation was getting out of hand. Further resignations, he said, were 'unthinkable'. There was a company to be run, the integration of the two banks to be completed and shareholders and employees to be protected. A mass resignation would destabilise the whole bank and would not help him, or anyone else – including Gordon Brown. At the end of the meeting, he told the board he would stick to the decision he had made after a great deal of thought: he would announce his retirement that weekend and leave before the next AGM.

Although several directors protested, the board finally agreed. 'It was apparent to us that there was going to be a victim,' said one of the directors. 'People were looking for someone to blame. And unfortunately it was Victor. And I think Victor did the very honourable thing.'

Before that, however, he thought he should tell the Prime Minister how he felt about it all, and called Shriti Vadera to ask her to arrange for him to see Brown as soon as possible. She called back shortly afterwards to say if he came to the back entrance to Downing Street on Horse Guards Parade she would be waiting for him. It was the first – and last – time Blank entered Downing Street through the back door, but he quickly found Vadera who guided him down a maze of passages and into a meeting room where she left him alone.

Brown appeared a few minutes later, profusely offering apologies for the events of the past few days. Blank had not told anyone other than his board what he intended to do and he could see Brown was nervous. He was having a bad day: all week long he had been involved in yet another political scandal, the *Daily Telegraph* disclosures of MPs' expenses, and earlier that day he had engaged in a shouting match with the *Telegraph*'s editor Will Lewis over claims, which proved unfounded, over his own personal expenses. 'The language was intemperate: it was one of those occasions when Brown simply lost it,' according to the authors Seldon and Lodge (*Brown at 10*). The last thing Brown wanted at that moment was another row – or another political crisis.

Blank put him out of his misery by telling him he planned to announce his early retirement over the weekend and would leave Lloyds before the AGM a year later. A greatly relieved Brown was effusive in his thanks. 'I'm enormously appreciative of everything you've done and you've supported me and you've supported the banking system,' he said. 'This is helping me a lot. I'm terribly sorry about this but my hands are tied.' The UKFI recommendation, now embodied in a letter sent to Darling and copied to him, left him no choice. 'We have just set up this thing to hold the bank shares and this is their first recommendation. If we ignore it, the whole thing will fold.'

When Blank reminded him of the phone call he had taken in the bath and his pledge of support for him and Daniels, the Prime Minister became even more apologetic, repeating again and again: 'I'm so sorry.'

('If he said that once, he must have said it ten times,' Blank related afterwards.) Brown was still protesting how grateful he was as Blank walked out the door and back out the way he had come.

Back in the office his first call was to Julian Horn-Smith, who served with him on the Lloyds nominations committee, suggesting he start the process of finding his successor. On Sunday 17 May 2010, he issued a brief press release headed: 'Sir Victor Blank to retire as chairman of Lloyds Banking Group by the Annual General Meeting in 2010'. Two weeks later, Kingman also issued a press release which carefully avoided any mention of Blank. 'UKFI has made it clear that we fully support the Lloyds board, strategy and team led by Eric Daniels,' he said. 'We have decided to vote in favour of all resolutions at the AGM.' That included the resolution to re-elect Blank for another year.

. . .

In the event, Blank left Lloyds Banking Group in September 2009, nine months earlier than he needed to, donating the final few months of his salary (for the months when he would not be working) to charity. In another little twist to the story, he was succeeded by his old friend Sir Win Bischoff – the same man who, as chairman of Citigroup, had hosted that party so long ago in Spencer House.

Eric Daniels, about to turn sixty, followed eighteen months later after a long and eventually successful campaign to escape the Treasury's muchhated asset protection scheme, achieving his objective of keeping the government shareholding to 43 per cent, its high point. It required a massive effort and a capital raise of £22.5 billion, the biggest ever, through a combination of equity (£13.5 billion) and the world's first underwritten liability management exercise. The Treasury took an equally huge fee – even though it didn't actually do anything – of £2.5 billion. Daniels, supported by the Lloyds board and shareholders, reckoned it was worth it to get off the hook. The capital-raising was initiated in Blank's time but it was Daniels who carried it through. 'It was a very lonely task,' says one of the former executives. 'Eric was the only one who thought he could do it and until the very end no one really believed him.'

By the time Daniels left, Lloyds's finances were in pretty good shape and it was back in profit. Tim Tookey, urged on by Daniels, trebled the size of the bank's treasury team which pulled off some of the most spectacularly successful money-raising exercises of the day. In 2010 alone, Lloyds issued £50 billion of non-guaranteed term funding and reduced the riskier HBOS assets by some £200 billion. Tookey arranged for the full repayment of the Bank of England's special liquidity scheme funding as well as the government-guaranteed debt which the bank, mainly on the HBOS side, had taken on during the crisis. Lloyds was funding normally again and didn't need any favours from the Bank.

By the middle of 2016, the government had raised more than £16 billion from selling down its holding from 42 per cent shareholding to less than 10 per cent, and George Osborne promised to sell the rest when markets allowed. Its remaining shareholding was worth another £5 billion, which meant the government will make a small profit on its £20.5 billion investment when the sale is completed. The bank also returned to the dividend list with a pay-out of £2 billion and announced that PPI losses were finally capped (at over £15 billion). Daniels was replaced in the spring of 2011 by António Horta-Osório, the former UK CEO of Santander. Tim Tookey resigned in the summer of 2011 to join Friends Life but at Lloyds's request he extended his notice period to cover for Horta-Osório when the new chief executive was forced to take two months' medical leave later that year. Helen Weir moved to John Lewis as finance director and then to Marks & Spencer, Truett Tate went back to the US and Archie Kane was appointed Governor of the Bank of Ireland. Terri Dial died of cancer in 2012, aged sixty-two.

CONCLUSION

NO TAKEOVER IN British corporate history ever received so much official support as Lloyds TSB's bid for HBOS in the autumn of 2008. It was blessed by the highest authorities in the land who removed every obstacle and wished it Godspeed. Liquidity, which had been denied in the case of the Northern Rock bid, was provided by the Bank of England in virtually unlimited quantities. At the Prime Minister's personal request, the competition rules were changed and Lord Mandelson's first act back in Parliament was to introduce an emergency order permitting the merger on the grounds of 'the stability of the UK financial system'. The Chancellor of the Exchequer stood four-square behind it and the FSA almost performed somersaults in its keenness to make it happen.

It was unanimously approved by the boards of both banks and overwhelmingly supported by their shareholders. Half the City's top legal, accounting, investment banking and stockbroking firms, advising either Lloyds, HBOS or the Treasury, signed off on it. The country's most senior officers in the Treasury, the Bank and the FSA slaved through long days and nights to facilitate the merger, basically because they feared – as did the Prime Minister and Chancellor – financial Armageddon if it failed. From No. 10 Downing Street, Shriti Vadera and Gordon Brown followed it every step of the way, ready to intervene instantly if it looked like faltering.

The City loved it too, at least at the beginning. When the merger was announced, Finsbury, the PR firm employed by Lloyds, did a sweep of thirteen 'sell-side' bank analysts who, it reported back to the Lloyds board, were 'unanimous about the transaction being a good deal for Lloyds TSB'. The analysts saw it as 'a unique opportunity [for Lloyds] with a strong strategic rationale that established the group as a clear retail market leader'. Several positively gushed: 'If you can get the government to abandon competition policy, you grab the opportunity with both hands,' said one. 'The deal is an absolute steal,' said another, while one analyst, slightly more cautiously, ventured: 'I think it's a great deal, but the wider picture has to be a concern.' That's about as negative as it got.

From Edinburgh the 'tartan twosome', Sir Peter Burt and Sir George Mathewson, the former chief executives of the two Scottish banks, sourly remarked that 'the deal has been billed as the deal of the century. It is a very good deal for Lloyds. We wish them well through gritted teeth.'

It was difficult to find a critical voice anywhere, inside or outside the bank, who thought it was bad for Lloyds. Government, City, financial press and the Lloyds board all thought it was just what Lloyds needed at that particular juncture in its history. HBOS shareholders, who would have got nothing if the deal had failed, were even more enthusiastic.

When the deal was announced, the financial press portrayed Blank and Daniels as the saviours of HBOS and maybe even the banking system. Both men were profiled in just about every major newspaper where they were hailed as Britain's new super-bankers, particularly Daniels, whose caution and conservatism, in contrast to the more flamboyant Fred Goodwin, James Crosby and Andy Hornby, finally seemed to have paid off. Such criticisms as there were basically related to the competition implications of creating such a large bank.

But the announcement of the merger in September 2008 marked the apogee in Victor Blank's banking career. When he had first arrived at Lloyds two years earlier, he was already a City grandee, a distinguished figure in business and financial circles where he was highly regarded and respected by his peers. He expected to do a five-year stint at Lloyds and then, still in his sixties, either retire or take on one last major role. He had been asked to consider becoming President of the Confederation of British Industry (CBI) where his friend Digby Jones was the director general, and was invited to join the Court of the Bank of England (offered to him, ironically, by John Kingman, on behalf of the Prime Minister). There were other offers too, but he turned all of them down because, as he told Jones, 'I don't think I could put in the time needed because of my Lloyds commitment.' There was talk of him as a future chairman of the BBC or of a big multinational company but if he chose to retire instead, which was his intention, he would have found plenty to do.

Then, virtually overnight, the world changed. The economy went into freefall, Lehman went bust, the banking crisis deepened and the climate turned brutally against banks and bankers. No one paused to differentiate between good and bad bankers – as far as the politicians, the press and the public were concerned, there *were* no good bankers. By January 2009, they had become social outcasts, blamed for everything from collapsing the economy and starving small businesses of loans to ripping off loyal customers. They were depicted as greedy, selfish, incompetent fat cats who took huge risks with other people's money. Some of them, of course, deserved all they got. But there were others who believed they had not done much wrong and were bewildered to be put into the same punishment corner as the real baddies. Their biggest crime was to be paid huge salaries and bonuses at a time when unemployment was rising rapidly and the country was getting poorer – and they don't deserve any sympathy for that. But the Lloyds directors in particular felt they had not caused the crisis, had helped avert an even bigger one and by far the biggest culprit was a worldwide recession caused by irresponsible monetary policies by authorities in the US, Britain and elsewhere. The Labour government, however, was never going to take any of the blame for that – that too had to be the fault of the banks and the bankers.

To say that the Lloyds directors were taken aback by the change in sentiment, particularly from the government, would be an understatement. 'That weekend in the Treasury,' says one of the Lloyds team mournfully,

> it was a case of 'we'll give you everything if you do the HBOS deal and we'll sort out the formalities later. Just let's get it over the line.' You know, it was 'we'll still respect you in the morning'. And naively, I actually expected the government to hold to its promises. By Tuesday it was as if they hadn't promised us anything and we were an RBS lookalike. And they hadn't sorted out Europe, and never really tried, they misled us over Barclays, leaving a stigma which sticks to us still, they changed the rules on salaries and bonuses and they misled us about not using their 43 per cent stake to interfere with the running of the company. If we had known all that, we might well have looked at things differently.

Treasury ministers, supportive in September, had turned hostile by January and seemed to the Lloyds team to be actively encouraging an ugly climate of anti-bank sentiment. By February 2009, as Lloyds became aware of the devastating impact of the recession on HBOS's assets and issued its first profit warning, Blank and Daniels had gone from heroes to zeros. They were the men who, in the words of one columnist, 'took Britain's safest bank and turned it into a basket case', or, as the *Sunday Times* preferred it, they were 'the men who steered Lloyds, the pride of British banking, onto the rocks'.

History may judge the deal, and the men behind it, more kindly – or at least differently. For it hasn't been all bad. In 2016, Lloyds Banking Group was the biggest financial institution in Europe and the fourteenth biggest bank in the world. It was twice the size of Barclays and bigger than Santander, BBVA, Morgan Stanley, Goldman Sachs, Deutsche Bank or any of the big Swiss banks. Its market value was nearly £50 billion, larger than Lloyds and HBOS put together a year before the merger, and its underlying profit was £8 billion a year, twice what it made at its pre-crisis peak. In 1999, in Pitman's best days, it was Britain's ninth biggest company; in 2016, it was still Britain's ninth biggest company (by market value).

Its earning power has been substantially enhanced through its increased market share and its four powerful brands, Lloyds, Bank of Scotland, the Halifax and Scottish Widows. Despite having to hive off 650 branches into the new TSB independent bank, it has more than 25 per cent of current accounts, mortgage balances and bank deposits in Britain, a bigger share than any other bank. The savings resulting from the HBOS merger by 2015 were running at over £2 billion a year, with another £1 billion to go by 2017 (the human cost of that is 45,000 jobs – but that is still a lot less than might have been lost if HBOS had gone down). These were the targets Lloyds set out to achieve when it first focused on HBOS and, by and large, they have been delivered.

The share price performance, however, has been the biggest disappointment and has still to reflect the market leadership position and the reduced cost base. On 8 April 1998, Lloyds shares stood at an (adjusted) all-time high of 506p, a level they are unlikely to see ever again. In February 2009 they had dropped to an all-time low of 28p, a fall of 94.5 per cent, before beginning the long climb back. By May 2015 they had recovered to almost 90p, close to the price immediately before the bid, allowing the government to dispose of a tranche of its shares at a decent profit. The continued drain of PPI once again returned them to the doldrums in 2016, although they were still handsomely outperforming most other British and European banking shares.

The taxpayer has at least not lost money. In March 2009, the government converted its preference shares at 38.4p and in December subscribed for its full entitlement in the rights issue, acquiring another 16 billion shares at a price of 37p (Lloyds by that stage didn't need – or want – its money but the Treasury insisted they take it anyway). It also insisted on charging an underwriting fee of £38 million (for underwriting itself) and another £2.5 billion for *not* participating in the APS scheme, which by a neat Treasury sleight of hand happened to be the cost of the government's participation in the rights. That brought the net price it paid, taking all its fees into account, to 73p.

Lloyds Bank Share Price

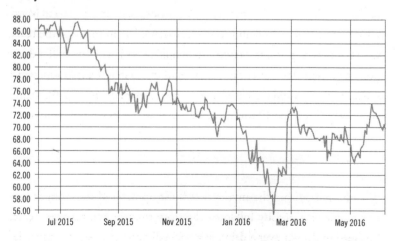

© MoneyAM.com

It has been tough for Lloyds's old shareholders, particularly as they lost their dividend seven years in a row. For five consecutive years before 2008 Lloyds paid out 34.2p (17.1p in adjusted form) on shares which often yielded over 9 per cent, a happy state for small shareholders who lived off the income. By the spring of 2009, however, the Lloyds share price was equivalent to its old dividend, or as one of the analysts caustically remarked, 'The share that paid a 34.2p dividend had become the 34.2p share.' That was the low point.

Lloyds shareholders were not the only sufferers. Bank shareholders around the world have had a pretty torrid time since the great sub-prime crisis began in 2007, particularly after Lehman went down. In the early summer of 2016, Lloyds shares were showing a loss of around 60 per cent against their mid-2008 level, but not all of that was due to HBOS: Barclays over the same period was down 52 per cent and even the lofty HSBC, which wrote off $30 billion on its sub-prime investment in the US, was 43 per cent below its 2008 share price. RBS was still a basket case, down 92 per cent, but that's a different story. For the record, the STOXX 600 Bank Index of European bank shares fell 50 per cent over the same period, September 2008 to March 2015. In Sweden, Ireland and Iceland, shareholders in many of the banks were basically wiped out. So were shareholders in Fortis and half a dozen other European and American banks. And the shares of Citigroup, which still ranks as the world's seventh biggest bank by market value (HSBC is third after Wells Fargo and JP Morgan), are less than 10 per cent of their peak.

. . .

In the meantime, the myths that built up around the merger have become part of City folklore. The story that the merger was created by Gordon Brown over a drink at a cocktail party has become unshake-ably fixed in the public psyche and will probably stay there for as long as people remember the former Prime Minister. The City had not had a better story than this one since Guinness and commentators and historians are never going to let it go. Here are the opinions of two widely respected journalists, which illustrate the point:

'Engineered by the then Prime Minister, Gordon Brown, in an ultimately doomed attempt to save HBOS from collapse, the merger turned into one of the most value destructive deals of all time.' – Jeremy Warner, *Daily Telegraph*, 13 March 2015.

Even Warner, one of the most informed financial commentators writing today, could not resist the temptation to perpetuate the Gordon Brown myth.

HBOS, thanks to Lloyds, never did (quite) collapse; and at least half the value destroyed has been recovered.

And then there was Ferdinand Mount, a former *Spectator* editor and head of Margaret Thatcher's Policy Unit, who in his book *The New Few* lambasted Eric Daniels for his 'hubris' in acquiring HBOS's 'festering morass of bad debts'. He then added:

> It was offered as an excuse that Gordon Brown had suggested the idea to Daniels's chairman, Sir Victor Blank, at a party. But no grown-up executive would bet the future of a bank as large and venerable as Lloyds on the strength of a passing whim of a Prime Minister.

Poor Gordon. But he had only himself to blame: the cocktail party story originated from Downing Street a few days after the announcement when aides sought to present their leader as the man who saved the banking system. Brown encouraged it for just so long as it made him look good and by the time sentiment swung against it, it was too late. Now he is stuck with it unto eternity and it will no doubt appear, many years from now, in his obituaries.

In fact, Brown did nothing wrong, at least as far as this transaction was concerned (although one could argue that it was his economic policies which contributed to the crisis in the first place). HBOS was in trouble, Lloyds wanted to take it over, the competition rules wouldn't allow it and Victor Blank asked him to intervene. Brown, perfectly correctly, went through the proper channels and discussed it with all the involved parties, including the Treasury, the Bank of England and the FSA which unanimously agreed that it was in the best interests of the financial system, and therefore of the country, that the bid should be permitted. When Lehman went bust, the process had to be accelerated dramatically and Brown then took the first opportunity, which happened to be the cocktail party, to tell Blank that 'if you still want to do it' the government would help smooth the way. Nothing bad about any of that.

From that moment on Lloyds found its arm twisted, sometimes brutally, by the government to get the deal done, but it can't blame Brown for that – it had asked for help and the government wanted something back. 'This was not a merger where people were innocently led into something where they were not in a position to judge the value of the deal or its strategic importance,' Paul Myners told the parliamentary Select Committee later. But that didn't mean that, once the button had been pressed, there wasn't pressure. 'The government never ordered Lloyds to do the deal,' says one of the Treasury's City advisers. 'But they made it very difficult for them to back out.' And one of the senior former executives of Lloyds supports the point:

Did we want to do the deal? Yes, in September we did, because it provided us with a strategic step-change. Were we forced to do the deal? No. Were we told to do the deal? No. But in mid-October, when we were all in the Treasury, did we have a choice? By then, in reality, there was no choice. The recapitalisation package and the stress tests were designed to make sure we continued with the merger. They told us to raise £7 billion if we didn't buy

HBOS, or £5.5 billion if we did, by Monday morning, which was impossible. And they said: 'And, by the way, we'll provide the cheapest money known to man, an 8.5 per cent discount on your Friday night closing share price.' So we had both arms so far up behind our backs it was painful.

Lloyds could of course have stood firm, taken the £7 billion of new capital it was being offered on such attractive terms and gone back into its strategic cage to think again – but with the government owning a 43 per cent stake. The directors did think about that. And they discussed asking the Treasury to give them more time, maybe six months, to raise the capital required, during which they could have approached Wells Fargo, where Daniels had connections, or one of the well-capitalised Canadian banks, to seek a merger. But what would have happened then? The government's only fall-back plan was to nationalise HBOS, which would almost certainly have led to the nationalisation of RBS too. The collapse in confidence would have shaken the whole banking system and maybe toppled some of the other banks as well. Barclays was very vulnerable that weekend and if it had gone down, Lloyds would have struggled to survive. That was the situation that Victor Blank, Eric Daniels and the Lloyds board had to confront that weekend when they took the decision – supported unanimously by all the directors – to carry on.

They have been heavily criticised for it since, even by their own peers. Win Bischoff, a friend and admirer of Blank as well as his successor as chairman of Lloyds, referred to the deal as 'a poor judgement call', arguing that Lloyds should have extracted conditions, possibly a guarantee to limit its downside, as some of the American banks had done. Horta-Osório told Alex Brummer (*Bad Banks: Greed, Incompetence and the Next Global Crisis*), 'I would never have bought HBOS. I would have bought the branches and the deposits but not the loans.' He likened the deal to 'a snake eating a poisonous bull'. The problem with that is the branches were not for sale – and if they had been, Lloyds, because of the competition issues, would probably have been the last bank the government (which didn't own them at the time) would have sold them to.

Deep in their retirement, two old Lloyds grandees, Sir Jeremy Morse and Sir Nicholas Goodison, also harrumphed their disapproval, although Morse didn't blame it all on the bank: 'Lloyds pulled that chestnut out of the fire for the authorities and then got thoroughly scapegoated, along with everyone else, for causing the crisis. The government, particularly the Bank of England, must take its share of the blame too.'

None of the critics was sitting in the Treasury that 'drive-by shooting' weekend with the world falling in around their ears and the tensions at boiling point. 'You have to put yourself into that microcosm of time around those few weeks in October 2008,' says a Lloyds director,

> and say would any sensible businessman have made a different decision? And if the answer is yes, then we can be criticised for bad decisions. But I don't think we can ever be criticised for bad process or any of that – none of it. If you take the view that any other reasonable person would take the same decision, then you have to ask: what went wrong?

So what did go wrong? Basically the economy went wrong and HBOS was in far worse shape to cope with it than Lloyds realised until it was too late. In his scathing report on its failure, the Bank of England's Andrew Bailey concluded that HBOS's 'flawed strategy led to a business model that was excessively vulnerable to an economic downturn and a dislocation in wholesale funding markets'. In 2008, the wholesale market, on which HBOS was over-dependent, dried up and the economies of the UK and Ireland fell faster than they had done in a century. Ireland, the first European country into recession, tore a great hole in the balance sheet when its banks and over-geared property sector collapsed. There were plenty of warning signs that the Irish housing market was over-heated but HBOS ignored them, and Lloyds, which under-estimated it, was badly caught out by the unprecedented scale of it.

Which leads us on to another myth: that Lloyds didn't do proper due diligence. In fact it did plenty of it, more than had been done in any previous banking merger, deploying all the skills the City, the accounting and legal professions and its own internal teams, specialists in banking assets and loan books, could provide. The results of the due diligence can perhaps be criticised and so can the assumptions behind them as well as the judgements made – but not the quantity.

The myth about the lack of due diligence in part stemmed from Eric Daniels's remark to the Treasury Select Committee on 11 February 2009 that, *if it had been given the chance*, Lloyds would have 'put in somewhere around three to five times as much time as we put in'. Unfortunately competition and data protection restrictions didn't let him. And even if they had, there is no evidence he would have discovered anything more than he did – most of the losses only tumbled out when the UK and Irish economies collapsed a month after the process was completed. Daniels elaborated on his earlier statement when he appeared in front of the Parliamentary Banking Commission: 'We did a very thorough job in terms of our diligence. We understood what we thought were the strengths and weaknesses of HBOS at the time.' But the damage was done and will probably never be undone. His protests that he was asked a hypothetical 'what if' question and his answer was taken out of context – which is true – have already been forgotten. He will be burdened by that unfortunate slip for the rest of his life.

But it is also true that the due diligence, even with the legal constraints the teams had to work around, did not discover the real horrors in the HBOS portfolio. 'To be honest, we were still uncovering stuff in 2009 which surprised us,' says a former executive. 'Some of the vertically owned investments stuff, which were virtually gearing up on their own lending, we didn't discover in the due diligence. But then if we'd had another month, I don't think we would have either.'

The main flaws in the due diligence process were the optimistic economic assumptions on which it was based, and HBOS's vulnerability to a recession. In the summer of 2008, as Lloyds was about to set out on its journey to acquire HBOS, the consensus forecast of City, Treasury, Bank of England and independent economic advisers was for two consecutive quarterly falls in GDP (0.5 per cent per quarter) in the last half of the year. But overall growth in 2008 was still forecast to hit 1.2 per cent – that was the average prediction of the twenty-eight City and sixteen non-City forecasters, including the CBI, EIU, IMF and OECD, monitored by the Treasury. Their actual range was 0.6–1.6 per cent growth and Lloyds's in-house economist, Patrick Foley, was pretty much in the middle of them at +1 per cent. The actual figure turned out to be –2 per cent, which in economic terms is an enormous difference. And that was about to get even worse.

In September 2008, when the due diligence process began, the Treasury economists were forecasting a slowdown in 2009 but they still believed it would be in positive territory: +0.5 per cent for the year after a reasonable recovery in the second half, which would have been in line with past recessions. Foley was actually more pessimistic than the consensus, revising down his estimate for 2009 from +0.5 per cent to –0.5 per cent since the summer. That was the so-called 'mid-case' scenario on which Tookey prepared his medium-term profit forecast, projecting a profit of £3 billion in 2009, and on which the due diligence was started in the week after the Lehman crash.

By December 2008, by which stage the due diligence was done and the deal approved by shareholders, the Lloyds economics team had revised their forecast down even further, this time well into negative territory. Again, that was in line with the consensus of official and independent forecasts. And again, like all the forecasts (literally all), it was hopelessly wrong.

The initial stress tests used by Daniels and the due diligence teams assumed a normal 1-in-15 years economic cycle, such as the 1991–92 recession under Norman Lamont as Chancellor when the economy fell 2.4 per cent and which seemed pretty bad at the time. Later, as the recession deepened, the due diligence team used a much tougher stress test, a 1-in-25 years scenario, similar to the early Thatcher years (4.6 per cent), but even that was thought to be improbable, the bottom end of the range.

UK GDP Growth 1949–2012

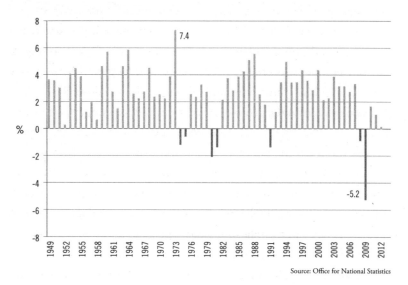

Source: Office for National Statistics

In September 2008, when Lloyds began its due diligence on HBOS, the consensus forecast for UK economic growth by fifty-four economists monitored by the Treasury was for +1.1 per cent in 2008 and +0.5 per cent in 2009. The actual figures were -0.3 per cent and -5.2 per cent – an unprecedented swing. The overall fall of 7.5 per cent (later revised to 6.5 per cent) was greater than in 1929–33.

The actual figures, when they emerged months later, were much, much worse: in the final three months of 2008 the economy declined by nearly 2 per cent, or an annual rate of 8 per cent, and by another 2.6 per cent in the first three months of 2009. Just that six-month period in the winter of 2008/09 by itself would have constituted the biggest fall in the British economy since the miners' strike in the early 1980s. And there was more to come, another two quarters of it, bringing the final total negative decline over five quarters to 7.5 per cent (later revised to 6.5 per cent), larger even that the Great Depression of the 1930s. In October, when the due diligence was completed, no economic forecaster was looking at anything even approaching that – the consensus of the economists was for economic growth of 2 per cent over the same period. It is safe to say that never in the history of economic forecasters did they get it as wrong as they did in the autumn of 2008. But then economic forecasters had never had to deal with a recession as long and deep as this one.

Worse still were the assumptions for the Irish economy where Peter Cummings had lent heavily to property developers and construction companies when the Celtic Tiger was still roaring and growth was in the 5–7 per cent range. In one quarter alone, in the middle of 2009, the Irish economy fell by more than 10 per cent and an overall 16 per cent from top to bottom. Dublin house prices fell by 24 per cent in 2009 and another 15 per cent the following year, wiping out many of Cummings's biggest borrowers. The House of Lords Banking Standards Commission later estimated that between 2008 and 2011 HBOS's impairments on its Irish loan book totalled £10.9 billion and there was another £3.6 billion of impairments in Australia. 'Most of the big losses occurred after the deal was closed and could not have been entirely anticipated. The property and construction sectors were full of aggressive, late-cycle lending,' says one of the banking analysts. 'While Lloyds expected some level of impairments in Ireland, I don't think they expected anything like the catastrophic levels they experienced.'

'The management of a firm is not required to have perfect foresight,' commented Andrew Bailey. 'The criticism in the Report is not that [HBOS's] management failed to predict that there would be a global financial crisis. Rather, they should have put in place strategies that could respond to changes in external circumstances. HBOS lacked these strategies.' Lloyds's bad luck was that the deal, which started out when economic times were uncertain but not disastrous, ended up being completed at the bottom of the worst recession in almost a century. A valuation made one week could be out of date by the next, and the teams were always behind the curve – 'it was like trying to catch a falling knife', one of them said later.

Lloyds, with its very clear and hard-headed strategies, never understood that. This doesn't excuse a bad decision, but it does help explain it.

. . .

In many ways, fate and the ghost of Brian Pitman guided Lloyds down the path to HBOS's door, the inevitable conclusion to the strategy he had put in train two decades before. Pitman created the modern Lloyds through the sheer force of his personality and obsessive pursuit of shareholder returns, something unknown in the complacent world of banking up to that point. He turned Lloyds, briefly, into the biggest bank in the world, but he also left it marooned, almost entirely dependent on the UK retail market which was rapidly becoming overcrowded with new and aggressive entrants, such as Northern Rock – and HBOS. Pitman could have re-balanced the bank and solved its growth issues for a generation if he had just had the courage to buy Standard Chartered Bank when it was served up to him by John Richardson in 1987, or the skills to merge with Midland, an acquisition which transformed the previously peripheral bank HSBC. But he bottled one and fumbled the other and his successors suffered the consequences.

Eric Daniels inherited a bank which, as he remarked at the time, had 'lost the will to grow'. Turning around a vehicle as large as a major clearing bank is unimaginably hard, but, professional banker that he was, he set himself the task of rebuilding the run-down branch structure, upgrading an IT system which was inadequate for the task and concentrating on getting more 'share of wallet' from his existing loyal customers. This was the era when he earned his reputation as a dogged, highly professional but overcautious banker unwilling to gear up his balance sheet, and shunning the more fashionable markets in which the more adventurous Bob Diamond, James Crosby and, of course, Fred Goodwin, were willing to ply their trade. No one in the City loved him for it but, as events were to prove, it was the right thing to do.

By the time Victor Blank arrived in 2006, Lloyds TSB had been stabilised but it was still trying to find growth.

> Pitman had infected the whole place with banking as a boring business and the job was to pay a dividend. There were lots of widows and orphans out there who appreciated that fat dividend cheque and we were a deeply boring bank, yielding 7 per cent and not growing very quickly,

says one of the former Lloyds directors, 'and that left Victor and Eric in a sort of strategic bind.' For the next two years, Blank and Daniels worked together, not always comfortably, to find the path back to growth. Blank was never convinced that path lay in Europe – that was a strategy put in place in Van den Bergh and Ellwood's time – but, in the absence of anything better he supported Daniels's decision to pursue it. And for two years, Daniels, although he didn't have much faith in the process either, diligently hunted for a cross-border acquisition.

Except there weren't any acquisitions, or at least any which made any sense. Blank's experience with Count Lippens, who refused to surrender either of the top jobs at Fortis, was typical of the many abortive discussions that took place. Lloyds, prepared to accept a marriage of equals, held merger discussions with most of the big European players: the Spanish bank BBVA, ABN Amro and with BNP Paribas, Commerzbank and Postbank. They talked to banks of a dozen different nationalities, including Hungarian, Turkish, Greek and Austrian. At one stage they even considered buying an Irish building society.

None of them came to anything, sometimes because of the 'social' issues, but more often because the European banks were demanding premiums that could not be justified. Every single deal Lloyds looked at was seriously earnings-dilutive and would have resulted in a lower dividend for Lloyds shareholders, who were therefore unlikely to vote for it. Several of them were also high-risk – as they would later prove when so many European banks went wrong in 2008–09.

By the summer of 2008, when HBOS came onto the scene, Lloyds had nowhere left to go. But the (almost) bid for Northern Rock inadvertently presented the bank with a new strategy, which was really a return to the old Pitman model – in certain circumstances they just might be able to find a way through the competition regulations which had blocked the Abbey National acquisition. Daniels and Andy Hornby had already discussed merging their two banks two years earlier, but concluded the competition problems were insurmountable and all the legal advice was: don't even think about it.

But the directors did think about Northern Rock when it came along and were within a few hours of landing it before the Governor killed it. The story of the Rock is one of the most poignant in the history of the banking crisis, basically because it could so easily have been rescued and confidence in Britain's banking system might have been preserved, at least for a bit longer, taking some of the pressure off the other former building societies, including HBOS. Unfortunately, Mervyn King, with his intellectual aloofness, visceral disdain for bankers and obsession with moral hazard, was not the right man in the Bank of England at that particular moment. Under a more practical Governor, Lloyds could have seamlessly absorbed Northern Rock, Britain's first bank run in a century would have been avoided – and Lloyds would probably not have bid for HBOS. All the Lloyds team today agree that they could never have taken over both Northern Rock and HBOS – not even Gordon Brown could have finessed that with the competition authorities, and one acquisition would have been enough for Lloyds to absorb in a twelve-month period. On this argument Northern Rock would today be part of Lloyds and HBOS would have gone down or been nationalised – and that might have created an even bigger crisis.

But there we enter into the realm of counter-factuals, 'what-ifs' and the roads not taken, which drive business leaders demented and take us nowhere.

The fact is the competition issues of the merger were temporarily buried in the need to get the deal done but were always likely to re-emerge even if the EU hadn't intervened. Horta-Osório, although at one stage he was trying to flog TSB to the Co-op for a price of around £1.5 billion, finally managed to turn adversity to his advantage through an IPO – originally Daniels's idea – and then a £2 billion takeover of TSB by the Spanish bank Sabadell. 'The disposal of TSB became politically expedient because the debate had moved on, from saving the financial system when HBOS was teetering on the brink, to promoting competition through niche banks, and no more nasty bankers and what can we do to change behaviour,' says the bank analyst JP Crutchley. 'TSB became a fig leaf for that shift in political emphasis.'

Lloyds, post-Daniels, adopted the view that the sale of TSB was the cost of doing business in terms of retaining its leading market position in the key credit categories. 'What they have done with TSB is do one of the UK's largest branch disposal programmes on the sly,' says

Crutchley admiringly, 'because we all know that the nature of banking is shifting from physical to virtual channels. You still need a substantial branch network to support your franchise but Lloyds probably had too many branches, and in TSB it created something that is cost heavy and revenue light.'

So, even that has not turned out too badly.

.   .   .

The true figures for the HBOS losses are almost impossible to extract from the consolidated Lloyds accounts, but we can make a reasoned guess – and they were a great deal more than Lloyds TSB bargained for. Early in 2008, HBOS announced that its (audited) profits before tax for the previous year were £5.5 billion and its interim statement, published on 31 July, a few days after the meetings in the St James flat, showed it was still profitable despite impairment losses of £1.3 billion. In February HBOS also announced an interim dividend costing £1.2 billion. These were the last published (and audited) figures before the merger was announced on 18 September 2008. In the event, early in 2009, HBOS revealed it had made a loss of £11 billion, compared to Tim Tookey's November forecast of £660 million, after massive impairment charges of £13.5 billion. More than half of it was in the corporate division where impairments totalled £6.7 billion as some of the bank's big bets on highly geared property developments were savaged as the economy collapsed. 'The deterioration in the quality of HBOS's loan book and the speed with which it all happened, are a notable part of the HBOS story,' the Bank of England's official report recorded. 'The policies and actions [of the HBOS management] created a business model that was highly cyclical and amplified the effects of the recession leading up to significant losses.' That is an understatement on a grand scale. In 2009 alone, Lloyds made provisions of £23 billion, 82 per cent of which related to HBOS whose assets had to be impaired by another £10.9 billion in 2010 and £7.1 billion in 2011. HBOS's cumulative impairments from 2008 to 2011 totalled a massive £52.6 billion, of which £21.9 billion was in corporate – 18 per cent of 2008 loans – which was 'sufficient in its own right', as the Bank of England report noted dryly, 'to cause the failure of the firm absent further capital injection'. The Bank's report showed that the performance of the international division was even worse: its impairment losses were £15.5 billion, 25 per cent of its loans, most of it a result of lending to speculative builders in Ireland where HBOS was swept along by the same insanity that destroyed almost the entire Irish banking industry. By contrast the core retail business, largely the old Halifax operation, sailed through the recession almost unscathed: only 3 per cent of its loans went bad, £6.6 billion out of a total loan book of £258 billion. Right through the worst of the recession and the years of austerity, private mortgage-holders kept up their interest payments and even for Northern Rock, with its 125 per cent mortgages, the level of defaults was remarkably low. It was the big property bets, many of them in Ireland, which brought the bank down. As the British and Irish economies emerged from their recessions, some of the HBOS impairment losses were recovered, but by 2013 Lloyds had decided that £39.6 billion would 'ultimately be irrecoverable' and wrote them off. That's probably about the extent of the actual, realised losses: around £40 billion, a quarter of it in Ireland.

In a less hostile environment, they didn't need to be as big as that. The steep increases in capital requirements set by the authorities forced Lloyds to shrink its balance sheet, which it did by unloading over £200 billion of HBOS's riskier assets. The regulators took a particularly dim view of the investments made by Bank of Scotland Integrated Finance, run by the entrepreneurial Graeme Shankland as part of Peter Cummings's corporate division, and in 2010 Lloyds sold a portfolio of shareholdings in forty-two

British companies, which included House of Fraser, the shirt-maker TM Lewin, the convenience store chain Martin McColl and the David Lloyd gym business. HBOS had invested £1.8 billion in the portfolio, much of it at the top of the market, and Lloyds offloaded it for 40p in the pound, retaining a 30 per cent stake itself and writing off the rest. Shankland and some of his key team left with it and under its new owner, Coller Capital, by cutting back, restructuring and selling off assets, recouped cash of more than £2.5 billion over the next four years. Loans of £3 billion to the same companies, which were heavily impaired in 2009, were almost all repaid.

'Look, this was not a collection of basket case companies, it just wasn't,' Shankland told the *Sunday Times* in December 2013. 'We weren't a big part of the [HBOS] balance sheet. When we were delivering, we were delivering sizeable profits and an excellent return on capital.'

In the atmosphere that reigned in the first eighteen months or so after the merger, Lloyds was forced to dump other assets at knockdown prices, which later recovered along with the economy. In a different climate, and with more sympathetic regulators, it would have carried them through the worst of the cycle. Lloyds had to crystallise its losses early by 'marking to market', basically valuing its entire balance sheet on the basis of the market value of the small part of it which was actually traded. Barclays, HSBC, Santander and others, which also had major losses, preferred to trade their way through the cycle, taking losses only as they occurred and waiting for values to turn up again as they always had – and which, indeed, they eventually did.

Later on, after Daniels had left, Horta-Osório, like most new chief executives, made still further provisions – or, in the phrase of one of the old Lloyds financial teams, he 'kitchen-sinked the place' – which for a time made the figures look worse still. Lloyds has enjoyed the benefit of that in the past few years as some of the provisions were unwound again. But many of the assets had been offloaded near the bottom of the market and Lloyds will never get the benefit of their recovery.

· · ·

Perhaps the key questions for the Lloyds directors are: with the benefit of hindsight, would they have done the deal? And, what would have happened to Lloyds if they had pulled out in October 2008?

'Based on what we knew at the time, we made what we genuinely thought was the proper recommendation,' says one of the senior executives.

> But if we had known what was coming down the track – the capital requirements, zero funding availability, economic crash, house price collapse, state aid, Brussels, government interference – I don't think we would have bought it. In September 2008, we took what we thought was the right decision. Hindsight has turned out to be different.

Even Blank, probably the deal's strongest advocate, eventually came to a similar conclusion, although he still felt that in the circumstances going ahead was the right thing to do. On that frenetic weekend in October 2008, the alternatives looked even less palatable. Blank firmly believed that abandoning the bid and letting HBOS go down would have done such damage to the system that Lloyds's shareholders would have suffered even more.

Whichever direction it took, Lloyds was never going to come through the crisis unscathed – that's another myth. If Lloyds had decided to stand alone that weekend in October 2008, says one of the senior team,

> we would have survived the tsunami but the dividend would have gone and we would have had to raise new capital through a rights issue because of the government's stress tests. The idea that we could have carried on without a rights issue is fiction. So we would have to recapitalise and rebase the dividend – it wouldn't have been nice but it would probably have been less painful – assuming the financial system survived.

Lloyds would also have been a much smaller bank, once again stuck in its old strategic trap. 'You could argue the price was too high,' says another former director, 'but the object of the bid has been achieved, even if the benefits have been slower in coming through. We should not forget that.'

At the end of the day the reality is that in October 2008 the British banking system teetered on the precipice and if Lloyds had decided to abandon HBOS to its fate, it could well have fallen over. Lloyds did the deal, it survived and today it is a bigger, healthier and more profitable bank than it has ever been; HBOS didn't go bust, its shareholders were left with some value, the government got – or will get – its money back and an even more serious banking crisis was avoided.

None of this is much consolation for Lloyds shareholders. But at least they can now glimpse sunnier uplands: Lloyds has returned to the dividend list, the PPI damage is almost behind it and its market and competitive position on the high street have never been stronger. Things should look very different a few years from now.

For those who lived through it, the banking crisis of 2008/09 was a life-changing, nightmarish experience they would not want to repeat. But in the long-term history of Lloyds Banking Group the events of that period may be no more than a hiccup along a bumpy and generally profitable road, at least for those who bought their shares post-crisis. As one of his former colleagues remarks: 'Victor, even when he knew he would have to step down, never gave up the faith and always believed that the Lloyds HBOS deal would deliver a stronger institution eventually.'

He may well be right.

INDEX